Politics and Religion
in the
White South

Religion in the South

John B. Boles
Series Editor

POLITICS

AND

RELIGION

IN THE

WHITE

SOUTH

Edited by

GLENN FELDMAN

THE UNIVERSITY PRESS OF KENTUCKY

Publication of this volume was made possible in part by a grant
from the National Endowment for the Humanities.

Editorial and Sales Offices: The University Press of Kentucky
663 South Limestone Street, Lexington, Kentucky 40508-4008
www.kentuckypress.com

09 08 07 06 05   5 4 3 2 1

Library of Congress Cataloging-in-Publication Data

Politics and religion in the White South / edited by Glenn Feldman.
    p. cm. — (Religion in the South)
  Includes bibliographical references (p.   ) and index.
  ISBN 0-8131-2363-1 (hardcover : alk. paper)
    1. Christianity and politics—Southern states. 2. Southern States
—Church history. 3. Church and state—Southern States.   I. Feldman,
Glenn. II. Series.
  BR535.P58 2005
  322'.1'0975—dc22   2005014128

This book is printed on acid-free recycled paper meeting
the requirements of the American National Standard
for Permanence in Paper for Printed Library Materials.

Manufactured in the United States of America.

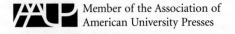 Member of the Association of
American University Presses

For Mary Margaret Morgan, Jody Coombs, Patricia
Weaver, Carol Ann Vaughn, Julie Brown, Wendy Price,
Kris Kristofferson, Jim Aycock, and my wife, Jeannie
Feldman, all people of faith who worship with their
eyes open. . . .

And

Most of all, for my mother, Julia Garate Burgos Feldman,
who through her living witness of the Beatitudes, taught
me that religion was for loving not hating, helping not
hurting, understanding not judging, embracing not
excluding, tolerating not shunning, forgiving not
damning, lifting up not putting down, for redeeming sin
not claiming sainthood, and for bringing us together as
children of God instead of lording it over one another.

In despotic statecraft, the true and essential mystery is to fool the subjects, and to mask the fear, which keeps them down, with specious garb of religion, such that they fight for their slavery as if it were their freedom, and count it not shame but highest honor to sacrifice their blood and lives for the vainglory of a tyrant.

—Benedict Spinoza,
A Theologico-Political Treatise (1670)

CONTENTS

TABLES

ACKNOWLEDGMENTS

First and foremost, I would like to thank Joyce Harrison, editor-in-chief at the University Press of Kentucky, for believing in this project. That always means the world to me, and I am deeply grateful to her. John B. Boles, editor of the *Religion in the South* series, provided sage advice and encouragement throughout. I owe him much. Nichole Lainhart, editing supervisor at Kentucky, was especially helpful, as were Ann Malcolm in acquisitions and Allison Webster in marketing. Karen Hellekson did an excellent job at copyediting. Ted Jelen read the manuscript and provided insightful suggestions that strengthened it. I am also thankful to the contributors for taking the time and interest to provide their expertise for what they viewed as an important project, and for their encouragement and enthusiasm as well. As usual, I reserve my most sincere thanks to my wife, Jeannie, for walking with me every step of the way, and to the two wonderful angels I get to call my daughters, Hallie and Rebecca. They make everything worthwhile. It is my deepest hope that one day they will read and get something out of this book. And, finally, for the example my friends and mother have set. It is to them that this book is dedicated.

Glenn Feldman
Birmingham, Alabama

Introduction

Glenn Feldman

There are few, if any, subjects that hold more intrinsic interest than the relationship between politics and religion: how religion affects, and is affected by, political thought and behavior. The interplay between the two, both capable of eliciting the most intense of emotions, may be found in virtually all time periods and every imaginable setting. That said, there is perhaps no area of the United States where this intersection is more important—both in daily life and at the ballot box—than the American South.

The South has always been a special place. The history of the South is the history of a place where adherence to courtesy and formal manners co-exists with the most shocking outbursts of violence and the settlement of personal differences by resort to physical force; where a slower and easier pace of life is found alongside the most intense and passionate forms of religious and political expression; where a region blessed by bountiful natural resources and stunning physical beauty is beset by pockets of abject poverty, one-crop agriculture, systemic economic problems, and a stubborn strain of anti-intellectualism and indifference to the public and private advantages of education; where the personal warmth of the people and their capacity for private charity and goodwill is outmatched only by a staggering and unquestioning faith in the tenets of "rugged individualism," laissez-faire, and even variants of the most callous forms of Social Darwinism. This is the South—all of these things, and more. It is a place of profound contradiction and, beneath its sunny exterior, of often the most serious struggle and tension between varying allegiances, competing philosophies, and divergent worldviews. Perhaps no other place in the nation is as inherently interesting a setting to study the ancient and ongoing interplay between spiritual beliefs and values, and realpolitik.

This book is an attempt to get at the intersection of politics and religion in the South. It is not an effort to cover all of the denominations in Southern history equally, nor is it an attempt to explore every manifestation of theological belief that has existed in the region. Some of the choices and inclusion of chapters are, necessarily, the product of the availability and, more importantly, the *willingness* of expert students of history, politics, and religion to participate. That said, denominations other than just Baptists and Methodists are included. There is a full chapter on Jews. Jews, as well as Catholics, are studied in important ways in a number of chapters. Smaller Protestant denominations—Presbyterians, Episcopalians, Disciples of Christ, Church of Christ, and others—are represented, as are more fundamentalist and charismatic sects: Holiness Pentecostal, Assembly of God, Church of God.

The book adopts an interdisciplinary approach, to an extent, yet is first and foremost a work of history. Eight of the twelve chapters are authored by historians. Even the few that are not include distinguishable elements of historical perspective, outlook, and research. But the goal was to examine how religion and politics have interacted in the South over time, not necessarily to adhere to the strict disciplinary boundaries of a single avenue of inquiry. In the spirit of believing that other academic disciplines have something useful to say to historians (and vice versa)—economics, sociology, anthropology, demography, literature, psychology, to name a few—four of the chapters, mostly those dealing with recent events, are contributed by political scientists.

The essays in this book, taken as a whole, strongly suggest that in the South, religion has worked hand in hand with political and social conservatism. The region's politics have, in turn, reflected its fundamentally conservative religious temperament. The relationship is not absolute; it is not unchanging. Nor has it gone unchallenged, at times even successfully, in the region's history. Yet, on balance, in the South, religion and political conservatism have been allies far more often than enemies. They have done much more than merely exist alongside each other. They have been mutually supportive and cooperative along with the other major historical factors of causation—a point explored more fully in the book's final chapter. Allegiance to party has been fleeting and ephemeral in the South—another point discussed in the final chapter, and alluded to as well in the chapter by Natalie M. Davis. *Partisan* change, though, should not be confused for *political* change—at least where the white South is concerned. Parties come and parties go, but conservatism has been forever.

The political party that most successfully positions itself as the "conservative" party is the party that will, odds are, day in and day out, win the

South—which, up until the past few decades, has meant exclusively the white South. This has been the case for over a century and a half. It is not less true today.

A number of the essays in this collection make clear the extent of this conservative religious victory in the world of Southern politics. Fred Arthur Bailey's elegant opening chapter explores Southern Baptist racial ideology during the late nineteenth and early twentieth centuries and in the process does much to delineate what have been enduring ties between racial conservatism and related regional orthodoxies in politics, morality, and economics. Politics, morality, and race, although intellectually separable in the South, and more practically divorceable in other regions, have a long history of interconnectedness and overlap in Southern mind, manners, and sensibilities—an indelible relationship that resonates strongly into the present. Bailey's chapter does much to explain how upper-class domination of what passed for official religion coalesced seamlessly with political, racial, and moral orthodoxy, and how it influenced important policy matters on such issues as lynching, disfranchisement, employment, law, and education, especially for blacks. Paul Harvey's examination of the Southern Baptist Convention from 1945 to 1990 traces the evolution of the SBC, the largest and probably most representative denominational institution in the South. Harvey's insightful exposition reveals that "although forces associated with the Religious Right decisively lost the battle over civil rights, they won the larger cultural war for the soul of white Southern believers." In a partisan sense, this victory took the form of the modern Republican Party. In a denominational sense, according to Harvey, it meant the "complete rout" of the moderates by the conservatives in the SBC.

James L. Guth echoes and extends Harvey's analysis through the 2000 elections and elaborates on what he terms the "deeply conservative" ideology of Southern Baptists. Guth evaluates this ideology as historically "usually buttressing the social, racial, and political status quo" in the Southern states. Even during the vaunted era of Southern progressivism, Guth stipulates, the Social Gospel made "relatively few inroads among Southern Baptist ministers." The civil rights movement captivated a few college professors and institutional leaders associated with what Guth calls the "Established Church" in the South but did not resonate with the bulk of white clergy and laity. Perhaps most intriguing in the Guth piece is his discussion of a "civic gospel" that has recently appealed to the most conservative, "dispensationalist" clergy—traditionally among the most other-worldly and politically abstinent. This "new social theology," like the old Social Gospel, summons clerics

to political action, only from the most conservative outlook and temperament. Political activism, according to this new theology, is mandated to clerics
as an affirmative duty to prevent the continued "slide of American society
down and away from its Christian origins toward a new, secular, and sinful
identity." This kind of theological mandate is clearly present in Ted Ownby's
treatment of Donald Wildmon and his "confrontational ministry" against
what he considers to be gratuitous sex, nudity, indecency, and anti-Christian
bias in various forms of the "liberal" American media.

Several other essays in this collection echo the theme of conservative
religious/political predominance in the American South. Charles S. Bullock
III and Mark C. Smith outline a theory they call "core constituency" that
further explicates the relationship between conservative theology and politics in the South. Bullock and Smith offer intriguing insights into the relationship of political parties, specifically the GOP, with their core conservative
religious supporters. Their study highlights the ongoing balancing act that
often takes place between the interests and goals of religious/social conservatives and cosmopolitan Republicans moved more by secular, economic
conservatism than moral issues. They examine the problems candidates
sometimes have in appealing to a religiously conservative core in the party
primary without jeopardizing mainstream, swing-vote support in the November general election. The essay conveys two very important lessons that
have a great deal of relevance to recent politics. To be successful politically,
Republican candidates have learned, through trial and error, to keep religious and social differences, where they do exist, as quiet as possible within
party ranks—a lesson that seems not to have been lost on Religious Right
activists who rallied early and almost unanimously to a presidential candidate not so publicly associated with the Christian Right, yet a man they
thought had the pedigree, organization, and financing to win in 2000. Republicans have learned, as well, to aid their own success by encouraging
members of the Religious Right to get behind the full gamut of the party
platform—including planks of an economic conservatism that do not always hold as much strong intrinsic appeal, and even less biblical justification.

This second lesson is explored in my chapter on women and the Ku
Klux Klan as well as in the book's final chapter. The discussion there mentions the tendency of many Catholics in the South, increasingly since 1973,
to allow the abortion question to serve as the "Eclipse Issue": one capable of
compelling allegiance to the GOP on a whole array of economic issues because the party has successfully positioned itself, first and foremost in the

minds of Catholics, as the defender of "life" against Democratic "baby kill-ers." The same obsession with abortion furnishes a "get out of jail free card" to American Catholics—evident in the South more than any other region—a kind of papal dispensation from having to know anything about, or pay attention to, economic issues and the traditional Catholic concerns of pov-erty, social justice, capital punishment, war, and worker exploitation.[1] As famed Irish-Catholic New York journalist Jimmy Breslin recently noted, under Pope John Paul II, the Catholic Church has four major concerns: "abor-tion, abortion, abortion, and Poland."[2]

The more fundamental issue, in both the KKK chapter and the final chapter, deals with the question of the power of a "politics of emotion" as opposed to a "politics of reason" in determining voter behavior—and the recent ascendance of what may be termed the "new racism": the replace-ment of overt racist appeals by religious and moral judgmentalism as the primary emotional issue that can move masses of Southern whites to vote for economically elitist policies. Other chapters touch on various aspects of the problem. Paul Harvey realizes that the ascendant right wing of the SBC, although specifically rejecting segregation in the here and now, can trace their lineage and "forebears" to the old anti–civil rights guard of the de-nomination. He argues that today, white supremacy has largely been replaced by "gendered hierarchies."

Two studies—Mark J. Rozell and Clyde Wilcox's on Virginia and Natalie M. Davis's on Alabama—analyze the relationship between politics and reli-gion on a state level. Davis discusses the conflict between liberalism and conservatism, what she terms "modernism versus fundamentalism," in terms of a metaphor—the Mercedes Culture versus the Pine Tree Culture—and muses that party might no longer be the "driving force in American poli-tics"; instead, it might be replaced by religion. Rozell and Wilcox examine Virginia politics in the last several decades and conclude, much like Bullock and Smith, that a Christian Right politics can be, and has been, successful at the polls, but it does have its limits. It tends to falter electorally if waged with utter impunity and a heavy-handed lack of finesse. In Virginia, until the early 1990s, Democratic candidates were able to win state elections largely by tying conservative Christian Republicans to the "extremism" of the Vir-ginia-based activist ministries of the Moral Majority's Jerry Falwell and the Christian Coalition's Pat Robertson—themselves rivals. But no more. Al-though the state has been home to, at one time or another, many of the nation's leading Christian Right activists—among them Ralph Reed, Rich-ard Viguerie, Oliver North, and Paul Weyrich—Religious Right politics in the Old Dominion has learned to flourish only by having its preferred candidates demonstrate a willingness to compromise and by shrewdly emphasizing the most popular parts of their conservative agenda—that is, advocacy of a moment of silence at the beginning of the school day as opposed to the teaching of evolution; calling for a ban on partial-birth abortions and public funding for abortion as opposed to a blanket ban or criminalization of the practice, even for the victims of rape and incest.

The essays in this volume, much like the history of the South more broadly, are not unqualified or unanimous in their judgments. To do so would be to imply that the South is a monolith, and it is certainly not that. Several deal with what may be called minority currents. Mark K. Bauman's chapter explores the heavy Jewish involvement in the factional city politics surrounding Atlanta from the end of the Civil War through the Progressive Era. In the essay, "Jewishness" is as much a cultural phenomenon as a religious one. Atlanta's "German Jews," principally mid-nineteenth-century immigrants from Germany and Austria, emerge as well-established, politically and commercially savvy, and successful in the department store and dry goods businesses, the banking industry, textile manufacturing, and other mercantile activities. Bauman also conveys considerable tension between older German Jews and newer, poorer, Russian Jews emigrating from southern and eastern Europe. The German Jews are ambivalent about the newcomers: they are embarrassed by their poverty and customs, anxious about losing their hard-won accepted status by being lumped in with the newcomers, yet empathetic to the plight of fellow Jews—a dynamic that has parallels to the present-day tension between new Mexican and Latino immigrants and older, established, often comfortable and conservative Hispanics from Cuba and South America. Perhaps most interesting is the political and economic conservatism of the established and dominant (among Atlanta's Jewry) German Jews. They are quite active in urban politics and consistently ally themselves with the city's older industrial and commercial business conservatives against organized labor. Here, religion—or, more accurately, the business-friendly side of Jewish culture—contributes to the furtherance of conservatism.[3] Tensions exist throughout the period between the German Jews and both labor unions and blacks.

Chapters by Andrew M. Manis and Steven P. Miller more self-consciously address the liberal and progressive potentialities of Southern religion. Yet both also recognize, and perhaps make even clearer, the limits and uniqueness of that kind of activism in the Southern past. Manis's story of Dorothy Tilly and her Methodist women's Fellowship of the Concerned is truly inspiring. Tilly exemplified her Christian faith and the social reform potential of Wesleyan tradition of Protestantism to its fullest. She lived a life that encouraged and fostered change, racial toleration, and inclusiveness while exhibiting a sensitivity to her region's people and the difficulty that people in any time and place often have living up to the rhetoric of their national ideals and the better angels of their nature. Tilly nudged white Southerners to do the right thing on race relations much as a mother might encourage her children, as painful as it might be, to do the right thing—hence Manis's adoption of Jessie Ash Arndt's moniker of "city mothers" for Tilly and her group. Miller's essay deals with a more moderate, yet more famous, white Southerner: Billy Graham. In his chapter, Miller explores Graham's efforts, sometimes dramatic, to encourage the South to peacefully accept the demise of racial segregation as part of his perennial emphasis on individual personal conversion, salvation, a personal relationship with Christ, decency, civility, moderation, and God's desire for law and order here on earth.

Yet both essays, and others, recognize the exceptionalism and the limits of even this kind of religious progressivism in the Southern experience. Graham, in particular, comes across as little more than a moderate in Miller's estimation. At times he is defensive about Southerners and their customs, never missing an opportunity to conflate militant segregationists and civil rights advocates as one and the same type of "extremist"; he advises Martin Luther King Jr. and others not to push too far or too fast; reminds people that race is a national, not peculiarly Southern, problem; and he denounces Northern hypocrisy and racial extremism on both sides from a place he thought was squarely in the middle of the controversy. More than that, though, Miller effectively evaluates Graham as a white Southerner who became a national and even global figure whose commitment to the demise of racial segregation had much to do with the realization that his credibility on the national and international stages could never survive a defense of his native region's reactionary racial customs. Perhaps most troubling about Graham's career in this regard, though, is his activist role in aiding and abetting Richard Nixon's "Southern Strategy," including playing an important role in the 1970 defeat of Tennessee senator Al Gore Sr. by Republican Bill Brock—a campaign in which Republican manipulation of the race issue hurt Gore badly. Although Graham is to be commended for his public stand against segregation when most of the white South did not approve, including his insistence on racially integrated crusades, it is difficult to believe that anyone with Graham's intellect could not have known that the Nixon strategy appealed to white supremacists in the South on a veiled and muted, yet still very real, level. Andrew Manis, meanwhile, openly acknowledges that the pro-*Brown* decision statements of some Southern Methodist bishops were a "minority view" among the lay faithful, that a great deal of the Methodist rank and file was pro-segregation, and that Dorothy Tilly and her group represented not the mainstream, but "the most progressive element in the white South." Prominent Methodist white supremacists such as Georgia's Rebecca Latimer Felton, of the Holiness movement, and Alabama's Hugo Locke, jurist, political operative, and Methodist deacon, furnish a stark counterpoint to the example of Dorothy Tilly. Both Paul Harvey and Steven Miller also comment on the notable gulf between some Protestant denominational leaders in the wake of *Brown* and a markedly more reactionary Southern white laity of deacons and others who practiced a folk (in Harvey's words) "theology of segregationism."

Two recent books—both of them very good—have done much to swing the recent historiographical center of gravity toward the proposition that Southern religion should be viewed, basically, as a force for liberal reform. Charles Marsh's *God's Long Summer* looks compellingly at the role of evangelical religion in providing meaning and inspiration for some of the civil rights movement's most notable figures. David L. Chappell argues in *A Stone of Hope* that the white South never did fashion a strong, organized, coherent defense of segregation from the point of view of religious theology, unlike its experience during the antebellum abolition crisis.[4] Although both books are important works that have much of value to offer, there is the very real danger that their arguments, taken together, might morph into a kind of misleading generalization by less than careful readers—and the overlooking of a couple of realities about the South that remain unchanged *even if* the central arguments of both books are accepted. First, when Marsh and Chappell speak of the potential for religion to inform Southern progressivism, they are speaking, predominantly, of *black-led* and Northern liberal reform—not that of white Southerners. Both books spend much time and energy on the central role of religion as a catalyst for the modern civil rights movement, but the vast bulk of this tie between progressive reform and theology deals with African Americans and their understanding of evangelical religion. Chappell's argument about the lack of a strong, cohesive, and organized religious defense of segregation from white Southerners also actually focuses on the elites who made up church leadership in the pulpits and denominations. What is left unsaid is that folk religion among ordinary whites was an undeniably powerful buttress for "massive resistance" and the defense of white supremacy. Church leaders may have been reluctant to engage the question directly from a religious standpoint, and a good number even ventured varying degrees of support for desegregation. But there is much in the Southern past to suggest that the rank and file of white Southern believers did not construct an elaborate religious defense of white supremacy *precisely because* it already functioned at a perfectly adequate level. Why bother to create and formalize something that was already so powerful and pervasive as part of a less formal folk religion? After all, white Southerners failed in the defense of their "way of life" because they were overwhelmed by black direct-action and federal intervention, not because they somehow suffered a failure of religious resolve to carry on.

The essays also make clear the sometimes very heavy "social penalty for noncomformity," as Paul Harvey calls it, of bucking the predominant regional conservatism. Harvey writes of such people as Georgia's Joseph Rabun, a Baptist minister and Marine Corps combat veteran, driven from his pulpit for criticizing Eugene Talmadge's defense of the white primary. Andrew Manis tells of the necessity for Dorothy Tilly and her Fellowship of the Concerned to use secrecy to deal with the Southern white majority's fury at having laws changed from outside their region, an outrage that channeled itself against her husband's business prospects and social standing. Mrs. Tilly herself, as Southern as she could possibly be, found herself denounced as an "outside agitator," an abettor of "Socialism and Communism . . . not worthy to live in the South," and a "cheap publicity seeker and nigger lover" who should "leave the South to the Southerners"—a theme also explored in the chapter on women and the KKK. Manis admits that, however inspiring and admirable, it is "difficult" to assess the effectiveness of Tilly's work in the South.

In the end, it is difficult not to notice the kinship between the old racial superiority of white religious Southerners—that is, most Southerners—and the more recent sense of religious exclusivity and moral monopoly of people such as Donald Wildmon, Jerry Falwell, George W. Bush and figures in his administration, and many less vocal and intense Southerners who identify with the Religious Right.[5] Ted Ownby writes of the conviction of Wildmon and others like him that the existence of what they define as "sin" in their world and community is not an individual affair, but a cancer that imperils the spiritual health and salvation of the whole—a corporatist belief not unlike that in vogue during the supremely violent, centuries-long obscenity that was the French Wars of Religion between Catholic and Huguenot. Acceptance of a view that ties together individual piety with societal health and orthodoxy, even on a small and subliminal level, implies a call to action, political involvement, activism, and religious and political evangelism for anyone who would seek to call himself "Christian."

NOTES

1. See, for example, the popular flyer "It's Time to Elect Candidates Who Will Protect Life!" (2004), distributed by Priests for Life for the 2004 presidential and national elections (flyer in possession of the author). In it, the group provides a blueprint for voting for Republican candidates without jeopardizing their 501(c) tax-exempt status without mentioning the party by name. First the flyer quotes the United States Bishops' "Living the Gospel of Life": "Every voice matters in the public forum. Every vote counts . . . We encourage all citizens, particularly Catholics, to embrace their citizenship not merely as a duty and privilege, but as an opportunity meaningfully to participate in building the culture of life." Then the flyer informs the Catholic faithful that "As we approach our national elections, Priests for Life has prepared resources to help you to carry out your civic responsibilities . . . in the light of moral law." What is more, these "resources will help you" to learn to put abortion above and beyond any other possible competing issue and to "Understand why the Right to Life is the primary election issue." Once the faithful Catholic has put abortion at the pinnacle of his list on how to vote, he may feel free to remove all other competing issues from his conscience because he has done his duty as a good Catholic. The flyer closes by inserting a quote from Pope John Paul II's 1988 encyclical, *Christifideles Laici:* "The common outcry, which is justly made on behalf of human rights—for example, the right to health, to home, to work, to family, to culture—is false and illusory if the right to life, the most basic and fundamental right . . . is not defended with maximum determination."

2. Jimmy Breslin, *The Church That Forgot Christ* (New York: Free Press, 2004), 1 (quoted).

3. For a lucid and interesting, if not always persuasive, account of the relationship between Jews and capitalism in the European mind, see Jerry Z. Muller, *The Mind and the Market: Capitalism in Modern European Thought* (New York: Alfred A. Knopf, 2002).

4. Charles Marsh, *God's Long Summer: Stories of Faith and Civil Rights* (Princeton: Princeton University Press, 1997); and David L. Chappell, *A Stone of Hope: Prophetic Religion and the Death of Jim Crow* (Chapel Hill: University of North Carolina Press, 2004).

5. For more on this subject, see chapter 12 in this book.

That Which God Hath Put Asunder

White Baptists, Black Aliens, and the Southern Social Order, 1890 –1920

Fred Arthur Bailey

Emboldened by a distinctive religious fervor, Southern Baptists leaders called down divine blessings upon racial segregation as the nineteenth century merged with the twentieth.[1] "We think it may be safely asserted that God's hand is in the clear-drawn line between the races," pontificated a Virginia editor in 1901. "That which God hath put asunder, let not man attempt to join." Representatives of the South's largest Christian denomination, Southern Baptist ministers, editors, and lay leaders combined their belief in Calvinistic theology with the logic of Social Darwinism and the traditions of black slavery to affirm God's will on ethnic policies. All spoke from a comfortable position as white supremacists at ease with their overmastery of a suppressed black class and claimed divine endorsement of their privileges. Asserting election by God, they preached that the Almighty had intentionally placed both Southern Baptists and Southern Negroes in the same geographic region. "Upon Southern Baptists God has laid the responsibility for evangelization and training of the negroes in our midst," reasoned delegates to an Arkansas convocation. "In the providence of God, they have been laid at our doors, and in his simple faith the negro is naturally a Baptist."[2]

At first glance, the confluence of racial separation and evangelistic outreach may appear to have been simple hypocrisy or an impossible contradiction. But in the mind of early twentieth-century Baptist leaders, the two concepts merged without seam. However much white religionists prayed for African Americans, they preached and practiced an upper-class theology bent more on educating Southern blacks to be obeisant workers than on saving their souls. From the perspective of Southern Baptist spokesmen, the relegation of blacks to an inferior social status was not only a needful corrective to decades of perceived social disorder, but also within their norms of a virtuous Christian society.[3]

Although the Southern Baptist Church cast a broad outreach to the South's white population, its articulated views on ethnic relations arose as much from class divisions within the white community as they did from social cleavages premised on race. In common with the other Southern churches, the Southern Baptists faced internal class struggles that mirrored larger themes within their society. Southern Baptists embraced a cross section of a white society that had been recently fractured by the late nineteenth-century agrarian revolt against Redeemer or aristocratic rule.[4]

Under the banner of the Populist Party's crusade, white and black farmers merged in their discontent with upper-class oppression, used the institutions of democracy to challenge the South's entrenched aristocracy, and had in 1896 approached the overthrow of the Redeemer establishment. But their movement failed. Redeemer politicians, together with their cohorts in the press and the pulpit, shrewdly and effectively used the fearful rhetoric of Negrophobia to split the white masses from their black allies. Successful in the destruction of the Populist challenge, the South's aristocratic leaders appreciated the need to avert future threats to their suzerainty.[5] Good social order, they understood, required all Southerners—white as well as black—to appreciate the virtues of place and power. Church leaders gladly cast the authority of religion into the support of these upper-class dictums, preaching as essential the virtues of a society strictly articulated by class and race.

Yet in some important forms, late nineteenth-century evangelicalism had contributed to the power of agrarian radicalism. As Bruce Palmer showed in *"Man over Money": The Southern Populist Critique of American Capitalism,* an important part of the Populist critique of capitalism was evangelical in nature and dealt with the fundamental unfairness and exploitation involved in Gilded Age politics and society. Populists did not hesitate to attack clergymen who bolstered the economic and political status quo of the Redeemers. As Frederick A. Bode explained, North Carolina populists attacked this "pure religion" of the upper classes on precisely religious grounds as "another part of a hegemonic and consensual ethos" that the Bourbons relied on to sustain control.[6] Briefly and furiously challenged, the elites soon regained control of the political—and religious—situation.

From the Civil War's conclusion to the century's end, the Southern Baptist Church underwent an internal class struggle that paralleled the dynamic divisions extant within the South's broader society. The church's elites—college-educated clergy, wealthy planters, and urban professionals—dominated its extracongregational superstructure: state and general conventions, religious presses, theological seminaries. Financially comfortable, culturally sophisticated, and theologically tolerant, they offended many among their less affluent rural brethren who questioned the elites' commitment to Baptist orthodoxy.[7]

Identified as "Landmark" Baptist, countryside evangelists propounded a narrow doctrine that held to the primitive practices of the first-century church as constituting true Christianity and maintaining that nineteenth-century Southern Baptists perpetuated this faith in its purest form. Accepting no fellowship beyond their narrow communion, they insisted on near-absolute congregational autonomy, seeing in their denomination's larger polity the easy acceptance of liberal theology and ecumenism. But those opposed to "Landmarkism" condemned the movement for its propensity to array country against urban brethren and criticized its leaders for their castigation of intellectuals, merchants, and bankers. Such class-based rhetoric, the critics argued, threatened to undermine the progress being made by the New South and its businessmen who were also its architects.[8]

From the inception of Landmarkism in the 1850s, its leaders preached a stinging message threatening to the South's established aristocracy. Tennessee's James Robert Graves, its most articulate voice, demonstrated an intense commitment to civil and ecclesiastical democracy, a disdain for social hierarchies, and an empathy for the impoverished masses. He saw in the rise of global popular revolutions in general and the earlier American Revolution in particular the triumph of democracy and true Christianity over tyranny and caste. Envisioning his movement as an important element of a worldwide uprising of the poor and the downtrodden against their wealthy oppressors, he commanded his followers to be on guard against "kingcraft," "priest craft," and all similar hierarchies. By the 1890s Landmarkers had become increasingly alienated from a Southern Baptist Church dominated by social elites and in 1905 formalized their separation from it with the creation of the General Association of Landmark Baptists.[9]

The Landmark Baptists' social radicalism easily melded into the South's late nineteenth-century agrarian crusades with their characteristic emphasis on both class and race struggle. Rural evangelism and the Populist campaign flourished in the same soil, merging brush arbor rhetoric with stump

oratory as radical politicians and sympathetic ministers urged their followers to social action. They condemned the Southern elites for oppressing the
masses, lambasted the un-Christian usury demanded by bankers and merchants, and called for a social revolution to overthrow the entrenched interests.[10] They found common cause with black clergy, among them black
Baptists, who cherished their long tradition of blending piety with politics.
Whether the black ministers supported an alliance between Republicans and
Populists or embraced Populism without restraint, they and their parishioners lent needful support for white radicals intent on change.

Ironically, this black-white connection ultimately worked to the advantage of the Redeemer class. Appealing to white fears of Negro domination,
Southern elites counterattacked, thereby undermining Populist support, and
emerged victorious in the elections of 1896 and 1898. Secure in their domination over state legislatures, they rushed through statutes denying the franchise to most blacks and many whites, and enacted oppressive Jim Crow
laws that virtually forbade social commerce between the races. Ensconced at
the top of a privileged class, Southern thought-leaders—especially the
clergy—determined to justify their entitlements to themselves and to those
less fortunate Southerners over whom they held sway. White supremacy,
buttressed by a powerful indictment of unfettered democracy, underscored
the essential elements of their intellectual paradigm. Standing before a Texas
Baptist convention in 1905, a prominent minister fearfully proclaimed that
"never before in the history of the race was the Negro more determined on
political equality. Never before was the Saxon more determined to dominate. The Negro has brute force and numbers; the Saxon all the qualities
that make kings."[11]

Turn-of-the-century Baptist spokesmen, identifying with the interests
of the Southern patriciate, and now rid of the Landmark egalitarians, sur-
veyed their social order and found it in disarray. They quaked at the thought
of Negro empowerment, renounced any political culture amendable to black-
white equality, and blessed those state officials who crusaded for franchise
constriction. "The giant of the negro problem stalks forth and challenges us
to subdue him," trumpeted delegates to the Mississippi state convention in
1912. These religionists shared with their white compatriots across the South
a fundamental disdain for the Negro's intellectual and moral capacities. One
Texas clergyman succinctly enumerated that as a people, their "low intelligence and high animal propensities are greatly against them," they "have
very imperfect religious teaching at best" and "are full of all manners of
superstitions," and, most dangerous of all, they "are only a few generations

removed from the jungle, and many of their inherent tendencies are toward savagery." Who knows, he asked, "what wishful images arises in their dreamy minds for the wild freedom of an ancestry they do not know?" A perceived black threat to the Southern weal demanded firm action. "Our own safety, as well as every instinct of Christianity," points to the "necessity for christianising [*sic*]" the Negro, shrilly proclaimed the Georgia Baptist Convention in 1906.[12]

Linking their religion's missionary imperative to their cultural preferences, the Southern Baptists denomination considered black subordination to whites an essential element in this "Christianizing" experience. Its General Convention admonished Baptists in 1912 that in the act of "saving and helping the Negroes to their best self-expression as a race, we shall save Anglo-Saxon supremacy." This concept was accepted as a fundamental article of faith everywhere in the white South. "We are [the Negro's] superior, made so by God," affirmed the editor of the *Alabama Baptist* in 1901, and later an Alabama minister assured his Birmingham congregation that "the white man, being the superior race by birth and training, will . . . rule the inferior race." South Carolina churchmen pledged that "we owe to the Negro a large debt—at least the debt of the strong to the weak"; Arkansas Baptists prayed that "this weaker race" would feel the impact of the white man's effort "to lift, push and elevate" their lives; and Mississippi delegates urged their state convention to remember that "as the superior race, it is our duty . . . to accord to [the Negro] that magnanimity of conduct due from the strong to the weak."[13]

Considering African-descended Southerners aliens in the midst of a God-ordained, stratified Anglo-Saxon civilization, Baptist elites championed franchise restrictions that virtually eliminated black voting while at the same time denying suffrage to significant segments of nonelite whites. These patricians identified as democracy's essential flaw the empowerment of the downtrodden and the dispossessed, which led them to threaten an entrenched oligarchy. "The cry of unrestricted suffrage is a fad and a fiction which never has been and never ought to be," lectured an Alabama Baptist clothed in the pseudonym "Clericus Civio." He proclaimed that even as the "Anglo-Saxon must meet his mission in America," the black race must accept its natural subordination in the South. "The best solution of the Negro problem for the present is an honest, uncorrupted and incorruptible white rule. Then the Negro himself will be content to be relieved of this burden of state." The editor of a Virginia Baptist publication declared in agreement that his state's post–Civil War experiment in democracy proved "manhood suffrage . . . a failure" and demanded that reasonable "limitation must be put on the right" to vote.[14]

In Georgia, Virginia, and Alabama, Baptist clergy and lay leaders alike were particularly outspoken in their insistence that their states diminish black rights. "The colossal mistake of the [nineteenth] century was made when the right of unqualified suffrage was guaranteed to the uneducated, liberated slave," railed a correspondent to the Atlanta-published *Christian Index* in 1899. He assured his readers that "in the love of constitutional liberty," the "dominant and self-assertive Anglo-Saxon" would soon abridge "the right of unlimited suffrage in the hands of our African neighbors." J. B. Gambrel, president of Georgia's Mercer College, agreed. "We have baptized [Negroes], communed with them, prayed with them," he wrote. But Southern white men knew for a fact that Negroes were "not suited to control the Southern States." In Virginia, a Baptist physician declared that the "negro, put into politics, has made a breach between the races," while a Richmond College professor condemned the "negro's hankering after politics [which] grows out of the desire . . . to get something for nothing," and a prominent religious editor claimed that as "the steadfast friend of the negro," he did "not hesitate to say that his retirement from active politics would be an unspeakable blessing." The editor of Alabama's principal Baptist publication demanded a state constitutional convention to end Negro suffrage, proclaiming that it would "go a long way toward solving the race question." Rejoicing at the success of such efforts across the South, the Baptist General Convention of 1904 observed that the "altered political status" of the Negroes in many Southern States had resulted in a "relief of friction and a kindlier disposition in general on the part of both races."[15]

However harsh the Baptist rhetoric of Anglo-Saxon supremacy, it was accompanied by a wistful longing for an idealized past that had never existed. As the chief beneficiaries of the Old South's social order, antebellum aristocrats had feared the Northern spirit of individual liberty and its concomitant universal manhood suffrage. To their horror, Union victory in 1865 exposed the South to Yankee-imposed reforms, ushered in unwelcome democracy, and stirred profound discontent among Southern nonelites, black and white. In their aristocratic mind, all of this had corrupted the symbiotic relationships that had once characterized a slave-based civilization. Immersed in this paradigm, one Virginia Baptist castigated those he believed forced on Southern blacks "the position of full citizenship." Did "we not forget that it is written, 'A servant of servants shall thou be to thy brother?'" he queried. He then emphasized that had the tragic mistake of unbiblical emancipation never occurred, the Negro "would have been useful to us," and he would have "continued to love us as of yore."[16] Such fancied nostalgia was premised on a distinctly upper-class historiography. In the pulpit and on the pages of periodicals and proceedings, Baptist leaders worshiped an assumed old order and railed against its destruction.

Cloaking their canted interpretation of the past with the blessings of religion, Southern Baptist ministers assured their congregations that Divine Wisdom ordained the institution of Negro slavery as an outreach to the Dark Continent's lost souls. "The negroes in Africa were unlettered, ignorant, fetish worshipers of the basest kind," wrote a Tennessee leader. In a reversal of the Great Commandment's commission to go forth to "teach all nations," he claimed that they "were brought to this Christian land, . . . sold to Christian masters," and through their "constant contact with Christian civilization," repented of "their idolatry." Seeing God's moving hand manifested in the apparent coincidences of history, a Texas delegate to his state's Baptist convention of 1894 marveled at the "remarkable fact [that] the first slave ship that ever brought African slaves to our thirteen colonies was . . . called Jesus, because it was intended to save African slaves from canabalism [*sic*] and the grossest heathenism." Comforted by such lessons, a writer for Nashville's *Baptist and Reflector* proclaimed that Southern blacks "were, by the permissive and overruling providence of God, greatly elevated by their slavery to Christian masters in a Christian land," and the South Carolina Baptist Convention of 1900 echoed that through "the frowning providence of slavery," God brought Africans "to this country . . . to the glorious end that they might receive the gospel."[17]

Baptist leaders lauded those paternalistic features of the Old South civilization which they imagined had encouraged religious outreach to Southern blacks. In 1904, the *Alabama Baptist* provided its female readers with a simple historical catechism useful in explaining to children slavery's more positive benefits:

> Question: When and for what purpose were Africans brought to the United States?
> Answer: Twenty Africans were brought here in 1620 and sold as slaves. . . . .
> Question: How long have Southern Baptists been interested in these people?
> Answer: Ever since they were brought to this country.
> Question: How were the slaves treated?
> Answer: In many families they were given religious instruction. They attended the same church with their masters, and some were educated that they might teach others.

Ebullient in his praise of the antebellum master class, a Texas spokesman gushed that "Our hearts are truly grateful . . . that the masters . . . in the days of slavery, looked upon [Negroes] not as chattel merely, but as human beings, with possibilities greater than manual labor; and either taught them themselves, in literary and spiritual matters, or arranged for such teaching." More sedate in their rhetoric, Arkansas Baptists in convention acknowledged the positive role of the clergy in instructing the slave. "Before the negroes were free," they wrote, "almost every white pastor in the South felt at least a sort of responsibility for the negroes in his community . . . splendid evangelistic work was done among them." Celebrating the overall concern of pre–Civil War aristocrats for the "sons of Ethiopia," in 1901 a Georgia churchman took satisfaction from the fact that "our former slaves and their children" turned naturally "to their former masters asking, like Lazarus, for only the crumbs of our benevolence."[18]

Baptist patricians thus clung to their belief that antebellum paternalism had earned black loyalty before, during, and immediately after the Civil War. Unwilling and unable to embrace the concept of racial equality, and confronted daily with ethnic tensions, Baptist leaders looked back with longing to an imagined time when a superior and an inferior race resided together in felicity. Delegates to the Baptist General Convention of 1896 maintained that a proper restoration of the relationship between blacks and whites would "renew afresh our kindly feelings for the race which in our time of sorest trial and greatest hardship and bitter anxiety stood in its place, stormy though it was, and waited patiently for deliverance to come." Other Baptists were less sanguine. A correspondent to Atlanta's *Christian Index* simply lamented that "the old master and his Negroes will soon be silent in the grave, and with them will lie buried the last vestiges of toleration and kindness between the races."[19]

Southern elites, and the Baptist clergy sympathetic to them, saw planted in the Reconstruction era seeds detrimental to this once cherished "toleration and kindness between the races." Had it not been "for the influence of the carpet-baggers," roared a Tennessee writer, "we would have had but little trouble with our former slaves." These Yankee interlopers used "the negroes . . . to pull out political chestnuts for them." The president of Baptist-sponsored Mercer College assured his constituents that the region had not forgotten the lesson of "untutored Africans" placed in control of society. He promised that alert Southern whites would use their "strength of . . . numbers, intelligence, prestige, spirit and wealth" to save the states of the late Confederacy "from being reduced to the condition" of anarchy. Such men argued that Southern whites, more specifically the Christian elites, understood the Negro race better than Northern interlopers. "Foreigners know nothing of the true inwardness of the negro character as a race," they explained. Reconstruction's unsagacious attempt to grant blacks equality with whites had the negative effect of appealing to the Negro's more negative characteristics. Emphasizing these lessons, an Alabama Baptist warned that wise men must not "do anything that will increase [the Negro's] vanity, self-importance, and, we may add, impudence." Claiming a critical need to restore proper race relations in the South, in 1901 the Southern Baptist General Convention reminded its delegates that the origins of the "Negro problem" could be traced back more than thirty years, when first carpetbaggers and then "Northern philanthropists and Christians" interfered with the South's ethnic dynamics, even though they "knew practically nothing about the Negro."[20]

One Baptist preacher castigated the Reconstruction epoch with particular vitriol. Thomas Dixon, a scion of North Carolina aristocracy, graduated from Wake Forrest University in 1883 and then followed his father and older brother into the ministry. A spellbinding orator, he commenced his work at Goldsboro, North Carolina, and moved quickly through a series of progressively larger and wealthier congregations in Raleigh, Boston, and New York. Across the North, Dixon delighted in finding audiences receptive not only to his proclamation of the Baptist gospel, but also to his discourses on white supremacy. "The prejudice against the negro is the instinct of self-preservation" of "our Germanic race," he lectured an attentive New York crowd. "You can't swallow a single nigger without changing your complexion." Although many in the North warmed to his message, a resilient spirit of Yankee abolitionism repulsed Dixon. Considering this an ungodly ideology that had fueled the crusade against the South in 1861 and that had rudely informed Reconstruction policies after Confederate defeat, he determined to strike down this persistent and pernicious "anti-South" disposition. Dixon retired from the ministry in 1899, purchased a five-hundred-acre estate on Virginia's Chesapeake Bay, and settled into its opulent mansion to author works congenial to a Southern upper-class revision of history.[21]

Dixon's novels—*The Leopard's Spots* (1902), *The Clansman* (1905), and *The Traitor* (1907)—written after he was a practicing Baptist minister, were best sellers; together, they constituted a thrilling depiction of the Reconstruction era that drew millions to a sympathetic view of the patrician South. Each book was a simple romance set in the context of a white South prostrated by misguided and generally corrupt reconstructionists. These men held sway over gullible Southern blacks who, no longer restrained by slavery's civilizing power, reverted to the status of savages, at best indolent, at worst ravishers of white women. Only the heroic intervention of the South's better class of people, cloaked with the robes of the Ku Klux Klan, rescued the region from infamy. Northern "fanatics, blinded by passion, armed millions of ignorant Negroes and thrust them into mortal combat with the proud, half-starving Anglo-Saxon race of the South," Dixon charged in *The Leopard's Spots*. In a later novel, however, the Klan emerged victorious over the perfidious Yankees and their black minions. "Civilisation has been saved," a Dixon hero proclaimed, "and the South has been redeemed from shame."[22]

Dixon, a master manipulator of popular culture, found additional venues for his message. In 1907 his stage play, *The Clansman,* drew massive crowds across the United States; eight years later, his *Birth of a Nation* screenplay riveted millions who gasped at the flickering images of Civil War battles, booed the depiction of brutish Negro legislators enacting statues "providing for the intermarriage of blacks and whites," and cheered as the Ku Klux Klan forcibly restored white rule. Viewing *Birth of a Nation* in the White House, Dixon's friend Woodrow Wilson reputedly exclaimed that it was "like writing history with lightening. And my only regret is that it is all so terribly true."[23]

The white South accepted Dixon's novels as the embodiment of historical truth, and his fellow Baptists readily endorsed them. In 1902, reviewers for Richmond's *Religious Herald* and Montgomery's *Southern and Alabama Baptist* praised his *The Leopard's Spots,* one praying that it would "be bought and read by the hundred thousand." Acknowledging that some skeptics "will claim Mr. Dixon has given mere fancy pictures" concerning the Reconstruction period, the *Religious Herald*'s reviewer testified that he personally knew of "many communities in the South that had experiences just as wretched as [the author] portrayed." Dixon hardly exaggerated when he described carpetbaggers as wolves and scalawags as hyenas because they "used the negroes as their tools, and prompted them to villainies such as they would have never conceived" on their own. Reviewer Henry W. Battle, writing for the Alabama publication, cast a more literary tone, comparing Dixon's work to Harriet Beecher Stowe's antislavery novel. "Thomas Dixon has written perhaps the most notable book . . . since Uncle Tom's Cabin precipitated" the Civil War, he mused. But in contrast to the "little Yankee woman" and her abolitionist homily, which was "utterly out of harmony with the history of slavery in the South," Dixon constructed his work on the harsh lessons of a verifiable past. He then "fused them in the white heat of intense feeling into a story," which is "so strong, sincere, and masterful that he who reads it must pause to think—perhaps to weep." In spite of these effusive assessments, however, a few Baptist leaders acknowledged the historical veracity of Dixon's works, but at the same time professed discomfort at the passions evoked by them. One Arkansas clergyman cautioned his state convention that "such literature as 'The Clansman,' both as a book to read and in its dramatized form," served to "only increase the friction between the races."[24]

All Southern Baptist spokesmen recognized an intense "friction between the races," but most blamed Southern blacks, seeing a generational decline in morals precipitated by emancipation. Across the former Confederacy, church pundits contrasted the "virtuous Old Negro" who had matured under the Christianizing guidance of the plantation master with the degraded "new issue" of Negroes who had grown up influenced only by members of their own race, or, worse, under the sway of meddlesome Yankees. "The 'old issue' darkey is gone," lamented a writer from the Old Dominion state. Those delightful people who had once "imitated the manners and reflected the morals of Virginia gentlemen" had largely died out, to be replaced by "their insolent and indolent grandsons, who pass us without a nod, puffing smoke in our faces." A Mississippi churchman regretted that under freedom, "the great mass of untutored negroes" were sinking into "the grosser and more venal sins," most of which had been uncommon under slavery. An Arkansas leader agreed, affirming that "if anyone doubts the truth of this statement, let him compare the morals and the religion and the reliability of the average anti-bellum [sic] negro with the morals of the average new generation"; and an Alabama editor simply concluded that the new issue's vanity "encourages his encroachment upon our social structure."[25]

The historical paradigm developed by Southern patricians and readily endorsed by the Southern Baptist Church provided whites a rational explanation for the discordant world of the late nineteenth-century South and pointed to appropriate solutions that would restore the imagined virtues of the antebellum order. Holding that the black race lacked sufficient maturity to flourish under freedom, Southern elites preached a doctrine that demanded not only racial separation, but, more importantly, also urged that the superior white race rigidly control the inferior black race. From the patrician perspective, Negroes had thrived only within slavery's sheltering boundaries, but once emancipated, they floundered, confusing liberty with license. Firm in this conviction, white thought-leaders assumed that the safety and happiness of Southern Anglo-Saxons necessitated protection from Negro malefactors, supervision over Negro morals, and restrictions on Negro employment. From Virginia to Texas, Baptist ministers joined with white clergy across denominational lines to embrace these assumptions and to clothe them with the mantel of Christian virtue.

The intense white fear of African American criminality grew naturally from the Redeemer's anti-Populist campaign. Patrician-controlled newspapers, which had largely ignored the black race throughout the 1880s, had in the 1890s emblazoned their publications with lurid accounts of "Negro fiends" ravishing white women and of righteous white mobs lynching the "crazed brutes." These journals appealed to the pre–Civil War anxiety that freed Negroes would revert to savagery, killing, and stealing without remorse. Although the resulting Negrophobia had the desired effect of diminishing black-white cooperation under the Populist banner, it had the negative consequence of revealing to the outside world a decadent white South as uncivilized as it was cruel. Such imagery undermined the Southern class system, suggesting that the region's patriciate lacked the requisite moral authority necessary to maintain order. Southern elites called on their religious leaders to help restore Southern integrity; Baptist churchmen vigorously played their role.

In an episode illustrative of this nexus between religion and the image problem created by lynching, in September 1915, Clarence Poe, editor of North Carolina's *Progressive Farmer,* wrote to a Nashville acquaintance urging him to intercede with Baylor University President S. P. Brooks and to ask the Texan to use his influence as a respected Baptist leader to oppose mob rule. "I believe that the lynch law is a blot on the fair name of the South," Poe explained. He despised the fact that outsiders had castigated "our people" as "sinners above all that dwell in Jerusalem" and made the average white Southerner seem "a barbarian as compared with the men of the North and West." Poe was confident that "if Dr. Brooks" would "prepare a statement" defending "the spirit of the Southern people but at the same time" pointing out the evil "we must free ourselves from, it may do good."[26]

Brooks agreed. He called to his campus an assemblage of chief executives from church-related colleges across Texas. Tasked to debate the "question of mob lawlessness and lynching in the South," they respectfully listened to the Baylor president's antilynching address, endorsed it, and ordered it published in the proceedings of the next Texas assembly of the Southern Baptist Convention. For more than thirty years, Brooks averred, "a spirit of vengeance and race hatred" had fueled extralegal violence. Scrupulously avoiding any direct reference to the ethnicity of mob victims, he charged that individuals accused of crimes had been denied due process of law even as they were murdered "by shooting or hanging or burning, or some brutal combination" of all three. Brooks focused instead on the failure of the South's "best citizens" to intervene and stop the outrages. As a consequence, "the whole South has suffered in the judgment of the civilized world," he lectured. "Let us in honor of our beloved Southland . . . do our utmost best . . . to put an end forever to these dreadful outbursts of vengeance and passion in which our laws have been defied, our civilization abused, and the good name of our section brought into disgrace."[27]

Such chauvinistic Southern Baptist spokesmen took umbrage at outside critics' condemnation of their homeland. Shaken by a British editorial chastening Southern whites for their brutish inclinations, a Virginia minister asked whether "those who resort to mob violence know that they are forcing their beloved Southland to forfeit in the eyes of the world that portion of chivalry, justice, and civilization which is the glory of our past and the chief possession of the present?" Pointing to a Richmond statue of Stonewall Jackson, recently presented to the city "by a company of English gentlemen," he reminded his audience that the better class of Englishmen had favored the late Confederacy. But at the twentieth century's opening, English "respect for the chivalry of the South [was] endangered by the frequency of the fiendish acts of mobs." Voicing similar thoughts in South Carolina, the *Baptist Courier*'s editor reflected that although a recently lynched Negro murderer had "richly deserved punishment," those men "who hung him had no right to inflict the punishment." This lawless act was but "another blot on the fair name of our state."[28]

However distasteful lynching might be, Baptist churchmen assumed its cause sprang from a natural response to the Negro's primitive moral character. A culture in which two races lived together in enforced equality emboldened the inferior to prey on the vulnerabilities of the superior. Viewing society from the top down, the editor of Montgomery's *Alabama Baptist* remonstrated that the South's better class of whites were "trying to deal with the most formidable problem that civilized mankind ever had to face." Not only did they cope with a "mighty mass of negroes," but they also over watched "a great many ignorant and often degraded white people." The savage nature of the former excited in the latter "the anarchistic madness of mob violence." A Mississippi minister pointed out with regret that lynching would likely continue so long as "the fiend exists to despoil the home"; Southern "mothers and daughters" quaked in fear of renegade Negro men, "the monster in human form." Sharing in this pessimism, one Virginia evangelist lamented that until the "religion of our Lord Jesus Christ" was properly taught to the black race, the "horrible crimes perpetuated by negroes" would be followed "by speedy punishments, sometimes almost as revolting as the crimes they expiate." Another Baptist preacher from the same state reasoned that given the black man's vestigial temperament, lynching proved counter-productive. "Perhaps [its] most ominous aspect," he reasoned, "lies in the fact that it tends to destroy in the mind of the negro that respect for law which must be our ultimate reliance in restraining his animal instincts."[29]

Fear of chaos combined with a desire to maintain their own position of supremacy by defining appropriate ethnic relationships in a racially divided South underscored Baptist opposition to mob-inspired justice. A Richmond college professor, pointing out that lynching brutalizes the community and dulls public conscience, condemned it as anarchy. No matter how heinous the crimes committed by blacks, he emphasized, they are not an excuse for lynching. This act not only created disrespect for law, but it also threatened the moral superiority of the white race. An Alabama Baptist leader warned that "if this happened the white will not lift the negro; both will go down together to the vengeance taking level." Common sense, such men reasoned, mandated that white elites take their paternal responsibilities seriously, dis-suade violence, and develop more positive approaches to the race problem. "Lynching impeaches the spirit of fairness in the Anglo-Saxon," rationalized a Virginia delegate to his state's general convention. Because the "Saxon [has taken the] responsibility of government, the more careful must we be that full justice and protection be given the negro. We deny him equality; we must therefore guarantee him equity." On the opposite end of the former Confederacy, the Texas General Convention agreed. "We thoroughly believe in three things for the negro: Justice, kindness and salvation," they professed in 1909. "To give him just treatment is necessary to the welfare of the domi-nant race."[30]

Baptist elites assumed that white Christians must accept the responsi-bility of educating Southern blacks to their proper subordination. "When the negro can be made to feel that his is an inferior race and must be satis-fied to remain such," reasoned a Virginia physician, "then, and only then will his real improvement begin." Confident that the master class's long associa-tion with slaves endowed Southern whites with special understanding of the Negro's character and capabilities, Baptist leaders lectured that Southern whites, and only Southern whites, fully appreciated the black man's peculiar needs. "We are responsible, for the negro being brought into this land in an ignorant state," declared the Florida Baptist Convention in 1912. For that reason, the black race "naturally and rightfully looks to us for the light." Six years later, Louisiana Baptists repeated the assertion. "God has opened [the Negroes] hearts toward us," they proclaimed. Blacks "yet look to us in a large measure for spiritual leadership, as they have looked in other matters." Virginia Baptists wrote more succinctly that "nobody understands the negro race better than the Southern people"; their Arkansas brethren claimed that the "white people of the South understood [Negroes] better and are more interested in them than other sections of the country"; and the Southern Baptist General Convention of 1904 ordained that "reforms in Negro education" must be "in accord with the judgment and experience of Southern white people."[31]

"The judgment and experience" of Southern Baptist churchmen suggested that schooling blacks in ways appropriate to the intellectual development of whites misdirected the energies of blacks. "We have grave doubts as to whether a finished education, a classical education, makes the negro as a race a stronger factor in our civilization," surmised the *Alabama Baptist*'s editor. "Learning is a very dangerous thing to the negro." In the mind of this journalist, and in the collective mind of the Southern patriciate as a whole, God had preordained blacks to be "hewers of wood and drawers of water" for whites. Inappropriate classroom curricula only aroused within the Negro discontent with his white-determined proper place, engendered within him unrequitable ambitions, and stirred within him rebellion. "An educated negro makes a poor servant," asserted a Tennessee churchman. "These educated negroes are the very ones most apt to turn upon Southern whites and give them trouble." Another clergyman who shared this belief pointed with disdain to the "throngs of young negroes in the towns and cities who go to the public schools and who cannot be induced to work."[32]

"Properly trained and well managed, the negro finds a useful place which no other race can fulfill," lectured an Alabama minister in 1902, and his fellow religionists echoed the sentiment.[33] Deeming a religiously based education as the salvation of the black race, Southern Baptists hailed its potential to mold African Americans into the safe, obedient, and subservient caste desired by upper-class whites. To that end, they identified two distinct audiences among the Negro population: the black masses who needed instruction in accord with their proper station, and black ministers who had to be trained to lead their congregations in accord with white wishes.

White Baptists, who were unwilling to envision the black masses as composed of anything other than minor artisans, domestics, and common laborers, heralded industrial training schools as best suited for the African American's improvement. Certainly these institutions must integrate a strong

religious element into a curriculum dedicated to the white perspective of
the Negro's proper role in Southern society. As one Baptist cleric cogently
observed, in these industrial schools, blacks "can learn to labor and to perfect themselves along such lines of work as they are best fitted for, being
servants in our Southern homes." Dismissing education for the Negro race
"without religious training" as "a curse affording increased facilities for the
commission of crime," a Virginia Baptist insisted on the necessity for "moral
training" as a restraint on "the vicious mind." In the same state, the editor of
the *Religious Herald* encouraged "proper" education for black youth. "It is,
of course, understood by education and religion for the negro we mean very
practical things. His religion must be moral and his education must be
manual." With equal emphasis, the editor of Tennessee's *Baptist and Reflector* scoffed that "education without religion will only make the negro a smart
rascal," but he was convinced that "religion with education will make him a
useful citizen."[34]

Believing that black ministers could be either a bane or a blessing to the
white Southern weal, Baptist clergymen complained that all too often "the
low state of religion among [Negroes] is in a great degree due to [their]
ignorant and immoral leadership." Only through the proper training of black
clergy, training suited to white patrician interests, could black Southerners
be inculcated with values appropriate to an orderly society. "The way to benefit the negro is not by working directly with the masses," lectured a Texas
evangelist. Uplift would only occur "by working with their leaders and
through them reaching the masses." Condemning the typical black preacher
as "more of a politician than anything else," an Alabama leader demanded
that such ministers forsake "political mischief" and focus instead on the
practical needs of their own people, "to raise their standard of home life,
quicken their moral sense, and teach them genuine morality." Reasoning
that a "people never rise above their priest," another Alabama churchman
concluded that whites "must lend a helping hand to the negro preacher."[35]

In 1894, the Southern Baptist Convention embraced this cause with enthusiasm, cooperating with the Northern-sponsored American Baptist Home
Mission Society and with various black Baptist state conventions in the creation of "New Era Institutes" across the South. With financial assistance from
their Northern brethren, Southern Baptists ministers created hundreds of
short-term institutes to school unlettered black evangelists in the truths of
the Gospel. The course of study, however, went far beyond simple lessons in
theology. The Southern Baptist Convention, championing their successes in
1896, were not only pleased at the quality of the institutes' Bible curriculum,

but they also boasted that the white ministers added "as may be wise other topics as . . . demanded by the peculiar needs of given localities." Conscientious white evangelists lectured their black colleagues on proper attitudes toward politics, personal morality, financial responsibility, and, especially, racial decorum. Having attended several New Era Institutes in Virginia, North Carolina, South Carolina, and Alabama, one white administrator enthused that "the plan of co-operation" with the Negroes had "wrought a revolution in the condition of affairs among the colored Baptists."[36]

Such optimism proved premature. Their black brethren, discerning the fundamentally racist intentions of white Baptists, gradually withdrew from the movement, chafing at their status as second-class citizens in the Kingdom of Christ as well as the kingdom of men. White Baptists, however, found the movement's decline was rooted in the black community's inherent imperfections. In 1902 the Board of Home Missions of the Virginia Baptist Convention admitted discouragement, blaming the New Era Institute's imminent demise in their state on "dissensions among the negroes and the apparent apathy of those who most need [its] training." That same year, the Texas General Convention complained that "the negroes in Texas [had] discontinued [the work] because of divisions among them"; and the following year, the Southern Baptist General Convention lamented even more failures. "In South Carolina there [was] no co-operative work with the Negroes of any kind, the Negroes themselves having declined to accept the arrangement proposed to them"; and in Georgia the movement had expired "on account of division among the Negroes." Four years later, the General Convention acknowledged the New Era Institute's complete collapse and urged new, less formal outreaches to their black brethren.[37]

In the twentieth century's early days, the Southern Baptist Church and its thought-leaders played their seminal role in maintaining a white supremacist social order sharply articulated by race and class. In common with white clergy across denominational lines, they gave the sanction of religion to a society in which white men of substance were born to rule, lesser whites to follow, and blacks to obey. Unable to free themselves from their own social structures, white Baptists would not espouse, perhaps could not imagine, a gospel in which Christians of all races and social condition resided together in a state of equality, "neither slave nor free." Instead, Southern Baptist churchmen served the needs of the region's ruling aristocracy and enjoyed the fruits of their own preferred place in society.

Although in 1912 a Texas minister could prayerfully petition God that the "unregenerate negro, black, like his skin, . . . be washed and made white in the blood of the Lamb," in his mind-set, and in that of his coreligionists, the spiritual whiteness of the regenerate Negro's soul neither bleached his skin nor fitted him for the entitlements enjoyed by his white brothers. A Georgia Baptist more correctly assessed the social requisites for a redeemed black Christian in an orderly South: "Let each know his place, stay in it, and do his duty there and we shall have no trouble, otherwise, there will be conflict, bloodshed, extinction."[38]

Southern Baptists' constant portrayals of blacks as a degenerate and dangerous black race threatening to the welfare of the white weal encouraged racial animosity and prevented meaningful interactions between Southern whites and Southern blacks. Deep into the twentieth century, the Southern Baptist Church drew on this heritage to remain a staunch defender of the white power structure. When faced with the civil rights revolution beginning in the 1950s, it continued as a bastion of the racist old order.

NOTES

1. This thesis is at odds with David L. Chappell's in his recent book, *A Stone of Hope: Prophetic Religion and the Death of Jim Crow* (Chapel Hill: University of North Carolina Press, 2004). This essay and Chappell's book clearly cover different time periods. But for commentary on Chappell's book, see the Introduction above, especially the text associated with note 4.

2. "An Ancient Race Problem, with a Modern Application," *Religious Herald* 74 (November 7, 1901): 8 (first quotation); *Proceedings of the Arkansas Baptist State Convention, Sixty-second Annual Session* (n. p., [1911]), 54 (second quotation). For a discussion of the Southern Baptist use of Calvinistic doctrine to justify slavery, see Wayne Flynt, *Alabama Baptists: Southern Baptists in the Heart of Dixie* (Tuscaloosa: University of Alabama Press, 1998), 123–24.

3. Although leaders of the Southern Baptist Church shouldered what they considered their burden to the South's black population, their essential cosmology was far from unique. For a broader examination of Southern white Protestant beliefs on racial issues of this period, see Fred Arthur Bailey, "'The Work among the Colored Brethren': Race, Religion, and Social Order in the New South, 1890–1920," *West Tennessee Historical Society Papers* 55 (2002): 55–71.

4. Keith Lynn King, "Religious Dimensions of the Agrarian Protest in Texas, 1870–1908" (Ph.D. diss., University of Illinois, 1985), 15, 21–22, 93–94; Anthony L. Dunnavant, "David Lipscomb and the 'Preferential Option for the Poor' among Post-Bellum Churches of Christ," in *Poverty and Ecclesiology: Nineteenth-century Evangelicals in the Light of Liberation Theology*, ed. Anthony L. Dunnavant (Collegeville, Minn.: Liturgical Press, 1992), 27–50; William C. Kostlevy, "Benjamin Titus Roberts and the 'Preferential Option for the Poor' in the Early Free Methodist Church," in Dunnavant, *Poverty and Ecclesiology*, 51–67.

5. C. Vann Woodward, *Origins of the New South, 1877–1913* (Baton Rouge: Louisiana State University Press, 1951), 254–58; Edward L. Ayers, *The Promise of*

the New South: Life after Reconstruction (New York: Oxford University Press, 1992), 274.

6. Bruce M. Palmer, *"Man over Money": The Southern Populist Critique of American Capitalism* (Chapel Hill: University of North Carolina Press, 1980); Frederick A. Bode, "Religion and Class Hegemony: A Populist Critique in North Carolina," *Journal of Southern History* 37 (August 1971): 417–38 (quotation 438).

7. J. Wayne Flynt, "Southern Baptists: Rural to Urban Transition," *Baptist History and Heritage* 16 (January 1981): 26–27.

8. King, "Religious Dimensions," 65–76; Flynt, *Alabama Baptists,* 83–84, 152, 224; Frederick A. Bode, *Protestantism and the New South: North Carolina Baptists and Methodists in Political Crisis, 1894–1903* (Charlottesville: University Press of Virginia, 1975), 39–60.

9. Bill J. Leonard, *"Comunidades Eclesiales de Base* and Autonomous Local Churches: Catholic Liberationists Meet Baptist Landmarkers," in Dunnavant, *Poverty and Ecclesiology,* 78, 84–85, 87; W. Morgan Patterson, "Landmarkism," in *Encyclopedia of Southern Baptists,* ed. Clifton J. Allen et al. (2 vols.; Nashville: Broadman Press, 1958), 2:757.

10. Richard Goode, "The Godly Insurrection in Limestone County: Social Gospel, Populism, and Southern Culture in the Late Nineteenth Century," *Religion and American Culture* 3 (Summer 1993): 155–69.

11. E. S. P. Pool, "Report on Negro Problem," in *Proceedings of the Fifty-eighth Annual Session of the Baptist General Convention of Texas* (Brownwood, Tex.: Mayes Printing, 1906), 88.

12. C. V. Edwards et al., "Report on Home Missions," in *Proceedings of the Seventy-fourth Session of the Mississippi Baptist Convention* (Memphis: Press of Filcher Printing, [1912]), 71 (first quotation); Pool, "Report on Negro Problem," 88 (second quotation); J. J. Bennett, "Board of Missions," in *Minutes of the Eighty-fifth Anniversary of the Baptist Convention of the State of Georgia* (Atlanta: Foote and Davies, 1906), 75 (third quotation).

13. "Work among the Negroes," in *Annual of Southern Baptist Convention 1912* (Nashville: Marshall and Bruce, 1912), 297 (first quotation); "The Race Conference," *Alabama Baptist* 27 (May 17, 1900): 3 (second quotation); A. J. Dickinson, "The Negro Problem Can Not Now Be Solved," *Alabama Baptist* 40 (September 6, 1905): 6 (third quotation); "Report of Home Missions," in *Minutes of the Ninety-fourth Annual Session of the State Convention of the Baptist Denomination in South Carolina* (Greenville: Baptist Courier, 1915), 99 (fourth quotation); J. L. Barrett et al., "Work among Negroes," in *Proceedings of the Arkansas Baptist State Convention, Sixty sev enth Annual Session* (n.p. [1921]), 94 (fifth quotation); B. W. Griffith et al., "Report of Committee on 'The Condition of the Negro Race': Their Religious Needs and Duty of Our People toward Them," in *Proceedings of the Sixty-fifth Session of the Mississippi Baptist Convention* (Hazlehurst, Miss.: Courier, 1903), 51 (sixth quotation).

14. Clericus Civio, "Christian Civics—No. 2," *Alabama Baptist* 26 (April 20, 1897): 3 (first quotation); Clericus Civio, "Christian Civics—No. 3," *Alabama Baptist* 27 (April 27, 1897): 3 (second quotation); "A Great Opportunity and a Great Peril," *Religious Herald* 74 (February 28, 1901): 8 (third quotation).

15. J. G. McCall, "The Negro Problem," *Christian Index* 79 (May 25, 1899): 3 (first, second quotations); J. B. Gambrell, "Dr. Gambrell to Gen. Morgan," *Religious Herald* 67 (May 10, 1894): 1 (third quotation); Jesse Ewell, "Some Current Ques-

tions," *Religious Herald* 73 (September 10, 1900): 3 (fourth quotation); S. C. Mitchell, "Some Aspects of Democracy," *Religious Herald* 74 (July 18, 1901): 2 (fifth quotation); "Great Opportunity," 8 (sixth quotation); "Race Conference" (May 17, 1900), 3 (seventh quotation); "Work among the Negroes," in *Annual of Southern Baptist Convention 1912,* 165 (eighth quotation). For a discussion of the disenfranchisement efforts in Virginia, Alabama, and Georgia, see J. Morgan Kousser, *The Shaping of Southern Politics: Suffrage Restriction and the Establishment of the One-Party South, 1880–1910* (New Haven, Conn.: Yale University Press, 1974), 130–38, 171–81, 209–23.

16. Ewell, "Some Current Questions," 3.

17. A. B. Cabaniss, "Rash Assertions," *Baptist and Reflector* 60 (March 18, 1897): 4 (first, third quotations); "Report on Colored Population," in *Proceedings of the Forty-sixth Annual Session of the Baptist General Convention of Texas* (Waco, Tex.: Baptist Standard Printing House, 1894), 62 (second quotation); "Report of Home Missions," in *Minutes of the Eightieth Annual Session of the State Convention of the Baptist Denomination in South Carolina* (Spartansburg, S.C.: W. F. Barnes, 1901), 55 (fourth quotation).

18. "The Colored People," *Alabama Baptist* 32 (April 13, 1904): 5 (first quotation); W. H. Sims et al., "Negro Population," in *Proceedings of the Sixty-eighth Annual Session of the Baptist General Convention of Texas* (n.p., [1917]), 59 (second quotation); C. W. Daniels et al., "Negro Work," in *Proceedings of the Arkansas Baptist State Convention, Fifty-second Annual Session* (Little Rock: Arkansas Baptist Job Department, 1900), 48 (third quotation); J. Pope Brown et al., "Board of Missions," in *Minutes of the Seventy-ninth Anniversary of the Baptist Convention of the State of Georgia* (Atlanta: Foote and Davies, 1901), 22 (fourth quotation).

19. "The Negroes," in *Proceedings of the Southern Baptist Convention . . . 1896* (Atlanta: Franklin Printing and Publishing, 1896), lxiii (first quotation); McCall, "Negro Problem," 3 (second quotation).

20. Cabaniss, "Rash Assertions," 4 (first quotation); Gambrell, "Dr. Gambrell to Gen. Morgan," 1 (second quotation); "The Race Conference," *Alabama Baptist* 27 (April 26, 1900): 4 (third quotation); "Work among the Negroes," in *Annual of Southern Baptist Convention 1901* (Nashville: Marshall and Bruce, 1901), 143 (fourth quotation).

21. M. Karen Crowe, ed., "Southern Horizons: The Autobiography of Thomas Dixon—A Critical Edition" (Ph.D. diss., New York University, 1982), 1, 25, 55, 148, 270–71; Raymond A. Cook, *Fire from the Flint: The Amazing Career of Thomas Dixon* (Winston-Salem, N.C.: John F. Blair, 1968), 33–40, 51–52, 71; Raymond A. Cook, *Thomas Dixon* (New York: Twayne, 1974), 28–29, 32–35; *New York Times,* June 9, 1903 (quotation).

22. Thomas Dixon Jr., *The Leopard's Spots: A Romance of the White Man's Burden, 1865–1900* (New York: Doubleday, Page, 1902), 85 (first quotation); Thomas Dixon Jr., *The Clansman: An Historical Romance of the Ku Klux Klan* (New York: Doubleday, Page, 1905), 374 (second quotation); Thomas Dixon Jr., *The Traitor: The Story of the Fall of the Invisible Empire* (New York: Doubleday, Page, 1907).

23. Thomas Dixon Jr., *The Birth of a Nation* (screenplay, 1915), reprinted in Robert Lang, ed., *The Birth of a Nation: D. W. Griffith, Director* (New Brunswick, N.J.: Rutgers University Press, 1993), 43–156; Thomas Dixon Jr. to Woodrow Wilson, February 20, 1915, Woodrow Wilson Papers, Library of Congress, Washington, D.C. The film was presented in the White House, February 1915, after which Wilson

greeted with enthusiasm Dixon, the film's director D. W. Griffith, and the projection staff who accompanied them. Arthur S. Link, Wilson's best-known biographer, casts doubts, however, on the authenticity of Wilson's quotation, pointing out that the exact quotation first appeared in Milton MacKaye, "The Birth of a Nation," *Scribner's Magazine* 102 (November 1937): 69. Certainly Dixon used Wilson's endorsement of the film, if not the exact quotation, to promote and to defend the movie, until political pressure forced Wilson to publicly separate himself from the movie. Dixon, a novelist, and Wilson, a historian as well as president of the United States, shared a common understanding of the dynamics of the Civil War and Reconstruction era. Arthur S. Link, *Wilson: The New Freedom* (Princeton: Princeton University Press, 1956), 252–54; Arthur S. Link, ed., *The Papers of Woodrow Wilson* (33 vols. to date; Princeton: Princeton University Press, 1980–present), 32:142; Michael Paul Rogin, *Ronald Reagan, the Movie and Other Episodes in Political Demonology* (Berkeley: University of California Press, 1987), 191–93; John Hope Franklin, "*Birth of a Nation*—Propaganda as History," *Massachusetts Review* 20 (Autumn 1979): 417–34. Born in Virginia and raised in Georgia, Wilson's views on the Civil War and Reconstruction paralleled those of Dixon. See Woodrow Wilson, *A History of the American People: Documentary Edition* (10 vols.; New York: Harper and Brothers, 1918 [1901]), 9:49–50, 9:59, 9:61–62.

24. G. review of *The Leopard's Spots: A Story of the Whiteman's Burden, 1865–1900* by Thomas Dixon, *Religious Herald* 75 (April 10, 1902): 7 (first, second, third quotations); Henry W. Battle, "The Leopard's Spots, or the White Man's Burden," *Southern and Alabama Baptist* 29 (June 11, 1902): 7 (fourth, fifth, sixth quotations); J. B. Searcy, "Report on the Colored Work," in *Proceedings of the Arkansas Baptist State Convention, Fifty-eighth Annual Session* (Pine Bluff, Ark.: Commercial Print, [1907]), 49 (seventh quotation).

25. M, "Are the Negroes Improving?" *Religious Herald* 71 (March 10, 1898): 3 (first quotation); Griffith et al., "Report of Committee," 49–50 (second quotation); Daniels et al., "Negro Work," 48 (third quotation); "Race Conference" (April 26, 1900), 4 (fourth quotation); "Work among the Negroes," in *Annual of Southern Baptist Convention 1900* (Nashville: Marshall and Bruce, 1900), cxxviii.

26. Clarence Poe to J. E. McCulloch, September 22, 1915, S. P. Brooks Papers, Baylor Archives, Carroll Library, Baylor University, Waco, Tex.

27. S. P. Brooks, "Evils of the Mob, an Address to the People of Texas," in *Annual of the Baptist General Convention Texas. . . . 1915 Containing the Proceedings of the Sixty-seventh Annual Session* (n.p. [1915]), 120–21.

28. M. Ashby Jones et al., "A Protest against Lynching," in *Minutes of the Eighty-first Annual Session of the Baptist General Association of Virginia* (n.p., [1904]), 60, 61 (first quotations); "Another Lynching," *Baptist Courier* 26 (December 20, 1894): 2 (second quotation). For a discussion of the relationship of Southern religion and the "Lost Cause" myth, see Charles Reagan Wilson, *Baptized in Blood: The Religion of the Lost Cause, 1865–1920* (Athens: University of Georgia Press, 1980), 34–57.

29. "Shall Lynchings Go On?" *Alabama Baptist* 21 (February 22, 1894): 2 (first quotation); Griffith et al., "Report of Committee" 50 (second quotation); C. B. Fleet, "Report of the Home Missions Board," in *Minutes of the Seventy-seventh Annual Session of the Baptist General Association of Virginia* (Richmond: Dispatch Printing House, 1900), 32 (third quotation); Jones et al., "Protest against Lynching," 60 (fifth quotation).

30. "Are Lynchings Ever Justified," 2 (first quotation); Jones et al., "Protest against

Lynching," 61–62 (second quotation); W. M. Harris and R. F. Jenkins, "Report on Negro Population," in *Proceedings of the Sixty-first Annual Session of the Baptist General Convention of Texas* (n.p. [1909]), 89 (third quotation).

31. Ewell, "Some Current Questions," 3 (first quotation); J. L. Hampton, "Home Missions," in *Proceedings of the Fifty-seventh Annual Session of the Florida Baptist Convention* (n.p., [1912]), 76 (second quotation); "Work among the Negroes," in *Annual of the Louisiana State Baptist Convention 1918 Containing the Proceedings of the Seventieth Session* (n.p., 1918) (third quotation); C. B. Fleet, "Report of the Home Missions Board," in *Minutes of the Eighty-third Annual Session of the Baptist General Association of Virginia* (n.p., [1906]), 78 (fourth quotation); Thomas H. Plemmons et al., "Work among Negroes," in *Proceedings of the Arkansas Baptist Convention, Sixty-fourth Annual Session* (n.p. [1917]), 103 (fifth quotation); "Work among the Negroes," in *Annual of Southern Baptist Convention 1904* (Nashville: Marshall and Bruce, 1904), 165 (sixth quotation).

32. "Race Conference" (May 17, 1900), 3 (first quotation); "The Negro and the Southern People," *Baptist and Reflector* 64 (June 28, 1906): 9 (second quotation); S. M. Provence, "The South and the New Education," *Southern and Alabama Baptist* 29 (June 11, 1902): 5 (third quotation).

33. Provence, "The South and the New Education," 5.

34. C. C. Brown, "Extracts from 'The Negro in the South,'" *Southern and Alabama Baptist* 29 (February 19, 1902): 3 (first quotation); C. B. Fleet, "Report of the Home Missions Board," in *Minutes of the Sixty-ninth Annual Session of the Baptist General Association of Virginia* (Richmond: Dispatch Steam Printing House, 1892), 63–64 (second quotation); "The South's Sceptre," *Richmond Herald* 67 (September 3, 1903): 8 (third quotation); "The Negro," *Baptist and Reflector* 64 (April 14, 1904): 8 (fourth quotation).

35. Griffith et al., "Report of Committee," 50 (first quotation); Pool, "Report on Negro Problem," 89 (second quotation); "Negro Preacher in Politics," *Southern and Alabama Baptist* 29 (October 22, 1902): 8 (third quotation); Brown, "Extracts from 'The Negro in the South,'" 3 (fourth quotation); "Colored People," *Alabama Baptist* 22 (February 21, 1895): 1 (fifth quotation).

36. Paul Harvey, *Redeeming the South: Religious Cultures and Racial Identities among Southern Baptists, 1865–1925* (Chapel Hill: University of North Carolina Press, 1997), 183–84; C. Durham, "Institutes for Colored Preachers," *Biblical Record* 67 (June 22, 1892): 3; Fleet, "Report of the Home Missions Board" (1892), 63; "Negroes," in *Proceedings of the Southern Baptist Convention . . . 1894* (Atlanta: Franklin Printing and Publishing, 1894), lviii; "The Negroes," in *Proceedings of the Southern Baptist Convention . . . 1896*, lxii (first quotation); H. L. Morehouse, "Our Co-operative Work for the Negroes," *Alabama Baptist* 24 (December 16, 1897): 1 (second quotation).

37. C. B. Fleet, "Report of the Home Missions Board," in *Minutes of the Seventy-ninth Annual Session of the Baptist General Association of Virginia* (n.p., [1902]), 24 (first quotation); "Annual Report of the Board of Directors to the Baptist General Convention of Texas," in *Proceedings Fifty-fourth Annual Session of the Baptist General Convention of Texas* (n.p., [1902]), 23 (second quotation); "Negroes," in *Annual of Southern Baptist Convention 1912* (Nashville: Marshall and Bruce, 1912), 161 (fourth quotation); "Work among the Negroes," in *Annual of Southern Baptist Convention 1907* (Nashville: Marshall and Bruce, 1907), 193.

38. M. E. Weaver et al., "Negro Population," in *Proceedings of the Sixty-fourth*

Annual Session of the Baptist General Convention of Texas (n.p., [1912]), 126 (first quotation); "The Color Line Drawn," *Christian Index* (May 26, 1892), 4 (second quotation).

Factionalism and Ethnic Politics in Atlanta

German Jews from the Civil War through the Progressive Era

Mark K. Bauman

Most historians of Southern urbanization pay scant attention to ethnic or immigrant group politics.[1] It is generally assumed that, lacking the numbers and concentrations associated with Northern cities, such groups failed either to coalesce or to exert much impact. The presence and obvious persecution of African Americans also negated any appeal to ethnic identity by the Southern power structure. According to historian Thomas M. Deaton, blacks served as "surrogate immigrants," allowing foreigners to rise at relatively the same rate as native whites and experience less "ethnic sensitivity."[2]

In this essay, I argue that a least one ethnic immigrant group formed effective alliances, "clustered" in particular areas in sufficient numbers, and exerted power beyond its size so that it wielded considerable political influence and preferment. The German Jewish community of Atlanta from the Civil War to World War I serves as a case study of Southern urban political dynamics that were evident in Memphis, New Orleans, Savannah, and other cities.[3]

The Atlanta Jewish Community

Jews had resided in Atlanta virtually from its founding. The first subcommunity to arrive migrated from central Europe, particularly the Germanic states and Poland, during the late antebellum period. These people acculturated, became a major force for commercial development, and served the city disproportionately in many capacities. From 1880 onward, an influx of Jews from Southern and Eastern Europe, mostly Russia, and after 1906 by a much smaller contingent from the crumbling Ottoman Empire, joined them. The "Russian Jews" overwhelmed the older immigrants in number, and almost as many forces divided the three subcommunities as unified them.[4] Because many of the newer immigrants remained in the struggling stage of adjustment, they participated only intermittently in politics and are thus not the focus of this study.[5]

The Jewish community never attained more than about 3 percent of Atlanta's population. Yet this statistic is misleading for three reasons. First, Jews tended to cluster in certain wards where they could provide the balance of power. Historian Ronald Bayor explains that the cluster pattern continued with geographic mobility. Finding "migration and re-clustering," Bayor concludes that "clearly the uniqueness of the urban South, in terms of having solely a racial rather than a racial and ethnic residential experience as in the North, must be brought into question and further investigated." What Bayor identified for residential patterns, the evidence in my essay here suggests, was true for political patterns as well.[6] Second, the newer East European Jews during the decades covered here clustered in areas of major black population densities.[7] The proximity facilitated significant interaction that opened both groups to outbursts of persecution. Finally, the German Jews achieved a level of affluence and civic involvement that made them far more active and influential than their numbers alone would have warranted. Although their small population did not allow the replication of the ethnic politics associated with immigrant groups in Northern metropolises, other variables contributed to a parallel phenomenon.

THE PATTERN OF SUCCESS AND FAILURE

Historian Steven Hertzberg traces Jewish involvement in Atlanta politics from the presidential election of 1868. In that year the local Democratic Party showed concern that area Jews might vote for Republican Ulysses S. Grant instead of their candidate, Horatio Seymour. The president of the Hebrew Benevolent Congregation reassured the Democrats' city executive committee of Jewish loyalty, and Jews worked on committees for a party rally. Soon thereafter, Jews entered Atlanta electoral politics themselves. In 1873, Aaron Haas won election as a ward alderman, and he filled an at-large seat with the next election. During the next four years, Jews held city council positions, and Samuel Weil represented Fulton County in the state house. In 1908,

Fulton County chose Henry A. Alexander for the state legislature. Besides regular positions on the school board and city council, the clerk's position at the Division 2 draft board seems to have been reserved as a Jewish seat. When Joseph N. Hirsch resigned in 1917, Simon H. Freitag replaced him.[8] Atlanta Jews also frequently assisted the city with bond issues.[9]

Yet the political success of Jews was not guaranteed. In 1896, while Thomas Watson and the Populists were defeated on the national level as they supported the free silver issue, Jewish Atlantans supported sound money. A year later, Hoke Smith's forces gained dominance on the school board and Aaron Haas failed to receive the Democratic nod for city council, something cousin Jacob (a former councilman) also failed to do in 1899. Joseph Hirsch won election to the city council in 1892, 1894, 1896, 1899, 1904, and 1906. Noteworthy are the years when his attempts failed—years of Hoke Smith factional success. In 1900 Frank J. Cohen observed that "there is not a Jew holding office in Atlanta." Four Jews ran for Democratic nominations for city posts unsuccessfully over the next eight years. Although Hertzberg blames religious discrimination for these failures, he also credits voter rejection of Jewish candidates to their opposition to prohibition and free silver.[10] Anti-Semitism was at work, but it was intertwined with political factionalism and the parallel persecution of African Americans. Those dynamics fostered the mentality fomenting the Leo Frank case in the same way that the climate of popular opinion and political rhetoric contributed to the Atlanta race riot of 1906.

THE NETWORK OF JEWISH MOVERS AND SHAKERS

The background and context of these positive and negative experiences are traceable to a complex political, economic, and religious-cultural matrix. Politics in Atlanta during the late nineteenth and early twentieth centuries can be defined as Byzantine. Although support for Republican, Independent, and Populist Parties intermittently emerged, the Democratic Party dominated. In this one-party situation, intraparty factionalism replaced interparty competition. Although alliances within the Democratic Party sometimes shifted, and political opportunists like Tom Watson and Hugh M. Dorsey occasionally clouded the picture, conservative and progressive factions are identifiable over the long term.[11]

A small group of German Jewish businessmen in Atlanta apparently participated within the conservative faction. Their involvement is traceable through the activities of a group of closely allied individuals as early as the

Civil War. The earliest link to later activism was David Mayer, arguably Atlanta's foremost Jewish leader of the nineteenth century.[12] Mayer, born in Bechtheim by Worms-am-Rhein in the Germanic states in 1815, trained as a dentist before his emigration to New York in 1839. He moved south for greater economic opportunity, working first in Tennessee and then in Washington, Georgia, before selling a stock of goods in Atlanta in 1847 and returning a year later to settle. By 1862, Mayer was a Whitehall Street merchant with assets over $59,000, including a home near his store and six slaves. Besides selling clothing and dry goods, he traded slaves and later also sold alcoholic beverages in partnership with a son.

On the eve of the Civil War, Mayer encouraged local merchants to refrain from business contacts with Northern Republicans and abolitionists, and he joined the local Minute Man Association espousing secession from the Union. During the war, Mayer donated rice to the poor and protected supplies from Union troops, earning himself a position as the supply officer on Governor Joseph E. Brown's staff. When Brown was temporarily incarcerated in Washington, D.C., after the war, he spent a day or two with Mayer on his way home. Robert Toombs and brothers Alexander and Linton Stephens, all key players in Confederate and state politics, also visited Mayer.[13] When Atlanta fell to Sherman's forces, the Mayer family temporarily relocated to New York. Apparently his Confederate sympathies stopped neither this move nor the marriage of two of his daughters to Jacob and David Steinheimer—brothers who had fled the South rather than fight.[14]

Mayer immersed himself in both Jewish and non-Jewish civic activity after the war. He was an early supporter of the Hebrew Benevolent Congregation (later called "the Temple"), serving as vice president in 1870 and then winning election to the presidency. As president of the Atlanta Hebrew Benevolent Society, Mayer convinced the city council to give the fledgling Jewish community a complimentary plot in the Oakland cemetery.

He was prominent in nonsectarian organizations as well. After having been inducted into the Masonic Order while in Tennessee, Mayer became a charter member of Atlanta's first lodge and its second-ranking officer. Although he was only one of two Jews in the fifty-member group, he moved up to the master position in 1859. On the state level, he served as senior grand warden and chaired the finance committee.[15] He served as vice president of the Organization of Foreign-born Citizens and helped organize Schiller Lodge of the Odd Fellows. When the Baptist convention met in Atlanta in 1879, the Mayers offered home hospitality to visiting clergy.

Mayer acted as treasurer of the Atlanta Benevolent Home during the 1880s. In 1890, the trustees voted to deed the property to the city, which sold it and applied the proceeds to a new medical facility named for the recently deceased Henry W. Grady. Another German Jew, Joseph Hirsch, a prominent businessman and city councilman, introduced the motion for the construction of Grady Hospital and chaired its fund-raising committee, which included such notables as Hoke Smith, former governor Rufus Bulloch, and Mayor John T. Glenn. Hirsch chaired the board of trustees when the hospital was dedicated in 1892.[16]

By 1880 Mayer served as director of the Capital City Bank, an offshoot of the Capital City Land and Improvement Company. Jacob and Aaron Haas were equally involved. Aaron Haas, who had moved to Atlanta from Newnan in 1860, had secured passes for his and Mayer's families when they traveled north together at the end of the Civil War. The Haas and Hirsch families were related through marriage and, along with Mayers and Steinheimers, had roots in Worms in Germany, where the families knew each other. Aaron Haas first visited Atlanta in 1849 while working as a store clerk in Newnan. He settled in Atlanta eleven years later.[17] During the Civil War, Aaron Haas assumed charge of selling Confederate cotton to help finance the cause. While running the blockade to England, he was captured in 1863, but a bribe to the jailer in Cincinnati facilitated his escape. After the war, Aaron moved from the wholesale grocery and liquor business to commission brokerage (Haas and Guthman) to part ownership of the Union (Street) Rail Lines. In 1891 he sold the latter and founded Haas and Dodd, an insurance business. As family members joined, this firm expanded into real estate, finance, and property management. Aaron became a trustee of the city water works (1879–1897) and president of the Young Men's Hebrew Association. He won election to the city council in 1874 and to the aldermanic board the following year. He also served as the first mayor pro tem of Atlanta. In 1877, he married Fanny Rich and thus joined ties with that rising department store family. During the 1890s they resided in the prestigious new suburb of Inman Park along with business moguls Asa Candler, Joel Hurt, Ernest Woodruff, and Joseph Maddox. Like David Mayer, Aaron Haas did not eschew his ethnic roots. Grand president of the Fifth District Grand Lodge of B'nai B'rith, he helped create the organization's Hebrew Orphans' Home, serving on its board from its inception. He also helped organize the Turn Verein, an ethnic German organization.[18]

Aaron's first cousin Jacob Haas achieved equal prominence in business and civic affairs. Born in Rhein-Hessen in 1844, he arrived in America in

1860 in time to become a private in the Confederate army and subsequently receive an illness discharge. He peddled in Cleveland, Tennessee, and traveled extensively before settling in Atlanta in 1877. He married his cousin, Caroline Haas. A Southern representative of a Northern cigar and tobacco business, Jacob later helped develop Atlanta's south side through the land and improvement company. By the 1880s, he was part owner of the Union Rail Lines and president of the Germania Loan and Banking Company. By 1900 he presided over the Capitol City Bank, the Temple, and the Concordia Club, the German Jewish social haven. He backed the first Atlanta "citizen's ticket," which tended to represent the upper class in opposition to the working class. One of Jacob Haas's sons, Herbert, helped obtain financing for the city's sewer system and police station.[19]

Jacob Elsas, born in Wurttenberg in the Alsacian region in 1842, moved to the United States in 1860. Elsas worked first as a peddler in Cincinnati, but he soon moved to Cartersville, Georgia, where he opened a dry goods store. Noting a scarcity of bags for flour, salt, sugar, and other goods, Elsas moved to Atlanta in 1868 and organized Elsas, May and Company to meet the need. The company built its first mill in 1870, partly financed through industrial bonds, to produce both the cloth bags and paper sacks that made it an effective competitor with other manufacturers. Elsas bought out Isaac May and reorganized as the Fulton Cotton Spinning Company. Partners separated from him in the late 1880s to form the Atlanta Paper Company; his firm emerged as the Fulton Bag and Cotton Company. The company changed from steam to electrical power as it became the largest industrial employer in Atlanta, with branches in New Orleans and other cities.[20] As discussed below, he and his son, Oscar, used a mixture of paternalism and industrial espionage to control the workforce.[21]

When David Mayer died in 1890, the city council nominated Aaron Haas, Jacob Elsas, and Joseph Hirsch to replace him on the school board. Hirsch won election and remained in office until 1897. Oscar Pappenheimer then replaced Hirsch on the school board and served five years. Steven Hertzberg reported that what had become the "Jewish seat" went into hiatus until 1913, when Walter A. Rich filled the position for a three-year term. Joseph Hirsch, so instrumental in the establishment of Grady Hospital, had been a Marietta merchant before the war and founded Hirsch Brothers Clothiers and Tailors with brothers Henry and Morris in 1863. Their business, which was burned out by Sherman in 1864, later grew into a successful department store; Henry bought out his two brothers' shares in 1890. Joseph Hirsch later served as president of the Hebrew Orphans' Home.[22]

Clearly Mayer and those with whom he associated epitomized the success, relative acceptance, acculturation, and contributions of Atlanta Jewry, and they served as symbols of the New South Creed.[23] Their interaction also illustrates the almost incestuous relationships that developed within this small ethnic community and the city of Atlanta. Tied together by family, national origin, and business, these Jews formed a power structure within their community with social, economic, civic, and political ramifications. It paralleled and intertwined with the power structure of the larger society.[24] Several interrelated issues are illustrative.

PUBLIC SCHOOLS, PROGRESSIVISM, PROHIBITION, FACTIONALISM, AND THE ATLANTA RIOT

The first example relates to the Atlanta public schools. In September 1869, the city council created a commission of ten, including Mayer and chaired by Joseph F. Brown, to investigate the formation of such a system. The city required an educated workforce in the competitive environment of the New South, and community leaders posited correlations between ignorance and poverty, crime and vice. Furthermore, the establishment of several black schools during Reconstruction angered whites, who argued that if African Americans could be educated, so too should whites. The referendum to create the school passed overwhelmingly on a nonpartisan basis with the support of a Republican-black coalition.[25] Brown became the president of the school board, and Mayer served as a member. Mayer used his position on the board to establish a policy of separation of church and state, and Brown joined him in opposition to school prayer.[26]

The first board members represented the established conservative faction, including William Hemphill, the *Atlanta Constitution*'s business manager, and Lemuel P. Grant, superintendent of the Western and Atlantic Railroad, who donated the land to the city that became Grant Park. Lemuel and John T. Grant had been business partners during the 1850s and 1860s. In 1868, John T. organized a railroad construction business with his son, William, and Henry Alexander, an influential Jewish businessman. They leased the entire prison system to rebuild the roads destroyed by the war. Future governor John Slaton married Sally F. Grant, William's daughter, in 1898. Lemuel Grant and Joseph E. Brown both built houses on Washington Street when it emerged as an affluent residential neighborhood after the war. Former governor Brown served as director of the Western and Atlantic, and his son worked his way up in the same line from freight clerk to traffic manager. Like most everything else, railroads were an integral part of the family, business, and political octopus.[27]

A power struggle between the school board and Superintendent Bernard Mallon resulted in the latter's resignation in 1879. Mallon was replaced by William F. Slaton, the future governor's father and principal of Boys' High School (1872–1879). Slaton's appointment and policies appeased board members, including his allies David Mayer and Joseph Brown.[28] The conflict and switch also reflected the division in city and state Democratic politics between Brown's "conservative" faction and Hoke Smith's "progressive" faction.[29]

Factional politics within the school system influenced the variation in curriculum between the city's schools and those elsewhere in the country. Education historian Wayne J. Urban contends that the Atlanta curriculum never became as vocationally oriented as those elsewhere. On the surface, this is surprising because a key national proponent of vocational education was Hoke Smith. Smith had served on the school board from 1886 to 1893 when he became secretary of the interior in Grover Cleveland's cabinet, and when he returned to Atlanta, he served as the board's president from 1896 to 1906, when he was elected governor. As a U.S. senator, he sponsored both the Smith-Lever (1914) and Smith-Hughes Acts (1917), which provided federal funds for agricultural and industrial educational. As early as 1885, Smith advocated manual training and the expansion of vocationalism. The latter did not win approval until 1899 while he presided over the school board. Although Smith's efforts were not in the forefront of vocational reform, they did differ from the directions of his opponents.[30]

On the mayoral level, James W. English, a conservative industrialist with ties to the chamber of commerce, opposed W. H. Brotherton, a prosperous merchant associated with the anti-immigrant American Protective Association, the Prohibition Club, and the labor unions—issues anathema to the Jewish community. English served on the original school board as a Brown-Mayer ally. Under Mayor Charles A. Collier, elected in 1897 as a Smith-Brotherton faction member, the reform group took control of the schools.[31]

Smith's primary ally in behalf of reform and vocational education—and more importantly, Democratic factional politics—was Robert Guinn, president of the school board from 1914 to 1918. Guinn's quest for curriculum change depended on the ouster of school superintendent William S. Slaton, who had succeeded his father in 1907. The younger brother of future governor John Slaton had been principal of Boys' High School (1892–1907) when Hoke Smith and the school board authorized the creation of technical and commercial courses there in 1903. Guinn ousted the brother in 1914, the same year he managed the campaign of Slaton's opponent for the U.S. Senate. John Slaton contended that William's firing resulted from the political antagonism of Guinn, his own political adversary.[32]

Conflict over the firing of William S. Slaton, who was supported by the teachers' union and the *Atlanta Constitution,* and "reforms" that further antagonized both parents and teachers ultimately resulted in city charter alterations by the state legislature. A smaller board would again be elected by the voters. Conservatives replaced the reformers after the ensuing election, and the board gained direct control over the school budget.[33]

As president of the Atlanta Chamber of Commerce in 1916, Victor H. Kriegshaber, the key Jewish layman in the city after David Mayer's death, may have been the only nonpartisan. Kriegshaber had been elected chamber president in 1915. The honor reflected much hard work and a natural rise through chamber ranks. Yet it was also a way for the city's business community to placate the Jewish community in the wake of Leo Frank's lynching earlier that year. Kriegshaber acted as community builder or ethnic broker, bridging gaps across dividing lines. Thus he eschewed direct identification with a warring camp.[34]

Conflicts over education reflected broader divisions associated with forces opposed to, as well as within, Southern progressivism. In his study of that movement, Jack Temple Kirby provides an excellent model to understand the dynamics at work in Atlanta. Division within the progressive ranks existed between radical, rural reform identifiable with Tom Watson and his supporters, and a more moderate middle class, urban progressivism associated with Hoke Smith. The radical element favored public schools, road improvements, and farm services, and opposed saloons, black rights, and monopolies. The moderates also supported educational reform frequently through "scientific experts" like Guinn, agricultural improvements, disfranchisement, and antitrust and child labor laws. When Hoke Smith ran for governor in 1905, he gained Watson's support on the basis of jointly held positions, but especially a pledge to disenfranchise African Americans, as well as jointly held positions on other issues. In the next election, Watson broke with Smith for fear that poor and working-class whites would also lose their vote. The business progressives and radical reformers might work together, but overriding constituent needs could tear them asunder.[35] Both progressive elements opposed the conservative faction that included the German Jews.

Prohibition was another issue illustrating such linkages. George B. Tindall describes prohibition as "the chief factional issue dividing the Democratic Party" in the South.[36] Using prohibition as a critical component of progressivism, Dewey W. Grantham argues that "the twentieth-century prohibition movement in the South—and in the nation—began in Georgia with the enactment of a statewide ban in August 1907." When Hoke Smith pressed for passage by linking prohibition with disfranchisement in his gubernatorial campaign in the summer of 1906, he exacerbated the tensions leading to the race riot in September.[37] If historians have explained Southern progressivism as a movement toward greater social control and order, then prohibition and the accompanying battle against prostitution may be seen as attempts to regulate behavior and to affect perceived moral values. Often the efforts were directed against African Americans, thus unifying racism and social "reform."[38]

Atlanta's Decatur Street became a symbol to prohibitionists and anti-prostitution crusaders alike, as well as a rallying point for violence. On the eve of the Atlanta race riot in September 1906, Methodist evangelist Sam Jones contributed to the tensions that fomented the riot by giving a series of sermons associating demon rum with loss of restraint among blacks, which contributed to the tensions that fomented the riot. Historian Joel Williamson observes that whenever "there was a serious disturbance among black people . . . whites usually insisted that it arose not from any intrinsic failing in the Southern social order, but rather from the machinations of evil outside forces—the Germans in World War I and II, communists after the Russian Revolution in 1917, and Jews, Catholics, and labor organizers all along." Although he links prohibition and the temporary alliance between Smith and Watson with the race riot and these with the "paranoid style" and lynching of Leo Frank, Williamson does not grasp the entire relationship.[39]

Decatur Street, an area of cheap housing and mixed business use, was not only an arena for lower-class black life; it also served as a home for East European Jewish immigrants and their businesses, which often catered to a black clientele. Moreover, although dictates existed against overindulgence, there was nothing in Jewish law or custom supporting prohibition. To the contrary, drinking wine is an integral part of ceremonies and Jews—including members of the German Jewish elite previously identified—manufactured and sold alcoholic beverages. When the state prohibition law went into effect on January 1, 1908, historian Deaton contends, "Decatur and Peters Streets were nearly wiped out," although wholesale houses like Jewish-owned Rose's obtained a windfall because it stocked up before sales were restricted. Sam Jones tinged his rhetoric with anti-Semitism and put Jews clearly on the side of the wets. The Civic League, established to heal wounds after the race riot, included black and white "conservatives" as well as David Marx, spiritual leader of the Temple, and Clark Howell. Factionalism was omnipresent.[40]

Efforts at disenfranchisement were typically viewed as a primary step toward overcoming Bourbon (the conservative faction I discuss here) power and what was perceived as Northern corporate influence. The more substantive reforms included the creation or strengthening of extant railroad and insurance commissions, and the passage of child labor restrictions.[41]

The mayoral election of 1900 featured a businessmen's ticket sponsored by a Businessmen's League with the support of the *Atlanta Constitution*.[42] The league served as a vehicle for Preston Arkwright, Joel Hurt, and the Atlanta Railway and Power Company group to challenge Hoke Smith's forces, including Henry M. Atkinson, president of Georgia Electric Company and new owner of the *Atlanta Journal*. Although the Smith faction rode the waves of antimonopoly, prolabor rhetoric, a reflection of Watsonian populism, Jews had been the dominant business owners since the 1880s in the residential-commercial area south of Marietta Street, between Fair and Washington Streets, and were thus natural opponents of the Smith faction's attacks.[43]

MORE FACTIONALISM, RACE, STRIKES, AND THE LEO FRANK CASE

In 1908 James G. Woodward ran for his third term as mayor of Atlanta. Woodward, trained as a printer, was a strong labor unionist employed by the *Atlanta Journal*. As mayor, he had supported school reform, child labor laws, and street improvements, and he had opposed the monopolistic tendencies of the Atlanta Railway and Power Company franchises. The mayor allied with the Smith-Atkinson faction. His public displays of inebriation, however, did not sit well with prohibitionists, including Dr. Leonard G. Broughton of Tabernacle Baptist Church. Another of Woodward's primary opponents had been Joseph Hirsch, an advocate of the "clean, honest and economical business administration." Although he won the normally crucial primary, Woodward was challenged in the general election by conservative business candidate Robert F. Maddox, pressed into service by Coca-Cola's Asa G. Candler, Jacob Haas, and Victor Kriegshaber, among others. The independent Maddox triumphed.[44]

The Businessmen's League had successfully settled several labor disputes, although a series of strikes had ensued during the early 1900s. Two unsuccessful strikes had hit Elsas's Fulton Bag and Cotton Mill in 1897. Women and children had composed the majority of the workforce for decades. The immediate cause of the strikes was an attempt by the company to employ twenty African American women to sort and fold bags, jobs traditionally held by whites. Hoke Smith negotiated the strike settlement in favor of the strikers, although the mill owners did succeed in protecting the jobs of African Americans—including a "second boss" hired before the incident. A few months later, the mill fired some of the strike leaders, thereby breaking the settlement and fomenting another strike. The strikers were fearful that the company wanted to lower wages and replace white with black workers, even though the latter received the same pay for the work in the same position. Elsas won this phase of the strike through the use of strikebreakers.[45]

When the white textile workers attempted to unionize and strike again in 1914–1915, the mill, now managed by Jacob Elsas's son Oscar, employed spies and African Americans to evict the strikers from company housing. Benjamin Z. Phillips, Oscar Elsas's son-in-law and John Slaton's law partner, represented the Elsas's interests against the strikers. By 1914, 8 percent of the workforce was composed of African American women, with African Americans making up 20 percent of the total. Although these strikes centered on typical union issues, the African American workers remained loyal to the company. The company successfully used race to counteract class. The *Atlanta Constitution* supported the corporation, whereas the Men and Religion Forward movement advocated unionization and fair treatment of the white workers. The same division appeared in 1916 when a strike hit Arkwright's Georgia Railway and Power Company as the progressive faction advocated municipal ownership of the lines.[46]

The workers contended that city police were used to defeat the 1914–1915 strikes, and the charge became part of the Fulton County sheriff's campaign of 1914. Politics, not surprisingly, permeated the police board. Here the parallel division was between the ongoing W. H. Brotherton–Police Chief Beaver's faction on the Police Board of Commissioners and the James Key–Police Board Commissioner Captain James English faction. It was Beaver's "flying squads" that attacked the African American red-light districts with the support of the Men and Religion Forward movement and of English, who attempted to bring calm and work with black leaders in the aftermath of the race riot.[47]

Race was as much a constant in these issues as factionalism. As I have noted in passing, circumstantial evidence points to the conservative side—and Jews—as far more benign (or, arguably, paternalistic) than the progressives. Labor unions were antiblack, and the conservative-Jewish faction opposed unions. Even before the strike of 1897, Jacob Elsas, who remembered an African American who had befriended him when he traveled the countryside as a peddler, had employed a few African Americans in positions normally filled by whites. By 1918 the Fulton Bag and Cotton Company was the largest industrial employer of African American women in Atlanta, and the Jewish-owned Norris Candy Company ranked fifth in the same category. William J. Lowenstein, a Jew who chaired the Chamber of Commerce Education Committee, advocated compulsory education even when opponents countered that this would encourage black enrollment.[48]

Several historians have persuasively illustrated the interwoven fabric of the Atlanta race riot, the Fulton Bag and Cotton Factory strikes, and the Leo Frank case. Along with the attacks on selected red-light districts, lynchings, Jim Crow laws, and disenfranchisement, both the riot and the strikes have been viewed in part as attempts by whites, especially those displaced from the countryside into the city and their political and ideological allies, to put African Americans "in their places," and to remove them as perceived arbiters of political power. What is less recognized is the factional dimension. Blacks tended to be supported by (in a limited and often paternalistic fashion) and to support the conservatives. The many linkages clearly call into question the neutralizing effect the presence of African Americans—and especially the prejudices against them—had on immigrant and ethnic minorities. In this case, it is likely that Jewish interaction with African Americans contributed to anti-Semitism.

The Leo Frank case became a cause célèbre a few months before the 1914 mill strike, and Governor John Slaton's commutation of Frank was granted two months after the strike ended. Some of the people screaming loudest for Frank's execution were involved with the strike and the workers' cause. Hatred of Elsas's business spilled over to Frank.

The Leo Frank case is perhaps one of the best known in Southern and American history.[49] Mary Phagan, a young worker in a pencil factory, was brutally murdered on Confederate Memorial Day in 1913. Leo Frank, the factory manager, who had been born in Texas but raised in New York, was accused, convicted, and condemned to death on the basis of flimsy and contradictory evidence. Hysteria prevailed as Frank became a symbol of conflict between rural values and the commercialism of the cities, of the Jew as businessman-exploiter, and of Southern hatred of big business, Northerners, and immigrants. Just before the end of his tenure in office in June 1915, after careful study, Governor John M. Slaton commuted Frank's sentence to life in prison.[50] A mob marched on the governor's mansion in protest as Slaton fled the state. Frank was subsequently taken from prison and lynched in August 1915.

The incident contributed to the founding of both the modern Ku Klux Klan and the Anti-Defamation League of B'nai B'rith. In 1915 the primary election was held on Rosh Hashanah, the Jewish New Year, thus disenfranchising observant Jews (much as blacks had been disenfranchised), albeit on a temporary basis.[51] When a council seat from the second ward became vacant in 1915, a Jewish businessman went down to defeat at the hands of a railway conductor in an election largely determined by prejudice.[52]

As indicated above, the Slaton family had closely associated with the conservative faction and Atlanta's Jewish establishment. Beyond the educational arena and personal ties, the bonds between Governor Slaton and certain elements of the Jewish community were also professional. In 1913, two weeks before the murder of Mary Phagan but after his election to the governorship, Slaton's law firm, Slaton, Slaton, and Phillips, merged with Rosser and Brandon. Benjamin Z. Phillips and Luther Z. Rosser served as Leo Frank's chief defense counsels.[53]

Thus, although Slaton made a courageous and justifiable decision in commuting Leo Frank's sentence of execution to life in prison, he also drew on decades of direct interaction and contact with Atlanta's Jewish elite.[54] This is not to say that Slaton made his decision as a political payoff, but rather that enduring ties to the Jewish community likely made him more amenable to their entreaties.[55]

The Frank case facilitated the rise and decline of several important political careers joined to factionalism. As for Frank's opponents, prosecutor Hugh Dorsey became governor, and Tom Watson's political career revived.[56] Although Slaton returned to Georgia after the riot and pursued a successful legal practice, he never returned to public office.

Ethnic politics remained alive and well in ensuing decades. Several Jewish attorneys, including Walter W. Visanska, established a Civic Educational League in 1914 to nurture unity and overcome the apathy of the East European Jews, many of whom had not applied for citizenship or registered to vote. They stressed responsibility and rights in the trying time of the Frank case. They also eschewed bloc voting, a policy opposite actual practice.[57] To cite only a few other examples, attorney Leonard J. Grossman, active along with his wife in favor of women's suffrage, won a state legislative seat from Fulton County in 1918, and J. R. Bachman and Joseph Berman served on the city council during the 1920s.[58]

I explore a series of avenues that beg further study. First, besides examining the tentative conclusions drawn here through my analysis of district voting, more work needs to be done concerning the role of Jews and other ethnic groups in urban politics elsewhere in the South. Second, although the intertwining of the place of origin, family, business, and civic activities of Atlanta's German Jews will not surprise those in the field, comparison and contrast with other ethnic communities in the South are largely lacking. Studies such as these should help place in perspective the impact of any Southern-specific culture on ethnic group behavior. Third, far from shielding Jews from prejudice, the black-white dynamic and black-Jewish interaction contributed to hostility toward the Jews of Atlanta. Was this also true in other locations, in other circumstances, and with other ethnic groups? And finally, urban "reform" has long been associated with racism in the South and ethnocentrism elsewhere. But were such efforts fueled by ethnocentrism in other Southern cities, as they appear to have been in Atlanta? As historians continue to examine these and related issues, perhaps we will find that the North and South shared greater similarities than differences and that there have been indeed a variety of Southern experiences.

NOTES

"Factionalism and Ethnic Politics in Atlanta: German Jews from the Civil War through the Progressive Era" by Mark K. Bauman appeared originally in *Georgia Historical Quarterly* 82 (Fall 1998): 533–58. Courtesy of the *Georgia Historical Quarterly*.

1. See, for example, Lawrence H. Larsen, *Rise of the Urban South* (Lexington: University Press of Kentucky, 1985); Eugene J. Watts, *The Social Bases of City Politics: Atlanta, 1865–1903* (Westport, Conn.: Greenwood Press, 1978); David R. Goldfield, *Cotton Fields and Skyscrapers, Southern City and Region, 1607–1980* (Baton Rouge: Louisiana State University Press, 1982). Blaine A. Brownell, however, writes, "the impact of foreign born groups was often greater than their numbers suggested." Brownell, "The Urban South Comes of Age, 1900–1940," in *The City in Southern History: The Growth of Urban Civilization in the South,* ed. Blaine A. Brownell and David R. Goldfield (Port Washington, N.Y.: Kennikat Press, 1977), 137. According to Howard N. Rabinowitz, "The small number of immigrants has often led historians incorrectly to minimize their impact on Southern life." He identifies Irish politics in New Orleans, Richmond, and Memphis; Jewish participation in Atlanta; and Jewish Radical and Redeemer mayors in Montgomery. Howard N. Rabinowitz, "Continuity and Change: Southern Urban Development, 1860–1900" in Brownell and Goldfield, *The City in Southern History*, 116.

2. Thomas M. Deaton, "Atlanta during the Progressive Era" (Ph.D. diss., University of Georgia, 1969), 31–32. According to David N. Plank and Paul E. Peterson, Atlanta's educational experience differed substantially from the model of reform in Northern cities partly because of its lack of a large immigrant population, the presence of a large African American community, and the political factionalism within

the upper class. David N. Plank and Paul E. Peterson, "Does Urban Reform Imply Class Conflict? The Case of Atlanta's Schools," *History of Education Quarterly* 23 (Summer 1983): 141–73; David N. Plank, "Educational Reform and Organizational Change: Atlanta in the Progressive Era," in *Southern Cities, Southern Schools: Public Education in the Urban South,* ed. David N. Plank and Rick Ginsberg (Westport, Conn.: Greenwood Press, 1990).

3. See Emily A. Baer, "Breaking Patterns, Creating Patterns: Images of the Pinch in Memphis, Tennessee, 1900–1948" (Ph.D. diss., Memphis State University, 1992) (citation provided by Berkley Kalin). For Jewish "cluster" patterns, "political and ethnic coalition building" (84), and active Jewish participation in politics with the business reform faction of the Democratic Party in New Orleans, see Bobbie Malone, "Standing 'Unswayed in the Storm': Rabbi Max Heller, Reform and Zionism in the American South, 1860–1929" (Ph.D. diss., Tulane University, 1994), 74, 80–84, 99, 99 n. 35. On Savannah Jewry, see Mark I. Greenberg, "Creating Ethnic, Class and Southern Identity in Nineteenth-century America: The Jews of Savannah, Georgia, 1830–1880" (Ph.D. diss., University of Florida, 1997).

4. Steven Hertzberg, *Strangers within the Gate City: Jews in Atlanta, 1845–1915* (Philadelphia: Jewish Publication Society of America, 1978); Mark K. Bauman, "Centripetal and Centrifugal Forces Facing the People of Many Communities: Atlanta Jewry from the Frank Case to the Great Depression," *Atlanta Historical Journal* 23 (Fall 1979): 25–54.

5. Leon Eplan and Morris Lichtenstein, two ethnic community leaders, encouraged naturalization and led an Independent Citizens Club in 1895, which claimed power over 250 immigrant votes. Hertzberg, *Strangers within the Gate City,* 159; Mark K. Bauman, "Role Theory and History: Ethnic Brokerage in the Atlanta Jewish Community," *American Jewish History* 73 (September 1983): 71–95.

6. Ronald H. Bayor, "Ethnic Residential Patterns in Atlanta, 1880–1940," *Georgia Historical Quarterly* 64 (Winter 1979): 435–46 (first quotation, 439; second quotation, 444); see also Hannah Blau, "Atlanta Jews: The Development of a Progressive Southern Jewish Community" (sociology seminar paper, Georgia State University, Winter 1976–1977; copy provided by Charles Jaret).

7. Deaton, "Atlanta during the Progressive Era," 166–67, map after p. 172; Gretchen Ehrmann MacLachlan, "Women's Work: Atlanta's Industrialization and Urbanization, 1879–1929" (Ph.D. diss., Emory University, 1992), 265.

8. Hertzberg, *Strangers within the Gate City,* 156–59. Hertzberg related Jewish office holding to Jewish contributions, acceptance, and anti-Semitism, not to ethnic politics or factionalism within the Democratic Party. In terms of Alexander's election, for example, Hertzberg states that he was elected in 1908 when few knew that he was Jewish but was defeated in the next election because his religious beliefs became known. Hertzberg characterized the Jewish office holders and seekers as both "conservative" and "progressive." Eugene J. Watts reported that Aaron Haas faced Know-Nothing opposition in the election of 1874. Watts, *Social Bases,* 56.

9. Bauman, "Centripetal and Centrifugal Forces," 44; *Atlanta Journal,* September 15, 1917.

10. Hertzberg, *Strangers within the Gate City,* 162–63. 157. Hertzberg noted surprising *Atlanta Constitution* advocacy of the Populist position on coinage.

11. The terms *conservative* and *progressive* do not necessarily reflect actual positions on issues or the role of government and should be viewed largely as names.

The conservatives were often—but not always—the "Bourbon" Democrats. On the latter, see Judson C. Ward, "Georgia under the Bourbon Democrats, 1872–1890" (Ph.D. diss., University of North Carolina at Chapel Hill, 1948).

12. For Mayer's life and career, see Hertzberg, *Strangers within the Gate City;* Steven Hertzberg, "The Jewish Community of Atlanta from the End of the Civil War Until the Eve of the Frank Case," *American Jewish Historical Quarterly* 62 (March 1973): 250–85; Janice Rothschild Blumberg, *As But a Day to a Hundred and Twenty, 1867–1987* (1966; reprint, Atlanta: Hebrew Benevolent Congregation, 1987); Janice Rothschild Blumberg, "Pre-1867 Atlanta Jewry," *American Jewish Historical Quarterly* 62 (March 1973): 242–49; David Marx, "The History of the Jews in Atlanta," *Reform Advocate,* November 4, 1911; "1880 Hebrews of Atlanta," *Southern Israelite,* December 1948 (reprinted from *Atlanta Constitution,* December 1880). Substantial additional material, including copies of his and his wife's wills, a letter he wrote to his parents and siblings dated October 19, 1839, a detailed genealogy from the family Bible, and newspaper clippings, are available at the Ida Pearle and Joseph Cuba Jewish Community Archives, Jewish Federation of Metropolitan Atlanta (hereinafter cited as Jewish Community Archives). I am indebted to archivist Sandra Berman for research assistance.

13. Derrell C. Roberts, *Joseph E. Brown and the Politics of Reconstruction* (Tuscaloosa: University of Alabama Press, 1973), 8–11, 18–32, 41, 56, 72. See also Wallace T. Hettle, "An Ambiguous Democrat Joseph Brown and Georgia's Road to Secession," *Georgia Historical Quarterly* 81 (Fall 1997): 577–92, which depicts Brown in opposition to the anti-immigrant Know-Nothing Party.

14. David Steinheimer also refused to fight for the North when an attempt was made to conscript him into the Union army. A copy of Steinheimer's account is available at the Jewish Community Archives. Mayer's clerk, Leo Cahn, also left the region after the passage of the 1862 Conscription Act. Hertzberg. *Strangers within the Gate City,* 25.

15. *Proceedings of the Grand Lodge* [Georgia Masons] (Atlanta, 1890), 67. T. C. McDonald, "David Mayer" and "Freemasonry and Its Progress in Atlanta and Fulton County, Georgia" (typescript), both in Mayer Collection, Jewish Community Archives.

16. "1892—Grady Hospital Celebrates Its 75th Anniversary—1967," *Grady News* 19, no. 1 (January 1967) (reprinted from *Atlanta Constitution,* December 23, 1890). Clark Howell, *History of Georgia,* 4 vols. (Chicago: S. J. Clarke Publishing, 1926), 2:122–26.

17. Reminiscences written by Aaron Haas to "Dear Doctor" between 1907 and 1911, Jewish Community Archives. The "Doctor" was probably Rabbi David Marx, who was preparing a short history of Atlanta Jewry about the same time. "Copy of a diary kept by David Mayer on His return to Germany May 19, 1875 to Sept. 7, 1876," Jewish Community Archives. At one time Jacob Haas was part owner with Hoke Smith of the *Atlanta Journal.* Dewey W. Grantham, *Hoke Smith and the Politics of the New South* (Baton Rouge: Louisiana State University Press, 1958), 26–27.

18. *Reform Advocate,* 1911, 53; Haas and Dodd Company brochure (Atlanta, 1961), Haas Family Papers, Jewish Community Archives. Don H. Doyle, *New Men, New Cities, New South: Atlanta, Nashville, Charleston, and Mobile, 1860–1910* (Chapel Hill: University of North Carolina Press, 1990), 195.

19. On Jacob Haas, see "One Hundred Years Accomplishment of Southern Jewry" (pamphlet; Atlanta, 1934), 22. On the "citizen's ticket," see Watts, *Social Bases,* 27–29.

20. Louis Jacob Elsas II, "Explanation of Jacob Elsas' Family Pedigree," n.d.; Elsas, "Brief History of Jacob Elsas and the Fulton Rag and Cotton Mill," n.d. Leonard Ray Teel provided an unverified account of Elsas serving as a Union soldier assigned to guard Sherman's supply lines in the summer of 1864 as the latter marched to the sea. Teel, "How a Yankee Brought Textiles to Georgia," *Georgia Trend,* January 1986, 108–13; Gary M. Fink, "The New South: A Century Later," *Atlanta's Might,* all in Oscar Elsas Family Papers, Jewish Community Archives.

21. Albert Steiner, another member of this group, was born in Taacan, Bohemia, emigrated to America in 1866, and started a lime works in Dadeville, Alabama. After moving to Atlanta in 1882, he ultimately presided over the Atlanta Brewery and Ice Company, the National Paper Company, and the Viaduct Place Corporation. A director of the Fourth National Bank, Steiner served on the Temple building committee and as vice president for nine years. The Steiner Foundation established a clinic at Grady Hospital and supported cancer research, a disease that eventually claimed him, his wife, and son. *Reform Advocate,* 1911, 53, Haas Family Papers; Celstine Sibley, "So Who Was Albert Steiner?" *Atlanta Constitution,* n.d.; Albert Steiner Papers, all in Jewish Community Archives.

22. Henry bought the shares of his brothers, Henry and Morris, in 1890. On Joseph Hirsch, see "Four Hirsch Generations See Plaque Unveiling," *Atlanta Constitution,* September 19, 1963, 51; *Atlanta Constitution,* July 9, 1882; 100th anniversary pamphlet, 1863–1963; Henry Hirsch disability discharge certificate, Confederate States of America, June 13, 1861; "1880 Hebrews of Atlanta"; *American Jewish Review,* April 1914; all in Morris Hirsch Family Papers, 1861–1976, Jewish Community Archives. Hertzberg, *Strangers within the Gate City,* 164. The school board financed a night school in 1906 and a few years later an elementary school at Elsas's factory. Melvin W. Eckes, *From Ivy Street to Kennedy Center: Centennial History of the Atlanta Public School System* (Atlanta, n.p., 1972). Herbert Elsas served as one of Leo Frank's defense attorneys, as did Leonard Haas, Aaron's son. "The Fighting Idealist—A Portrait of Herbert Joseph Haas," *Southern Israelite,* December 31, 1935.

23. For this much-abused term, see Paul M. Gaston, *The New South Creed: A Study in Southern Mythmaking* (New York: Alfred A. Knopf, 1970).

24. Richard J. Hopkins, "Patterns of Persistence and Occupational Mobility in a Southern City: Atlanta, 1870–1920" (Ph.D. diss., Emory University, 1972). Don Doyle finds that although the foreign-born made up 4 percent of the total population, they comprised 12 percent of the elite in Atlanta in 1880 (*New Men,* 90). Although Doyle describes the business class and the role of Jews well, he fails to recognize the factionalism. Eugene Watts asserts that foreign-born candidates were more likely to have arrived in the city before the Civil War, to have resided in the city for a long time, and to have owned substantial property. Thus they fit the characteristics of the majority of the candidates, particularly those who were successful. In essence, the Jews discussed in this article, like the immigrants identified by Watts, became well established before entering politics. Once nominated, Watts stated, immigrants had a reasonable chance of victory. Watts, *Social Bases,* 80–82, 162.

25. Philip N. Racine, "Public Education in the New South: A School System for Atlanta, 1868–1879," in Plank and Ginsberg, *Southern Cities, Southern Schools,* 37, 41, 43; Marcia E. Turner, "Black School Politics in Atlanta Georgia, 1969–1942," in Plank and Ginsberg, *Southern Cities, Southern Schools,* 177–97.

26. *Atlanta Constitution,* November 29, 1925; Roberts, *Joseph E. Brown,* 96, 98;

Racine, "Public Education," 50. Brown served as president of the school board from its inception to 1888 and as an honorary member from 1888 to 1894.

27. Eckes, *From Ivy Street to Kennedy Center,* 5; James F. Cook, "Governors of Georgia: The Shadow of Leo Frank," *Georgia Journal* (Fall 1991): 15; James M. Russell, "Grant, John Thomas," in *Dictionary of Georgia Biography,* ed. Kenneth Coleman and Charles Stephen Gurr (Athens: University of Georgia Press, 1983), 362–64: Thomas H. Martin, *Atlanta and Its Builders* (n.p., 1902), 655–57, 658–60; Philip N. Racine, "Atlanta's Schools: A History of the Public School System, 1869–1955" (Ph.D. diss., Emory University, 1969), 56; James F. Cook, "Governors of Georgia: Leaders for a New Century," *Georgia Journal* (Fall 1991): 20. For additional ramifications and the role of Governor Nathaniel Harris, often a Brown faction member, see Nathaniel E. Harris, *Autobiography* (Macon, Ga.: n.p., 1925), 154–55, 239, 258, 288–89, 301, 304, 329, 346, 344, 350–51, 359–61. At one time Harris had a Jewish law partner, Washington Dessau. See also Francil Beach Hudson, "The Smith-Brown Controversy" (M.A. thesis, Emory University, 1929); Mary Richards Colvin, "Hoke Smith and Joseph M. Brown, Political Rivals" (M.A. thesis, University of Georgia, 1958); Grantham, *Hoke Smith,* 23, 134–55, 163, 180, 187, 199, 206, 212, 266–75; C. Vann Woodward, *Tom Watson: Agrarian Rebel* (New York: Macmillan, 1938); Cook, "Leaders for a New Century," 16–20; Grady Sylvester Culpepper, "The Political Career of John Brown Gordon, 1868 to 1897" (Ph.D. diss., Emory University, 1981).

28. Eckes, *From Ivy Street to Kennedy Center,* 46–49; Racine, "Atlanta's Schools," 15–19, 44–45. In 1879, a "Prof. Slaton" introduced Rabbi E. F. M. Browne, spiritual leader of the Hebrew Benevolent Congregation, as speaker at an Atlanta high school graduation exercise; *Jewish South,* July 4, 1879.

29. Plank, "Educational Reform," 135, 139; Wayne J. Urban, "Educational Reform in a New South City: Atlanta, 1890–1925," *Education and the Rise of the New South,* ed. Ronald K. Goodenow and Arthur O. White (Boston: G. K. Hall, 1981), 122; Willie Bolden, "The Political Structure of Charter Reform Movements in Atlanta during the Progressive Era" (Ph.D. diss., Emory University, 1978); Eckes, *From Ivy Street to Kennedy Center,* 33, 73.

30. Urban labels the factions within the school board as "traditional" and "progressive"; Urban, "Educational Reform," 115, 117–18; Cook, "Leaders for a New Century," 16; Grantham, *Hoke Smith,* 30, 118. In 1898 the first board of visitors was created. The mayor nominated people who were subject to election by the city council. Mrs. Joseph Jacobs, wife of a prominent Jewish druggist, represented the second ward; Eckes, *From Ivy Street to Kennedy Center,* 71.

31. Like the articles by Wayne J. Urban, this essay stresses greater division over patronage and politics than on policies. Plank, "Educational Reform," 136–37; Plank and Peterson, "Does Urban Reform Imply Class Conflict?," 151–73. For an explanation of the city government and continuing battles on the city level between the factions, see Deaton, "Atlanta during the Progressive Era," 37–67. Family and friendship tied key individuals into the school system. Hoke's father, Hildred Smith, and a sister had been appointed principals during the 1880s. Besides William S. Slaton's principal position under his father, his sister Martha "Mattie" Slaton taught French at Girls' High School. According to one student, the latter showed partiality toward Jewish students. Racine, "Atlanta's Schools," 88; Mark K. Bauman, "The Youthful Musings of a Jewish Community Activist: Josephine Joel Heyman," *Atlanta History* 39 (Summer 1995): 48. Heyman's original diary is housed at the Jewish Community

Archives. See also two unidentified newspaper clippings, one dated November 29, 1925, the other undated, Heyman Papers, Jewish Community Archives, for indications of the close relationship between the Slaton and Mayer families.

32. Eckes, *From Ivy Street to Kennedy Center,* 119, 120–22; Racine, "Atlanta's Schools," 137. Plank, "Educational Reform," 135, 139. Wayne Urban describes Guinn's background and the influence of four educators associated with the University of Chicago that Guinn brought into Georgia education. He also exhibited the division between the Hoke Smith, Guinn, and *Atlanta Journal* group versus the Slaton, Clark Howell, and *Atlanta Constitution* faction and related these further to pro-English versus pro-German positions vis-à-vis World War I. According to Urban, infighting and change within the Atlanta school system cannot be separated from state politics. Wayne J. Urban, "Progressive Education in the New South: The Reform of the Atlanta Schools, 1914–1918," in *The Age of Urban Reform,* ed. Michael H. Elmer and Eugene M. Tobin (Port Washington, N.Y.: Kennikat Press, 1977), 131–41; Wayne J. Urban, "Organized Teachers and Educational Reform during the Progressive Era: 1890–1920," *History of Education Quarterly* 16 (Spring 1976): 35–52. When Clark Howell died, the *Southern Israelite* (November 20, 1936) eulogized him as a symbol of democracy and religious freedom.

33. Plank, "Educational Reform," 138–40; Plank and Peterson, "Does Urban Reform Imply Class Conflict?" 141–73.

34. Bauman, "Centripetal and Centrifugal Forces," 44–45; "Victor H. Kriegshaber, Community Builder," *American Jewish History* 79 (Autumn 1989): 94–110; Charles Paul Garofalo, "Business Ideas in Atlanta, 1916–1935" (Ph.D. diss., Emory University, 1972).

35. Jack Temple Kirby, *Darkness at the Dawning: Race and Reform in the Progressive South* (Philadelphia: J. J. Lippincott, 1972), chap. 1, 26–27, 36, 44, 142–43; John Dittmer, *Black Georgia in the Progressive Era, 1900–1920* (Urbana: University of Illinois Press, 1977), 103–4.

36. George Brown Tindall, *The Emergence of the New South, 1913–1945* (Baton Rouge: Louisiana State University Press, 1967), 18.

37. Dewey W. Grantham, *Southern Progressivism: The Reconciliation of Progress and Tradition* (Knoxville: University of Tennessee Press, 1983), 161, 54.

38. Dittmer, *Black Georgia,* iii; Ronald H. Bayor, *Race and the Shaping of Twentieth-Century Atlanta* (Chapel Hill: University of North Carolina Press, 1996), 5–6.

39. Dittmer, *Black Georgia,* 124; Joel Williamson, *The Crucible of Race: Black-White Relations in the American South since Emancipation* (New York: Oxford University Press, 1984), 209, 464, 468 (quotation). See also Thomas R. Pegram, "Temperance Politics and Regional Politics Culture: The Anti-Saloon League in Maryland and the South, 1907–1915," *Journal of Southern History* 63 (February 1997): 57–90.

40. Williamson, *Crucible of Race,* 221; Deaton, "Atlanta during the Progressive Era," 338–39; Hertzberg, *Strangers within the Gate City,* 160–61; Bauman, "Centripetal and Centrifugal Forces," 25–54; Mark K. Bauman and Arnold Shankman, "The Rabbi as Ethnic Broker: The Case of David Marx," *Journal of American Ethnic History* (Spring 1983): 71–95.

41. Dewey W. Grantham, *The South in Modern America: A Region at Odds* (New York: HarperCollins, 1994); 47–51; Grantham, *Southern Progressivism,* 145–99.

42. Deaton, "Atlanta during the Progressive Era," 67–71.

43. Although most Jewish and non-Jewish textile factories had been unionized

by 1904, Nathan Abelson's factory remained the exception. MacLachlan, "Women's Work," 60, 133.

44. Much of the following is from Thomas Deaton's excellent dissertation, "Atlanta during the Progressive Era"; see chap. 8, "Mayors and Progress." See also Grantham, *Southern Progressivism*, chaps. 2, 6, and 7; Hertzberg, *Strangers within the Gate City*, 158 (for Hirsch quotation).

45. On this and the 1914–1915 strikes, see Gary M. Fink, *The Fulton Bag and Cotton Mills Strike of 1914–1915: Espionage, Labor Conflict and New South Industrial Relations* (Ithaca, N.Y.: Cornell University Press, 1993); Clifford M. Kuhn, "'A Full History of the Strike as I Saw It': Atlanta's Fulton Bag and Cotton Mills Workers and Their Representatives through the 1914–1915 Strike" (Ph.D. diss., University of North Carolina at Chapel Hill, 1993); Clifford M. Kuhn, *Contesting the New South Order: The 1914–1915 Strike at Atlanta's Fulton Mills* (Chapel Hill: University of North Carolina Press, 2001); Jacquelyn Dowd Hall, "Private Eyes, Public Women: Images of Class and Sex in the Urban South, Atlanta, Georgia, 1913–1915," *Atlanta History* 36 (Winter 1993): 24–29. I am indebted to Gary Fink, Clifford Kuhn, and Robert McMath for many helpful insights.

46. Hertzberg, *Strangers within the Gate City*, 125–32; Doyle, *New Men*, 265. The following draws especially from MacLachlan, "Women's Work"; Fink, *Fulton Bag and Cotton Mills Strike*; Gary M. Fink, "Labor Espionage and the Organization of Southern Textiles: The Fulton Bag and Cotton Mill Strike of 1914–1915," *Labor's Heritage*, April 1989, 10–35.

47. Deaton, "Atlanta during the Progressive Era," 125–27; Harry G. Lefever, "Prostitution, Politics and Religion: The Crusade against Vice in Atlanta in 1912," *Atlanta Historical Journal* 24 (1980): 7–29; MacLachlan, "Women's Work," 207, 217–25. See Dominic J. Capeci Jr. and Jack C. Knight, "Reckoning with Violence: W. E. B. Du Bois and the 1906 Atlanta Race Riot," *Journal of Southern History* 63 (November 1996): 744–45, 747, for a negative view of the league organizers, especially James English; Gregory Mixon, "'Good Negro—Bad Negro': The Dynamics of Race and Class in Atlanta during the Era of the 1906 Riot," *Georgia Historical Quarterly* 81 (Fall 1997): 612. Mixon's article also refers to a critical case just after the riot in which Judge Roan presided and Luther Z. Rosser was a member of the defense team—roles the men replayed in the Leo Frank case (618). Clifford Kuhn posits a relationship between the Men and Religion Forward movement and Police Chief Beavers in opposition to both Elsas and Frank. If he is correct, it would raise the issue of the activities of the police and the prosecution of Frank as politically motivated, a point dramatically developed in Steve Oney, *And the Dead Shall Rise: The Murder of May Phagan and the Lynching of Leo Frank* (New York: Pantheon, 2003).

48. Dittmer, *Black Georgia*, 30–31, 111, 117, MacLachlan, "Women's Work," 82, 91. For the conservative/black coalition, see also Kirby, *Darkness at the Dawning*, 9. Doyle used the term *New Paternalism* when referring to efforts to uplift African Americans economically. *New Men*, 266. For black-Jewish relations in Atlanta, see Mark K. Bauman, introduction to *The Quiet Voices: Southern Rabbis and Black Civil Rights, 1880s to 1990s*, ed. Mark K. Bauman and Berkley Kalin (Tuscaloosa: University of Alabama Press, 1997); Steven Hertzberg, "Southern Jews and Their Encounter with Blacks: Atlanta, 1850–1915," *Atlanta Historical Journal* (Fall 1970): 7–24. See also the important work by Clive J. Webb, *Fight against Fear: Southern Jews and Black Civil Rights* (Athens: University of Georgia Press, 2001).

49. The literature on the Frank case is extensive. The definitive studies are Leonard Dinnerstein's *The Leo Frank Case* (New York: Columbia University Press, 1968); and Oney, *And the Dead Shall Rise*. Interesting studies include Nancy MacLean, "The Leo Frank Case Reconsidered: Gender and Sexual Politics in the Making of Reactionary Populism," *Journal of American History* 78 (December 1991): 917–48; Jeffrey Melnick, *Black-Jewish Relations on Trial: Leo Frank and Jim Conley in the New South* (Jackson: University Press of Mississippi, 2000); Eugene Levy, "'Is the Jew a White Man?' Press Reaction to the Leo Frank Case, 1913–1915," *Phylon* 35 (June 1974): 212–22; and Harry Golden, *A Little Girl Is Dead* (Cleveland, Ohio: World Publishing, 1965). Oney's work especially expands on the many ties and conflicts depicted here.

50. Stephen J. Goldfarb, "The Slaton Memorandum: A Governor Looks Back at His Decision to Commute the Death Sentence of Leo Frank," *American Jewish History* 88 (September 2000): 325–40.

51. Slaton was unanimously elected president of the Georgia Bar Association in 1928. Dinnerstein, *Leo Frank Case*, 159. Slaton received an honorary doctorate from the University of Georgia in 1936. Cook, "Shadow of Leo Frank," 16. Slaton gave many speeches before Jewish groups in Atlanta through the years and was selected an honorary member of Nu Beta Epsilon, a national Jewish legal fraternity, in 1942. In 1937, Slaton was described as "the noted liberal" when he spoke before Congregation Ahavath Achim in a celebration of the 150th anniversary of the adoption of the U.S. Constitution. *Southern Israelite,* October 4, November 15, 1929, February 28, 1930 (for some of his speaking engagements), October 1, 1937 (for Constitution anniversary speech), June 26, 1942 (for induction into the fraternity). On the date of the primary, see Hertzberg, *Strangers within the Gate City,* 158.

52. Hertzberg, *Strangers within the Gate City,* 213–14.

53. Dinnerstein, *Leo Frank Case,* 123; Howell, *History of Georgia* 2:122–26. Law firm affiliations did not always influence politics. Prosecutor Hugh Dorsey started his legal practice in Atlanta in his father's firm, which included a Jewish partner. Cook, "Shadow of Leo Frank," 18. Reuben Arnold, another defense counsel, supported Hoke Smith; Hudson, "Smith-Brown Controversy," 77, n. 1.

54. Dinnerstein wrote, "Slaton, a man with a keen sense of justice, faced the issue squarely in spite of the possible political consequences." *Leo Frank Case,* 123, 126. See also James E. Dorsey, "Slaton, John Marshall," *Dictionary of Georgia Biography,* 893; Golden, *A Little Girl Is Dead,* 20–21; Cook, "Shadow of Leo Frank," 15; James F. Cook, *The Governors of Georgia, 1754–1995* (Macon, Ga.: Mercer University Press, 1995). Frank received a posthumous pardon in 1986 when new evidence from a witness to many of the events surrounding Mary Phagan's murder provided additional testimony.

55. For further infighting that muddles the picture, see Dinnerstein, *Leo Frank Case,* 29–31, 94, 122–23, 126, 118: Golden, *A Little Girl Is Dead,* 216, 248–50, 255.

56. In still another twist, Joseph M. Brown, the son of Joseph E. Brown, was one of the lynching conspirators. For the political impact on the conspirators, see Oney, *And the Dead Shall Rise.*

57. Hertzberg, *Strangers within the Gate City,* 159–60, 212; *American Jewish Review,* September 1914, March 1915.

58. Bauman, "Centripetal and Centrifugal Forces," 43–33, 46, 48.

Home and Hearth

Women, the Klan, Conservative Religion,
and Traditional Family Values

Glenn Feldman

Much has been written in recent years about race, some on the Klan, and still more on women. But little has been written about women, the Klan, and the intersection of the conservative theology that often served as the underpinning of various manifestations of the KKK.[1] This is so largely because the KKK was a white Anglo-Saxon Protestant, male organization. Members had to be men, by the very definition of the organization itself. Not surprisingly, most historians have logically concentrated on the actual members of the organization—men, that is—until recently. Only in the last decade have scholars done direct work on the relationship of women to the KKK as an organization.[2]

Yet anyone who knows anything about how life functions, especially in the South, knows that women, far from being invisible, played a very important role in the KKK. At one time, the Klan was a highly organized, immensely effective group—as a political, civic, fraternal, patriotic, educational, social, religious, and—yes—violently intolerant organization. And anyone who knows anything about how the South works knows that behind the best-run and most highly organized events, there are women—usually very busy women.

The Invisible Empire was no different. Although women were barred from formal membership, they played important roles in the religious and secular life of the hooded order. As the wives, girlfriends, mothers, sisters, and daughters of the 115,000 adult male members of the 1920s Alabama Klan,[3] for example, women shaped the order; its ideology, goals, and selective interpretation of theology; and the implementation of its program (sometimes at the end of a whip). Some actually joined the Klan movement, if not the KKK itself, as members (along with children) in its auxiliaries.[4] But many who did not, even semiformally, played a more crucial, if less visibly obtrusive, role in shaping and carrying out the Klan's program, principally in the spheres that were most thought to affect them: religion, morality, family, and education.

Although the activities of Klanswomen and fellow female travelers usually focused on the moral, civic, and educational thrusts of the Klan, there was tremendous overlap between race, class, ethnicity, gender, and religious concerns. Klan activity, male and female, had much to do with the preservation of societal order against a host of perceived and real changes. Despite its differing shapes over time, the KKK had to do with preserving a familiar social order. In the South, this meant the protection and preservation of a whole Southern way of life that included white supremacy, patriarchy, ethnic purity, and social and political conservatism, all of which relied on the bonds of a moral and religious orthodoxy that usually bolstered, rather than challenged, the status quo and its component parts.[5]

What is more, women—black and white—also played a vital role as victims of the KKK. The sheeted order is often thought of (with good reason) as a militant and terrorist wing of white supremacy. It was. But it was also much more than that, especially during the first half of the twentieth century. Along with black victims, the KKK targeted virtually any person, regardless of sex, who represented an aberration (and thus a threat) to Alabama's majority and to its exceptionally homogenous society.[6] Anyone who was an "outsider"—racially, religiously, ethnically, culturally, and morally, as well as with respect to traditional gender roles—risked becoming a target of repression and violence. Female victims of the Klan, often targeted by other women, supplied visible, corporeal, and even visceral examples of women who had "gotten out of their proper place," and who thus posed a threat to the stability of the wider community.

In intensely religious environs like Alabama, a Calvinist notion of concern for personal morality reigned, largely because of a curious reading of St. Paul's admonition to the early Christians to treat the body of faith as a whole community.[7] Actually, St. Paul's admonition can profitably be read as a call for the toleration and acceptance of diversity in society—even the religious community. Yet the relevant passages were much more commonly employed in the white evangelical South as the opposite: a license, indeed a heavenly mandate, for intolerance and the rooting out of nonconformity. Translated into Southern evangelical society, this admonition rapidly gained

momentum as a permit for ordinary folks to police the personal morality—
indeed, the customs, habits, and idiosyncrasies—of their neighbors in the
name of keeping their society pure, decent, and intact. This kind of community monitoring was in keeping with Calvinist notions of an "elect." No one
could know for sure that they were members of the elect—that their salvation was preordained—but "signs" did exist, they believed. Thus, the temptation to look for such signs was strong: membership in a moral elite, for
example, by comparison with one's backsliding neighbors, a desire to be
"holier than thou." Fearing contamination from "sinners" in the community, many Southern whites accepted the notion that a "sin" on behalf of one
member of the community threatened, in the same way that a cancer did,
the health and perhaps the survival of the larger whole. It was not a far leap
from such an intellectual formulation to the widespread acceptance of "moral
authoritarianism"—the policing and even sometimes violent repression of
individual "sin," or at least moral unconvention, in the name of maintaining
the greater community's spiritual health.

Women—frequently responsible in many places and times for the spiritual welfare of the family and community—played a vitally important role
in this regard, both as the policers and the policed. Men, more often than
not, wielded the blunt instruments that drove the morality lessons home.
But it was women, in vital conjunction with and in concert with men, who
decided what the religious and moral curriculum should be. In doing so,
women functioned both as the coauthors and the victims of a kind of mi-
sogynistic terror that kept women tethered to the most narrow and traditional of roles outlined for them by the South's patriarchal society.[8] Klan
repression of women concerned the maintenance of "proper" relations between the races, to be sure. But it also included the preservation of the "proper
place" of women in society and the maintenance of widespread notions of
what constituted acceptable ethical behavior. As several historians have
shown, the line between racial order and sexual order was not only hard to
distinguish, but it was also at times mutually supportive and even symbiotic.[9] Along with class hierarchy, caste, gender, and ethnic order were variants of a comprehensive social order that was comfortable to the
overwhelming majority of the South's white inhabitants.

To this rectangular formulation may be added a fifth side: a narrowly
defined notion of family values that buttressed traditional race, class, and
gender relations (in other words, white supremacy, class hierarchy, and patriarchy). This religious-based morality, an overarching kind of Southern
community morality system, long served as a foundation for Southern soci-

ety in the same ways that white supremacy, material privilege, and male domination did. In fact, it was this religious-based system of conservative mores that often served as the crucial bridge between white supremacy, class hierarchy, paternalism, and ethnic homogeneity, a moral status quo that interlocked the pillars of caste, class, gender, and ethnicity into a mutually supportive foundation on which Southern society itself rested.[10] For the majority of white Southerners, this critical moral link made the race, class, gender, and ethnic status quos seem God-ordained, granting both the orthodoxies and their protectors an exalted status, and girding the whole system in an almost impregnable way against fundamental change.

Emotion and intolerance were important by-products of the Southern reliance on religious orthodoxy to provide the cement with which to bond white supremacy, class hierarchy, patriarchy, and nativism in a solid social order. Threats to this order were discerned in the most innocuous events. Where there were minimal threats present—the mildest of liberal reform impulses, for example—a "slippery slope" approach or extreme version of guilt by association was used to discredit that threat. Social Gospel advocates and labor organizers were branded at the drop of a hat with the foolproof epithet of "communist agitator."[11] W. J. Cash wrote that "Southerners didn't think; they felt," and for that, he has been roundly castigated by some of the most distinguished minds ever to address the subject.[12] But Cash was onto something, even if he never articulated it quite this way. Emotion and its cousin of irrational intolerance were powerful by-products of the Southern reliance on old-time religion and religious conformity to undergird its social order.[13] In such a society, assaults on the status quo were more than just efforts at reform; they were rejections of the word of God. Heresies, in fact, that had to be rooted out like the cancers they were, lest they spread their poison throughout the body politic and the body social. The momentousness of such a task, preserving the Good Society itself, made the defensive effort a highly emotional one, an American jihad in which the stakes were so high that virtually no method was off limits.

Sister, You Were Not Punished Tonight in a Spirit of Anger

During the 1920s, Alabama experienced an orgy of Klan violence. Although much of it was racial in nature, a good deal was tied to the forcible maintenance of traditional gender roles and religious-based notions of conventional morality. A large part of the racial violence had clear moral and gender components. During the frenzy of Klan violence in Alabama, Kluxers routinely targeted women, mostly for violating narrow social conventions and ideas of traditional morality, but sometimes for being too racially tolerant and thus jeopardizing the sacred color line and pure white-blood basis for white supremacy and privilege in Southern society. Aside from the obvious contradiction of its own self-conscious tenets about chivalry, the Klan's targeting of women said much about the kinds of people who belonged to the order. Women, it should be recalled, had only just received the franchise in 1920. The perception of the flapper and her rejection of traditional gender constraints—despite her rarity in actuality—terrified men and women more comfortable with the old roles and confinement to separate spheres for the sexes. The automobile and contraception heralded growing female independence. Divorce rates rose, and growing numbers of women entered the workforce. Gender relations, like racial and ethnic purity, came under a withering assault. Men and women tied to the Klan worked to ensure that the clock would be turned back to a simpler time, a purer time—a time when women "knew their place," darkies were obedient, religion was orthodox, immigrants were Nordic, and Yankees stayed home.[14]

Viewed in this context, the "protection" of white womanhood may be more properly understood as the circumscription of certain behaviors from women. After World War I, female suffrage, sexual experimentation, labor unrest, Freudian psychology, the "New Immigration," modernist values, and the debate over alcohol all contributed to an uncertain atmosphere. Although the Klan may have been the purest, and perhaps the most extreme, expression of a native white Protestant backlash against these changes, it was by no means aberrant from the greater native white Protestant majority. It was just more pronounced. The Klan's representative nature was the main reason for its numerical popularity and geographical diffuseness in the 1920s, as well as for the lack of much criminal, legal, or moral opposition to the order—opposition that was usually expedient, pragmatic, and self-serving in nature.[15]

To repel assaults on this order, the KKK enforced the preponderant conventions of local communities with social pressure, religious ostracism, and, if need be, violence. Although men usually wielded the whips and blunt instruments, if it came to that, women functioned as the essential eyes and ears of KKK dens in learning about infractions of mores and customs that needed correction.[16] Just as every feminist is not a woman and every antifeminist is not a man, the enforcement of conventional morality, including women's behavior, was not a job limited to men. In their role as the eyes and ears of the Klan morality police, women played a large role in setting the agenda of morality enforcement and community orthodoxy, much of which perpetuated traditional theological beliefs and male-female relations. Offenses varied in severity and whether or not they were actual infractions of the law or only personal vices. Kluxers might visit a man who had been accused of adultery, spousal abuse, or nonsupport and visit a woman for adultery or prostitution. Other offenses were not nearly so serious or public. The Klan visited people for transgressions as capricious as drinking, dancing, gambling, parking, and being too courteous to blacks, or as personal as dating after divorce or deciding to remarry. The thin and arbitrary line between policing orthodox religion and morals versus neighborhood quarrels and petty jealousies was an easy and tempting one to cross.

Some became addicted to their roles as morality commissars and to the feeling of moral superiority inherent in pointing out the shortcomings of their neighbors. Exclusive membership in a moral elite—if only in the eye and mind of the beholder—was a powerful incentive for some to join the Klan and its morality police. In one South Alabama county overrun with KKK violence, a small-town mayor named five of the most active Kluxers as two blacksmiths, a barber, a bricklayer, and a shoe repairman. He described the sixth as the former village drunk. "Ever since he's sworn off," the mayor explained, "he's been all hell in favor of virtue."[17]

During the Klan's heyday in Alabama, violent incidents of morality policing exploded in number and severity. Although the state had clearly experienced vigilantism before, nothing had been seen on this scale since Reconstruction. Various estimates of Klan floggings alone in 1920s Alabama—not to mention cross burnings, kidnappings, threats, and actual disappearances and killings—numbered between 600 and 800.[18] Although black men made up Klan targets, in fidelity to the popular image of sheeted violence, white women (usually singled out for immorality) also comprised a large number. In 1927, for example, Florence night riders dragged Bertha Slay from her bed to her front yard, tied her husband and sisters to chairs to watch, bent her over a barrel, and whipped her with such gusto that they exhausted themselves and had to take a break. Trading their switches for an automobile fan belt, the hooded group resumed the beating and demanded a "confession" for Slay's part in a neighborhood scandal.[19] In St. Clair County, masked Knights lashed a sickly teenage girl and her mother for allowing a black man to teach them how to drive. Chilton County Klansmen repeatedly terrorized an elderly woman because she insisted on running a restaurant after her husband's death.

In a case that combined sadism, sexuality, and moral conventionality with controlling women not under the direct eye of a male authority figure, the Crenshaw County Klan visited Fannie Clement Daniels twice. A seventeen-year-old divorcée who had moved back home to take care of her mother after her father died, Fannie Daniels violated local sensibilities by dating a young farmer. On their first visit, the Klan warned her to stop seeing the young man. At a second midnight visit, Knights broke down her front door, snatched a shotgun from her mother, bruised the old woman, and ordered Fannie to dress suitably to search for her boyfriend. As she changed out of her nightclothes, several of the hooded men stayed to leer. Growing impatient, they threw her across the bed, hiked up her dress, and whipped her. When Fannie showed signs of being unbowed, one struck her across the face. "Give her some more," another called out, "she ain't had enough."[20]

Klansmen dealt just as roughly with divorced women who attempted to date or remarry. Such anomalies to the ideal of lifelong monogamous marriage threatened social order and orthodox religion because marriage was viewed by the majority as the divinely inspired bedrock of a stable and hierarchical society.[21] One Alabama episode illustrates just how grotesquely community mores could be twisted once they were subject to a pathological obsession with the private moral decisions and behaviors of others. A Baptist preacher officiated at the wedding of a couple who had both been previously married, and apparently, he later officiated at their brutal Klan flogging. After a savage beating of the young couple, administered in front of their several small children, the minister took up a collection for the bleeding woman and offered her $3.50, a jar of ointment, and some pastoral words of wisdom. "Sister, you were not punished in anger this evening," the preacher told her, "you were punished in a spirit of kindness and correction to set your feet aright and to show your children how a good mother should go."[22]

Many white Alabama women supported and participated, as informers, in this sort of community morality policing and enforcement of an idealized religious status quo. Time after time, Klansmen from across the state described how their wives and other women fingered persons in the local community whom they thought should be visited by the KKK.[23] Two Alabama women recalled years later that during the 1920s, everyone in their social circle knew who was, and was not, a member of the "secret" order, and both argued that the Klan was a good thing: it punished people for worthy ethical offenses like drinking, adultery, and nonsupport. Others recalled that often the locals were happy the Klan had dealt with ethical infractions.[24] Such expressions of support for the Klan—even the most violent aspects of the order—reflected a larger consensus about traditional values and gender roles in Alabama. Birmingham's police commissioner publicly applauded Klan raids on teenage dances that sometimes included alcohol and petting, even when the raids turned violent. W. B. Cloe's defense of the Klan was an almost perfect articulation of the connection between racism, nativism, and religious intolerance and the drive to preserve societal order. In a statement in which he disparaged blacks, Jews, and Asians, Cloe defended vigilante morality monitoring. "Klansmen are a good bunch of men," Cloe explained; otherwise "they wouldn't be knocked so much. . . . I say God bless them. It may be your sons or daughters who are going to hell."[25] R. F. Elmore, judge of Alabama's Seventeenth Circuit Court, instructed a grand jury investigating a string of Klan assaults that the order was worth supporting, even to the point of jury nullification, because it bolstered morality, hierarchy, and social order. The KKK, Judge Elmore charged the jurors from the bench, "stand[s] for just what you and I stand for: . . . the constitution . . . white supremacy . . . the public school . . . [and the] chastity of women."[26] An Etowah County court allowed Kluxers to deliver a popular broadsheet on morality to jurors while they were actually in session.[27]

Many Alabamians agreed that vigilantism and perhaps hypocrisy were preferable to the greater evil of immorality and religious nonconformism. Some women naively compared vicious Klan assaults to childhood whippings. Others felt that local communities had a right—indeed, a civic and religious responsibility—to regulate personal conduct. Some evangelicals felt it was their moral duty to note and correct the ethical shortcomings of their neighbors and preserve social order, by force if necessary. One Klanswoman remembered that the policing of community morality "gave people a feeling that they were doing the right thing . . . like they were doing the[ir] Christian duty."[28] This ethos was reinforced in a society in which well-received Klan groups called on Protestant congregations in the midst of Sunday morning services and presented grateful pastors with envelopes stuffed with cash. Klan lecturers such as Methodist minister Earl Hotalen crisscrossed the state to defend white supremacy as essential to the preservation of an unpolluted heritage and praised the Klan at gatherings that blended religious and civic conformity as an organization dedicated to the precepts of morality, chivalry, Bible study, and free public schools. The KKK wore robes, Hotalen claimed, not to conceal the identities of those committing violent crimes, but to bolster the social order and symbolize the purity of Jesus Christ. The Klan would unmask, he explained, only when "our Lord, the Prince of Peace, shall come again, . . . when Satan . . . shall have been bound in chains, and when bootleggers . . . rapists . . . [and] gamblers . . . no longer encumbered the earth."[29]

Behavior that specifically threatened the maintenance of the family—especially the existence of undiluted white bloodlines—came in for special attention. In January 1925, for example, Klan chapters around the state launched a campaign to close down suspected houses of ill repute. Within a week, masked Kluxers burned crosses in front of ten Birmingham homes. A raid on one brothel yielded a special prize when Knights discovered a former policeman enjoying the sexual favors of black prostitutes.[30] In other episodes, Talladega Knights flogged an elderly farmer for housing prostitutes, making moonshine, and hosting dances.[31] In Birmingham, armed Klansmen organized a truck-and-car caravan and issued an invitation to the press to accompany the mob on its raids. Birmingham's commissioner of public safety publicly endorsed the raids and told the press that the police welcomed the Klan's aid in combating prostitution.[32]

Adultery and prostitution warranted close attention. As the eyes and ears of hooded morality police, women were often the driving force behind the Klan's regulation of extramarital sex. Shortly after New Year's Day 1926, a dozen armed Klansmen, accompanied by an off-duty deputy sheriff, invaded three Chinese restaurants in downtown Birmingham to search for alcohol and to raid couples, which ended up consisting of only one married person, found in one of the small private dining rooms said to be havens for adulterous couples. The raid combined nativism, the prohibitionist impulse, and a concern about adultery and preservation of the family as gun-wielding Klansmen bullied, searched, and finally "arrested" three women and three men and took them to the county jail. Once there, though, the party came to an end as Jefferson County's chief deputy tore up the "warrants," released the "prisoners," and declared the whole thing to be a huge mistake.[33] Alabama Klansmen lashed men and women suspected of adultery, forced several shotgun weddings to take place, and beat husbands accused of nonsupport and spousal abuse. They beat a man who refused to allow his wife to visit her sick mother, assaulted a man who refused to remarry his former wife, kidnapped a man for legally separating from his wife, caned teen couples for parking on lovers' lanes, lashed a separated mother of four for having improper sexual relations with men she was dating, brutalized a janitor for spying on school-age girls in the bathroom, tried to hang a farmhand for cursing in front of a woman, and used brass knuckles on a doctor they charged with having sexual relations with a female patient.[34] All of them were white. In June 1922 a robed Klan party attacked a white married couple for sharing a physician's home with him. The Kluxers beat the husband with a blunt instrument as he slept, leaving him unconscious in a pool of blood, and choked his wife until she blacked out.[35] In a particularly tragic incident, a Klan mob raided a 207-acre truck farm in Blount County in the middle of the night. Aroused by rumors that the farmer's wife, Lily, was an adulteress, fifty sheeted and gowned Knights attacked the African American parents of eight while they were sleeping. The farmer, Emory, seized his shotgun and returned the gunfire, but Lily fell, mortally wounded in the exchange.[36]

Incidents that crossed lines of color, ethnicity, or religion raised special passions. Although race was the most emotional of all issues in the South, it was not just an emotional issue. White supremacy had a definite rational, if repellant, logic to its maintenance. Concrete economic rewards accompanied white supremacy and institutionalized racism: better parks, playgrounds, libraries, schools, public amenities, health care, and housing; safer neighborhoods; access to credit; a continued source of cheap labor for employers; and a leg up on job competition for whites. These economic trappings of white supremacy were every bit as important and powerful as the social and psychological benefits whites felt from this legal and institutionalized caste system. It is little wonder, then, why so many whites from all walks of life clung to segregation and white supremacy with such tenacity in the face of the changes that came in the middle of the twentieth century. On some occasions, race, gender, and ethical concerns melded perfectly. During the 1920s, Klan mobs in Alabama got wind about, and brutally flogged, a black porter for "associating too closely" with white women, a white woman for being too friendly to blacks, a white woman and her daughter for allowing a black man to teach them how to drive, a black man for having domestic troubles, several black physicians for treating white women, a German grocery store owner for allowing his teenage daughter to wait on blacks, and a black man and two black women whom they made strip naked and run a gauntlet around a baseball diamond.[37]

Ethnic and religious purity raised similar passions. Knights terrorized a Greek man for marrying a native white woman, a Jew for trying to marry a Protestant woman, a Rumanian confectionary store owner and a German tailor for trying to date native women, and a Catholic druggist who said he could date married Protestant women.[38] "The Saddest Story Ever Told," according to a poem distributed by a female fellow traveler, was the story of young white women who shook the racial, religious, and sexual order to the core by marrying outside of her race.[39]

Of course, such things did not go on completely uncriticized. Virginia Foster Durr, noted Montgomery liberal and sister-in-law to later Supreme Court justice Hugo Black, had nothing but contempt for the Invisible Empire and its crusade of moral enforcement.[40] More commonly, though, criticism of the Klan and its activities emanated from the most economically conservative sources in the state: the Big Mule/Black Belt coalition of powerful and wealthy industrialists and planters. Jealous of the Klan's political strength and the resonance of its moral and religious program with many plain whites—and especially worried that unsubtle Klan enforcement of the racial status quo might risk federal intervention and bring about real racial change—these conservatives mounted an eloquent critique of the order's violent enforcement of morality, ethics, and orthodox religion. Predictably, though, their opposition to the order's violence was itself rooted in preference for time-tested notions of what constituted proper relations between the sexes and the races. An enraged Covington County editor denounced the beating of women—for any excuse—as uncivilized, and demanded that Southern gentlemen take up arms to protect white womanhood from the depredations of hooded mobs. "Where are they now . . . [the] men . . . the pride of the Southland?" he lamented, "men whose honor is worth more to them than their life's blood. . . . Do they sleep . . . ? Is the spirit of the Old South waning?"[41] Prominent Black Belt Democrat John Bainbridge damned the 1920s Klan while praising the Reconstruction order and its racial conservatism (not an unusual combination among Alabama elites). He described morality-obsessed Klansmen as indulging their Freudian fantasies to "spank some neighborhood [Mary] Magdalene" and recommended a liberal use of buckshot as suitable remedy.[42] The state's leading patrician mouthpiece, Grover Hall of the *Montgomery Advertiser*, lambasted the Klan's morality enforcement as "appalling . . . [the work of a] gang of hooded demons . . . fiends . . . heartless ruffians . . . beasts." "Every blow of the lash . . . on the body of a defenseless . . . woman," Hall wrote, "is a blow at . . . [the] State and [the] law.[43]

Actually, women were not as defenseless as the popular press depicted. On several occasions, women took up arms against attacking Klansmen. A Decatur madam repulsed one Klan mob by wielding a shotgun and calling out the names of regular customers she recognized in the mob.[44] The daughter of an elderly striking railroad worker came to his defense, only to be flogged herself by his attackers. A wife who stood between Kluxers and her husband wound up with her clothes being ripped off. A young woman eagerly learned how to operate a firearm after her husband was brutalized. An elderly woman attempted to foil the flogging of her daughter by brandishing a shotgun, but had it ripped from her hands. A similar result occurred when a woman aimed a shotgun at a mob of a hundred hooded Klansmen outside her home. Two spinster sisters were more successful, though. They drove off a Crenshaw Klan mob with a pair of shotguns, only to have their furniture shot full of holes in their later absence.[45]

More telling, though, was the reaction of Alabama law enforcement and juries, made up of the friends, neighbors, and fellow church members of Klansmen. Rarely, if ever, did local law enforcement arrest Knights for such acts, no matter how violent they were. In those few instances in which arrests did happen, acquittals usually occurred. In the rarest of cases where convictions resulted, virtually all were overturned at higher levels. At a fundamental level, the goals of the hooded order, if not their methods, were seen as noble and worthy of societal and religious endorsement. Of all the travesties of justice in 1920s Alabama, perhaps none was more egregious than the flogging and killing of Annie Mae Simmons, an elderly black woman. In a sensational 1927 case, brought by an ambitious state attorney general, her killers walked scot-free despite the incriminating testimony of three (black) eyewitnesses and the confession of the flogging squad's ringleader. Still, a Crenshaw County jury returned a verdict of not guilty in a case that featured squabbling between state police officers and apparent complicity between law enforcement and the defense team. But mostly, as one defense attorney accurately, if incredibly stated in open court, the killers of Annie Mae Simmons would not be convicted because as a black woman, she occupied the lowest rung on society's ladder and her death was of no consequence.[46] Perhaps as disturbing was the moral commentary afforded by Oscar Adams, the black publisher of the *Birmingham Reporter*. A black accommodationist who profited handsomely from his close relationship with the white power structure, Adams refused to denounce the Klan. "While the means of correction are unlawful," he wrote of the lynching of an interracial couple, "the spirit behind the act must be considered righteous and altogether pleasing."[47]

ONE HUNDRED PERCENT AMERICANISM

Women in Alabama—as Klan auxiliaries, members of the Women of the KKK (WKKK), and as individuals connected in less formal ways—played a major role in the era's civil religion and the Klan's activities to encourage religiosity, patriotism, "100 percent Americanism," and public education. Altruism and civic involvement in its purest sense was thoroughly mixed with more pragmatic goals for these women. Much of the activity of this period gained its impetus from the exuberant unspent patriotism associated with American involvement in World War I, fear and suspicion of immigration from Southern and Eastern Europe, and outright nativism. As part of this general clime, Alabama women spearheaded KKK and WKKK drives to ensure that all children were properly schooled in the prevailing white Anglo-Saxon Protestant variant of American patriotism. Again, the goal of the political socialization was to short-circuit threats to the race, class, ethnic, gender, and religious status quo in a rapidly changing world. One manifestation of this concern was the Klan drive to ensure that all Alabama children of classroom age had American flags in their schoolrooms. In Talladega County and other places around the state, local women affiliated with the KKK bought individual American flags and bestowed them on public schools with great flourish and ceremony. Speeches, fireworks, parades, barbecues, and other demonstrations of patriotic fervor accompanied these rituals.[48]

Initiations of new Klan members gave the order ideal opportunities to overawe rural and small-town communities with the religious-based values and ethos of the order. In 1922, Anniston's KKK held festivities on a large sandbar in Oxford Lake, featuring a barbecue beneath a huge electric cross, fireworks, and several parades as four hundred area men formally joined the outfit. Over a thousand robed Klansmen and women attended the event, carried to Anniston on special trains from around the state. In 1925 and 1926, "Klan Day" at the Lee County Fair drew 10,000 spectators, including 2,000 costumed. The galas featured fireworks, two Klan bands, races, a carnival, a 1,500-person parade, martial music, robed horses, fiery crosses, American flags at every turn, and speeches by Alabama's grand dragon. All of this was undergirded by the authority of old-time religion as Alabama's best-known "lecturer," a Methodist minister, made his presence ubiquitous. Hundreds of WKKK women, dressed in full Klan regalia, took active part in all of the festivities, accompanied by men and children, also in full Klan dress.[49]

Klan leaders went to great lengths to recruit women formally into the life of Ku Kluxism. During the early 1920s rival efforts at recruiting women actually reached a fever pitch in Alabama. Methodist minister Joseph Simmons, founder of the Knights of the KKK, recruited Birmingham women into a group called the "Kamelias," after the famous male white supremacist organization of the Reconstruction era. Alabama dentist Hiram W. Evans, who was soon to displace Simmons as the nation's leading Klansman, responded by organizing his own Alabama branch of the Women of the Ku Klux Klan. The WKKK group grew to absorb a host of like-minded religious and civic women's groups: the Ladies of the Invisible Empire, Queens of the Golden Mask, the Grand League of Protestant Women, the Order of American Women, the Puritan Daughters of America, the White American Protestants, and the Dixie Protestant Women's Political League. Klan speakers, interested in recruiting women to the various auxiliary orders, tailored their remarks on public education, Protestant Christianity, private morality, and temperance to women of various ages at the large open-air celebrations and Klan initiations held around the state during the 1920s.[50]

For some, the Klan and its values was an essential part of family and religious life. At its peak, Birmingham's huge Robert E. Lee Klavern claimed 10,000 members, half the city's police force (including the city's police chief), most of its Protestant ministers, and a good number of its judges and other public officials. The oldest active klavern in the country, it ran an orphanage called "Klanhaven," printed a newspaper, sponsored a drum and bugle corps, supplemented public school finances by sponsoring plays, concerts, and other fund-raising activities, and community charities, and even owned a posh athletic club that provided bathing facilities, recreation, and meeting rooms for Klansmen and their wives and children. Around the state, Klan chapters engaged in a variety of civic projects commonly associated with women's religious groups and sodalities. Klan women and men donated money to hospitals, visited sick children, bought food and clothing for widows, and bought toys for the needy at Christmastime. The Clay County chapter paid for funerals, the Tuscaloosa den raised money to pay for a new Boy Scouts campground, and a Huntsville klavern sponsored a memorial room at the city hospital.[51]

As admirable as some of the Klan's civic projects undoubtedly were, education-minded Klansmen and women were motivated by more than a simple love of learning.[52] Many supported public education because they feared parochial education and the "un-American" and "undemocratic" indoctrination and the ethnic, working-class character of the Catholic religion and its schools. Although civic and educational efforts appealed to some Klan types whose motives were beyond reproach, these activities also struck a common chord among nativists, religious bigots, and members of the middle class who feared threats from below.[53] Supporting public education was another way of fighting Catholic theology and education, just as efforts at the inculcation of "American" values were often imbued with a dread of immigration, alcohol, political machines, and religious faiths other than Protestant Christianity. Many Alabamians harbored a profound fear of a church they saw as evil, foreign, and menacing to the "American" way of life.

Klan literature betrayed an obsession with "aliens"; many whites interpreted "Americanism" in the narrowest fashion to include only white Anglo-Saxon Protestant culture.[54]

It is impossible to divorce Klan support of public education in Alabama from an environment in which the Klan also abused Catholics, Jews, Greeks, Italians, and others whose religion or ethnicity varied from the Anglo-Protestant norm. Klan leaders from imperial wizard on down won thousands to their standard by accusing Catholics of making secret treaties to bring on World War I, plotting to assassinate Abraham Lincoln, opposing republican forms of government, controlling the press, stockpiling arms for a Catholic takeover of Washington, and planning to convert or exterminate all Protestant Americans. Hooded speakers regaled receptive audiences with tales of how Catholics buried a rifle under their churches every time a boy was born for a takeover of America, and how Catholics dominated the World Court for use in "Romanizing" the United States and forcing "papal aliens" into the country. When they "learned" that the 1917 U.S. dollar bill was really covered with secret Catholic symbols, dutiful Klansmen ripped off the corner of bills where they believed the Pope's picture was hidden. A favorite theme concerned the "unnatural" male domination of women in convents as priests took the rightful place reserved to Protestant men as the biblically mandated head of the household and were privy to the graphic and salacious details of women's sex lives in the privacy of the confessional. Decades before the actual Catholic priest-pedophilia crisis, klaverns in Alabama hosted itinerant "escaped nuns"—female Klan lecturers who posed as former Catholic nuns—to titillate audiences with tales about the carnal lust of priests and to display leather bags, which, they told their wide-eyed audiences, were used to cremate the infant products of priest-nun sexual unions in the basement furnaces of Catholic churches. Other stories emphasized the plight of helpless young girls locked in dungeonlike convents with high walls, iron windows, and bolted doors, eliciting actual tears of rage from emotionally overwrought Protestant audiences.[55]

Klan groups in Alabama responded to this kind of stimulation by burning a Catholic church and school at Pratt City, organizing boycotts of Catholic-owned stores, pressuring businesses to fire Catholic employees, blocking construction of Catholic churches, burning crosses in front of Catholic churches and schools, and, on one occasion, raiding a Mobile playground where frightened Catholic kindergarten children mistook the sheeted men for ghosts. Birmingham's boisterous city elections of 1917 turned on anti-Catholic prejudice, and Thomas E. Kilby won the governorship in 1919 partially by exploiting the issue. Two years later, Sylacauga Klansmen beat a Catholic druggist senseless, breaking his jaw and knocking out most of his teeth, because he bragged about dating Protestant women. The anti-Catholic fervor, like white supremacy, was intimately bound up in "protecting" white American Protestant women from infection by unclean and un-American "outsiders." Race, gender, class, and ethnic issues were integral to the Catholic question, all bound up neatly by the emotional "rope of religion" and evangelical notions of Protestant morality. The mania reached a low point in 1921 when an itinerant preacher, called "The Marrying Parson," shot and killed a Catholic priest in broad daylight in downtown Birmingham because the priest had officiated at the wedding of the parson's daughter to a white Puerto Rican Catholic. Himself a member of the Klan, the Baptist preacher admitted the deed, but he profited from a Klan defense fund to secure the talents of an ambitious young attorney named Hugo Black. The jury, anchored by a foreman who was also a Knight, returned a verdict of not guilty largely because Black dimmed the courtroom's lights, insinuated that the groom was part African American, and had jury members examine his skin complexion, nostrils, and fingernails.[56]

EMISSARIES OF THE DEVIL

Because most American Catholics were of Irish, Italian, or Eastern European descent, the immigration and alcohol issues were indelibly imprinted on the Catholic question. Along with concern about papal domination came the worry that people only one generation removed from the old country would not harbor the same loyalties to American government, values, or society as the Northern and Western European stock that had earlier emigrated to the United States. These anxieties reflected the powerful insecurities of immigrants whose memories of their parents' odysseys to America were remarkably short-lived. The Klan damned the hierarchy of the Roman Catholic Church and allegiance to a "foreign prince" while demanding loyalty above all to a hierarchical Invisible Empire. Likewise, the order spewed republican ideology while notoriously failing to practice it within the KKK.[57] Sensational events, such as the Red Scare of 1919–1920 and the Sacco and Vanzetti trial, fueled popular nervousness. In 1928, immigration, Catholicism, white supremacy, and alcohol found their purest expression in the presidential candidacy of New York governor Alfred E. Smith. A "wet," Catholic Irish product of New York's Tammany Hall and a relative liberal on the race issue, Smith's nomination as the national Democratic standard-bearer precipitated the deepest crack in the "solid Democratic South" since Reconstruction. In places like Alabama, it meant virtual war between those who insisted that Smith had to be accepted to ensure traditional Democratic protection of white supremacy and those like the Klan who viewed his candidacy as intolerable on a variety of grounds: religious, ethnic, moral, and racial.

In Alabama, Klan forces united with prohibitionists, women temperance advocates, and evangelical Protestants to wage a ferocious campaign against Smith's candidacy. But for some familiar Black Belt electoral shenanigans, they would have carried the state for Republican Herbert Hoover.[58] Women, far from being demure observers of the millennial conflict in Alabama, took part as major players in the unfolding drama. As male Klan leaders damned "Popish plots . . . the papal menace . . . and the papal monster" and warned Alabamians that Catholics would use mind control, Jesuit assassins, and hoarded gold reserves to win the day, female allies in the powerful Anti-Saloon League and the Women's Christian Temperance Union (WCTU) locked arms with the KKK.[59] Leading racial and religious bigots and Klan leaders Horace C. Wilkinson and Hugh A. Locke organized the "Anti-Smith Democrats" (it was still counterproductive at this time to openly declare oneself as a Republican in the South) with the conspicuous assistance of women from the Anti-Saloon League and the WCTU. The rump group negotiated a bizarre compact with former Populist O. D. Street and the Alabama Republican Party to list twelve prominent Democrats as Alabama electors for Herbert Hoover. Reflecting their growing political power and intimate involvement in the 1928 "bolt," two women made the critical elector slate: Mary T. Jeffries, president of the Alabama WCTU, and Zue Musgrove Long, sister of multimillionaire coal operator, Klansman, failed senatorial candidate, and Methodist prohibitionist extraordinaire L. B. Musgrove.[60]

The 1928 campaign brought out the worst in Alabama as both sides—conservative Democratic and upstart Klan/Hoovercrat—stooped to the lowest forms of a "politics of emotion." The term refers to the manipulation and/or exploitation of ingrained feelings on emotional issues, like race and "God and Country" issues such as abortion, prayer in schools, gay rights, patriotism, gun control, the personal morality of candidates, and exhibition of the Confederate flag and the Ten Commandments. Throughout Southern history, elite white Southerners—Bourbons, Redeemers, planters and industrialists (Conservative Democrats), and most recently the Southern GOP—have persuaded many plain whites to ally themselves with their class "betters" by appealing to these emotional, rather than substantive, issues.

Race, though, because of its perks in American society, qualifies as part of both a "politics of emotion" and a contrasting "politics of reason."[61]

Both sides in the 1928 bolt used the powerful ammunition of emotional appeals. Bourbon Democrats, including Marie Bankhead Owen—whose father and two brothers served in the U.S. Senate and House of Representatives—resorted to religious baiting and racial demagoguery to bash the candidacy of Republican Herbert Hoover.[62] The Klan/Hoovercrat alliance, though, proved itself every bit the equal of its Bourbon adversaries. Bob Jones—founder of the conservative university that bears his name, a noted Montgomery evangelist, and Klan fellow traveler—bragged on Birmingham as the most typical Anglo-Saxon city in America and criticized large Northern cities as being made up mostly of unwashed "foreigners." "If Catholic Al Smith is elected," he warned direly, "the gates to immigration will be thrown open. I had rather see a saloon on every corner . . . than to see the foreigners elect their candidate." The Reverend Jones also urged rejection of Al Smith by informing Alabamians that "God Almighty" had called on Southerners to be His chosen people for the sacred mission of saving America from the wickedness of immigrants and big cities.[63] A. J. Barton, member of the Southern Baptist Convention's social service committee, stumped against Al Smith by reassuring mixed Klan and women temperance audiences that "They say we are intolerant, but I have never been so happy in all my life as I am in supporting Herbert Hoover. He is not a negro lover."[64] U.S. senator and Klan darling J. Thomas Heflin did yeoman service against Al Smith by damning the "insidious papal monster . . . [and] the invisible government of Rome" at every opportunity, warning that Smith's election meant the systematic genocide of all American Protestants by the Knights of Columbus, and several times predicting his own assassination at Jesuit hands. A firm believer in white supremacy who had once enforced his understanding of Jim Crow by gunning down a black man on a Washington, D.C., streetcar, Heflin and other Klan speakers appealed to Alabama women by using language expressly calculated to press their "domestic sphere" buttons. Heflin had earlier raised his profile by defending the lynching of "fiendish brutes in human form" in classic terms: because "Southern womanhood is the priceless jewel of the Southern household [and] we will safeguard it and protect it with the last drop of our blood." Women now had an affirmative duty to oppose Al Smith and traditional Democracy because Rome was "aim[ing] her brutal, arrogant and unholy propaganda at the sacred circle of the American . . . Protestant home . . . [and] real Americans."[65] State Republican and Masonic leader O. D. Street's variant of opposition to Al Smith and traditional Democracy bordered on outright misogyny. Street's anti-Catholic bigotry was so raw, in fact, that it earned him official censure from the national chair of the Republican Party. In addition to the usual insults directed at the Catholic faith, Street distributed 200,000 copies of a broadsheet entitled "Governor Smith's Membership in the Roman Catholic Church and Its Proper Place as an Issue in this Campaign." In it, Street included an imprint from the Spanish Inquisition that depicted Catholic priests amputating a Protestant woman's breasts; it bore the caption, "She nursed a heretic child."[66]

The Klan/women's groups/evangelical racism aimed against Al Smith was savage, as befitting the infighting in a holy war. Broadsheets reached every corner of Alabama charging Smith with having to pander to "Harlem negroes" to be elected. Various titles were used, none of them very subtle: "Al Smith, the Negro Bootlicker," "Al Smith, the Negro Lover," "Nigger, Nigger, Nigger," "Smith's Negro Babies," "Tammany and the Negro," and "More Nigger."[67]

The 1928 presidential campaign was so divisive and so emotional in Alabama that certain of its episodes rival any in American political history for their bizarre nature. Long accustomed to feeding on the emotional issue of race in its politics, Alabamians of both sexes again hewed to a "politics of emotion" in 1928 rather than a "politics of reason"—and, in effect, rehearsed their roles for what would be common political practice in the state for years to come. Because of the long-standing race issue, as well as related issues from the state's periodic bouts with a "Reconstruction syndrome,"[68] emotion was a deeply engraved part of Alabama's political culture and a large part of the political socialization of plain Alabamians. In the critical 1928 election, though, race was fortified by the related emotional issues of religious "regularity," ethnic purity, moral conformity, and threats to white womanhood bound up in the Irish-Catholic Al Smith and prohibition issues. The emotion was palpable and raw, and it permeated political discussion in the state. Despite its proliferation and almost banality, in 1928, a pathological low point of sorts was reached in August when the powerful Nathan Bedford Forrest Klan Den of Wahouma, a middle-class suburb of Birmingham, held a political rally for the whole family. As two hundred men, women, and children cheered, one after another local Klan leader stood to denounce Al Smith for his Catholicism, his moral depravity in opposing prohibition, and the impurity of his New York–Irish heritage. After the speakers had whipped the crowd into a frenzy, a Klan leader held up a Smith mannequin before the crowd and asked them what they wanted to do with it. "Lynch him! Lynch him," they chorused in a macabre (but unconscious)

imitation of Christ's passion at the hands of Pontius Pilate. At that, the pre-
siding Klansman took out a long knife and slit the dummy's throat. Red
mercurochrome spurted forth to simulate blood. Assisting Knights rushed
the stage to tie a noose around the mannequin's neck and drag it around the
hall. Men, women, and children kicked and shot the Smith doll as a Klan
emcee assured his audience that come November, Al Smith would be lynched
"with good Christian votes."[69]

At less debased gatherings, the race, gender, and ethnic issues still combined with an explosive moral and religious dynamite. Women temperance
activists joined Klan leaders and leading evangelicals to denounce Smith's
candidacy. One prominent Methodist minister warned that if Smith were
elected, the Democratic Party would become the "party of Rome and rum
for the next hundred years." Around the state, Protestant preachers urged
their flocks to "vote as you pray" or "vote as Jesus our Captain would have us
vote." Baptist rallies featured speakers from the Anti-Saloon League railing
against "boss-ridden city masses—largely foreign and thirsty." One wife to a
Baptist preacher, herself a member of the WCTU, concluded that every
woman who planned to vote for Al Smith was an "emissar[y] of the Devil."
"It is useless," she sobbed, "to pray that the wicked will change their votes."[70]

The loyalist opposition to the 1928 bolters did not itself shy away from
preying on the emotional insecurities and fears of Alabama natives, male
and female alike. In fact, the planter-industrialist oligarchy that formed the
nucleus of conservative Democracy in Alabama, as in other Southern states,
was well versed in the craft of race baiting to convince plain whites to forgo
their class interests to help them preserve the stratified status quo. Although
patrician and Klan-connected women found themselves on opposite sides
of the Smith-Hoover question, women on both sides hewed to, and pursued
the maintenance of, narrow and traditional versions of race and gender relations. In doing so, planter and industrialist types invoked the emotional
specter of Reconstruction drummed into every Southern schoolboy and girl
by the age of ten. The caricature, which relied on the canted texts of the
"Dunning School" of Reconstruction historiography, was replete with corruption, "ignorant" black rule, Yankee and federal oppression, and dire threats
to white womanhood.[71]

The imagery was powerful, pervasive, and of long-standing effectiveness in the South. "We have a white man's government in Alabama, and we
are going to keep it unless federal bayonets again tear our heritage from us,"
one leading Bourbon declared. Future Alabama governor Frank M. Dixon
warned that Hoover's election would reconstitute Reconstruction Republi-

can "Negro rule" in the South and again bring "down the heels of the ex-slaves on the throats of Southern men and women." Another future gover-nor, Benjamin Meek Miller, agreed that "no nigger" had helped to nominate the Democratic standard-bearer, but rather "900 Anglo Saxons." Former gov-ernor Bill Brandon raised himself from his sickbed in Tuscaloosa to warn of "negro domination . . . the perils of Republican misrule . . . [and] the slimy trail of the carpetbagger." State Democratic chairman W. B. "Buck" Oliver cautioned that Hoover's election meant that Republicans would "use fed-eral bayonets to 'put the black heel on the white neck' just as they had done during Reconstruction."[72]

Women were part and parcel of this brand of conservative Democracy, just as they were intimately bound up with the Klan-evangelical attempt to derail the candidacy of Al Smith. Marie Bankhead Owen resorted to reli-gious baiting. Mabel Jones West, president of the Alabama Women's League for White Supremacy, endorsed Smith and repudiated the Klan, an act that spoke volumes because she herself had been a leading member of the Women of the KKK. As paradoxical as it may now appear, for Mabel Jones West and thousands of others who remained loyal to Alabama's Democratic Party in 1928, the preservation of white supremacy meant rejection of the Invisible Empire. "When the time comes when we must choose between the Ku Klux Klan and . . . white supremacy," she announced, "let the Ku Klux Klan go to the devil."[73] Other Alabama women who put white supremacy above all things—even religious orthodoxy—denounced the KKK-prohibitionist heresy of backing a Republican. "Think of a Secretary of Commerce hav-ing to stoop to niggers . . . [and] nigger politicians . . . to win," one com-plained about Hoover's desegregation of the Commerce Department. "I wonder how Mr. Hoover would like to have the women of his family use the same toilet that colored people use." They are "'Hoover's Chocolates' . . . and [we] all wish we could make him eat them."[74]

Other Alabama women found the wellspring of their support for the 1920s Klan in religion and nostalgia for the Reconstruction Klan of their fathers. It was an order that had long been branded on the Southern psyche as the gallant defenders of a God-ordained system of racial order and soci-etal hierarchy. One self-described "Old Lady of the South" praised the 1920s Klan because her father had been in the Reconstruction order that "cleansed our public offices of Negroes, carpetbaggers, and scalawags." "I can very well remember the Reconstruction Days," the old woman recalled, "when the White people of the South were oppressed and mistreated by this ungodly corruptible group. I can remember my father saying the Ku Klux Klan will never die. 'It was here yesterday, today, and forever.' And I firmly believe that God has a working hand through this organization. . . . If it wasn't for the Ku Klux Klan in the Reconstruction Days, America would have been a mongrelized nation." "So today," because of rampant immorality and assaults on conventional norms and gender roles, "God sees the need of a Ku Klux Klan as never before."[75] This feeling of a traditional society in moral crisis was part and parcel of the Klan ethos during the 1920s.[76]

ALABAMA IS WORTH MORE THAN THE "HONOR" OF TWO 50-CENT PROSTITUTES

During the 1930s, a smaller KKK shifted gears to focus on Jews, communists, labor unionists, and other threats to the class-based status quo. Class had been a part of the 1920s KKK appeal and raison d'être. Members of the Invisible Empire often disparaged Roman Catholics as members of a dirty working class, attacked unionists in the labor unrest after World War I, and painted Jews as the radical "brains" of an international conspiracy out to use blacks as the dupes of global revolution.[77] Still, at its root, the ostensible change in Klan targets was only that—ostensible. As in previous incarnations, Alabama's Klan activity still revolved around a xenophobia understood in its broadest terms: people who in some way represented foreign threats to cultural homogeneity—white supremacy, ethnic purity, and religious regularity. Jews, "Godless communists," and labor organizers, especially the new biracial Congress of Industrial Organizations, were all dangerously suspect in the South because they were closely associated with class insurgency and religious minorities. But their most egregious sin was in threatening racial purity by promoting biracial activity for reform.

The Scottsboro Boys tragedy encompassed all of these threats, plus some: black men accused of raping white women, Jewish attorneys from New York, communist defense funds. The KKK leapt into the proceedings, surrounding Alabama courthouses, threatening to lynch defendants and attorneys, clashing with black and white communists in Birmingham.[78]

The explosive combination of race, religion, radicalism, and sex led to heightened tensions during the Depression. Birmingham erupted in 1931 in full-blown hysteria when a deranged black radical kidnapped four young white women from Mountain Brook, easily the wealthiest neighborhood in the state. The communist held the women hostage for four hours while occasionally spouting radical propaganda, and he eventually shot three of them, killing one. Simmering tensions boiled over, giving way to a summer reign of terror in which Klansmen, police officers, and corporation security guards wreaked havoc on the city's black population. Before the outbreak ended, white mobs burned and bombed black businesses, shot several African Americans at random, and assaulted many others.[79] A similar outbreak of community terror occurred just hours away in Tuscaloosa when an eighty-four-year-old bedridden black man was falsely accused of raping a white woman.[80]

Many Alabamians were certain that Jewish labor organizers and communist activists wanted to break down—forcibly, if necessary—the wall between black men and white women. As the "hardest hit Depression town in America," and as the new home of the Southern branch of the Communist Party (however small), Birmingham became an emotion-filled religious and racial battleground during the 1930s.[81] The vaunted atheism connected to communism lent a millennial quality to the fight against radicalism and white supremacy. Native Alabamian and imperial wizard Hiram Evans warned blacks in Birmingham to stop "breathing [the] hot communistic airs of racial equality or there would be trouble." "The negroes are made to believe that the communists practice complete racial and social equality," Klan publications lectured. "[They] 'dangle' before the ignorant, lustful and brutish negroes . . . a tempting bait . . . that negro men should take white women and live with them, declaring that this is their God-given right under a communist regime.[82] In east Alabama, a Klan leader concurred, instructing local whites that "the Communist preach[es] absolute equality of race. He goes to where you are . . . puts his arm upon your shoulder and with that arm still warm . . . puts the same arm around the niggers . . . and says to them: 'Don't you know [that] . . . you can have a white wife?'"[83] In the central part of the state, an Autauga County woman explained her support for, and belief in, the KKK in terms of a religious and patriotic duty because America had become "a nation of contemptible filth." The sheeted order rode not for mere amusement, but because they were on a mission from God. "Instead of the carpetbaggers and scalawags of years past," she complained, today we have to contend with "Communism . . . the NAACP and other Jewish controlled organizations as peddlers to create hate and brainwash the minds of the American people [and] destroy our Christian faith . . . and the American Way of Life."[84]

As in the 1920s, the Depression-era Klan was not an aberrant fringe group but rather the most extreme manifestation of very common views in the South. Alabama's dominant white society, as represented by the Klan as well as its opponents, held women to chivalrous ideals of ladyhood and pure

white womanhood, but it punished transgressions from this norm vigorously—even violently—and saw no inherent contradiction. Leading Klan
opponent and voice of the gentry, Grover Hall, lobbied for the release of the
Scottsboro Boys, not for reasons of justice, equity, or due process but because "this Scottsboro thing has done more to injure Alabama in the public
mind, outside of Alabama . . . than any other experience it has had before."[85]
Worried that continued Klan vitality and cases like Scottsboro might invite
eventual federal intervention into Alabama's race relations, Hall demonstrated a fairly low estimation of blacks and the women involved in the affair. The boys had to be pardoned, Hall pressured the governor, editors, and
religious notables, not because they were innocent, "for the . . . Scottsboro
culprits . . . are [certainly] not innocent," but because the "reputation . . . of
our beloved State of Alabama is worth more than the 'honor' of two 50-cent
prostitutes."[86] Hall was quite willing, he wrote, to trade Alabama's reputation—and continued Northern investment and laissez-faire on race relations—for the rape of "two alley cats . . . on a gondola in High Jackson
[County]."[87] The editor damned Ku Klux involvement in the Scottsboro cause
célèbre, but also opposed black jury service because the race was "not yet
prepared," referred to the defendants publicly as "gorillas" and privately as
"fool niggers," and encouraged Alabama's emotional hypersensitivity to the
outside criticism that was making it infamous. Hall voiced full-throated
opposition to national censure and deplored the involvement of "kept agitators" and "outside interferences" in the case. "I do not know whether [the
boys] are guilty or innocent of the rape of two cut-rate prostitutes," the 1928
Pulitzer winner wrote. "I do not care. What I do care for is . . . that the character of Alabama and its people is at stake before the world and that these
moronic beasts are the most expensive guests that Alabama [has ever]
entertain[ed]."[88]

As Klan and police clashed with Alabama's few thousand black communists during the Depression, in the minds of the combatants, societal
orthodoxy itself—racial, religious, class, ethnic, and sexual—was at stake.
Women gave and received right along with the men. In the streets of Birmingham, antiradical vigilantes beat female communists into unconscious-
ness with blunt objects and rubber hoses. Black women excitedly asked
communist organizers when the next rally was going to be held so they could
"whup them a cop." Joint Klan and police groups went on nocturnal raids
for black radicals and sometimes satisfied themselves with assaulting whatever women and "dirty black bitch[es]" they found.[89] As sharecropper clashed
with landlord and Klan ally in the Black Belt, women became casualties right

along with men. A Klan attorney, although "not an advocate of lynch law," told Clarke County whites that he still had "red blood in my veins and I believe it is no more contemptible to string up a Negro in the face of high heaven than it is to pounce upon an unprotected white woman and defile her." "The proper thing to do," he lectured, "is to crack their necks with the least possible delay."[90]

Eventually, Alabama's embattled radicals realized that although their calls for social equality appealed to the state's depressed black working class, their traditional impiety did not. Remarkably, in 1936, a drawing of Jesus Christ appeared in the July issue of the communist *Southern Worker* along with a caption that sought to infuse some of the inherently socialistic elements of Christianity with regional religious preferences. The editors used the sketch of Christ to create a "wanted" poster with the following description:

> Jesus Christ. WANTED—For Sedition, Criminal Anarchy, Vagrancy, and Conspiring to Overthrow Established Government. Dresses poorly, said to be a carpenter by trade, ill-nourished, has visionary ideas, associates with common working people, the unemployed, and bums, Alien—believed to be a Jew—ALIAS "Prince of Peace," "Son of Man," "Light of the World," etc. Professional agitator, red beard, marks on hands and feet the result of injuries inflicted by angry mob of respectable citizens and legal authorities.[91]

It Sure Was Pretty

Although the "second Klan" faded as a political entity after the 1928 election, it continued to exist as a social, cultural, religious, and economic force to be reckoned with well into the 1930s and beyond. World War II marked a relative hiatus in Klan activities. Thirty or so klaverns and a thousand hardcore members remained in Alabama through the war, but the organization increasingly attempted to dissociate itself from unflattering comparisons with Adolf Hitler and Nazism. In 1945, though, pent-up racial tensions exploded and gave rise to another period of intense Klan activity. Although this period has not been as closely studied as other eras, the KKK was very active, and in ways quite reminiscent of the 1920s order.[92]

The post–World War II Klan demonstrated profound concern for the growing racial independence of returning black soldiers and the attempts of African Americans to secure the voting rights that had been denied them so long. Like the 1920s order, though, the 1940s KKK exhibited intense interest in preserving traditional religion, morality, and gender roles—roles that had changed when women entered the workforce in numbers to help win the war. When race was involved, the mixture became pure TNT. The Klan, its membership markedly lower and more working-class than its 1920s heyday, garnered strong support from fringe evangelical sects rather than the mainline Protestant denominations that had been its lifeblood. In a real sense, the 1940s KKK served as the militant plain-white arm of white supremacy in Alabama. The growing racial crisis drew plain-white Klansmen together with industrialist and planter in a broad white coalition to combat federal movements toward expanded civil rights. Overlap existed between the Klan and the Dixiecrat movement of the States' Rights Party, in which plain-white segregationists locked elbows with the privileged. The Klan's revisited obsession with "moral authoritarianism" was decidedly plebeian in nature, and it appealed strongly to the emotions and religious sensibilities of plain whites in Alabama. But like other plain-white movements in Alabama's past, the coalition most benefited the state's more powerful interests.

From its outset, the 1940s Klan organizers—themselves alumni of the 1920s order—reassured an increasingly nervous middle class that their goals were purely racial, sexual, religious, and moral: they sought only the "protection of white womanhood and white supremacy," in the words of Alabama grand dragon Will Morris.[93] Only "honky-tonk operators, common brier-patch prostitutes, and people of that type . . . [and] the colored man [that did not know] his place" need be concerned.[94] In June 1948 the KKK made good on its word. Upset over two white female instructors sleeping in close proximity to a group of black Girl Scouts, a huge midnight mob of robed and gowned Klansmen descended on a Bessemer Girl Scout camp, ransacked the tents of the two white instructors, accused them of practicing communism, and ordered them to leave the campgrounds within twenty-four hours. Badly shaken, the instructors canceled the two-week course and fled. Meanwhile, the county sheriff and his chief deputy told the press that the Klan raid was "a good thing" and failed to arrest anyone. Instead, they reported that their survey of a hundred local residents favored the raid because "folks around here don't like Negroes and whites living together."[95] A local Klan leader and physician carefully denied the group's involvement "as an organization," but defended the raid as one that upheld proper racial, religious, and sexual mores. "If I saw a mad dog or a snake I would shoot it," he explained. "And some people act like mad dogs and snakes."[96]

A year to the day of the Girl Scout raid, morality and gender took center stage in a sensational manner. One hundred armed and costumed Klansmen struck at the Jefferson County home of Edna McDanal, a white woman. As she pulled the masks off several of her assailants and tried to load a shotgun, Kluxers slugged her over the head with a blackjack and dragged her outside to watch a giant cross burning in her yard. They read a list of charges including prostitution, statutory rape, nude dancing, and selling alcohol and pornography, and threatened her with beating, hanging, and burning at the stake. Residents later testified that a Baptist preacher and two other ministers were in the mob and that Graysville's police chief escorted the Klan procession with lights and siren.[97]

In separate incidents, the postwar Klan regulated caste, sex, religion, and ethics. Kluxers brutally flogged two white men and a white woman because she had given birth to three children out of wedlock. An Assembly of God preacher removed his hood to pray over the victims before they were beaten. Walker County Klansmen savaged an elderly man who failed to provide for his family because he had broken his back in the mines. He suffered a nervous breakdown. Nearby, Klansmen kidnapped and terrorized three young couples—including simulating their hangings—because they did not approve of them dating.[98] Klansmen, meeting as the "Tuscaloosa Social Club" in a public building, made plans to punish black dishwashers and white waitresses for talking together in local restaurants.[99] Accused in court of being a member of a Klan flogging squad, one Holiness Pentecostal preacher got up, walked to the witness box, and struck his female accuser across the face. When he asked to be forgiven, the judge excused him.[100] In 1949, Kluxers abducted navy veteran Billy Guyton Stovall from his home and covered his back with welts because he violated local sensibilities by allowing his wife to take a part-time job. They charged Stovall with failing to support his family despite the fact that he had a full-time job at a pipe company, a part-time job, and attended school three nights a week.[101]

Female opinion was by no means universal. Elite women in the Birmingham League of Professional and Business Women and the Council of Church Women publicly criticized Klan violence, if not its actual goals and beliefs.[102] A woman of standing proposed that Birmingham adopt an antimask ordinance but was rebuffed by Mayor Cooper Green, himself a 1920s alumnus of the order.[103] More ordinary Alabama women spoke out as well. "We are … [ultimately] responsible for the Klan!" Jennie Bartran Gentleman admonished one Alabama governor. "Please … use your position to fight this thing of prejudice, ignorance, and hate … [and] give our children the heritage their fathers fought for." "I am not a Jew, Catholic, or Negro, just an American," she explained, and "I am sick to death of the Ku Klux Klan!"[104] Another plain Alabama woman, well acquainted with the popular wellspring of support for the order, put it as well as anyone: "The people themselves in Alabama are responsible for the Ku Klux Klan. It will also be the people who ultimately must change their way of thinking."[105]

Still, on balance, many Alabama women were sympathetic to the Klan's principles and ideology, if not its actual methods in all cases. One woman, who described herself as a virulent opponent of the KKK, revealed that her brand of opposition actually had more to do with Southern touchiness over its honor and reputation than the white supremacist tenets of the sheeted organization. "The harm . . . [that] the . . . Klan has done to Dixie is beyond the scope of mention, it has disgraced us." The stupidity of the Klansman was "not a God-given ignorance as the savages of the 'Dark Continent' possess," she explained. "Their's [is] a man made ignorance."[106] Many women were outright supporters of the Klan, even in the 1940s. "Every Southern white woman who has suffered a fate worse than death in the clutches of THE BLACK BEAST," one woman said in relying on the old rape excuse, "was outraged by an ANTI-KLANSMAN." A Gardendale woman favorably compared the Klan's moral violence to parental discipline and thanked the Kluxers publicly. Another applauded the particularly vicious attack on Edna McDanal. "When [the Klan] . . . take[s] one out and whip[s] them it is for some disgraceful act. . . . [The KKK is made up of] god-fearing men and god-loving men."[107]

Religious resistance to the Klan, where it could be found during the 1940s, went hand in glove with press and civic discontent, and reflected class cleavages. It was driven by church elites and populated primarily by main-line denominations that attracted upper- and middle-class whites. Fringe evangelical sects appealed more to lower- and working-class groups and poor whites and exhibited a closer proximity to the post–World War II Klan. Baptists, Presbyterians, and Episcopalians sat on a blue-ribbon committee of five hundred people formed to fight the KKK. Of course, Catholic clergy and Jews such as attorney Abraham Berkowitz also acted forcefully against the secret society. But most inspiring were the courageous actions of two Methodist preachers and their bishop in investigating a particularly nasty spree of Klan vigilantism in Clay County. In Birmingham, John Buchanan, the morally outraged and outspoken pastor of the Southside Baptist Church, and Henry M. Edmonds, the progressive pastor of the affluent Independent Presbyterian Church in Mountain Brook, led Protestant opposition to the

KKK. Tuscumbia attorney and later U.S. senator Howell Heflin demonstrated that he was related to his infamous uncle, "Cotton Tom" Heflin, more by blood than by sentiment as he called for the abolition of masks and the "spirit which hides behind the mask," lawlessness, and prejudice that "desecrate[s] the symbol of Calvary with the fire of hate." Montgomery editor Charlie Dobbins, a fierce enemy of the Dixiecrats, noted that the involvement of clerics in the KKK was sadly consistent with a long tradition of religious persecution that had its roots in the Christian Crusades, Islamic jihads, the Spanish Inquisition, the Protestant Reformation, and the Catholic Counterreformation. Repelled by Klan violence, yet still firmly opposed to racial change, Dobbins wrote that "people have committed murder thinking they were doing God's will, people have been burned at the stake by religious fanatics who thought they were serving the Lord."[108]

Elite opposition to the increasingly "redneck" KKK led to the rise of the Reverend "Dr." Lycurgus Spinks, a bizarre personality by any estimation. With a shoulder-length mane of silver hair, Spinks had made a living across the South by delivering sermons on "sexology," billed himself as the reincarnation of George Washington, and made a disastrous bid for the Mississippi governor's mansion. Arriving in Alabama in the late 1940s, Spinks realized the potential of personifying a popular revolt against the state's elite critics by organizing parades and waving Confederate battle flags. The minister eventually ran out of Klan favor when he made a national spectacle of himself on NBC's *Meet the Press,* arguing that Jesus Christ was a Klansman, that the Klan had never flogged anyone, and that it was the best friend Southern blacks had ever had.[109]

More telling popular religious support for the Klan took the form of preachers, usually associated with fundamentalist and Holiness Pentecostal sects, who defended the order, received regular Klan delegations and donations, and dismissed the order's violence as a trifle compared to issues such as liquor consumption and church attendance. "I am a KKK and proud of it," one such Jefferson County preacher declared, "and . . . if some of these fat, greasy, panty-waist preachers would get intestinal fortitude enough to preach the Gospel and keep their mouths out of things they know absolutely nothing about . . . the churches would have more people in them." A Church of God minister asked his flock to make room in their pews for Klan visitors, and another Holiness preacher earned an indictment for his part in a series of Klan floggings. When welcoming twenty-five visiting Klansmen to his Wylam Baptist church, Pastor H. L. Tully denounced middle-class, urban Baptist critics, admitted that he had been a Knight during the 1920s, defended morality-based Klan violence as "deserved," and said alcohol and Roman Catholicism were still the two greatest menaces in America.[110]

WOMEN AND THE KKK

Overall, the relationship between women and the Ku Klux Klan as an organization was multilayered and varied. Some women served the organization in vaguely positive, or at least neutral, forms. Some helped drive the organization's effectiveness as a blunt instrument of racial, religious, nativist, gender, and moral repression. Still others were victimized by the group—both in literal and figurative ways. Still others participated in the KKK as the perpetrators of victimization as individuals, only to paradoxically contribute to their own continued victimization as members of a repressed group.

It is important to note that the women who actively engaged in the Klan's more insidious program of moral authoritarianism—or enforced conformity—did so as more than just victims who came to identify with their male oppressors and thus embrace their values. Many of these women actively collaborated with Klansmen and consciously felt that they benefited. Some acted willingly to uphold the interrelated racial, religious, class, and gender hierarchy of Southern society. Others, in a curious kind of way, sought a different kind of advantage. Through their adherence to local moral orthodoxy—enforced, if the need arose, by violence—these women sought "conformity status" and "conformity comfort." By toeing the local line on religious and family values, and race and gender roles, many average women won for themselves enhanced status as upstanding, square, godly, reliable, and solid members of their communities. They won for themselves the comfort and possibly even the peace of mind that comes with conformity as they became part of the community approbation and sometimes the enforcement apparatus of a stratified society grounded on the pillars of patriarchy, ethnic purity, and white supremacy, all resting on the firm foundation of religious and moral orthodoxy. By doing so, these women found themselves welcomed by their sisters and brothers into the warm and nurturing sunlight of local acceptance. They did not have to worry about the social discomfort that is often the price of minority dissent, or concern themselves with the price such dissent might mean for their husbands' and fathers' livelihoods, their children's futures, and their own social lives. Men and women alike found the allure of this warm acceptance too appealing and too powerful to buck with what was almost certain to be futile dissent. But, in doing so, in becoming such reliable parts of the dominant white Southern community and its enforcement mechanisms, these very women were as much the active perpetuators and (at least perceived) beneficiaries of the Southern status quo as its victims.

Notes

"Home and Hearth: Women, the Klan, Conservative Religion, and Traditional Family Values" by Glenn Feldman appeared originally in his article "Keepers of the Hearth: Women, the Klan, and Traditional Family Values," in *Lives Full of Struggle and Triumph: Southern Women, Their Institutions, and Their Communities*, edited by Bruce L. Clayton and John Salmond (Gainesville: University Press of Florida, 2003). Reprinted with permission of the University Press of Florida.

1. Some of the classic works on the Ku Klux Klan are: David M. Chalmers, *Hooded Americanism: The History of the Ku Klux Klan* (1965; reprint, Durham: Duke University Press, 1987); Wyn Craig Wade, *The Fiery Cross: The Ku Klux Klan in America* (New York: Simon and Schuster, 1987); Patsy Sims, *The Klan* (New York: Stein and Day, 1978); Kenneth T. Jackson, *The Ku Klux Klan in the City, 1915–1930* (New York: Oxford University Press, 1967); and Arnold S. Rice, *The Ku Klux Klan in American Politics* (Washington, D.C.: Public Affairs Press, 1962). The "populist-civic school" of Klan historiography is best represented by Shawn Lay, ed., *The Invisible Empire in the West: Toward a New Historical Appraisal of the Ku Klux Klan of the 1920s* (Urbana: University of Illinois Press, 1992); and Leonard J. Moore, *Citizen Klansman: The Ku Klux Klan in Indiana* (Chapel Hill: University of North Carolina Press, 1991).

2. This topic is fortunate to have been the focus of Nancy MacLean's excellent study, *Behind the Mask of Chivalry: The Making of the Second Ku Klux Klan* (Oxford: Oxford University Press, 1994). Kathleen M. Blee first addressed the issue in fascinating detail in *Women of the Klan: Racism and Gender in the 1920s* (Berkeley: University of California Press, 1991).

3. Alabama grand dragon James Esdale claimed 150,000 members during the 1920s, but this figure is probably inflated. The figure of 115,000 is reasonable, although Wayne Flynt put it at around 95,000 in Leah Rawls Atkins, William Warren Rogers, Robert David Ward, and Wayne Flynt, *Alabama: The History of a Deep South State* (Tuscaloosa: University of Alabama Press, 1994), 431–32. Whichever figure is used, it should be remembered that many women, children, in-laws, and perhaps older parents belonged to "Klan families" and to the order itself, in terms of sentiment and identification, although these numbers are not included in strict estimates of physical membership. Historian Kathleen M. Blee quotes a Women of the KKK (WKKK) member as claiming that, even before the Klan's revival in the 1920s, "our mothers have been Klanswomen at heart, sharing with our fathers the progress and development of the country." *Women of the Klan, 35.*

4. William Robert Snell, "The Ku Klux Klan in Jefferson County" (M.A. thesis, Samford University, 1967), 55–56, 77.

5. "Klan leaders found . . . [in] the fundamentalist world view . . . the spiritual anchor for their ideology," Nancy MacLean writes in *Behind the Mask*. "The Klan advocated fundamentalism as a[n] . . . all-encompassing explanation of and prescription for social order . . . a vision backed by the authority of the Almighty. In the Klan's hands, Protestantism . . . provided answers to the basic questions about who

should wield power over whom, and how and why" (91). Georgia's grand dragon declared that "The Constitution of the United States is based upon the Holy Bible and the Christian religion and an attack upon one is an attack upon the other" (92).

6. In the 1920 census, Alabama was home to 2.35 million people, about 62 percent white and 38 percent nonwhite. That is where the state's heterogeneity ended. Almost 99 percent of the state's white population was native-born; 78 percent lived in rural settings; and 96 percent identified themselves as Protestant Christians. Over 84 percent of these Protestants were either Baptist or Methodist. The clear majority of Alabama's half-million urban residents could be found in only three cities: Birmingham, Mobile, and Montgomery. Catholics made up only 3.4 percent of the overall population; Jews comprised less than 1 percent. United States Department of Commerce, Bureau of the Census, *Fourteenth Census of the United States: Population, 1920, Vol. 3: Population, 1920; Composition and Characteristics of the Population by States* (Washington, D.C.: U.S. Government Printing Office, 1922), table 1, p. 54, tables 10 and 11, pp. 66–68; *Religious Bodies: 1916, Pt. 1: Summary and General Tables* (Washington, D.C.: U.S. Government Printing Office, 1919), 238–39; *Religious Bodies: 1926, Vol. 1: Summary and Detailed Tables* (Washington, D.C.: U.S. Government Printing Office, 1930), 142–45. The dean of Southern religious history, Samuel S. Hill Jr., wrote that it is "legitimate to speak of a transdenominational 'Southern church' embracing what may be called 'popular Southern Protestantism.'" *Southern Churches in Crisis* (New York: Holt, Rinehart, and Winston, 1967), 73. Consequently, Hill wrote, the South had a "limited options culture." See "Religion," 1269, in the *Encyclopedia of Southern Culture,* ed. Charles Reagan Wilson and William Ferris (Chapel Hill: University of North Carolina Press, 1989). Ted Ownby discusses these quotations and what they mean in "'Ethos without Ethic': Samuel S. Hill and the Search for Southern Religious History," in *Reading Southern History: Essays on Interpreters and Interpretations,* ed. Glenn Feldman (Tuscaloosa: University of Alabama Press, 2001), 250.

7. 1 Corinthians 10:6–33 may be read as a basis for intolerance of diversity in moral matters; 1 Corinthians 12:4–28 may fruitfully be read as a prescription for tolerance of diversity. See also Ownby, "Ethos without Ethic," 251–56. For an intriguing look at a similar climate of community monitoring and intolerance, set in Catholic Paris of the sixteenth century, see Barbara B. Diefendorf, *Beneath the Cross: Catholics and Huguenots in Sixteenth-century Paris* (Oxford: Oxford University Press, 1991), esp. 28–36, 37, 48, 53, and for incredible brutality performed in the name of religious orthodoxy, see 100–103. "We must remember that the 'Lutheran heresy,'" Diefendorf writes in this regard, "was not . . . a mere failure of religious orthodoxy; it was a threat to the social order and a danger to the entire community. The Protestants were believed to be not only religious deviants, but immoral and seditious . . . [and] debauched. . . . The laws encouraged people to keep watch on their neighbors. . . . Just as one might benefit from the prayers of others, so might one be threatened by their sins, which could bring down the wrath of God upon an entire people." Members of the religious majority believed that "heresy is a cancer or gangrene that has to be rooted out . . . [the majority's] safety and Salvation were in jeopardy if they continued to tolerate the heretics' presence." Diefendorf, *Beneath the Cross,* 37, 53, 54, and 150.

8. This point is in contradistinction to Kathleen M. Blee's interpretation of women's involvement in the Klan as having been a liberating experience that qualified as part of feminism. See Blee, *Women of the Klan,* 35, 51–52, 178. This may have

been the case in the regions that Blee concentrated on in her study, the Midwest and West, but it was not the case in Alabama, nor do I think, generally, in the South.

9. Jacquelyn Dowd Hall, *Revolt against Chivalry: Jesse Daniel Ames and the Women's Campaign against Lynching* (New York: Columbia University Press, 1979); and Jacquelyn Dowd Hall, "'The Mind That Burns in Each Body': Women, Rape, and Racial Violence," in *Powers of Desire: The Politics of Sexuality,* ed. Elizabeth Ann Snitow, Christine Stansell, and Sharon Thompson (New York: Monthly Review Press, 1983), 328–46; Joel R. Williamson, *The Crucible of Race: Black-White Relations in the American South since Emancipation* (New York: Oxford University Press, 1984); Glenda Elizabeth Gilmore, *Gender and Jim Crow: Women and the Politics of White Supremacy in North Carolina, 1896–1920* (Chapel Hill: University of North Carolina Press, 1996); and various essays, especially the ones by Laura F. Edwards, Stephen Kantrowitz, Jane Dailey, W. Fitzhugh Brundage, Nancy MacLean, and Kari Frederickson in *Jumpin' Jim Crow: Southern Politics from Civil War to Civil Rights,* ed. Jane Dailey, Glenda Elizabeth Gilmore, and Bryant Simon (Princeton: Princeton University Press, 2000).

10. Both Nancy MacLean's *Behind the Mask* and Kathleen M. Blee's *Women of the Klan* do an excellent job of tying together race, class, and gender issues in their analyses of the 1920s KKK. In a sense, though, MacLean's work does not fully acknowledge the power of religion to factor into this dynamic because she expressly rejects the notion of a distinctive South (xv–xvi), and she writes from a perspective of socialist activism as well as scholarship (viii, 189). It is difficult, if not impossible, to recognize the reality of Southern distinctiveness without also acknowledging the fantastic—indeed "distinctively" so—influence of religion in the region, and its ability to be the societal cement to bond white supremacy, class hierarchy, and paternalism in a solid Southern social order.

11. On fundamentalist and literalist intolerance of religious liberalism and the Social Gospel, see MacLean, *Behind the Mask,* 93–94, 120.

12. C. Vann Woodward, "The Elusive Mind of the South," in *American Counterpoint: Slavery and Racism in the Black-White Dialogue* (Boston: Little, Brown, 1971), 265–83. Bruce Clayton provides a more sympathetic reading of this Cash insight in "W. J. Cash: A Native Son Confronts the Past" in Feldman, *Reading Southern History,* 118. Similar terms sometimes used to discuss the forced conformity of the South are "siege mentality," the "savage ideal," and the "closed society." See also Bruce Clayton, *The Savage Ideal: Intolerance and Intellectual Leadership in the South, 1890–1914* (Baltimore: Johns Hopkins University Press, 1972).

13. Scholars of the Klan have touched on the ties between religious fundamentalism and emotion (and even intolerance). They have also discussed fundamentalist-based emotion as opposed to thought based on reason. But these connections have been cast in terms of the Klan and not specifically Southern society as a larger whole. "Central to the old-time religion," Nancy MacLean writes in *Behind the Mask,* "was belief in the literal truth of the Bible. 'The Klansman,' explained one manual, 'pins his faith to the Bible as the revealed will of God.' 'Human reason bows' before this 'Impregnable Rock,' 'afraid to doubt.' Such magical thinking helped Klan leaders subdue reason and elicit unquestioning loyalty to the status quo. Rational thought derived from philosophical materialism, in contrast, was deeply threatening . . . [for example] Darwin's theory of evolution . . . [and] the teaching of evolution. . . . The Klan's opposition to religious liberalism was thus eminently sensible. Once the right to interpret the Bible was conceded . . . [and] to enlist in the cause of social reform,

the whole structure of feeling that made fundamentalism such a formidable buttress of social order would collapse" (93). Religious revivals were "much more than [mere] religious events. They provided arenas in which believers worked out their social fears ... through potent, visceral experiences ... The emotional character of revivalism ... by fundamentalist preachers ... invested conservative political messages with divine sanction.... By tapping participants' fears of damnation and hopes for salvation, clergymen ... infused right-wing political commitments with an emotional force that made them impervious to rational disputation.... Klan fellow-traveler Billy Sunday claimed God's benediction for racial segregation, nativism, anti-communism, free enterprise, anti-Catholicism, anti-Semitism, Prohibition, and law and order" (94). "Klansmen's feelings of imminent disaster led them to renounce not only reason but tolerance as well. No 'man or woman who opposes the government ... has any right to protection. [They] should be deported or placed behind prison bars.... [Critics] must either shut up or get out'" (94). Blee, in *Women of the Klan,* also emphasized the "highly emotional harangues" used by anti-Catholic Klan speakers that led people to "'practically [break] out in tears about some of the things that were being taught to the children in the [Catholic] school" (90, 91). Of course W. J. Cash argued, in his inimitable and colorful journalistic style, that the typical Southerner wanted "a faith as simple and emotional as himself" characterized by "primitive frenzy and blood sacrifice." See *The Mind of the South* (New York: Alfred A. Knopf, 1941), 58.

14. A dated, but still gripping, source for the contextual background of the dizzying changes that occurred during the 1920s is Frederick Lewis Allen's journalistic account, *Only Yesterday: An Informal History of the 1920s* (New York: Alfred A. Knopf, 1931). See also Leslie Woodcock Tentler, *Wage-Earning Women: Industrial Work and Family Life in the United States, 1900–1930* (New York: Oxford University Press, 1979); and MacLean, *Behind the Mask,* 31–33, 118–19.

15. See the concept of "pragmatic opposition" versus "principled opposition," in Glenn Feldman, *Politics, Society, and the Klan in Alabama, 1915–1949* (Tuscaloosa: University of Alabama Press, 1999), 8–9, 326–27.

16. Mildred Ruth Heaton and Lois Cowan Interview, conducted by Linda Jean Thorpe, February 1, 1974, p. 4. Oral History Collection, Mervyn Sterne Library, University of Alabama at Birmingham Archives. Vern M. Scott Reminiscences, 1988, p. 15, Talladega County Historical Association (hereafter TCHA), Talladega, Alabama; Snell, "Ku Klux Klan in Jefferson County," 144–45, 153; *Montgomery Advertiser,* July 23, 1927.

17. William G. Shepherd, "The Whip Wins," *Collier's Magazine* 81 (January 14, 1928): 31–32 (quoted).

18. Ku Klux Klan File, Tuskegee Institute News Clipping Files, reel 28 (1927), Tuskegee University Archives (hereafter TUA), Tuskegee, Alabama; *New York Times* July 12, 1927, and December 2, 1927, 22; *Montgomery Advertiser,* July 10, 12, 1927; William G. Shepherd, "The Whip Hand," *Collier's Magazine* 81 (January 7, 1928): 8; and Shepherd, "Whip Wins," 32; Editors, "The South Aroused to Midnight Floggers," *Literary Digest* 94 (July 30, 1927): 8–9

19. Despite their best efforts, they did not get a confession. Ku Klux Klan File, reel 28 (1927), TUA; *New York Times,* July 11, 1927; July 14, 1927, 25; July 18, 1927, 32; *Montgomery Advertiser,* July 10, 14, 20, 1927; *Atlanta Constitution,* July 22, 1927.

20. *Montgomery Advertiser,* October 2, 20, and November 26, 1927; *Montgomery Examiner,* July 7, 1949; Michael Newton and Judy Ann Newton, *The Ku Klux*

Klan: An Encyclopedia (New York: Garland Press, 1991), 142, 391; Shepherd, "Whip Wins," 32. Men and women becoming nervous about women unattached to men and not under the watchful eye of a male authority figure was a major component of targeting some women—widows, midwives, spinsters—for charges of witchcraft during the great European witch crazes and the Salem witch trials. See Joseph Klaits, *Servants of Satan: The Age of the Witch Hunts* (Bloomington: Indiana University Press, 1985), 69–71.

21. MacLean, *Behind the Mask,* 32–33, 113–14. Gender roles and traditional expectations for family life were also closely bound up with a broad social order. MacLean refers to this as "a conviction that ordered, hierarchical families undergirded ordered, hierarchical society.... Hierarchies of private life served public order ... regulation of women's sexuality buttressed white supremacy. Tolerance of sexual autonomy for women might erode the social order.... The politics of morality ... was never separate from the racism, nativism, and class prejudice.... Hostility to sexuality fused with concern about the security of the larger social order" (100, 103, 104). "Klansmen expected men to marry, to provide for their families, and to exercise control over their wives and children. 'God intended,' affirmed one Klan minister, 'that every man should possess insofar as possible, his own home and rule his own household.'" "Historically," MacLean reminds us, "honor, in fact, rested on a man's ability to control the sexuality of his female relations. Their 'purity' was a complement of his 'honor'" (114). This extended to female behavior in general. "Klansmen's ideal ... was the nineteenth-century petty proprietor—whether farmer, artisan, or merchant. His vaunted independence as a citizen presumed his control over the labor and behavior of the dependents in his household" (117). "The Klan wholeheartedly agreed ... that the hierarchical family was the basis and guarantor of ordered society.... The Klan's ... mask of chivalry concealed an unwillingness to surrender proprietary rights to women" (118). "'We pity the man,' taunted the Klan press, 'who permits the loss of manhood through fear of wife.' Similarly, the author of *Christ and Other Klansmen* censured women [who] blaspheme God by disobeying their husbands.... Klansmen tried to naturalize gender hierarchy. American women were [already] emancipated; change should go no further. Feminists should cease complaining about such 'pretended wrongs' as the burdens of housework. 'God or nature' dictated women's roles, not men and society, so nothing could change them" (115). "By romanticizing the idea of home life while pointing to women's untrustworthiness," Blee writes in *Women of the Klan,* "the Klan fraternity ... appeal[ed] ... as a substitute family ... an official family, with God the father and all Klansmen as brothers" (48).

22. *Montgomery Examiner,* July 7, 1949; Newton and Newton, *Ku Klux Klan,* 391, 412 (quoted).

23. Vern M. Scott Reminiscences, 1988, p. 15, TCHA; Snell, "Ku Klux Klan in Jefferson County," 144–45, 153; *Montgomery Advertiser* July 23, 1927. This practice was apparently the same in Georgia and elsewhere. During the 1920s, the Georgia Realm office reported getting twenty letters each week from women requesting that the Klan "threaten or use violence against people whose conduct they disapproved of." A Knight who worked in Imperial headquarters in Atlanta concurred that klaverns get "hundreds of letters from women asking that some man they don't like be whipped." Quotes from MacLean, *Behind the Mask,* 121.

24. Mildred Ruth Heaton and Lois Cowan Interview, p. 4, Oral History Collec-

tion, University of Alabama at Birmingham Archives; Vern M. Scott Reminiscences, 1988, TCHA.

25. *Birmingham News,* April 21, 1925 (quoted).

26. *Montgomery Advertiser,* November 1, 1927 (quoted).

27. "Remember," the Klan circular instructed the jurors, "every criminal, every gambler, every thug, every libertine, every girl ruined, every [home] wrecker, every wife beater, every dope peddler, every moonshiner . . . every pagan papal priest . . . every white slaver, every brothel madam, every Rome-controlled newspaper is fighting the Ku Klux Klan. Think it over. Which side are you on?" *Pittsburgh Courier,* November 6, 1926 (quoted).

28. Blee, *Women of the Klan,* 80 (quoted).

29. *Alabama Ku Klux Klan Newsletter* (March 5, 1927), 1 (quoted), in box G192, folder: "Ku Klux Klan, 1927," Alabama Governors Papers, Bibb Graves Papers, Alabama Department of Archives and History (hereafter ADAH), Montgomery, Alabama.

30. *Birmingham News,* January 17 and 21, 1925; Irving Beirman, "Birmingham: Steel Giant with a Glass Jaw," in *Our Fair City,* ed. Robert S. Allen (New York: Vanguard, 1947).

31. E. C. Sharp Interview by Ralph H. Compton, ca. 1974, Oral History Collection, Mervyn Sterne Library, University of Alabama at Birmingham Archives; Bibb County KKK File, Shelby County KKK File, and Talladega County KKK File, in KKK Research Files, Department of Special Collections, Harwell Goodwin Davis Library, Samford University (hereafter SUDSC), Birmingham, Alabama.

32. Ibid.

33. Ku Klux Klan File, reel 25 (1926), TUA; *New York Times,* January 5, 1926; *Atlanta Constitution,* January 5, 1926; *Birmingham Age-Herald,* January 4–14, 1926. The action of the chief deputy, also a member of the Klan, precipitated a cause célèbre within and without Birmingham's Klan ranks.

34. Lee County KKK File, KKK Research Files, SUDSC; KKK File, reel 20 (1924) and reel 23 (1925), TUA; *New York Telegraph,* July 19, 1927; *New York Graphic,* July 18, 1927; *Birmingham News,* February 26, 1; March 21, 27, 1925; *Atlanta Constitution,* October 9, December 6–7, 1921; Snell, "Ku Klux Klan in Jefferson County," 79–83, 116, 120

35. KKK File, reel 20 (1924), TUA.

36. *Pittsburgh Courier,* August 6, September 10, 1927; *St. Louis Argus,* August 5, 12, 1927

37. *Atlanta Georgian,* March 30, 1922; *Montgomery Advertiser,* April 12, May 21, September 4–8, 1922, and October 2–8, 1923; *Birmingham Age-Herald,* March 13, 1927; William R. Snell, "Masked Men in the Magic City: The Activities of the Revised Klan in Birmingham, Alabama, 1915–1940," *Alabama Historical Quarterly* 34 (Fall–Winter 1972): 221.

38. *Alabama Ku Klux Klan Newsletter* 4 (June 1926): 7, in box 16, folder 11, Associations Records, ADAH; Alabama Ku Klux Klan Scrapbooks, volume 1 and the Charles A. Fell Memoirs, vol. 2, part 1, pp. 101–28, both in the Birmingham Public Library Archives (hereafter BPLA), Birmingham, Alabama; Papers of the NAACP, part 1, reel 13, Library of Congress (hereafter LC), Washington, D.C., and Microforms and Documents Department (hereafter AU-MADD), Ralph Brown Draughon Library, Auburn University, Auburn, Alabama; Virginia Van der Veer Hamilton, *Hugo Black: The Alabama Years* (Baton Rouge: Louisiana State University Press, 1972), 84;

Glenn Feldman, *From Demagogue to Dixiecrat: Horace Wilkinson and the Politics of Race* (Lanham, Md.: University Press of America, 1995), 67. For some, Alabama was such a homogenous place that encounters with persons of diverse backgrounds were almost exotic. A Jewish man who lived over forty years in Montgomery, yet still was known, albeit affectionately, as "the foreigner," told of a 1920s sidewalk encounter with a woman who stopped him and askcd: "Are you a Jew?" When he responded in the affirmative, she stepped back, looked at him again, and said, "My, you're a real live Jew, aren't you?" See "Reminiscences," folder 1, p. 9, Eugene Feldman Papers, ADAH.

39. Ku Klux Klan-Prattville File (quoted), Boone Aiken Papers, Auburn, Alabama. In possession of the author. It reads: "I was my father's future hope, my mother's joy and pride, but I got lost on life's dark road, and there my spirit died. I smeared my all white heritage and left the white man's track, now my descendants for all time shall be forever black. . . . All other crimes my be forgiven when prayer its power fulfills, the scheming crook may find new hope, and even the man that kills. I try to hide from all the stars, the moon, the setting sun; for all mankind . . . condemn what I have done. My mother sleeps deep in her grave, my dad lies at her side; for both were crushed when I became a common negro's bride."

40. Virginia Foster Durr Interview, 7–8, Oral History Office. Columbia University, New York.

41. Covington County (Ala.) *News* in the *Montgomery Advertiser,* July 17, 1927 (quoted).

42. John Bainbridge to Editor, *Montgomery Advertiser,* September 13, 1927 (quoted).

43. "So long as masked men may go into an Alabama home to . . . satisfy . . . their lust for cruelty . . . so long will Alabama harbor anarchy and barbarism." *Montgomery Advertiser,* July 11–12, 1927 (quoted).

44. Decatur (Ala.) *Daily,* August 10, 1975; Ku Klux Klan Collection, Blount County Historical Society, Blountsville, Alabama.

45. Feldman, *Politics, Society,* 47–49, 61, 72, 100, 147, 301, 395 n. 28.

46. *New York Times,* November 21, 1927, 3, and November 25, 1927, 23; *Montgomery Advertiser,* October 2 and November 25, 1927.

47. *Birmingham Reporter,* January 13, 1923 (quoted) in James L. Sledge III, "Black Conservatism in the Twentieth-century South: Oscar Adams and the *Birmingham Reporter,*" *Proceedings of the Southern Conference on Afro-American History* 13 (February 1992): 8–9.

48. Talladega County KKK File, KKK Research Files, SUDSC; Sylacauga (Ala.) *Advance* February 4, 24; May 10–13, 22; June 21; July 26–29; October 18, 27–30, 1925; and October 20, 27, 1926.

49. *Alabama Ku Klux Klan Newsletter* 4 (June 1926): 7, in box 16, folder 11: Ku Klux Klan, Associations Records and 5 (March 1927): 2–4, in box G192, folder: Ku Klux Klan, 1927," Alabama Governors Papers, Bibb Graves Papers, both in the ADAH; E. C. Sharp Interview by Ralph H. Compton, ca. 1974, pp. 1–4, Oral History Collection, Mervyn Sterne Library, University of Alabama at Birmingham.

50. *Atlanta (Ga.) Imperial Knighthawk,* June 13, October 3, 1923, May 14, July 16, 23, and 30, October 29, 1924; *Memphis Commercial Appeal,* August 22, 1924; *Montgomery Advertiser,* September 27–28, 1921, January 20, March 28, June 21, August 22–24, and December 17, 1923; Snell, "Ku Klux Klan in Jefferson County," 55–56, 77. Women lobbied to be active in the Klan movement. They wanted to "stand

alongside our men and help" rather than be "patted on the head and told not to worry," one woman wrote in a Klan publication. An "unhappy wife" agreed by asking why native-born, white, Protestant women should be excluded from the KKK along with such unseemly groups as the "Knights of Columbus, Jews, or negroes?" Quoted in Blee, *Women of the Klan,* 24. By 1923, thirty-six states had WKKK groups operating in them. The WKKK banner included other related women's groups such as the Ladies of the Invisible Eye, Ladies of the Cu Clux Clan, Ladies of the Golden Den, Hooded Ladies of the Mystic Den, and the Ladies of the Golden Mask. Blee, *Women of the Klan,* 25–29.

51. Chalmers, *Hooded Americanism,* 79; Jackson, *The Ku Klux Klan in the City,* 82–83.

52. Not every Protestant minister in Alabama during the 1920s was a fan of the secret order, Klan claims notwithstanding. The clear majority were members or at least sympathizers. Still, there were a few solitary individuals who went beyond greeting the order with silence or cool indifference. They voiced genuine outrage at the Klan's methods and unease with its goals. The most notable of these was probably Dr. J. E. Dillard, pastor of Birmingham's Southside Baptist Church. Feldman, *Politics, Society,* 104.

53. Blee, *Women of the Klan,* 93; MacLean, *Behind the Mask,* 93, 96–97. MacLean theorizes that the Klan morality appealed to a middle class that believed "their moral standards were the visible sign of their difference from, and purported superiority to, both the working class and the elite" (99).

54. MacLean, *Behind the Mask,* 118–20. Georgia's Tom Watson, the well-known former Populist, was a leading mouthpiece on the evils of Catholicism in eroding proper marital relations and social order. Priests, through the confessional, became the "confidante of another man's wife" to whom she confessed the couple's "inmost secrets . . . [including] sexual procedures and techniques . . . extramarital activities, masturbation, homosexuality, and unnatural fornication." This invasion of the husband's privacy would "rot out the heart" of America (MacLean, *Behind the Mask,* 120). This passage also describes Klan dislike of socialism and communism because of its usurpation of male proprietary rights in the household.

55. Ibid. Some stories related how priests and nuns would engage in makeshift abortions, ripping open the stomachs of pregnant nuns to remove live fetuses. One escaped nun told how a cross had been burned on her back; another how nuns had burned off a fellow sister's fingers when they found that she had violated convent rules by wearing rings; and others how, "for the sexual pleasure of priests," nuns would be locked in "coffins filled with human excrement." See also Blee, *Women of the Klan,* 86–93, 90 (quoted), and 90, 91 for emotionalism. Also, see note 21 above for evangelical notions of proper household order and gender relations.

56. Dozier to Coyle, 1917, box 7, folder 25, Alabama Pamphlets Collection; and Emmetts to Kilby, August 1, 1921, folder: Law Enforcement, 1920–23, Alabama Governors Papers, William W. Brandon, both in the ADAH. See also Charles A. Fell Memoirs, vol. 2, part 1, 1–28, BPLA; *New York Telegraph,* October 20, 1921; *New York World,* October 17, 1921; *Memphis Commercial Appeal,* April 13, 1922; Marvin Y. Whiting, "'True Americans,' Pro and Con: Campaign Literature from the 1917 Race for the Presidency of the Birmingham City Commission," *Journal of the Birmingham Historical Society* 6 (July 1980): 11; Michael A. Breedlove, "Progressivism and Nativism: The Race for the Presidency of the City Commission of Birmingham, Ala-

bama in 1917," *Journal of the Birmingham Historical Society* 6 (July 1980): 3–4; Paul M. Pruitt Jr., "The Killing of Fr. Coyle: Private Tragedy, Public Shame," *Alabama Heritage* 30 (Fall 1993): 24–37.

57. MacLean, *Behind the Mask,* 92–93, 95–97; Blee, *Women of the Klan,* 92–93

58. J. Mills Thornton III, "Alabama Politics, J. Thomas Heflin, and the Expulsion Movement of 1929," *Alabama Review* 21 (April 1968): 83–112; and J. Wayne Flynt, "Organized Labor, Reform, and Alabama Politics, 1920," *Alabama Review* 23 (July 1970): 163–80.

59. *Alabama Ku Klux Klan Newsletter* 6 (April 1928): 2, (June 1928): 1 (quoted), (July 1928): 1, 7 (January 1929): 4; Oliver Day Street Papers, ADAH.

60. "Call for Conference of Anti-Smith Democrats" and "A Resolution Adopted by Conference of Anti-Smith Democrats," August 13, 1928, J. F. Hines Papers, SUDSC. See also box 26, whole folder: Intolerance and the *Alabama Ku Klux Klan Newsletter* 7 (January 1929): 3, both in Oliver Day Street Papers, ADAH.

61. Although race was perhaps the most powerful emotional issue for white folk, it was also a substantive issue in many respects. Because it is impossible to absolutely separate race from class concerns, despite the best efforts and desires of professional historians, race is an issue that may be found in both camps—unlike more purely emotional issues, such as gun control, school prayer, patriotism, and the moral "character" of candidates. Concrete economic rewards accompanied white supremacy, both for plain whites and for patricians. As the primary economic competitors with blacks, poor whites stood to gain much by the preservation of white supremacy—not just in the social and psychological terms of Jim Crow, but also in legal disfranchisement, and in the economic rewards associated with employment discrimination and institutionalized racism. As members of a select caste, no matter how humble, plain whites enjoyed more freedom and better schools, parks, libraries, neighborhoods, public amenities, and access to credit than did people of color. The South's planters and industrialists profited from the preservation of white supremacy as well, both in emotional terms and in concrete economic terms such as the perpetual supply of a cheap source of labor and a strong wedge dividing potential biracial action along class lines. The concepts of a "politics of emotion" and "God and Country Issues" are explained in Glenn Feldman, "Introduction: The Pursuit of Southern History," in Feldman, ed., *Reading Southern History,* 6; the term "politics of emotion" itself appears in the book's index. For an interesting discussion of economic differences based on race, see Melvin L. Oliver and Thomas M. Shapiro, *Black Wealth/White Wealth: A New Perspective on Racial Inequality* (New York: Routledge, 1995). Institutionalized racism is also becoming a more popular topic of comment as evinced in Tim Wise, "Racism, White Liberals, and the Limits of Tolerance," *Lip Magazine* (April 12, 2000), available at http://www.lipmagazine.org/articles/featwise 11.htm; Kendall Clark, "The Global Privileges of Whiteness," ca. 2000, available at http://www.monkeyfist.com/articles/764; Teresa Williams, "Progressive Racism: The Great Impediment towards Real Social Change," July 19 2001, available at http://www.livegem.net/sojourner communictions

62. Marie Bankhead Owen, "Hoover's Religion" statement, October 23, 1928, box 5, folder 14, William Brockman Bankhead Papers, ADAH.

63. *Birmingham Age-Herald* and *Birmingham News,* August 14, 1928 (all quotations).

64. Ibid. See also box 19, folder 4, State Democratic Executive Committee Records, ADAH; "A Resolution Adopted by Conference of Anti-Smith Democrats,"

August 13, 1928, J. F. Hines Papers, SUDSC; and the *Alabama Ku Klux Klan Newsletter* (April, September, October, and November issues), Oliver Day Street Papers, ADAH.

65. J. A. J., "Roman Treason against Our Homes," *Kourier Magazine* 3 (April 1927): 21 (first and third quotations); Senator J. Thomas Heflin in the *Congressional Record,* Senate, extract, February 18, 1927, and 63rd Cong., 2d sess., LI, p. 2893 (second quotation), J. Thomas Heflin Scrapbooks, MF-652, SUDSC.

66. "Governor Smith's Membership in the Roman Catholic Church and Its Proper Place as an Issue in This Campaign," box 26, folder: Intolerance, Oliver Day Street Papers, ADAH.

67. Feldman, *Politics, Society,* 185.

68. Much of the post-1865 South can be understood in terms of the chronic appearance of what may be termed a "Reconstruction syndrome"—a set of powerful negative attitudes that have shaped Southern history and culture for more than a hundred years. The attitudes that make up this syndrome, fortified by race, were originally born of the psychological trauma of military defeat, occupation, abolition, and the forcible imposition of a new political order. After the initial trauma, the syndrome has repeatedly manifested itself in the South, where it rises to the surface most clearly during times of acute stress. As a result, for more than a century after the Reconstruction trauma, the dominant white Anglo-Saxon Protestant South was largely distinguished and distinguishable by the syndrome's recurring component tendencies: very strong antiblack, anti–federal government, antiliberal, anti-Yankee, and antioutsider and antiforeigner beliefs that translated into little tolerance for diversity. The Second Reconstruction cemented and personalized these beliefs in the minds of a new generation of white Southerners and their children. To a large extent, these unfortunate tendencies still persist at, or just under, the surface of the present-day South, where they shape and color the region's approach to politics, economics, and social mores. Often these tendencies appear in softer, sanitized, and more euphemistic forms. Yet appear they still do, as an almost manic concern for states' rights, local autonomy, individual freedom, political conservatism, sectional pride, traditional values, religion, and gender roles—in fact, reverence for all things traditional, including pride in the white race's leadership and achievements, disdain for hyphenated Americanism in favor of ethnic, racial, and cultural homogeneity—in sum, for all of the things that "made this country great." See Feldman, "Introduction," 5–6; and also see Feldman, *Politics, Society,* 75, 187, 327.

69. *New York Times,* July 8, 1928, 2; *Birmingham Age-Herald* and *Birmingham News,* July 8, 1928.

70. Alabama Women's League for White Supremacy, clipping (woman quoted), box 210, folder: Birmingham City Commission. Alabama Governors Papers. Benjamin Meek Miller Papers. ADAH; Atkins et al., *Alabama,* 440 (other quotations).

71. For a good explication of the "Dunning School" of Reconstruction historiography, see almost anything by Fred Arthur Bailey, most recently "E. Merton Coulter and the Political Culture of Southern Historiography," 32–48, and his "Charles Sydnor's Quest for a Suitable Past," 88–111, both in Feldman, *Reading Southern History.*

72. Huddleston to Hammill, October 4, 1928, box 210, folder: Birmingham City Commission. Benjamin Meek Miller Papers, ADAH; *Birmingham News,* November 5, 1928; Hugh D. Reagen, "Race as a Factor in the Presidential Election of 1928 in Alabama," *Alabama Review* 30 (Fall 1993): 6–7, 12–17.

73. *Birmingham News,* November 4, 6, 1928; *Birmingham Age-Herald,* November 16, 1928.

74. "Anonymous" (Commerce Department Employee) to Cole Blease (quoted), ca. 1928, box 5, folder 14, William Brockman Bankhead Papers, ADAH.

75. Declaration (quoted), folder: KKK-Prattville, Boone Aiken Papers, Auburn, Alabama. In possession of the author. A decidedly minority counterpoint was expressed by liberal pariah Virginia Durr of Montgomery. Durr vehemently opposed the 1920s Klan, although her maternal grandfather had ridden with Nathan Bedford Forrest and, after the war, founded a local klavern. She also clearly remembered her Klan uncle reminiscing about beating blacks with baseball bats during Reconstruction because they attempted to vote. Virginia Foster Durr Interview, p. 7 (quoted), Oral History Office, Columbia University, New York.

76. Klan publication quoted in Blee, *Women of the Klan,* 32. "Klan recruiters portrayed themselves as a movement of righteous Protestants beleaguered by forces of immorality" (Blee, *Women of the Klan,* 80). Klan propaganda stressed the order's effectiveness at arresting the 1920s "drift toward immorality." "Whole communities that seemed traveling fast on the road to hell have suddenly turned toward Heaven" (MacLean, *Behind the Mask,* 99).

77. Blee addressed the connection between Catholicism and the working class in *Women of the Klan,* 93. MacLean described Klan dislike of socialism and communism for its usurpation of male proprietary rights over women and children in *Behind the Mask,* 118–19.

78. On one occasion, Klansmen grabbed hold of defense attorney Joseph Brodsky as he tried to make his way through a crowd ringing a Decatur courthouse and screamed in the lawyer's face, "Come on, yah Jew bitch! We'll show you how to defend nigger rapers." Angelo Herndon (circular), "The Scottsboro Boys: Four Freed! Five to Go!" ca. 1931 (quoted), box 5, folder 30, p. 9, Alabama Pamphlets Collection, ADAH.

79. *Birmingham Reporter,* August 15, 1931; Birmingham (Ala.) *Southern Worker,* August 15, 29, September 12, 1931; Robin D. G. Kelley, *Hammer and Hoe: Alabama Communists during the Great Depression* (Chapel Hill: University of North Carolina Press, 1990), 84.

80. NAACP Brief for Federal Prosecution against Tuscaloosa Sheriff, October 13, 1933, part 7, series A, reel 4, and Ransom et al. to Cummings, part 6, reel 2, and "Killing of Workers," part 10, reel 13 and part 7, series A, reel 8, Papers of the NAACP, LC, and AU-MADD; Colman to Editor (May 30, 1934), in "The Klan Revives," *The Nation* 139 (July 4, 1934): 20.

81. Feldman, *From Demagogue to Dixiecrat,* 104. As part of its heritage as a battleground for class and racial issues, Birmingham spawned such well-known black radicals as Hosea Hudson, Angelo Herndon, and, later, Angela Davis.

82. *Pittsburgh Courier,* December 21, 1940 (first quotation); "Communism and the Negro," *Kourier Magazine* 8 (September 1932): supplement, 5, 23 (second quotation); "Communists Stirring Southern Negroes," *Kourier Magazine* 9 (October 1933): 19–20 (third quotation).

83. *Birmingham Afro-American,* February 15, 1936 (quoted).

84. Declaration (quoted), folder: KKK-Prattville, Boone Aiken Papers, Auburn, Alabama. In possession of the author.

85. Hall to Graves, July 7, 1938 (quoted), box 67, folder 1, Grover C. Hall Sr. Papers, ADAH.

86. Ibid. (quoted).

87. *Montgomery Advertiser,* August 23, 1933 (quoted).

88. Hall had won his Pulitzer prize for a series of anti-KKK editorials written in 1927. Hall to Graves, November 14, 1938, and Hall to Chappell, November 15, 1938 (quoted), box 67, folder 1, Grover C. Hall Sr. Papers, ADAH.

89. Helen Long Affidavit, December 30, 1936, part 3, 967–69, Joseph Gelders Testimony, part 3, 775, Jane Speed, Kenneth Bridenthal, and Harriet Flood Affidavits, January 12, 1937, part 3, 961, 970–73, Belle W. Barton Affidavit, December 7, 1936, part 3, 973–76, all in the United States, Senate, Committee on Education and Labor, 75th Cong., 2nd sess., *Violations of Free Speech and Rights of Labor,* Hearings before Subcommittee (1937–1938).

90. *Birmingham Afro-American,* February 17, 1934 (quoted); KKK File, reel 46 (1934), TUA. Yet the same protections did not extend to black women. After a group of Klanlike vigilantes, with the apparent involvement of law enforcement, riddled the body of a black Share Croppers Union leader with bullets, the mob returned to his Lowndes County home that night. They hung his wife from a tree several times before cutting her down, and for good measure they lashed a female friend who had come to stay with the grieving woman. Near Dadeville, a black preacher informed the Klan that a black female communist was hoarding dynamite. That evening, they raided her home and beat her so ferociously that they broke her spine. Albert Jackson, "On the Alabama Front," *The Nation* 141 (September 18, 1935): 329–30. Birmingham (Ala.) *Southern Worker,* July 25 and August 1, 29, 1931; Kelley, *Hammer and Hoe,* 40–43.

91. Birmingham (Ala.) *Southern Worker,* July 1936 (quoted).

92. Glenn Feldman, "Soft Opposition: Elite Acquiescence and Klan-Sponsored Terrorism in Alabama, 1946–1950," *Historical Journal* 40, no. 3 (1997): 753–77.

93. *New York Times,* July 22, 1946 (quoted).

94. Louisville (Ky.) *Courier-Journal,* June 23, 1949 (quoted).

95. Testimony of Herbert M. Levy, in the United States, House, Committee of the Judiciary, Subcommittee No. 3, *Beatings and Cross-Burnings in Alabama Towns,* 81st Cong., 2nd sess. (1949), p. 129. See also Thompson to Selden, August 13, 1948, folder 2: Ku Klux Klan, 1948–1950. Alabama Governors Papers, James E. Folsom Sr., ADAH.

96. Columbus (Ga.) *Recorder,* June 24, 1948 (quoted); Morris to Whom it May Concern, June 22, 1948, box 8, folder 21, Birmingham Mayoral Papers, Cooper Green Papers, BPLA.

97. A male neighbor who had watched the entire midnight spectacle, when interviewed later, enthusiastically endorsed the action because Edna McDanal was an immoral woman. The Klan's fiery cross, he said with delight, "sure was pretty." "It Sure Was Pretty," *Time* 54 (November 7, 1949): 24 (quoted). See also Edna McDanal Interview, June 24, 1949, Hugh McDanal and J. E. Woods Interviews, June 12, 1949, Dester Lott and Jerry Ensor Interviews, June 13, 1949, Mr. and Mrs. Virgil Cook and Mr. and Mrs. Grady Ensor, Cal Nations, and W. E. Mitchell Interviews, June 14, 1949, and George Bensko to Torrence (statement), June 23, 1949, all in box SG 12644, folder: KKK, 1949, no. 5. Alabama Governors Papers, James E. Folsom Sr. Papers, ADAH.

98. KKK File, reel 108 (1949), TUA; Part 5, reels 19 and 20, Papers of the NAACP, LC, and AU-MADD; William Hamilton, William Rochester, Flossie Rochester,

Emmett Atkins, and Martha Gladys Rochester Interviews, June 23, 1949, box SG 12644, folder: KKK, 1949, no. 5. Alabama Governors Papers, James E. Folsom Sr. Papers, ADAH.

99. Anti-Negro Groups File, reel 108 (1949), and reel 112 (1950), Tuskegee Institute News Clipping Files, TUA; Tuscaloosa (Ala.) *News,* May 28–31, 1949.

100. Louisville (Ky.) *Courier-Journal,* October 28, 1949; New York *Daily Worker,* November 6, 1949; *Birmingham News,* October 26–29, 1949.

101. Stovall bought three guns, taught his wife how to use them, and promised to kill the next batch of hooded men who entered his home. Incensed by his beating, Stovall's young wife vowed to defend her home with the firearms. "I'd do it," she pledged, "I'd not mind at all seeing them drop one at a time." Testimony of [Mr.] Lake, in *Beatings and Cross-Burnings; Montgomery Advertiser,* June 16, 1949, 184–94 (quoted); *Birmingham News,* June 17, 1949 (quoted)

102. Program Convention, 1949, association box 8, Alabama Associations Records. American Legion Records, ADAH; Warner to Folsom, June 21, 1949, folder 3: Ku Klux Klan, 1949, Alabama Governors Papers, James E. Folsom Sr. Papers, ADAH; "Sheeted Jerks," *The Nation* 169 (July 2, 1949): 2.

103. Although he personally approved of such a law, the mayor claimed, his two fellow city commissioners, Jimmy Morgan and Eugene "Bull" Connor (later the notorious Birmingham police commissioner), were unmoved. Green to Parker, June 28, 1949, box 8, folder 21, Birmingham Mayoral Papers, Cooper Green Papers, BPLA.

104. Jennie Bartran Gentleman to Folsom, June 13, 1949 (quoted), box SG 12644, folder: KKK, 1949, no. 4, Alabama Governors Papers, James E. Folsom Sr. Papers, ADAH.

105. A Citizen to Folsom, July 3, 1949 (quoted), box SG 12644, folder: KKK, 1949, no. 8, Alabama Governors Papers, James E. Folsom Sr. Papers, ADAH.

106. Whitfield to Folsom, July 15, 1949 (quoted), box SG 12644, folder: KKK, 1949, no. 6, Alabama Governors Papers, James E. Folsom Sr. Papers, ADAH.

107. Anonymous to Folsom, June 18, 1949 (first quotation), box SG 12644, folder: KKK, 1949, no. 6 and Pitts to Folsom, June 27, 1949 (second quotation), box SG 13479, folder: KKK, 1949, both in Alabama Governors Papers, James E. Folsom Sr. Papers, ADAH.

108. The *Atlanta Constitution's* liberal editor, Ralph McGill, wrote that Klan preachers had forsaken the cross to march in the steps of Nazi storm troopers and challenged Alabamians to "try to imagine the Nazarene in a Ku Klux robe going in a mob to terrify helpless persons." Feldman, *Politics, Society,* 310–12.

109. Feldman, *Politics, Society,* 312–13, 318, 319.

110. Ibid., 322–24.

Religion, Race, and the Right in the South, 1945–1990

Paul Harvey

In the Southern Baptist Convention (SBC) from the late 1970s to the early 1990s, conservatives in the nation's largest Protestant denomination staged a complete rout of moderates and assumed control over the convention's numerous agencies and its $150 million budget. Conservatives had been caucusing and organizing over their grievances since the 1920s, but their anger at denominational leaders who endorsed *Brown v. Board of Education* and the broader civil rights agenda forced them to coalesce. As they perceived it, there *was* a denominational elite from which they were largely excluded. This elite, the conservatives believed, produced modernist books, endorsed integration, and were soft on communism. In later years the list of sins changed—endorsing abortion rights replaced sanctioning integration, for example—but the contending factions were essentially the same. The battle for the soul of the convention that raged through the 1980s was fought over nearly everything *except* race, even though the coalitions in the battle had been forged permanently by the race issues of the civil rights era. The forebears of today's religious/political right came unhinged from their traditional denominational loyalties through the battles over race and civil rights. By the 1960s and 1970s, Southern whites lost much of their traditional theological undergirding for their race politics, but they found new inspiration in the defense of traditional gender roles. In the process, the conservatives jettisoned the familiar racial arguments for racial hierarchy, replacing these now-discredited views with a renewed and updated defense of gendered hierarchies.

The Southern Religious Right dates back at least to the fundamentalist/modernist controversies of the early twentieth century, as well as to wars over denominational centralization, the role of women, and other issues that vexed most American denominations. The civil rights–era controversies helped to solidify these coalitions, with groupings that fought battles in the 1970s and 1980s centering on the structuring of gender roles. The progressives won the battle to end legal segregation, and the religious conservatives who defended Jim Crow conceded their defeat. A panoply of other issues have incited the more recent controversies and set the stage for the coalescing of major forces within the religious/political right. But although forces associated with the Religious Right decisively lost the battle over civil rights, they won the larger cultural war for the soul of white Southern believers. The importance of the battle over civil rights was that it helped to produce the coalitions and groupings on the right that would emerge victoriously in a later day.

The restructuring of Southern religion has paralleled the reconfiguration of Southern politics and culture. Southern religious conservatives fought unsuccessfully through the civil rights years, unable to turn back the tide of changes brought by the civil rights movement. Through the 1970s and 1980s, however, they came of age and successfully pursued their agenda of reshaping religious organizations such as the SBC and political groupings such as the Republican Party. No longer saddled with the burden of defending segregation, they took the offensive and linked themselves with a broader national conservative coalition. The transformation of the SBC into a bastion of the Religious Right is a case study in the travails and triumphs of Southern religious conservatism since World War II.

White supremacy was an ideology of power that enveloped white Southerners in an imagined community, one that encompassed and stretched beyond the social conflicts that divided them. Southern whites inherited a theological regime grounded in conservative notions of order, one in which a proper understanding of the racial hierarchy mirrored and helped to sustain the prescribed relationship of men and women. Both in the antebellum era and after the Civil War, white Southern theologies of class, blood, and sex—sometimes expressed formally, more often disseminated in everyday speech, Sunday sermons, self-published tracts, and pamphlets—buttressed white Southern practice. God ordained inequality, preached Southern theological figures from Richard Furman in the nineteenth century to W. A. Criswell, the combative pastor of First Baptist Church in Dallas, the largest congregation in America in the 1950s and 1960s.

Southern white supremacist Christians were not hypocrites. Such a stance implies that "true" Christianity would have required acceptance of the equality of humans, regardless of their social status—an important point theologically, but a dubious mode of analysis for historians. White Southern defenses of social hierarchy could be intellectually grounded in a conservative vision rather than merely hypocritical cant intended to void the clear biblical message. James Henley Thornwell's "The Christian Doctrine of Slavery" enunciated the Southern conservative vision in 1850, and that held even after the demise of slavery: God created the world. If inequality exists, then God must have a reason for it. Without inequality—without rulers and ruled, without hewers of wood and drawers of water—there could be only anarchy. Men cannot govern themselves on a plane of equality. Realizing this, God sanctions Himself to head the church, men to lead women and children, slave owners to direct the lives of slaves, and white people to guide the destiny of black people.

Religious institutions and practices in the nineteenth- and twentieth-century South reflected and reinforced the racism of the region's social life. A generation of scholars writing in the 1960s and 1970s referred to this as religion in cultural captivity, or a "culture-religion." According to this view, Southern whites, slumbering in a reactionary form of evangelicalism, faltered before the moral challenge posed by the civil rights movement. Writing in the midst of the stunning racial revolution of their time, scholars such as Samuel Hill and John Lee Eighmy could not help but see cultural captivity when stiff-necked deacons and ushers stood cross-armed at church house doors, defending segregation now, segregation forever. Compared with their forebears, Southern social critics and the cultural captivity school advanced a considerably less provincial understanding of the regional religion. In their minds, something outside Christianity had entrapped the Southern soul.[1]

Yet the religious notions of the dominant classes have rarely supported theologies of equality. Most commonly, they sanctify inequality. Historically, this was the case with white Southern believers and race. "We do not believe that 'all men are created equal' . . . nor that they will ever become equal in this world," a prominent Southern Baptist cleric said in the 1880s. The theology of class and blood was premised on God-ordained inequality. It was an unstable foundation in the context of American liberal democracy, but it was one common in human history.[2]

For biblical literalists such as most white Southerners were, defending slavery was relatively simple. The Bible, after all, spoke with abundant clearness of spiritual equality and temporal inequality, enjoining servants to obey masters, just as wives were to submit to husbands. It was the burden of the abolitionists, in fact, that they had to invoke relatively loose readings of the Bible to support their crusade against slavery, certainly an uphill battle in a Protestant culture that put a strict construction on the interpretation of biblical texts.

In the twentieth-century South, however, constructing a theological defense of the particular institution of segregation proved more complicated. Since the end of Reconstruction, the culture of segregation held up less because of any internal coherence or integrity than because it was not seriously questioned or challenged. The theology of segregationism was handed down naturally, as confirmed dogma, a set of assumptions about the divine ordering of the social world. When he was a boy, a North Carolinian wrote, it was nearly universal to learn in churches that God made different races and that "He expected them to stay that way, and that each should have his own churches and schools." Segregation was a "fundamental law of nature," another Tar Heel wrote; the state superintendent of education declared that a challenge to white supremacy would be a "violation of God's eternal laws as fixed in the stars." In the same vein, at the First Baptist Church in Jackson, Mississippi, the deacons declared that "the facts of history make it plain that the development of civilization and of Christianity itself has rested in the hands of the white race."[3]

After World War II, to justify the existence of inequality, they resorted to constitutional arguments ("interposition"), appeals to tradition, and outright demagoguery. They dug up references to "render unto Caesar" and formulated obscurantist renderings of Old Testament passages such as the Son of Ham mythologies. Increasingly, they sounded desperate and defensive. W. A. Criswell condemned *Brown* before the South Carolina legislature: "Let them integrate. Let them sit up there in their dirty shirts and make all their fine speeches. But they are all a bunch of infidels, dying from the neck up." A Birmingham minister said others envied Southern Baptists because "we have stoutly held the line against undemocratic and subversive influences."[4]

Even as Southern denominational leaders throughout the South endorsed *Brown,* defended public schools against the tide of massive resistance, and recognized the need for federal legislation to protect civil rights, laymen and ordinary ministers throughout the region articulated and often enacted a newly self-conscious theology of segregationism. Most of the conservatives melded theological, racial, and social ideas. In their eyes, integrationism, modernism, and communism constituted a single three-headed devil. Their theology was intentionally and self-consciously reactionary, a rearguard response that ultimately would falter. Increasingly they saw their failure as part of the biblical eschatology of the decline and fall of man leading up to the millennium. In this sense, they almost half-willed their own demise. The folk defense of white Southern racial politics, for a short time given institutional expression in citizens' councils and other groups that defended Southern apartheid, was relatively weak and incoherent compared with the passionate moral politics that emanated from the civil rights movement. With the Supreme Court behind *Brown*, conservative politicians such as Dwight Eisenhower willing to enforce plans of school desegregation, and denominational authorities acceding to, and some positively pushing for, the end of Jim Crow, segregation seemed to be a new Lost Cause.

Church leaders struggled over how to reconcile the fact that ordinary congregants assumed segregation was divinely ordained or simply the best and most workable social system for the South, even while their church leaders at the denominational level moved increasingly in the direction of endorsing desegregation. One issue for white Christians was simply whether segregation *was* a political issue or not. Many churches and ministers simply sought to avoid controversy altogether. When the SBC meeting of 1954 endorsed the *Brown* decision, minister Jack Stafford, who had attended the meeting, returned home to South Carolina to find that "no one would touch him with a ten-foot pole," not even his seminary professor. No matter their political bent, most ministers knew when to keep quiet and avoid political issues. As one woman recalled of her ministers, "most hid their heads in the sand and spoke the language of the people in the church, even if they didn't believe it." Parishioners wanted peace rather than admonition. Early fundamentalists such as Jerry Falwell began in the 1960s to preach against abortion and other political issues, but he himself was deliberately stepping out of his tradition of shying away from politics. Later, when Southern Baptists felt more embattled by a culture they saw slipping from them, fundamentalists (defined by one historian as militant and angry antimodernists) took the opportunity to politicize churches and parishioners—but that occurred in a later, post–civil rights generation.[5]

Ministers were infrequently found in the ranks of segregationist leaders, as historian David Chappell has noted. Certainly the denominational leaders at the national level would not associate with segregationism, which they identified as being the right-hand pole of the "extremists on both sides" whom they so often condemned (the NAACP usually serving as the opposite and equally blameworthy side). Most Southern ministers endeavored to unify congregations and communities, dwell on themes of reconciliation, and avoid divisive rhetoric or political activity. For these reasons and others, clergymen were not in the forefront, and indeed were strikingly under-represented, both in the civil rights movement and in the organized opposition to it. They were often the flaccid moderates memorably skewered by Martin Luther King Jr. in his "Letter from a Birmingham Jail." Few were active supporters of civil rights, as King noted. On the other hand, only a handful took leadership roles in the citizens' councils, religious organizations that defended segregation, and groups that fed the massive resistance campaigns to school desegregation sweeping the region from 1956 to the early 1960s.[6]

Leaders of the segregationist right mostly relied on secular arguments, largely distrusting the churches. They used religious arguments secondarily, if at all, and often seemed embarrassed by the kind of strained biblical diatribes preached by some segregationist believers. Religious segregationists peopled the white churches of the region, but they were difficult to organize into concerted action, particularly given the apolitical stance of so many of their ministers.

That is not to say that there was no theology of segregationism. There was, even if it could be found more among laymen's organizations and ministers outside the denominational hierarchy than in the circles of denominational leadership. It was important in making the white South so obsessed with purity. Only a proper ordering of the races would maintain white Southern purity against defilement—the sexual metaphors behind the race politics were obvious and restated endlessly. The frequent references to "filth" and "social disease" that pervaded segregationist literature clarify that segregationism was something deeper than custom, that it had been sanctified. It was about not being "forced to go into those *intimate* things that I don't wish to go," as W. A. Criswell put it, capturing perfectly the link between race and sex that haunted white Southern conservatives.[7]

Some ministers, such as Henry L. Lyon in Birmingham, defended segregation as positively God-ordained. In "Why Racial Integration Is UnChristian," an address he delivered repeatedly, he argued that "separation of the races is the commandment and law of God." Carey Daniel, pastor of the First Baptist Church of West Dallas, Texas, and active in the White Citizens' Council in his region, authored a widely reprinted and distributed pamphlet entitled "God the Original Segregationist," which articulated themes common to much of this literature. "Anyone familiar with the Biblical history of those cities during that period can readily understand why we here

in the South are determined to maintain segregation," he wrote, introducing a familiar litany of arguments drawn from the already exhausted "Son of
Ham" tradition. According to Daniel's view, the Canaanites ("the only children of Ham who were specifically cursed to be a servile race") were temporarily allowed to occupy a narrow strip of the Promised Land along the
Mediterranean, including the fateful lands of Sodom and Gomorrah. The
children of the servant people were to live in a different part of the country
from the children of Shem, the ancestors of white people, but "when they
later dared to violate God's sacred law of segregation by moving into and
claiming the land farther east," God commanded the chosen people to destroy them. "We have no reason to suppose that God did not make known to
Noah and his children His divine plan for racial segregation immediately
after the flood," although three generations hence the peoples to be segregated were living together. The burden of proof, Daniel concluded, rested
with those who would say that Jesus was not a segregationist because he
never specifically repudiated the system.[8]

Daniel's folk theology of segregation may be found recycled through
letters to editors, newspaper columns, and frequently in private correspondence. White supporters of civil rights quoted Acts 17:26: "Of one blood has
God made all nations." Segregationists, in response, explicated the second
half of the verse, which referred to God assigning to his creatures the "bounds
of their habitation." For biblical literalists such as most Southerners were,
passages such as Acts 17:26 correlated to the specific social customs of God's
Zion, the American South. "The plan of God is for diversity of races to continue through earthly time and into eternity," wrote a Baptist editor, meaning that those who would "try to break down or obliterate racial distinctions
and bring in a mongrel race or mongrel races go contrary to this plan of
God." This editor repeated the familiar folklore of God dividing the world
between Noah's sons, with Ham and his descendants consigned Africa and
the burden of servitude. The Israelites were chosen to be God's people and
forbidden to intermarry, providing the religious sanction for America's own
miscegenation laws. Denominational ethicists and theologians consistently
showed how these ancient and mysterious stories could in no way be used to
defend the specific social system of segregation. This was beside the point, for
the folk theoreticians of Jim Crow were suspicious of officially sanctioned
modes of biblical interpretation on the race issue. In endorsing *Brown*, after
all, the Southern church leadership had betrayed them.[9]

Some ministers and Sunday school teachers perpetuated this folk theology of segregation, as well—often in the guise of insisting that questions

of segregation and integration were political ones, best left out of the church. The president of Mississippi College, D. M. Nelson, argued that the purpose of integration was to "mongrelize the two dominant races of the South," and that integration was "based upon Karl Marx's doctrine of internationalism . . . the obliteration of all national and racial distinctions and the final amalgamation of all races." A Baptist faculty member of the college and frequent speaker at Citizens' Council meetings believed, along with Governor Ross Barnett of Mississippi, that "our Southern segregation way is the Christian way." Along the same lines, a South Carolina Baptist church declared that "in integrating the races in schools, we foster miscegenation, thereby changing God's plan and destroying His handiwork."[10]

Believers throughout the region, but especially in the Deep South, explained time and again the connection between the preservation of white racial and sexual purity and the defense of the social customs of segregation. For them, racial segregation invoked the most profound mythologies that underlay the white South's preconceptions of the proper ordering of the world. "God created and established the color line in the races," a Texas Baptist editor wrote, and man had "no right to try and eradicate it." The obvious fact that "God created the races and set barriers of color," another Texan explained, meant that "an intermingling and intermarriage (which is the definition for the word integration) of the races God separated himself, is unthinkable, disgusting, and contrary to His divine plan!" Segregationists routinely called on a simplified and distorted version of commonsense realism by insisting that the obvious natural truths of the world could not be tampered with without "destroying the handiwork of God in the creating of the races." Believers in the region also connected integrationism with the social gospel. Until denominational agencies realized "that we are in the business of saving souls rather than trying to solve social ills," a couple in Alabama feared, it would be "necessary for those Southern Baptists with firm convictions toward segregation to take drastic action to preserve what we feel is God's will." God had revealed His Truth in the scripture and in the natural workings of the world, and it was a modernist folly to read into the Bible what clearly was contrary to God's will.[11]

In the context of the cold war, white Southerners seized on the fight against communism, just as did those in favor of black civil rights. "Since God made the races, and appointed the bounds of their habitations," a Florida Baptist church added in what amounted to an amalgamation of all the Southern religious segregationist arguments, any "attempts to force racial union in social life would lead to the communist hope of producing a 'one world hybridized human,' against the Word and will of God." In the heart of Dixie, *Alabama Baptist* newspaper editor Leon Macon carried on the segregationist fight throughout his tenure, which ended only in 1964. "Integration is nothing but Communism, and it is strictly against God's Holy Word," he intoned in his state denominational newspaper. He found "strong evidence that world Communism is stirring the segregation problem in America," and also pointed to the "definite dread in the hearts of people relative to losing the identity of their races through inter-marriage and amalgamation."[12]

Some Christian segregationists simply wove together all strands of the argument. A rural pastor named T. J. Preston, for example, inveighing against school desegregation, argued that "in the first place the Bible teaches segregation and in the second place what the Supreme Court did is political and our Conventions had no right to try to deal with it. . . . If the Lord had wanted us to all live together in a social way, why did he separate us in the beginning . . . what the Supreme Court did would finally bring us under a dictatorship."[13] That integration would produce intermarriage and a mongrel race, that blacks themselves preferred segregation, that Negroes were unclean and simply socially inferior, that civil rights organizations (notably the NAACP) were communist- inspired—religious segregationists used a plethora of arguments in defense of a social system that they had regarded, mistakenly, as timeless.

The folk theology of segregation was rarely articulated at the level of denominational leadership or in seminaries, but it was fairly commonplace among churchgoers in the region and ordinary ministers. More so than ministers, many of who were relatively silent during the civil rights crises, or who attempted to use the language of "moderation" to paper over differences, laymen in the South articulated, defended, and enforced the theology of segregation. The work of deacons, laymen's association, and church auxiliaries in the church world paralleled the efforts of businessmen's groups and Citizens' Councils in the workaday world. In many cases the membership rolls of the religious and secular groups overlapped heavily, and both issued similar defenses of the theology and practice of segregation.

Laypeople were not about to follow the progressive elite in giving up the embattled social customs of the white South. Neither were many ministers. Those in the major denominations associated with desegregation, such as the leaders of social service commissions among Southern Baptists, Methodists, and Presbyterians, as well as ministers who made public stances, were inundated with extensive correspondence from religious segregationists, both laymen and ministers. At the height of the massive resistance in the late

1950s, segregationist Baptists flooded their state conventions with protests against the SBC Christian Life Commission's reports. Segregationists in various denominations complained bitterly of their social concerns agencies, tried to shut them down or freeze their finances, or at the very least tried to limit their reports or to order them to avoid controversial issues. Such religious segregationists commonly charged that the social turmoil associated with the civil rights movement fed the spirit of lawlessness and societal breakdown that worried conservatives generally.

Those who were on the fence could be persuaded or intimidated by activist laymen, as segregationist organizations quickly realized. James McBride Dabbs wrote that white supremacy groups feared preachers as their worst enemies, but in fact most pastors were silent, or silenced. Efforts by white moderates to enlist ministerial support for gradual desegregation met with limited success during the era of massive resistance. Many ministers said that moderate laypeople simply did not want their views to be public knowledge. Harry Wilson, a Danville Baptist pastor, found no ministers who spoke out against segregation. He discovered that white pastors generally were apprehensive about encouraging racial brotherhood. The Reverend Carl Pritchett, a progressive Southern Baptist in South Carolina, met resistance in his efforts to organize meetings of the South Carolina Council on Human Relations. Black schoolteachers were afraid to attend, and white ministers were indifferent or hostile. The head of the council, Alice Norwood Spearman, tried to bridge the divide between the state's white liberals and black leaders and asked ministers to mend the racial divide in the state. "So many of our ministers have just as much racial prejudice as anyone else," the Reverend Pritchett regretfully concluded. "The social penalty for nonconformity is still so high it discourages forthright thinking and outspoken Christian interpretation." By 1959, a black South Carolina minister pronounced the state's Council on Human Relations dead, a victim of white timidity in the face of massive resistance.[14]

Those white ministers who Martin Luther King Jr. had assumed would join the cause of racial brotherhood instead mostly folded their hands. Looking at the determination of laypeople to silence white ministers who supported the movement, however, it is not so surprising that the church appeared to lack a moral conscience. Joseph Rabun, a Georgia minister and veteran of combat in the Pacific theater, came home from the war only to find himself in new skirmishes, this time with his own congregation. Rabun served as a chaplain with the Marine Corps during World War II. The war taught this Baptist preacher to be "more conscious of the precious importance of life and dignity." He regarded World War II as a conflict "fought against the anti-Christ, . . . fought against forces that would shackle and ground men down instead of set him free; that the war was fought against an ideology which held that because of race one man was better than another." Rabun's own experience in the war led him to understand Southern racism as parallel to Nazi and Japanese master race ideologies. His travails made clear also that the forces fighting racial justice were politically connected and powerful. In 1946, the veteran and minister found the Peach State's white supremacists united under Eugene Talmadge, head of a "Cracker" party that successfully employed racist demagoguery to capture the votes of ordinary whites. Talmadge's letter of church membership happened to be in Rabun's congregation in McRae. Influenced by Rabun, the Georgia Baptist Convention condemned Eugene Talmadge's campaign to save the white primary (then under attack in the state). While testifying against the white primary in the state legislature, Rabun noted that "the real issue is not a white primary, it is democracy." Rabun pointed out that he had "faced 100 days of battle-fire" and four years of war, and thus should be able to "exercise my right as such in a democracy, to speak in behalf" of his beliefs. Congregants attacked him, telling Talmadge that Rabun did not speak for them. In 1947, under duress, he resigned from his pulpit, a victim of the postwar racist reaction throughout much of the South. Rabun's martyrdom would be repeated frequently in the coming years, as ministers who appeared to be sympathetic to the civil rights crusades were unceremoniously deposed from pulpits and sometimes driven out of the South or out of the ministry.[15]

Antagonism and suspicion grew through the 1950s as positions hardened in response to *Brown,* the Montgomery boycott, and the flurry of national denominational resolutions even from conservative Southern denominations endorsing changes in the nation's racial policies. An ecumenical service in Little Rock, planned by the ministerial association there to advise peaceful compliance with the desegregation order, drew small crowds, whereas a rally of segregationists at Central Baptist Church drew an enthusiastic response. In North Carolina, hard-line Baptists refused to support school desegregation. Unless segregation could be shown to be "in conflict with the Sermon on the Mount, or other teachings of Jesus," one Baptist declared, "we should be able to uphold and to practice it; and to do so with a *good conscience.*" In Chapel Hill, Baptist chaplain J. C. Herrin was dismissed because of his efforts at racial reconciliation, and denominational progressives worked with very limited success to establish a voice within their convention.[16]

Most white Baptist congregations throughout the region silently complied with or actively supported the segregationist order, in defiance of pronouncements from denominational leaders. In Little Rock, a Baptist minister and radio personality (with a radio program entitled *The Little Country Church*) named James Wesley Pruden organized resistance to desegregating the city's soon-to-be-famous Central High School. For Pruden, who had been converted to the Baptist faith but found an interdenominational following through his radio program, segregation was intimately tied up with religion. Pruden met with Governor Orval Faubus to plan the segregationist strategy on the Central High case. Women in Pruden's congregation founded the Mothers' League of Central High, a group that comprised mostly working-class mothers offended that middle-class whites could send their children to safe suburban schools while Central High was their only choice. The Council of Church Women in Little Rock, made up of solidly middle-class women of the established churches, condemned Faubus, but fundamentalist ministers such as Pruden successfully connected the defense of segregation with the offense against all forms of modernism. Pruden's efforts found support in other congregations, including one Baptist church in North Little Rock, which sent a telegram protesting the "unholy invasion" of the National Guard and subsequent violation of the "customs, rights, and privileges" of white Southerners. "If you had been spending as much time on your knees in prayer as . . . on the golf course," they telegrammed the commander in chief, "you never would have sent troops into Arkansas."[17]

In Mississippi, the White Citizens' Council targeted moderate ministers, whom it called "our most deadly enemy." Again, the evidence leaned the other way, as a number of clergymen fought against desegregation. The council received support from prominent segregationist ministers such as G. T. Gillespie and, in turn, widely distributed his pamphlet, "A Christian View of Segregation." Douglas Hudgins, pastor of Jackson's critically important First Baptist Church, refused to speak out on *Brown* and avoided political issues. He was, as historian Charles Marsh has brilliantly limned him, the "theologian of a closed society."[18]

In addition to the frequent expressions of anger by the segregationists against mainstream denominational leaders, the Citizens' Councils pressured local congregations to maintain segregation in church life. Hodding Carter wrote that "the Citizens' Councils think and plan as a group and they are able to act as individuals within the various churches . . . to which they belong. This has already proved effective in various church denominations in Mississippi." Prominent Baptist clergymen supported the Citizens' Coun-

cils in various states, including Charles C. Jones in Jackson, Marion Woodson
of Olanta, South Carolina, and Henry L. Lyon of Montgomery's Highland
Avenue Baptist Church. A deacon in the First Baptist Church of Jackson,
Mississippi, was a leader in the Citizens' Council Association. Such examples
could be multiplied many times over. Those with substantial local churches,
but usually outside the highest channels of denominational leadership, often emerged as leaders of groups such as local Citizens' Councils, and allied
themselves with laypeople who resisted the growing sympathy the major
white Southern denominations gradually evinced toward desegregation.
There were some exceptions to the rule. William T. Bodenhamer of Georgia
pastored a Baptist church while serving as a state legislator and directing the
States' Rights Council of Georgia. For the most part, however, it was lay
leadership in state councils that enlisted ministers to attend meetings and
perform auxiliary roles such as giving invocations and talks, making announcements from the pulpit, and generally encouraging members to support their efforts. The Citizens' Councils thus exploited and sometimes
coerced ministers in much the same way as had the Klan during its heyday
earlier in the century.[19]

　　More virulent strains of the folk theology of segregation also existed
among white Christians. If less numerous than the silent segregationists,
violent defenders of Jim Crow certainly knew how to draw attention, both
through their words and their actions. The White Knights of the Ku Klux
Klan, reorganized under Sam Bowers, terrorized Mississippi blacks in the
early 1960s. Bowers insisted that "a Solemn, determined Spirit of Christian
Reverence must be stimulated in all members" of the White Knights. During his reign of terror, the state Klan was involved in thirty-five shooting
incidents, the bombing of sixty-five homes and other buildings, including
thirty-five churches, the notorious murders of three civil rights workers
during "Freedom Summer" in 1964, and other acts of intimidation. Bowers
and the Klan did not distinguish between those in the movement and those
who were not, aiming instead at a more generalized terrorism. These spasms
of violence moved young activists in the Student Non-Violent Coordinat-
ing Committee (SNCC) to question—and some to give up entirely—their
commitment to nonviolence. "We had told a lot of people to put down
their guns and not be violent in Mississippi," remembered Dave Dennis, a
Congress of Racial Equality and SNCC activist, "and I wasn't so sure that the
nonviolent approach was the right approach anymore. And I had to do a lot
of soul searching about that."[20]

　　Southern Christian defenders of segregation fought on in the 1960s but suffered serious ideological setbacks. If they were to continue as self-proclaimed defenders of law and order, they now faced the troubling reality that the law was on the side of desegregation, whereas blame for disorder increasingly lay squarely in the hands of fellow segregationists, who had been complicit with the violent terrorism of the likes of Bowers. Many religious segregationists still insisted that segregation was right in God's eyes, but they conceded that Christian citizens must render obedience to the powers that be. Leon Macon, editor of the *Alabama Baptist* for fifteen years and an outspoken opponent of civil rights measures, faced this dilemma by the end of his term. During congressional debate over the Voting Rights Act, he attacked President Lyndon Johnson's efforts to enlist clergymen in his behalf. As Macon saw it, this turned "our pulpits into political rostrums to advance the ideas of one man, or group of men." Civil rights legislation, he charged, was yet another step toward "an all-powerful centralized Federal government," one that would "out-socialize the Socialists" and destroy personal freedom. Likewise, he opposed statements emanating from the Christian Life Commission of the SBC that endorsed desegregation and insisted on opening the church doors to all. For Macon, this violated the principle of the autonomy of the local church. Most importantly, though, as he expressed it, "the basic fear and cause of the opposition to the integration which the Civil Rights Bill intends to bring about has been the mongrelization of our society through intermarriage," as it was God's desire to "keep our races pure" rather than tamper with the "difference and variety in His creation." At the same time, after the passage of the civil rights legislation of the mid-1960s, obedience to the laws simply required acquiescence to desegregation. Macon's only recourse was to suggest voluntary segregation, just as he believed the Jews had practiced for centuries. As a principled Baptist, moreover, Macon was unalterably opposed to state funding or tax advantages for private religious academies, thus taking the steam out of the efforts to construct an alternative to the public schools that could service more than a small elite of students.[21]

The civil rights victories at the national level did not mean that white Southern congregations would open their doors at the local level. Southern Baptist Theological Seminary, in Louisville, had to apologize for issuing an invitation to Martin Luther King Jr. to speak after threats from throughout the Baptist South to cut off funding to the SBC and its Christian Life Commission. As late as 1966, as an official in the Department of Interracial Cooperation in the North Carolina Baptist State convention wrote, white pastors were "afraid to preach what they [knew was] right in race relations for fear of losing their pulpits." Many pastors who tried to lead the way paid the price, often with a determined segregationist faction within churches steamrollering cowed congregations. Baptist congregations generally required large majorities to accept new members. Previously a pro forma procedure, it now engendered church splits, with determined minorities blocking efforts to enact more inclusive admissions policies to congregations.[22]

Into the mid-1960s, battles raged in local congregations as determined segregationist laypeople (and sometimes ministers) clung to the segregationist line—now reduced simply to protecting the citadels of their local churches. One of the better-known local controversies took place across the street from Mercer University in Macon, Georgia, pastored in 1964 and 1965 by Thomas J. Holmes. The young pastor arrived near the end of the career of Sam Omi, an African missionary student who had desegregated Mercer in 1962. At that time, most Mercer students attended services at Vineville Baptist, not as conveniently located as Tattnall but more open and accepting as a congregation. Once the dominant church in town with over 1,000 members, Tattnall Square Baptist Church had been reduced to 450 total members, less than half of whom normally attended on Sundays. Because Tattnall was located in a "transitional" neighborhood, Holmes recognized that something would have to be done to improve the church's tattered facilities and battered reputation.

Upon taking the pulpit in 1965, Holmes soon sensed that trouble would arise with the deacons, two of whom were Klansmen. Trouble was not long in coming. He spent the first year preaching from the Book of Acts, making clear the Bible's message about the unity of mankind. In response, recalcitrant deacons held secret meetings, plotting to rid themselves of Holmes. Supporters of the beleaguered pastor publicized the machinations of the deacons and gave Holmes a vote of confidence; but when the church voted on whether to admit blacks, opponents packed the pews and turned down the measure. Although personally devastated, Holmes complied with the church's vote. Sam Omi, already a veteran of desegregation wars from his days as a Mercer student, decided to challenge the segregation of the church. Deliberately refusing offers of help from other students at Mercer, he sought not a public demonstration but a simple personal act. One Sunday, as Holmes was preaching, Omi was dragged down the outside church stairs by deacons and taken away by waiting police officers, unbeknownst to Holmes himself. By September 1966, the deacons forced a vote on their controversial pastor; he lost the vote of confidence 250 to 189, and soon thereafter resigned.

Meanwhile, the story had been picked up by the press. The church's disgrace drew international attention. A few years later, Holmes penned a memoir about the controversy, *Ashes for Breakfast*, seeking to "bring to full public knowledge the grievous dimensions of a tragic chain of events which created a sensation in the press. . . . the story laid bare the ignominy of ministerial captivity by entrenched power structures within the church which have long fallen behind the thinking of the majority within the congregations." Holmes sought not to romanticize his personal suffering but to explain that "the tragedy of this church is the nearly universal disgrace of the churches—they might have led the way to community, but, alas, they would not!" The message, he insisted, was that there was yet time for church to "fulfill its divine commission of reconciliation between God and man, and between man and man . . . Only as the people of God affirm the basic personhood of all men can they heal the breach between class and race within the fellowship of Christ's church. Only then will they recover the spiritual force to turn the tides of public opinion and conduct into the Christian stream within the nation." Holmes saw good coming out of his experience, particularly after he became involved with a ministerial alliance that put him in contact with respected black ministerial colleagues such as William Holmes Borders in Atlanta. In that way, Holmes later wrote,

> God enabled he and his wife to sublimate our grief by merging it with that of other broken and bruised members of the human race. The fact that we were willing to suffer for a principle involving love and respect for Negro brothers and sisters has given us an introduction to the black community that we had never had before. The average Negro does not believe in the affirmations of the white community because he has seen too many pronouncements and not enough demonstration. But where there is evidence of genuine Christian love, black people respond magnanimously. We violated the mores of the segregated church and paid the penalty, but in the process we were liberated into the larger fellowship of God's people that transcends racial lines.[23]

By the late 1960s and early 1970s, the raw exercise of white supremacist power appeared naked, without any compelling theological justification. The foundation of God-ordained racial inequality crumbled, and around its ruins lay the simple hypocrisy of saying one thing and meaning another, of endorsing equality for all while practicing racism. Eventually the segregationist theologians retreated. The structure of evangelical racism could not withstand the moral force created by the civil rights movement. Although they did not renounce their views, segregationists knew better than to air them publicly. "I firmly believe in each race having its own schools, social organizations, and churches . . . Of course, what I am suggesting will be considered ridiculous and absurd by today's liberal and brainwashed public and I will be labeled a dirty old racist and bigot," wrote an Alabama Baptist in 1974. What had been mainstream thought was now extreme, and this Baptist knew it. Periodic controversies sometimes tormented white Southern Baptists, as when the Sunday School Board of the SBC pulled an issue of *Becoming,* its quarterly for adolescents, because a cover showed a black male teenager conversing with two white girls. The trustees of the board approved guidelines admonishing writers to avoid potentially inflammatory issues. That same year, however, Texas Baptist Jimmy Allen convened a huge interracial meeting in Houston's Astrodome, bringing together white, black, and Hispanic Baptists, thus pointing the way to what would be a repudiation of Southern religious racism.[24]

Religion, Race, and the New Right

The relationship between race and contemporary Southern Baptist identity was forged in the wake of civil rights–era controversies. That is not to say that race is the real issue behind the Southern Baptist wars of recent years; it is not. It is to say, however, that moderates and conservatives, as well as a few liberals, coalesced during the civil rights years, and those factions played out their battle over a very different terrain of issues from 1979 to the early 1990s. The conservatives came together in part against the moderate and gradualist leadership of many Southern Baptist agencies in regard to the race issue. They argued strenuously, and probably correctly, that when the Christian Life Commission issued statements in favor of desegregation, it did not speak for the majority of Southern Baptists; and that, accordingly, the democratic principle supposedly determinative in Southern Baptist life had been breached.

By the late 1960s, this argument had lost its potency, and Southern Baptists accommodated themselves with remarkable ease to the demise of white supremacy as fundamentally constitutive of their society. During those years, that is, the battles were bitter, but looked at historically, segregation crumbled remarkably easily. Thus, in the recent controversies within the SBC, race has been one of the very few items on the agenda that was *not* in dispute. Today's conservatives, for the most part, have repudiated the white supremacist views of their predecessors, as seen in the SBC's official apology for slavery and racism issued in 1995.

For religious conservatives generally, including the currently dominant power structure of the SBC, patriarchy has supplanted race as the defining first principle of God-ordained inequality. Of course, the Southern conservative view of race and gender was intertwined, particularly in the emphasis on social purity. Shielding the body politic from corruption always assumed the form of protecting the white female body from defilement. Nevertheless, the historical experience of the Civil War and Reconstruction, and the constant ongoing struggle to maintain the facade of white unity in the face of the ever-present threat of an alliance of poor and working-class whites and blacks, meant that race hierarchies looked unstable and fragile in comparison to the seemingly secure fortress of Southern manhood and womanhood.

Since the 1960s, the standard biblical arguments against racial equality, now looked upon as an embarrassment from a bygone age, have found their way rather easily into the contemporary religious conservative stance on gender. Since the 1960s, a theology that sanctifies gendered notions of place and station has become what whiteness was to earlier generations of Southern Baptists. Behind the recent battle for control of the SBC has been a deep divide between those for whom human equality and autonomy reign as fundamental principles, and those for whom communal norms and strictures and a divinely ordained hierarchy remain determinative of social life—in short, a classic battle between the kind of philosophical liberalism most associated with the philosopher John Rawls, and conservative doctrines descended from Edmund Burke, the Nashville Agrarians of the 1930s, and (for those on the right-wing edge of the right wing) the Christian Reconstructionists of more recent vintage. For the latter group, gendered patterns of hierarchy are fundamental to godly structures of religious, social, and political life.

In 1979, a group of fundamentalist men led by Paige Patterson and Paul Pressler, the former a theologian and the latter a lawyer and conservative district judge, set out to win control of the largest Protestant organization in the United States, the SBC. Earlier attempts by less well-connected fundamentalists in the early 1970s had failed. But this earlier effort did succeed in formulating a strategy for ultimate victory: place the right men in the presidency of the SBC, and then use the power of the presidency to appoint political and ideological allies to key positions of leadership. Patterson and Pressler, the two Texans who served respectively as the theologian and strategist of the movement, put into action their plan to purge the SBC of liberalism, estimating that in ten years, conservatives would own the majority on trustee boards of the seminaries and denominational agencies. An ugly battle for control of the SBC ensued, with upward of 30,000 to 40,000 messengers in some years attending convention meetings that turned into political brawls. By 1991, however, the conservatives had won a complete victory, and both sides recognized that a new era of Southern Baptist history had begun.[25]

The victorious group, those self-described as "conservatives" and called by their enemies "fundamentalists," argued that theological modernism and political liberalism were weaning Southern Baptists away from their historically conservative stance. The moderates (generally referred to by conservatives as "liberals," although sometimes privately classed as "rats" and "skunks") responded that the fundamentalists were conducting a classic political purge. The SBC now stands firmly in control of men who swear by the completely inerrant nature of the Bible "in all areas of reality," who castigate all liberalism, whether theological or political, and who conduct severe tests of political correctness for job candidates for seminary professorships or denominational posts. The moderates in this controversy, who once swore loyalty to the SBC, regrouped into a quasi-denominational Cooperative Baptist Fellowship.

Conservatives meant what they said: they wanted to put the SBC back in the hands of biblical inerrantists, those who (by their own self-description) read the Bible literally and took it at its word. Inerrancy served usefully as a political slogan, designed to smoke out skeptics who expressed any deviance from biblical literalism. The moderates also meant what they said: they sought to allow for some limited theological diversity among local churches who would cooperate for the cause of missions. The moderates, however, lacked any clear political leadership and could not, by the very nature of being moderate, fight with any single-mindedness of will. The conservatives went for the jugular, and it was the moderates' blood supply that would be stanched.

Through the 1980s, while claiming to eschew politics, the conservatives built a political machine with an effective and exclusivist patronage system. They demanded allegiance to Reaganite conservatism among SBC appointees. They fought with moderates who were themselves conservative biblical literalists but who disapproved of the political program of the fundamentalists. They secretly tape-recorded conversations, placed spies in Southern Baptist agencies, and engaged in astute parliamentary maneuvering to advance their cause. In short, they operated effectively as a political movement, in contrast to the hapless and ineffectual moderates. In the end, the

moderate and progressive Southern Baptists, who were often accused of being preoccupied with things of the world, turned out to be too spiritually
inclined and conciliatory to be able to organize themselves as a "movement
culture," or to engage successfully in power politicking in the convention.
Meanwhile, the conservatives and fundamentalists, who proclaimed themselves defenders of the spirituality of the church, in fact were savvy political
operators who successfully organized for a political victory in taking over
the nation's largest Protestant denomination. The fundamentalists were the
successful dissenters, and now they reigned as the power elite. Not coinci-
dentally, the "conservative resurgence" (their preferred description for what
the moderates referred to as a "coup d'état" or a "fundamentalist takeover")
coincided with the rise of Reaganism in national politics; the steady disinte-
gration of the Southern Democratic party; the creation of the powerful
Christian Coalition (led by the Southern minister and television celebrity
Pat Robertson and his academically trained political strategist, Ralph Reed,
also Southern-born); and the rise of the antiabortion ("pro-life") movement in national politics.

Southern religious conservatives came to national prominence after the
demise of race as the central issue of national life. Relieved of their historic
burden, Southern conservatives took hold of the national agenda. Underly-
ing their political movements, however, lay philosophical positions that up-
dated older and venerable defenses of social hierarchies as necessary for a
properly ordered liberty. No longer defenders of racial hierarchy, the conservatives could advance their positions in favor of an unapologetic patriarchy. In the late 1990s, when delegates to the SBC approved a change to their
"Baptist Faith and Message" that endorsed "wifely submission" to husbands,
the nation took note, but in fact this statement simply reiterated a time-
honored position in Southern evangelical culture.

The battle over the SBC, and the restructuring of American religious
groups as outlined by sociologist Robert Wuthnow, both followed a pattern
similar to the restructuring of American politics from the New Deal to
Reagan. During the New Deal, Southern conservatives led by such figures as
the Southern Baptist Josiah Bailey effectively had formed a Southern conservative coalition that stymied FDR's social reform plans for the remainder
of his presidency. Race was central to this Southern conservative coalition.
In particular, opposition to a federal antilynching law was an effective organizing tool for the proto-Dixiecrats. They argued that the Democratic Party
had become something very different than the party of their fathers. It had
become the vehicle for the New Deal, not the stalwart defender of decen-

tralization and limited government, as was the Southern Democratic conservative philosophy. Moreover, the Southern conservatives looked on with dismay as their party became a multiethnic coalition. They were especially uneasy as blacks deserted the party of Lincoln for the party of Roosevelt. A decade later, their efforts would take shape in the Dixiecrat revolt of 1948, and in later years, many of the same figures led the attack on the civil rights revolution.[26] This generation of political conservatives fought on, unsuccessfully, through the civil rights era. They lost, as the federal government compelled Southern states to accept desegregation of social life and voting rights for African Americans.

The descendants of this restructuring of Southern politics and religion led the conservative movements of the 1970s. This time they experienced more success, largely because they were free of the burden of defending an indefensible social system such as segregation. This has allowed the more recent Southern religious conservatives to take the offensive, to pursue strategic alliances in pursuit of ends shared by many other American religious interests, from attacking abortion rights to upholding family values. Although conservative Baptist patriarch W. A. Criswell fought civil rights every inch of the way until capitulating later in the 1960s, current conservatives eagerly form strategic pacts with political allies of all sorts—black conservatives, Mormons, antiabortionist Catholics, and a variety of others.

Divisions within the SBC had been evident during the Progressive Era, and of course during the evolution and modernist controversies of the 1920s. Yet it took the coalescing of divisions over race to fracture and create new coalitions, including groups such as the Christian Coalition. The civil rights struggle re-formed the SBC, splitting it along the lines of conservatives, moderates, and liberals. The arguments made about civil rights brought to light differences within denominations known to exist but generally finessed, papered over, or simply fought out and then forgotten. The new groupings on the right wing left behind the dishonorable racist past of the predecessors, but inherited well-honed theological defenses of hierarchy, submission, and order.

Future generations seem as likely to look on today's gender strictures with the same regret as today's conservative thinkers look back on proslavery and proapartheid theology—so much intellectual firepower and heartfelt biblical argumentation wasted on such a futile and ultimately indefensible cause. Over the long term, ideologies of inequality, and perhaps more importantly the blocking of opportunities, simply do not survive well in competition with the American creed of opportunity and equality. Nor can they thrive over the long term in an essentially free-market system of religious expression. The historic Baptist emphasis on soul liberty and soul competency reinforces this fact. Cries for liberty and opportunity historically win out over strictures and boundaries along the lines of race, class, and gender. Eventually, theologies must adjust themselves to that social reality—as has been the case with the demise of racial theologies among Southern Baptists.

NOTES

1. Scholars in the first modern generation of Southern religious history generally wrote in the "cultural captivity" vein. See especially Samuel Hill, *Southern Churches in Crisis* (New York: Holt, Rinehart, and Winston, 1967); Kenneth Bailey, *Southern White Protestantism in the Twentieth Century* (New York: Harper and Row, 1964); Rufus Spain, *At Ease in Zion: Social History of Southern Baptists* (Nashville: Vanderbilt University Press, 1967); and John Lee Eighmy, *Churches in Cultural Captivity: A History of the Social Attitudes of Southern Baptists* (Knoxville: University of Tennessee Press, 1972).

2. *Christian Index,* March 22, 1883.

3. Quotations from Timothy B. Tyson, *Radio Free Dixie: Robert F. Williams and the Roots of Black Power* (Chapel Hill: University of North Carolina Press, 1999), 21; John Dittmer, *Local People: The Struggle for Civil Rights in Mississippi* (Urbana: University of Illinois Press, 1994), 217.

4. Andrew M. Manis, *Southern Civil Religions in Conflict: Black and White Baptists and Civil Rights, 1947–1957* (Athens: University of Georgia Press, 1987), 65, 92, 83; Dittmer, *Local People,* 63.

5. Oran P. Smith, *The Rise of Baptist Republicanism* (New York: New York University Press, 1997), 45–47; Jerry Falwell, *Strength for the Journey: An Autobiography* (New York: Simon and Schuster, 1987), 334–49.

6. David L. Chappell has argued strongly that religion did not play a central role among segregationist activists, citing the relative lack of ministerial participation in the prosegregationist argument, which stands in stark contrast to the sanctification of slavery in the 1830s–1850s. For more on this, see *A Stone of Hope* (Chapel Hill: University of North Carolina Press, 2003). A précis of the original argument can be found in David L. Chappell, "Religious Ideas of the Segregationists," *Journal of American Studies* 32 (1998): 45–72.

7. "W. A. Crisswell, 1909–2002," http://www.thebaptistpage.com, March 13, 2005.

8. Joseph Crespino, "The Christian Conscience of Jim Crow: White Protestant Ministers and the Mississippi Citizens' Councils, 1954–1964," *Mississippi Folklife* 31 (Fall 1998): 36; Carey Daniel, "God the Original Segregationist," pamphlet found in John Owen Smith papers, box 1, Special Collections Library, Emory University. A note attached to the pamphlet, directed to Methodist bishop John Owen Smith read, "Please read the enclosed and then ask God to forgive you for trying to mix the races."

9. Quotations from Mark Newman, "Getting Right with God: Southern Baptists and Race Relations, 1945–1980" (Ph.D. diss., University of Mississippi, 1993), 93–94.

10. Randy Sparks, *Religion in Mississippi* (Jackson: University of Mississippi Press, 2001), 231; Jane Dailey, "Sex, Segregation, and the Sacred after *Brown*," *Journal of American History* 91 (June 2004): 119–44, quotation on pp. 125–26.

11. Mark Newman, *Getting Right with God: Southern Baptists and Desegregation, 1945–1995* (Tuscaloosa: University of Alabama Press, 2001), 51–56.

12. Newman, *Getting Right with God,* 56; Newman, "Getting Right with God," 99, 522.

13. Newman, "Getting Right with God," 549.

14. Ibid., 499; Pete Daniel, *Lost Revolutions: The South in the 1950s* (Chapel Hill: Smithsonian Institute and University of North Carolina Press, 2000), 233, 239, 249.

15. Jennifer E. Brooks, "Winning the Peace: Georgia Veterans and the Struggle to Define the Political Legacy of World War II," *Journal of Southern History* 66 (August 2000): 574, 576 n. 33; John Egerton, *Speak Now against the Day: The Generation before the Civil Rights Movement in the South* (Chapel Hill: University of North Carolina Press), 424.

16. Manis, *Southern Civil Religions,* 83; Mark Newman, "The Baptist State Convention of North Carolina and Desegregation, 1945–1980," *North Carolina Historical Review* 75 (January 1998): 1–28.

17. Daniel, *Lost Revolutions,* 55; Michael Friedland, *Lift Up Your Voice Like a Trumpet: White Clergy and the Civil Rights and Antiwar Movements, 1954–1973* (Chapel Hill: University of North Carolina Press, 1998), 34.

18. Daniel, *Lost Revolutions,* 236; for more on Hudgins, see Charles Marsh, *God's Long Summer: Stories of Faith and Civil Rights* (Princeton: Princeton University Press, 1997).

19. Sparks, *Religion in Mississippi* , 230–235.

20. Dittmer, *Local People,* 217, 268, 305–307.

21. Macon's editorials from *Alabama Baptist* quoted in Newman, "Getting Right with God," 520–525.

22. Newman, "Getting Right with God," 543, 699.

23. Thomas J. Holmes, *Ashes for Breakfast* (Valley Forge, Pa.: Judson Press, 1969), 10, 122–123.

24. Newman, "Getting Right with God," 107, 690–99.

25. For a narrative history of the struggle for control of the SBC, see David T. Morgan, *The New Crusades, the New Holy Land: Conflict in the Southern Baptist Convention, 1969–1991* (Tuscaloosa: University of Alabama Press, 1996); a useful compilation of primary documents in the controversy may be found in *Going for the Jugular: A Documentary History of the SBC Holy War*, Walter Shurden and Randy Shepley, eds. (Macon, Ga.: Mercer University Press, 1996). For a more sociological overview, see Nancy Ammerman, *Baptist Battles: Social Conflict and Religious Conflict in the Southern Baptist Convention* (New Brunswick, N.J.: Rutgers University Press, 1990). A penetrating new study of the Southern Baptist conservative mind is Barry Hankins, *Uneasy in Babylon: Southern Baptist Conservatives and American Culture* (Tuscaloosa: University of Alabama Press, 2002).

26. Patricia Sullivan, *Days of Hope: Race and Democracy in the New Deal Era* (Chapel Hill: University of North Carolina Press, 1996); Robert Wuthnow, *The Restructuring of American Religion: Society and Faith since World War Two* (Princeton: University Press, 1998).

"City Mothers"

Dorothy Tilly, Georgia Methodist Women, and Black Civil Rights

Andrew M. Manis

Sometime in the 1950s an editor of a large Southern newspaper advised a group of college students, "If you do not know what social action to take, watch the Methodist women, and where they lead, follow."[1] Similar instructions were issued in 1982 when John Patrick McDowell pointed historians toward Methodist women if they wanted to see evidence of the Social Gospel in the American South.[2] Both the editor and the scholar were correct in isolating the women of the Methodist Church as the vanguard of Southern white church people's efforts to sow seeds of racial change in the pre–civil rights era. More specifically, what in this chapter begins as a survey of Methodist attitudes and actions related to race and civil rights will move to a more individualized argument—that the work of Atlanta laywoman Dorothy Tilly and the Methodist women she led embodied white Protestant work to foster better race relations based on racial justice. This telling of Tilly's story focuses on her activities both within and outside the Methodist Church, highlighting her role in leading Georgia Methodist women to work for racial justice in America, both before and after *Brown v. Board of Education* outlawed segregation in 1954.

Dorothy Rogers was born in Hampton, Georgia, in 1883, the daughter of Methodist minister Richard Wade Rogers. A lifelong and committed Methodist, Tilly served as president of a youth mission organization when she was twelve years old. She graduated from Georgia Methodist schools, Reinhardt (Junior) College, and in 1901 from Macon's Wesleyan College, where her mother was also an alumna. Two years later she married a University of Georgia graduate, Milton Eben Tilly, who became a successful chemical distributor in Atlanta. The couple lived there for the rest of their lives, attending the Haygood Memorial Methodist Church and investing themselves in race relations work through various Methodist organizations. By the time of her death in 1970, she had been honored with Wesleyan College's Distinguished Achievement Award and been named the "outstanding Methodist woman of the first quarter century" by the Methodist Church's Women's Society for Christian Service of the Southeast Jurisdiction Church. Extending her efforts beyond her denomination, she had also become a friend of Eleanor Roosevelt, a member of President Harry Truman's Committee on Civil Rights, and one of the most influential women in the South.[3]

Her influence was built upon, but grew far beyond, her Methodist activities—to politics, to interracial dialogue, and to what she considered a religious calling to help Methodist and other Christian women monitor racial justice in local legal systems throughout Georgia and the South. This race relations "mission" came to be expressed most vigorously in the Fellowship of the Concerned (FOC), the organization she founded in 1949. By her own testimony, she compared this "calling" to the ministerial call that brought black Methodist missionary John Stewart into Christian service. As Stewart had received a "calling [that] gave no rest," so had the women of the FOC answered "calling voices that would not be stilled. Voices calling, 'Let the people know what is happening in the courts.'" Until the FOC died with its leader in 1970, Methodist and other Southern women, black and white, worked alongside each other and with the Southern Regional Council to help bring local Southern practices "in closer accord with the ideals of Christianity and Judaism, to strengthen and broaden democracy, to build a society in which every person can be confident of security and justice."[4] As a result, Tilly and her followers supplemented the work of "city fathers" to become "city mothers," keeping a watchful eye on law and order and racial justice in local communities across the South.[5]

Although Dorothy Tilly was not purely sui generis, she was mostly an original. The women who followed Tilly into the FOC were, of course, likeminded. As for other denominations, the Southern Baptists had members involved in the Women's Missionary Union (WMU) who were similar to Tilly. A generation before Tilly, Fannie E. S. Heck, a WMU leader in North Carolina, served as vice president of the Southern Sociological Congress and lived a life attuned to the Social Gospel. But Heck, other Baptist women, and even other Presbyterian women who shared some of the same attributes with Tilly never reached her stature and involvement in civil rights.[6]

Because of her lifelong Methodist affiliation and her Methodist education, and because her involvement with Methodist women's organizations launched Tilly into wider circles of influence, an examination of the actions and racial attitudes of the Methodist Church is warranted. From within the Methodist fellowship emerged women's organizations that became the vanguard of the Social Gospel and concern for race relations in the South. In time, these women's organizations would be the first Methodist groups to move beyond calling for truly "separate *but equal*" facilities to advocate the complete eradication of Jim Crow segregation. These organizations not only nurtured Dorothy Tilly and other Southern white women of social conscience, but set the pace in race relations for the dominant religious institutions of the post–World War II South.

THE METHODIST CHURCH AND SOUTHERN RACE RELATIONS

One must view the Methodist Church's record on race in at least three distinct periods. Two of these periods are those before and after the 1939 reunification of the Northern Methodist Episcopal Church with the Methodist Episcopal Church, South. The third is the period after the U.S. Supreme Court's landmark *Brown* ruling.

Methodist Opinion before *Brown*

After the political reunion of North and South in the Compromise of 1877, a more perfect reunion was effected culturally and militarily when Southern and Northern soldiers fought together against common enemies in the Spanish-American War and the Great War against the German Kaiser. By the end of the Progressive Era, Methodists and other white Southerners settled into a spectrum of three common racial views, none of which opted for equality between the races. The most virulent expression was what Joel Williamson has called the radical stance, which supported a vigorous defense of white supremacy. Radicals mounted a staunch defense of white privilege against images of the Negro as an inferior being quickly descending into bestiality in the absence of the erstwhile civilizing influence of slavery. In this response could be found a level of fear and hatred that expressed itself in terror, lynchings, and the use of the epithet *nigger*.[7]

　　The numerically dominant stance was that of a paternalism, which saw African Americans as a "child race," but one inclined toward retrogression unless aided industrially, intellectually, and morally by beneficent whites. Methodist writer Elmer T. Clark, reflecting this view, articulated what virtually became the race relations motto of the white South until deep into the civil rights movement: "The Christian white man of the South is the Negro's best friend and always has been."[8] This paternalism was, of course, committed to the preservation of segregation, as in 1926, when the *Alabama Christian Advocate* criticized Methodist bishops for dining with African Methodist bishops and their wives, commenting: "Now, when Negro men and their wives and white men and their wives sit down together at the same banquet table, it is what we in the South call social equality . . . [that] will lead to social equality of other sorts, and social equality ultimately leads to intermarriage."[9]

Out of this Christian paternalism, which included a dose of Social Gospel progressivism, came a strong Methodist critique of lynching and race riots. For Georgia progressives like Dorothy Tilly, the race-baiting 1906 gubernatorial contest between Hoke Smith and Clark Howell and the Atlanta race riot of the same year had a powerful effect. Two years later, the disfranchisement of black Georgians similarly stimulated a third approach to race relations that can be called interracialism. Early on, this approach accepted the concept of "separate but equal," but sought to work together with blacks to push local and state governments to shore up the equality of Jim Crow arrangements. As the century wore on, however, Methodists were in the forefront of these efforts, mostly through the denomination's women's groups and the person of Will W. Alexander, the founder of the Committee on Interracial Cooperation (CIC). This organization, founded in 1919, embodied the somewhat conservative interracialist spirit. After 1944, however, when it was transformed into the Southern Regional Council (SRC), the organization gradually developed a restrained critique of segregation itself.[10]

In this social context, Tilly was converted to working in race relations with the help of her husband, Milton. When she cast about for some meaningful Christian activity, Tilly was advised to consider the plight of African Americans in her own city. One night her husband drove her through Atlanta's black slums to the service entrance of the Piedmont Hotel. There she observed black children raiding garbage cans for food and determined, with her husband's encouragement, to go to work on the problem. Soon thereafter, she became involved with the CIC and its sister organization, the Association of Southern Women for the Prevention of Lynching.[11]

Leading the way in race work among Methodists was the Woman's Missionary Council (WMC). The WMC, which began in the early twentieth century, appointed a Committee on Race Relations to study the needs of Southern blacks. In July 1920, Carrie Parks Johnson and Estelle Haskin from the WMC met with ten members of the national Association of Colored

Women at Tuskegee Institute to discuss possibilities for working together. That meeting resulted in the Memphis Woman's Interracial Conference in October of that year.[12] Joining the women in opposition to lynching and the Klan were a number of Methodist newspapers in the South, among them the versions of the *Nashville Christian Advocate,* the *North Carolina Christian Advocate,* and the *Wesleyan (Macon, Ga.) Christian Advocate,* which wondered how Southerners could "identify secret methods, sectionalism, partisanism, and racial hatred with American democracy." The editor admonished his readers to resist the Klan as an "Un-American and undemocratic order."[13]

In the 1920s and 1930s, despite occasional sparring over segregation between some Northern Methodists and their Southern counterparts, the impulse toward reunion gradually drew the two wings together until a Plan of Reunification was approved and the two fellowships became the Methodist Church in May 1939.[14] Race, however, became the major sticking point over the place of black Methodists in the new structure. More than 300,000 blacks within the Methodist churches and annual conferences from several geographical jurisdictions were constituted into a separate, racially determined Central Jurisdiction. Only on such a basis were the Southern churches and conferences willing to agree to the plan. As a compromise, black Methodists overcame their initial misgivings. They became convinced that the arrangement would be a temporary compromise that would in the meantime give them a larger, more unified voice in church affairs.[15]

Reunification made the Methodist Church the largest Protestant denomination in the United States. Ironically, as W. Edward Orser has noted, on the eve of World War II, when segregation would be questioned in many areas of American society, the large and influential Methodist Church had achieved unification by institutionalizing segregation in its own structure. Orser further argued that this left the Methodists "virtually voiceless" on the race question.[16] The women of the denomination, however, constituted the important exception. Significantly, within the Methodist connection, the WMC's study group became the only white group within the Methodist Episcopal Church (MEC) or the Methodist Episcopal Church, South (MECS) to join black Methodists in opposing the Plan of Reunion and its proposed Central Jurisdiction. The women wondered whether the plan's "ethical imperfections" would be permanent or be flexible enough to allow future efforts "toward a more brotherly union."[17]

Events of the war years brought race into national consciousness to an unprecedented degree. The fight in the European theater against Hitler's patently racist ideology shed light on American racial discrimination as never before and raised the practical issues of discrimination in the armed services and in the defense industry.[18] The black press, with its powerful strain of isolationism, was initially divided on the war. "Our war," claimed the *Pittsburgh Courier*, "is not against Hitler in Europe, but against the Hitlers in America."[19] Eventually, however, while pointing out the irony of fighting Nazism while Jim Crow continued his reign over the Southern United States, the black press led the "Double V" campaign—calling for victory against racism, first in the war and second in America itself. The war had thus become an opportunity to point out the nation's hypocrisy and shame it toward racial justice.

The mainstream and the church press gradually followed the black press's lead, and arguments noting the similarity between segregationist and Nazi ideology slowly began appearing in white newspapers and magazines. In 1942, L. O. Hartman, editor of the Northern Methodist paper *Zion's Herald*, denounced the Methodist Church's acceptance of segregation, both in church and society, which he saw symbolized in its acceptance of the Central Jurisdiction: "In these days of war, with discrimination against the Negro becoming a nation-wide scandal, we are tongue-tied." Particularly tongue-tied was Methodism's official organ, the (Chicago) *Christian Advocate*, which "indicated the unwillingness of an important segment of the church to make an issue of what already had been settled."[20]

It is important, however, not to overstate this supposed silence, as even the often-cautious College of Methodist Bishops sounded similar themes as were found among the critics of segregation. In 1944 the bishops issued a statement on race, asserting, "The continent of Europe is drenched with blood because of the German doctrine of a superior race. In this country a minority group of 13 million Negroes is compelled to remain a detached racial unit, is accorded a sub-Christian status, is given an uncertain standard of livelihood, and all by the artificial standards which arise from racial grouping.... Racial minorities scattered throughout the earth are demanding to know what is meant by the affirmation of democracy that all men are created equal." Some of the denominational papers argued likewise, such as the 1947 article titled "White Supremacy—Master Race": "The notion of 'white supremacy' is a belief that the white race is inherently superior to all other races and should dominate other races politically, economically, and socially. It bears a striking resemblance to the phrase 'master race,' so frequently heard on the lips of the Nazis. It cannot stand . . . the indictment of the Christian faith. It is an idea against which millions of Americans fought a World War, and many died."[21] Methodist women, as we shall see, were even more forthright.

Even some traditionalists on race used the same arguments, as in the case of Benjamin F. Neal, a judge in Montezuma, Georgia. In the fall of 1948, when Georgia educators met in Milledgeville for a conference that included blacks, the proceedings were interrupted by shouts of "nigger" from the audience, and Klan insignia were drawn on the sides of buildings. In addition, the culprits attempted to intimidate the African American educators by following them out of town. Neal denounced such activities as reflecting "the spirit of Hitlerism," adding that "their ambitions and their methods are not unlike those used by Hitler to subjugate the races he claimed inferior to the Master Race."[22]

What is remarkable about these comments is that some two months earlier, the *Wesleyan Christian Advocate* had printed a conservative think piece on race and civil rights by the same judge. Neal argued that segregation in black church life was self-determined, so that the "black man" could "more freely give vent to the emotionalism of his nature." He defended the disfranchisement of blacks as a means of removing political corruption. He clung to notions of black inferiority, wherein the great mass of African Americans were "utterly incompetent to intelligently exercise the right of franchise and totally unfitted for jury duty." While claiming that whites had "given a pretty good home to the Negro," he bluntly asserted that "this is a white man's economy, a white man's civilization, and we in the South are unwilling for our standards of morality, for our social status, and for the future of our children and grandchildren to have its moral standards crushed and our ideals of common decency and the social relationships of life destroyed. . . . If our Jim Crow laws should be abolished and all segregation eliminated, the culture of the South would be destroyed; the morals of our people would degenerate beyond description, the religious life of both races would be demoralized and many of our churches destroyed."[23] Perspectives of this kind lay in wait for the announcement of the *Brown* decision.

Methodist Opinion after *Brown*

The postwar South was of course rocked by the Supreme Court's ruling in *Brown v. Board of Education*. The Methodist bishops knew the difficulty of implementing the decision quickly. Their initial statement supported the ruling as "in keeping with the attitudes of the Methodist Church," citing a 1952 General Conference statement on race. The bishops underscored the church's opportunity to provide leadership to the South, asserting: "We accept this responsibility, for one of the foundations stones of our faith is the belief that all men are brothers, equal in the sight of God. In that faith we declare our support of the ruling of the Supreme Court."[24] In stronger terms, the Methodist Board of Social and Economic Relations encouraged all Methodist churches "to move resolutely forward toward the goal of full participation of the people of all races in the life of the Church and the Community." Arguing that segregation clearly violated doctrines of the Fatherhood of God, the Brotherhood of Man, and the Kingdom of God, the board asserted: "We, therefore have no choice but to denounce it [segregation] as evil. This we do without equivocation."[25] Similarly, a group of young Methodists, meeting at the Southeastern Regional Leadership Training Conference at Lake Junaluska, North Carolina, unanimously approved a strong resolution of support on June 13, 1954, asserting, "We stand wholly in support of and applaud the Supreme Court ruling." The students further called on every level of the Methodist church to write letters to political and religious leaders in support of the decision.[26]

Unlike the Baptists and Presbyterians, the Methodist Church was at the time of *Brown* the only truly national denomination containing a Southern wing. Methodists in the South, confined mostly to the Southeastern Jurisdiction, found their defense of segregation a minority view within their Church. Thus, by the 1956 General Conference, Southern Methodists winced as the larger denomination received the bishops' word that "the principle of Christian brotherhood is no longer debatable" and approved a statement entitled, "The Methodist Church and Race." This document was a vigorous affirmation that the "Master permits no discrimination because of race, color, or national origin"; it concluded, "There must be no place in the Methodist Church for racial discrimination or enforced segregation."[27]

Understandably, the Church's Southern bishops, in their attempt to mediate between their segregationist members and the national denomination, expressed a cautious support of *Brown* while warning racial liberals not to push too far, too fast. Bishop William T. Watkins of Louisville, Kentucky, frankly told a group of Southern ministers in 1955 that "there are areas of brotherhood we are not in position to enter yet." He added: "We prefer to bring reflection on ourselves by confessing that we have not yet become fully Christian in the area of Christian brotherhood, rather than by casting an aspersion on the Christian religion by implying that it does not require us to be a full brother to the Negro." Then in language later incorporated in a statement by the bishops of the Southeastern Jurisdiction the next year, Watkins said, "The door to new areas of racial brotherhood simply cannot be blasted open. It must be opened from within. Any violent assault will not only fail but will keep the door closed indefinitely. Our slower pace is a swifter way to arrive at the goal. Whoever doubts this simply does not know the South."[28]

A North Georgia Conference resolution that echoed the caution of the bishops reminded church members that they were "Christian citizens in a democracy" who, according to the Methodist Discipline, were duty bound "to observe and obey the laws and commands of the governing or supreme authority in the country." Beyond this, the conference reiterated its support of the public schools and the need for white and black Christians to work to better understand each other.[29]

Public statements of even qualified support for *Brown* were hardly received without a murmur, especially in the Southeastern Jurisdiction. Before the bishops could even leave Chicago, their 1954 meeting place, a North Carolina attorney sent them a blistering telegram: "It is with righteous indignation I condemn you, as will all other self-respecting white and colored people in America condemn you, for undertaking to use the Methodist Church and its nine million communicants as an instrumentality in bringing about desegregation in American schools. . . . It is unthinkable that the Bishops . . . of the Methodist Church would allow themselves to be drawn into a political fight, which, if successful, would destroy the ethnological divisions of man created by God and give us a nation of mongrelized races."[30]

In Montgomery, Alabama, the Reverend Stanley Frazer, pastor of the St. James Methodist Church, mounted a spirited defense of segregation along with his criticisms of the Supreme Court and its supporters within the Methodist Church. In a lengthy article, Frazer called on lay members of the General Conference to "stand solidly against the choice of any one as a delegate who may help to bring about a situation that will create endless dissension in our Church." He argued that God had put his children in racial families with distinctive physical and ideological characteristics, establishing "'the bounds of their habitations' [Acts 17:26] on different continents." To call segregation an "un-Christian thing" was simply "not supported by the authority of the Holy Bible." In McCarthyite fashion, he indulged in guilt by association, accusing the NAACP or the Southern Conference Educational Fund as being communist organizations. He added: "If an 'un-Christian thing' is being done, it is by those who seek to use the Church to further political ends and to force on the rank and file of the American people a condition of strife that is distasteful to the thoughtful people of both races."[31]

Frazer ended 1954 by leading a meeting of Methodists opposed to the abolition of the Central Jurisdiction and in organizing Methodists from six different conferences into an interstate group called the Association of Methodist Ministers and Laymen. Their agenda was to oppose "any legislation or movement that seeks to 'liberalize' our present policy on racial matters." He began the next calendar year by complaining to Atlanta Bishop Arthur J. Moore about "the continuing pressure of the integrationists in every department of our Church work."[32] Over the next four years, Frazer's organization attracted more than 34,000 members. It also drafted and influenced the Alabama legislature to pass the Dumas Bill, which allowed any local church to go into state court to claim title to any church property if at least 65 percent of the adult membership agreed to secede from the national denomination. The bill, which had been designed to circumvent Methodist church law and allow a local church to withdraw from the Methodist church over the issue of racial segregation, was eventually declared unconstitutional.[33]

Alongside the laity's specific criticisms of the *Brown* ruling stood other, more veiled complaints. In 1952 the Board of Stewards of the Lindale (Georgia) Methodist Church approved a resolution "opposing this cancerous growth of Communism in our great Church . . . We deplore the socialistic and communistic actions and teachings of some of the contributors to the literature published by our Methodist Publishing House." The statement also called on Bishop Arthur J. Moore to make every effort to "rid our Church of persons who either knowingly or through ignorance would destroy our Church and our sacred way of life." Connecting such subversion with criticism of segregation, a few months later a laywoman from Sylvester, Georgia, complained about Methodist Sunday school literature: "Have we gone so far Leftist that our commentators *must* use a writer of Lillian Smith's caliber?" The writer enclosed a copy of the lesson, which included a quotation from the liberal Methodist's *Killers of the Dream.*[34] A few weeks before *Brown* was announced, another Georgia Methodist woman complained about what she saw as anti-Americanism in her denomination. She would be surprised, she asserted, to see a church conference enthusiastically salute the American flag. She connected this malady with a certain perspective on race matters, sarcastically complaining, "Our Methodist Church . . . [is] constantly belittling America. 'America is a big, rich bully' and 'poor, dear Russia is trying so hard.' Russia's millions of degraded human slaves are not mentioned but 'the *horrible* treatment accorded colored people in America' is of prime importance."[35]

These comments reveal that Georgia Methodist women were not unanimous in supporting progressive change in church and society on matters of segregation and race relations. Nonetheless, in January 1957, in the midst of the white South's "massive resistance" to desegregation, a group of prominent Methodists met in Atlanta for one of many denomination-wide Interracial Leadership Conferences. One of the conference workshops, which examined Methodist progress in race relations up to that point, credited the women and youth "for leading out in example against race prejudice and in integration of groups meetings of various kinds. They seem more liberal in this respect than the men's groups."[36] Thus, there is good evidence, especially when the involvements of Dorothy Tilly and her colleagues are considered, that women did more than merely issue statements of goodwill. Indeed, they led the way in the Methodist Church and became the most progressive element in the white South.

Dorothy Tilly and Methodist Women's Organizations

Since antebellum times, Christian activism among white Southern women found expression, at least to the extent allowed by the male heads of their households, in mission work among the slaves. The wife of Frederick Douglass's owner was certainly not unique in teaching their young slave to read, and by the time of the Civil War, Methodist women were busying themselves in similar pursuits. One Georgia woman implored her bishop, "The field, of all others, for the care and labor of Southern women is the mission to the colored people. . . . Bishop, give us work; we can do it, not at once perhaps, but let us begin."[37]

The Methodist tradition assured that women who entered the Civil War years with the slaves as their mission field would continue to work among the freed persons into the twentieth century. Wesleyan-Arminian theology avoided the extreme Calvinist conceptions of original sin and allowed for the possibility of human improvement. John Wesley's own ethical activities and preaching formed another element in the Methodist tradition that was conducive to social reform. The combination of this tradition and the practice of Southern women working among African Americans created just one area of the Social Gospel activities John Patrick McDowell has described.

By the 1920s, Methodist leader Carrie Parks Johnson served as part-time chairperson of the WMC's Commission on Race Relations and as the part-time Director of Woman's Work for the Commission on Interracial Cooperation. In this dual capacity, she informed Southern churchwomen about conditions among African Americans and organized women to work for better race relations in the South. She diligently recruited Methodists for

CIC work and used the CIC as a resource for Methodist work. Alice G. Knotts estimates that Methodist women made up more than half of all the women involved in interracial dialogues and race relations studies. A south Georgia Methodist women's auxiliary participated in a variety of interracial activities, including providing for blacks a public rest room, a clinic, a nurse, a playground, and day care facilities. Taking the equality seriously in "separate but equal," the women's groups would not move toward challenging Jim Crow until the World War II era. As Knotts argues, however, they legitimized interracial work and gradually, "knowingly or unknowingly," undermined segregation.[38] As the war and its aftermath brought issues of racial justice into clearer focus, Methodist women's organizations worked on a three-pronged race relations agenda that included education, the continued antilynching crusade, and eventually civil rights and politics. Out of this context emerged Southern Methodism's unlikely leader, Dorothy Tilly, and her Fellowship of the Concerned.

EDUCATIONAL WORK

By the mid-1940s, the Women's Division of the Board of Missions, particularly its department of Christian Social Relations and Local Church Activities (CSR/LCA), had increased its interest in human rights and publicly called upon church and society to ensure these inherent rights to persons of all races. Through various educational programs, the CSR/LCA sought to induce Methodists to exercise moral leadership in replacing racial and religious bigotry and oppression with civil liberties and peace. In addition, from 1943 on, the women's organization committed itself to interracial meetings several times a year, issuing invitations based on geographical location rather than race or jurisdiction. They also became the Methodist Church's strongest advocates for participation in World Communion Sunday and Race Relations Sunday.[39] In sharp contrast to general public opinion in the South, and to the generally cautious tones by the bishops, the Woman's Division in 1944 became the first agency within Methodism to declare segregation as evil.[40]

Soon thereafter, they began a large-scale campaign to change the denomination's attitudes and policies on race. In 1945 the Woman's Division called a denominational commission to "advocate full participation by people of all races in all aspects of the church's life in nondiscriminatory ways, including participation in 'non-racial congregations and conferences.'" That same year the CSR/LCA recommended that its societies "work immediately for the equalization of educational opportunity in the United States for all people without regard to race, creed, or place of residence."[41] The Women's Division went even further, becoming the first Methodist organization formally to call for the abolition of Central Jurisdiction. Their memorial asked the 1948 General Conference to "take such steps as may be necessary to abolish this pattern of segregation in the Methodist Church."[42]

In the 1950s, the Women's Division adopted a "Charter on Racial Policies," which became the organization's primary tool to influence public education and federal housing policies in the South. Committing itself to creating "a fellowship and social order without racial barriers," the women asserted, "Time marches on! The ground swell of human equality under God is becoming unmistakably the ground swell of human equality under law! ... We must plant the right seeds." Specifically, planting the seeds meant Methodist women working in their churches and communities to provide general information about segregation, in particular to publicize conditions in schools for blacks, to bring parents of both races together to discuss problems, and to solicit state and federal funds for all public schools "without discrimination in any form."[43]

In the first weeks after the *Brown* ruling, while many in the southeastern jurisdiction were temporizing and issuing cautious public statements, the General Assembly of Methodist Women quickly went on record as the first Methodist agency to support the decision. Their statement "rejoiced" in the ruling and affirmed a new urgency in working to eliminate segregation from the nation and the denomination.[44] Similarly, the Woman's Division welcomed the court's ruling as an opportunity to press forward in integrating Methodist schools. Two years later, the same organization petitioned the General Conference to request "that the institutions of the church, local churches, colleges, universities, theological schools, hospitals, and homes carefully study their policies and practices as they relate to race, making certain that these policies and practices are Christian."[45]

Reflecting this perspective, one Georgia Methodist woman refused to let Stanley Frazer's treatise in defense of segregation go unanswered, taking on the minister point by point. She reminded readers of the *Wesleyan Christian Advocate* that "large conferences of Methodist youth and Methodist women all over the South have been passing resolutions" to abolish segregation within the Methodist Church for "more than a decade now." She underscored the interracial and nonpaternalistic work of Methodist women, sharply noting:

It seems on analysis that the only group which falls into a category within the church, that has not been moving decidedly toward inter-racial co-operation is the men. . . . it is they who have failed to see how strong [and] deeply-rooted this feeling is among young adults, the youth, many of the women, and some of the older adults in Methodist churches in every state of the South. The same lack of sensitivity, unfortunately, has persisted among some of the men who are ministers in our Annual Conference. That they have listened politely to the resolutions presented by the women and passed over them as being "sentiment[al]" or "too hasty." That they have scorned the statements of the Methodist Youth Fellowship and groups of young adults as long the "hot-headedness of youth" and [the] "unfortunate results of agitators."

To Frazer's point that blacks preferred their own schools and churches, she raised what she considered the obvious question: "Would you really want membership in a church where you were not welcome, where your children would be shunned by some and ignored by others?" Those who want integration, "being human beings and not psychopaths, they will wait until they get an honest welcome." On Frazer's point that the *Brown* decision was politically motivated, she replied that the Court made its decision "to reassure the rest of the world, whose population is overwhelmingly colored, that our nation means what we declare in our intentions to work with them for a peaceful world." Finally, "with all the force of conviction" she could muster, she rejected the minister's biblical interpretation that segregation was by God's will and design, citing Peter and Paul's New Testament insights into the inclusiveness of the Christian gospel and Jesus' willingness to minister to Samaritans.[46]

Dorothy Tilly's activism emerged naturally out of this well-developed tradition of social concern. Beyond her local church membership in Atlanta, she was active in the North Georgia Conference, where she served on a number of committees concerned with children, tenancy, and race relations. She had served on the Women's Division's Committee on Rural Life since 1933. From 1940 to 1948 she was secretary of Christian Social Relations of the Woman's Society of Christian Service, through which she made contact with Methodist women of nine Southern states. Three times she was elected as a delegate to the General Conference.[47] Outside her specifically Methodist involvements, her activities also included serving as field secretary of the women's division of the SRC (which she regarded "as a mission of the Methodist Church in her part of the world"), the Georgia Interracial Committee, the Georgia Council of Church Women, and the Georgia Conference of Social Work. In 1944 she was a lobbyist in Washington to save the Farm Security Administration.[48]

In the late 1930s, she conducted leadership seminars at Paine College, a historically black Methodist school in Augusta, Georgia, designed to train black women for leadership in the churches.[49] She spearheaded a drive to establish a state school to train delinquent African American girls. She worked with black women's clubs in the state; her efforts raised money for the project, bought a plot of land, and put a building on it with additional aid from the federal government's Works Progress Administration. When a proposal for funding failed to pass the state legislature, she mobilized 28,000 angry churchwomen to lobby the legislators, who eventually passed the appropriation over the veto of Governor Eugene Talmadge. When the school opened in an interracial dedication service, a participating pastor said, "I dedicated that which has already been consecrated by the tears of the women of both races in Georgia.' . . . As many a preacher will tell you, when it comes to courage to do the right thing, the women are far ahead of the men."[50]

Antilynching

Not all Methodist women opposed lynching or developed progressive views of African Americans. Perhaps the most widely known woman in turn-of-the-century Georgia, Rebecca Latimer Felton, represented a radical counterpart to the likes of Dorothy Tilly or the Association of Southern Women for the Prevention of Lynching (ASWPL) president Jessie Daniel Ames. Active in the Holiness movement of Georgia Methodism, Felton also became a powerful force in Democratic politics after the death of her husband, Dr. William H. Felton, who had served as an influential member of the U.S. House from Georgia. Along with Tom Watson, she wielded wide influence in the state and became the first woman to serve in the U.S. Senate when she was appointed to fill Watson's term after his death in 1920.[51]

Felton was far from a progressive on race. She complained about the possible election of Teddy Roosevelt, who had drawn Southern fire for inviting Booker T. Washington to eat with him in the White House. She sardonically warned: "Voter, take your choice. Shall this be a white man's government, or a mixture of black, tan, and white?" In a 1898 letter to the *Atlanta Journal,* she weighed in on the lynching question: "When you take the negro into your embrace . . . and make him believe he is your man and brother, . . . so long will lynching prevail. . . . if it requires lynching to protect woman's dearest possession from . . . drunken human beasts, then I say lynch a thousand a week if necessary."[52]

By the time of Felton's death in 1930, women like Tilly and Jessie Daniel Ames had moved through their involvement with the Commission on Interracial Cooperation and had branched out into the ASWPL. Although the occurrence of lynchings had declined after the 1930s, the September 7, 1940, lynching of Austin Callaway in LaGrange, Georgia, marked the first in the state in two years and brought a wave of protests from across the nation. The Methodist women of the LaGrange district in annual session on September 16 issued a statement, as did the LaGrange Ministerial Association.[53] Methodist women all over Georgia then renewed their efforts to bring attention to failures of racial justice in the courts, lauding leaders who upheld justice, advocating clemency in race-based cases, and pressuring public officials to sign the antilynching pledges. In 1941 Ames wrote to Lillian Smith indicating that out of 43,000 pledge signatures filed with the ASWPL, all but 3,000 were identified as Methodist women.[54]

Tilly was centrally involved with these activities. Because Rebecca Felton's justification of lynching as protective of Southern white women was echoed all across the South, Tilly and the others made a persuasive counterargument that the collective voice of white women could carry great weight when "raised in protest against violence and to prove that no so such measures were required, effective, or to be tolerated in a civilized and democratic society."[55]

In 1941 she helped Methodist women mount an economic boycott of the businesses of every Klan member in the South Georgia Conference. The boycott also resulted in the first antilynching law passed by the state general assembly. On another occasion she faced down a Mississippi lynch mob. She stood in the doorway of the jail and quietly persuaded the mob to break up and return to their homes. Five years later she investigated a race riot in Columbia, Tennessee, along with the lynching of two couples in Monroe, Georgia. Two days after the incident, Tilly quietly canvassed the town and gradually gathered the full story. One woman told her she had heard rumors and had even observed what she had thought to be a rehearsal for the lynching. When Tilly asked the woman what she did in response, the woman simply confessed she had not known what to do. Having received a similar reply from a minister in Columbia, Tennessee, Tilly wrote a leaflet for future use to instruct concerned citizens: "Call the sheriff and tell him you expect him to do his duty. Call and tell the state patrol the same. Call the local editor, the state-wide papers, the ministers, the civic leaders, and the headquarters of the network—the Southern Regional Council in Atlanta."[56]

Politics and Civil Rights

Tilly's antilynching and educational activities often overlapped, as they also provided her entrée into politics. Her efforts to establish the school for African American girls had put her at cross-purposes with Governor Eugene Talmadge, and she led large numbers of Methodist women to support his opponent, Ellis Arnall, in the 1942 gubernatorial election. Along the campaign trail, Arnall had made a public remark that seemed to condone lynching. Women of the CIC mounted a letter campaign to convince Arnall that women in the state rejected lynching. Arnall's supporters arranged a meeting between the candidate and Tilly, who convinced him that he was in danger of losing the support of churchwomen throughout the state. To make amends, he agreed to issue a statement opposing "mob violence in all its insidious forms." In the midst of this crusade, a reporter asked her what was happening in the South. She replied, "Nothing that wasn't happening in my girlhood. There have always been Southerners who put humanity above color."[57]

In 1934, out of her work with the Farm Security Administration, Tilly became acquainted with Eleanor Roosevelt, who shared many of her concerns related to racial justice, particularly federal antilynching legislation. The first lady often spoke at meetings of women's organizations, and in April 1944, Tilly and several other Methodist women were invited to visit Mrs. Roosevelt in the White House. On that visit, Tilly invited her to speak at an assembly of Methodist women at Lake Junaluska, North Carolina, in July. In introducing Roosevelt to the group, Tilly said the seminar was focused on the condition of minority groups in America and designed to help the women "think through our Christian citizenship responsibilities for these groups and establish a program of action." Roosevelt's speech dealt with race relations as one of many problems awaiting the postwar world. The war, she argued, had underscored the issue of race relations, which she called a national as well as a Southern problem. "The thing that makes it important nationally," she continued, "is the way America is being watched by other countries to see if we cope with our minority problems better than they do. The whole question of our religious belief will be examined as well as our political beliefs. They expect us as the greatest and strongest Democracy to take the lead in giving the same rights to all people."[58]

Tilly and Mrs. Roosevelt continued their friendship over the years, with Tilly visiting her in her Hyde Park, New York, home in 1947. Two years later, in her memoir, Roosevelt indicated her deep regard for Tilly:

I had great admiration for the courage of Mrs. M. E. Tilly of Atlanta,
Georgia, who was the executive secretary of the Methodist women's
organization. I was told that whenever a lynching occurred, she went
alone or with a friend, as soon as she heard of it, to investigate the
circumstances. Only a Southern woman could have done this, but
even for a Southern woman it seemed to me to require great moral as
well as physical courage. She is a Christian who believes in all Christ's
teachings, including the concept that all men are brothers; and though
she is a white Southern woman she deeply resents the fact that white
Southern women are so often used as a pretext for lynching.[59]

It was likely through a recommendation from Eleanor Roosevelt that Tilly
was invited to serve on President Truman's Committee on Civil Rights.

To Secure These Rights

In late 1945, the phone rang at the Tilly residence in Atlanta. It was the White
House calling to invite Tilly to serve on the president's Committee on Civil
Rights. Hearing the invitation, the sixty-two-year-old woman buckled with
surprise and gasped, "Who, me?" Her excited husband stood next to her,
cheering her on, urging, "Say yes! You can do it!"[60] She quickly accepted the
assignment to travel to Washington almost every week for the next several
months to help the committee study racial conditions throughout the nation and to make recommendations to the president and Congress. The only
white woman and one of only two Southerners on the committee, she and
fellow Southerner Frank Porter Graham, president of the University of North
Carolina, fully supported the end of segregation; they worked to make sure
the committee saw it as a national problem, rather than merely a Southern
one. Together, they successfully softened the committee's final report so that
the South would not be singularly castigated for its racial policies. She also
argued strongly that federal aid to segregated schools be maintained.
Throughout their deliberations, Tilly worked to keep the other members of
the committee abreast of developments and the social realities in the South,
along with pointing out instances where other regions provided less than
sterling examples of race relations.[61]

The 178-page report, *To Secure These Rights*, which was published on
October 29, 1947, called for the "elimination of segregation based on race,
color, creed, or national origin, from American life." The committee cited
Supreme Court justice John Harlan's dissent to the *Plessy v. Ferguson* decision, which argued that racial segregation implied an unconstitutional badge

of inferiority. Both Harlan's dissent and the committee's report anticipated
the eventual language of the *Brown* ruling. The report thus argued that equality within segregation was "one of the outstanding myths of American history." The report further proposed a federal antilynching law; the abolition
of all obstacles to voting, especially the poll tax; the end of segregation in the
military, and in public housing and accommodations; and recommended
cutting off federal funds to all recipient bodies continuing to practice segregation. In addition, the report called for the establishment of a permanent
commission on civil rights, a joint congressional committee, a civil rights
division of the Justice Department, and a fair employment practices committee. In all, it was one of the most important government statements on
civil rights in American history. Tilly and Graham added a mild dissent,
indicating that although they favored the end of segregation, they opposed
"its imposition by federal laws and sanctions."[62]

Methodist women were bursting with pride in their "favorite daughter,"
and within weeks of the report's publication, they had Tilly make a comprehensive report of the committee's work to the Women's Division. The Department of CSR/LCA also convinced the entire Women's Division to support
the policies and to issue a statement commending President Truman and
urging him "to rectify current discriminations in health, education, and
employment" within the federal government. The Woman's Division eagerly
committed itself to helping circulate the report throughout the nation. Tilly
had made a sixty-page list of women she wanted to receive a copy of *To
Secure These Rights,* and she personally sent out copies to more than a hundred church leaders across the country. Following Tilly's lead, that spring,
the executive committee included in its budget additional funds to purchase
and distribute 6,000 copies of the report. One correspondent wrote Tilly
that she was "glad your Committee used the word 'immediately' in regards
to abolishing segregation. We too often try to excuse our inactivities, ab-
solving ourselves from all blame by thinking and preaching that action must
not take place until the next generation."[63]

Dorothy Tilly spent most of the two years after the publication of *To
Secure These Rights* discussing its proposals with church congregations and
lay audiences all over the United States. In 1949 she appeared in thirty
states. To sometimes critical white Southerners, she defended her support
of the committee's report: "I do not believe that there is anyone in the
United States, who, had he been with us and seen the things we did, would
have signed his name to any less strong a report." Large crowds attended
her talks, and fan letters poured in congratulating her for participating in

the study. She told reporters that she had "received only twelve letters opposing my work."[64]

She reviewed the report and was one of the main speakers at a SRC meeting in Atlanta in February 1948. Some 400 people from across eleven states attended the conference, which published a report called "The Condition of Our Rights." Six days later, Herman Talmadge's segregationist newspaper, *The Statesman,* devoted its entire news section to denounce the meeting.[65] Speaking on her home turf, she addressed the North Georgia Conference Wesleyan Service Guild on June 26–27, 1948, holding her audience spellbound as she called on her fellow Christian women to help battle hate in America: "More than 20,000,000 people are denied justice in this land because of national origin, color, or the faith of their fathers. We must work harder and pray harder to make this a land of liberty. . . . It is up to Christians to heal the sore spots all over our country. The hardest part of the golden rule is to want for someone else what you want for yourself. Democracy, brotherhood, and human rights are the practical expressions of the eternal worth of every child of God."[66]

She carried the same message to venues outside the South, recognizing the battle was national, not just regional. Speaking at the February 13, 1949, annual interracial service of the Springfield, Illinois Council of Churches, Tilly told the audience, "Brotherhood is the basis for peace, and brotherhood must begin with the church." A reporter for the *Springfield Register* told readers that Tilly was "representative of what Southern white women are doing to abolish 'Jim Crowism,' lynching, segregated schools, and other discriminatory customs." She implored the audience to help uproot hate, "America's public enemy No. 1":

In our nation 22 million persons are denied opportunity for employment in fields in which they have been trained; many are denied justice, medical care in hours of need, and a voice in your government. . . . Our heads have outgrown our hearts; our minds have developed faster than our morals and science has outstripped our spirits. We invented gunpowder and atomic bombs before we acquired the morality to use them wisely. We learned the secrets of chemistry before we grew enough spiritually to refuse to make poison gas. We brought in the machine age before we had the morals to manage it. . . . One hundred seventy-three years after the Declaration of Independence, which says that all persons are created equal, and 82 years after Lincoln's Gettysburg Address . . . , [it] now becomes our duty to see that our communities give civil rights to our citizens, regardless of race, color, or creed. Our world is a battle between those who would exploit the hatred in it and those who would strengthen the fellowship within it. Violence may be infectious, but liberty and courage are also infectious."[67]

Ever the optimist, Tilly was sure, in the words of a later sermon by Martin Luther King Jr., that the "arm of the moral universe" was bending "toward justice." In early 1950, she told a Louisville, Kentucky, audience that civil rights reforms were catching on at the grassroots level. "I am encouraged by progress seen in Kentucky where you have admitted Negroes to your state university, and by progress in my home state of Georgia, where we have whipped the white primary and the poll tax." Always recruiting new soldiers into the struggle, she assured them, "There are no sacrifices to fighting for what's right and the compensations are many. I have had the most satisfactory, thrilling, and stirring life possible."[68]

One pragmatic result of Tilly's far-flung advocacy tour was the boost she gave to President Truman's election plans in the hotly contested 1948 presidential contest. Truman, having seen his high-profile civil rights policies alienate large portions of the white South, desperately needed the help of influential Southerners like Tilly. Although she was reluctant to campaign for the president overtly, her membership on the Civil Rights Committee and vocal support of its conclusions constituted an implied endorsement. Just after Truman's upset victory, Channing Tobias, director of New York's Phelps-Stokes Fund and a fellow member of the Civil Rights Committee, wrote Tilly with his thanks: "I deeply appreciate your message referring to the election of President Truman. . . . I am glad that Georgia, in spite of its many weaknesses, rebuffed the Dixiecrats and came up strongly in the Truman column. I know you had a lot to do with this through the exercise of your strong influence with the church women of both races throughout the state."[69] Methodist women followed Tilly's lead and sought to use their influence in the next election cycle. In the 1952 presidential election, the department of CSR/LCA issued "A Call to Methodist Women," reminding them of their citizenship responsibilities to elect persons who would "seek to enact laws and protect rights of all persons regardless of race, creed, or nationality."[70]

In the aftermath of her service to the White House, Tilly capitalized on her fame by corresponding with Attorney General Tom C. Clark, along with many state governors, sheriffs, and judges throughout the South. She advocated improvements in the court system and more fairness in civil rights cases, especially lynchings.[71] Out of her solicitude for these issues, particularly lynching, and in light of the demise of the ASWPL, Tilly found her inspiration to create a new organization of churchwomen to continue these efforts.

The Fellowship of the Concerned

Before and after the *Brown* decision, it was in the activities of the FOC that Dorothy Tilly and her fellow Methodist women most clearly "mothered" their communities toward racial justice and better race relations. Like all good mothers who watch out for pain among their children and try to ease it, who guide their children in growing up to do the right thing in responsible citizenship, these "city mothers" kept vigilant watch over their communities and enabled them to experience growth in race matters.

In the summer of 1949, Tilly visited Greenville, South Carolina, to attend the trial of thirty-one whites charged with the lynching of an African American named Willie Earle. She watched as the racial jokes of the defense attorneys and the muffled laughter of the all-white jury made a mockery of the trial. She was particularly angered when the jury acquitted all of the defendants. Tilly became convinced that the presence of more fair-minded local church people, the sort of women in her own circle of contacts, would bring such injustice into the light of day, where it could be ameliorated. She hit on the idea of recruiting a cadre of Methodist and other churchwomen to become a presence in their communities to observe and inform the larger population of racial unfairness in their courts, police departments, and election systems. She believed that "there's so much goodness everywhere, there's not a spot we can't reach," and she determined to build a network of local watchdogs in every county seat in the South.[72]

She put her ideas into action by bringing together 165 leaders of religious women's groups on September 8–9, 1949, for a conference at Atlanta's Wesley Memorial Methodist Church. She told the conferees, "I am concerned that our constitutional freedoms are not shared by all our people. My religion convinces me that they must be and gives me courage to study, work, and lead others to the fulfillment of equal justice under the law." Many of the women drawn to the meeting had never before participated in an interracial luncheon. Reminding them that black citizens often suffered discrimination from white judges and juries, she asserted that America's moral leadership in the world, placed upon the nation by its religious convictions and its world position, demanded that such failures of democracy be corrected. "The remedies," she added, "lie with us in our own communities."[73] She recognized that her audience had come because of concerns similar to her own and proposed a new interracial, interdenominational organization that would take up and expand the work of the now defunct ASWPL. The organization would be called the Fellowship of the Concerned.

In the aftermath of the Greenville, South Carolina, lynching trial, one of the first projects Tilly took on was a counterattack on a Klan-sympathizing member of the South Carolina Assembly. Alexander Miller, a regional director of the Anti-Defamation League, phoned her to report that a legislator had invited grand dragon Sam Green of the Georgia Klan to speak to the Palmetto State's legislature. Tilly immediately consulted her massive index file of ministers and leaders of women's groups across the South. She quickly notified key people in South Carolina, who avalanched the assemblyman with hundreds of protest letters. He eventually rescinded his invitation to Green and denounced Tilly as "this foreign woman from Georgia for poking into South Carolina's affairs." A year later, South Carolina passed an anti-Klan law. Tilly was thus among the first white Southerners to be pilloried as an "outside agitator." To what she considered a ludicrous charge, she gave a simple reply: "What happens to any person in this country is the business of the whole country."[74]

Early on, working closely with the SRC, Tilly held workshops in Atlanta and elsewhere focused on school desegregation and justice in the courts. Like many civil rights activists and Supreme Court watchers in the period, she anticipated that segregation's days were numbered and believed that the women of the South should be the "shock absorbers" of social change. These early workshops were designed to train churchwomen what to look for and what questions to ask of local officials, along with tactics for nudging them toward racial justice. Tilly, who counted fund-raising among her skills, also tapped her contacts in foundations and religious organizations for donations to fund FOC conferences.[75]

FOC workshops trained members to visit local sheriffs, judges, and other officials, and to publicize their visits, particularly to report their findings to SRC headquarters, where a file was established on each community. Tilly developed a questionnaire for each area under scrutiny for the use of FOC contacts in each locality. For example, in the area of administration, FOC women asked officials about the organization and personnel of their police departments, their salary scales, how they attracted qualified officers, and whether they employed African American officers. As to training, they inquired into the hours of instruction given police, the subjects taught, and whether they were instructed in the laws, ordinances, and constitutional procedures relating to civil liberties. Regarding performance, their questionnaires uncovered the number of blacks arrested compared with the number of whites, and the number of homicides of both races. They asked whether there were marked differences in the nature of the homicides; they asked whether places of amusement were adequately patrolled; they asked whether police departments had any preventative activities designed to avoid racial conflict. In the area of community relations, they sought to determine African Americans' feelings about the police in their communities. Were there trouble areas in housing, recreation, or other public services?[76]

Tilly's troops informed themselves about local conditions in the courts as well, operating with a specific goal: "Know your courts as you know your schools." The FOC women made their influence felt as they encouraged better selection and training for police, and worked for the hiring of black police. They publicly commended officials who showed courage and integrity in race relations and they called attention to violations. Later, when their agenda expanded to overseeing election laws and practices, the women sought to make sure registration and voting procedures were fair, both in theory and in actual practice. They publicly opposed state registration measures that threatened the security of any voters, they urged officials to train poll workers "in the proper performance of their duties, and volunteered to serve as local election managers and clerks." They also worked to shape public opinion by discussing problems with local newspaper editors. In particular, they commended the adoption of improved journalistic practices in the handling of "racial news," for example, applying the titles "Mr." or "Mrs." to African Americans as well as whites.[77]

After they were trained, the women signed the FOC Pledge, part of which read: "I, as a church woman, am concerned that our constitutional freedoms are not shared by all of our people. . . . I am willing to sit in the courts and to visit police and other law enforcement agencies to learn how law is administered in my community. I will work with others in times of tension to see that the rights of all are protected."[78] Before long, whenever unjust practices were uncovered in a local community, word somehow got to Tilly, who in turn contacted someone on the scene, and often went there herself. On her organization's mothering success, she commented: "We may not always get justice, but we can get public opinion so stirred up that the same thing can't ever happen in that community again."[79]

Often the work of these women had to be carried out in secret. In 1956 Tilly had promised the editor of the *Methodist Woman* an article on what

Southern church women were doing to allay tensions in the South. In the interim, however, escalating tensions forced Tilly to inform the editor that for the protection of her FOC colleagues, she would not be able to discuss their activities fully. "The women are still meeting and working," she wrote, "but are giving no publicity to what they are doing. They are very bravely trying to work, in spite of opposition so great that it might affect their husband's business—and in some instances, it has already affected their standing in the community."[80] Sometimes women told their husbands they were going shopping or visiting relatives, rather than informing them that they were attending FOC workshops. Tilly reveled in their courage, saying that their slogan was "to find a conviction that will not rest, a faith that will not shrink, and courage that will not waiver [sic]."[81] In addition, some were silent members of the FOC network—the conscience-tortured wives of Klansmen, whose value to the movement, Tilly said, "lies in their keeping their eyes and ears open and their mouths shut."[82]

Naturally, the petite crusader in her flowery hats could not manage these "subversive activities" without virulent opposition and harassment. Just after the publication of *To Secure These Rights*, a newspaper editor denounced her as a "parasite who while living upon funds furnished by the Methodist Church had rendered much of her service to the cause of Socialism and Communism."[83] Before Tilly even managed to leave Washington to return home, her husband received a bomb threat. Atlanta mayor William Hartsfield provided police protection, and the Justice Department dispatched FBI agents around their home. Not knowing whether the cars cruising the alley behind his home were the Klan or the police, Milton Tilly lost a night's sleep in the aftermath of the threat.[84]

She also received hate mail and harassing phone calls. She received an anonymous letter with the heading, "To the Two Southern Residents of the Civil Rights (?) Committee." It read: "You are not worthy to live in the South. The Southern public knows that you are not Southerners. The damage that has already been done is irreparable. . . . You cheap publicity seekers and nigger lovers such as Eleanor Roosevelt, President (?) Truman, and others . . . will be the direct cause of more lynchings than have ever, or would have ever occurred." As to African Americans: "Their feeble minds, and yours, cannot grasp the resulting chaos your recommendations will bring. you are bringing about insolence, bigotry, as well as assault, rape, murder, and a number of other outrages. We admit that the murder of 4 Negroes in Georgia was a dreadful affair, but . . . something had to be done. by this action, possibly 4 thousand lives were saved. Leave the South to the Southerners. we have handled the situation for a century and we will continue to do so."[85]

Interestingly, Methodist women more generally were getting a taste of the same medicine. During the same month that Senator Joseph McCarthy began his anticommunist crusade, an article in *Reader's Digest* criticized "Methodism's Pink Fringe." Interracial meetings and civil rights legislation sponsored by the Woman's Division provided "evidence" for critics that Methodist women were communists.[86]

In 1958 segregationist editor Bill Cleghorn dispatched photographers to an FOC meeting in Montgomery, Alabama. Reporters went along to record the license plate numbers of the attendees, and Cleghorn published the names and business connections of the women's husbands. As a result, the Montgomery FOC women received harassing phone calls for the next several weeks. A livid Tilly wrote to Cleghorn, accusing him of trampling the women's basic constitutional rights. In response to such efforts at intimidation, she admonished her colleagues in Alabama: "The men in the car, the uninvited guest, and the editor are too *little* to intimidate praying women. Don't let them—defeat them. Don't give them that much power over your lives."[87] To counter her own crank phone calls, Tilly often tried to evangelize her callers or played a recording of the Lord's Prayer. "It always helps me," she noted, "and it silences the one at the other end of the phone."[88]

The FOC was largely the organizational extension of Dorothy Tilly's crusading spirit and indomitable personality. She managed the work of the organization single-handedly, with no other officers and no secretarial help. There were no membership dues, and meetings were held irregularly. By early 1950, however, more than 4,000 women, mostly from the Peach State, had affiliated with the FOC.[89]

Assessing the results of Tilly's work, particularly that with the FOC, is difficult, although she was perennially upbeat about the good she and her colleagues were doing. A few days after the formation of the FOC, six women visited the editors of the two Atlanta newspapers. They reminded the journalists of the unfavorable publicity their stories were giving the South. They reminded them of the racial slurs implicit when they told only of black crime but not black accomplishments. They further called on the editors to discontinue the practice of segregating stories about African Americans and urged them to use "Mr." and "Mrs." with the names of blacks. The following Sunday the *Atlanta Constitution* carried a prominent, two-column story (with photographs) of the inauguration of the president of the African American Gammon Theological Seminary.[90]

Another example of FOC success was an occasion when Tilly got word of a south Georgia community where a black schoolhouse had been burned. After whites had moved out of the community, an empty school building was donated to blacks in the community, who raised $100 to repair one of the two rooms as a community center. When the center was officially opened, a white man told the blacks, "You will never hold another meeting in that schoolhouse," and the next day the building was burned to the ground. Tilly rounded up two women from the community and contacted a local minister and the sheriff. The FOC committee raised money to rebuild the structure in order to "build back race relations." Tilly told reporters she did it simply by giving the facts to "a few good people in the community, who in turn stir up the consciences of the rest." After all, she often pointed out, "There is not a spot in the South without its good, liberal-minded people who are terribly hurt when disaster and disgrace fall on the community through broken human relationships. They are eager to do something that will say to the Negroes and to the outside world, 'We have had no part in this evil thing.'"[91]

Tilly, explaining the religious and civil rights work of the Methodist and other churchwomen she led, often spoke of seeking "a way to ease the tensions of our section and make it a proving ground for democracy."[92] In this manner, the FOC sowed seeds that would later come to fruition. They shined their lights on unfairness and pushed their Southern communities toward justice. Like good "city mothers," they used their powers of encouragement to help their communities reach their potential in matters of race relations. In their straight-laced, Methodist piety, they also embodied a powerful Social Gospel.

NOTES

"'City Mothers': Dorothy Tilly, Georgia Methodist Women, and Black Civil Rights" by Andrew M. Manis appeared originally in *Before Brown: Civil Rights and White Backlash in the Modern South,* edited by Glenn Feldman (University of Alabama Press, 2004). Reprinted with permission of the University of Alabama Press.

1. Quoted in Dorothy Tilly, "Christian Social Relations in the Southeastern Jurisdiction," *Methodist Woman,* n.d., n.p., copy in Dorothy Rogers Tilly Papers, Robert W. Woodruff Library, Emory University, Atlanta, Georgia (hereinafter referred to as Tilly Papers).

2. John Patrick McDowell, *The Social Gospel in the South: The Woman's Home Mission Movement in the Methodist Episcopal Church, Southern 1889–1939* (Baton Rouge: Louisiana State University Press, 1982).

3. Information on Tilly's early life is found in the biographical sketch introducing the Tilly Papers; Arnold Shankman, "Dorothy Tilly and the Fellowship of the

Concerned," in *From the Old South to the New: Essays on the Transitional South*, ed. Walter J. Fraser Jr. and Winfred B. Moore (Westport, Conn.: Greenwood Press, 1981), 241; Shankman, "Dorothy Rogers Tilly," in *Encyclopedia of Religion in the South*, ed. Samuel S. Hill (Macon, Ga.: Mercer University Press, 1984), 782; *Macon Telegraph,* June 3, 1962; *Wesleyan Christian Advocate* (hereafter *WCA*), March 18, 1965.

4. Dorothy Tilly, "The Fellowship of the Concerned" (hereafter Tilly, "FOC"), *Woman's Press,* February 5, 1950, 8; Shankman, "Dorothy Rogers Tilly," 782.

5. Apropos of Tilly and her FOC colleagues was the designation of "city mothers," first suggested by Jessie Ash Arndt, "Women's Crusade Spurs Fairer Treatment of Negroes in Southern U.S.," *Christian Science Monitor,* January 9, 1953, n.p., copy in Tilly Papers, Woodruff Library, Emory University.

6. W. C. James, *Fannie E. S. Heck: A Study of the Hidden Springs in a Rarely Useful and Victorious Life* (New York: Broadman Press, 1939).

7. See Joel Williamson, *The Crucible of Race: Black-White Relations in the American South since Emancipation* (Nashville: Oxford University Press, 1984). For a fuller discussion of Methodist racial views in this period, see Robert Watson Sledge, "A History of the Methodist Episcopal Church, South, 1914–1939" (Ph.D. diss., University of Texas, 1972), 197–200.

8. Elmer T. Clark, *The Negro and His Religion* (Nashville: Cokesbury Press, 1924), 48.

9. *Alabama Christian Advocate,* July 15, 1926, 2.

10. Sledge, "History"; Ann Wells Ellis, "The Commission on Interracial Cooperation, 1919–1944: Its Activities and Results" (Ph.D. diss., Georgia State University, 1975), preface. On the relation of the 1906 Georgia governor's race to the Atlanta riot, see C. Vann Woodward, *Tom Watson: Agrarian Rebel* (1938; reprint, Savannah, Ga.: Beehive Press, 1973), 327–28; Mark Bauerlein, *Negrophobia: A Race Riot in Atlanta, 1906* (San Francisco: Encounter Books, 2001).

11. Helena Huntington Smith, "Mrs. Tilly's Crusade," *Collier's,* December 30, 1950, 66; Shankman, "Dorothy Tilly," 242–43; Ellis, "Commission on Interracial Cooperation," 178–89. For a fuller examination of the Association of Southern Women for the Prevention of Lynching, see Jacquelyn Dowd Hall, *Revolt against Chivalry: Jessie Daniel Ames and the Women's Campaign against Lynching* (New York: Columbia University Press, 1979).

12. Alice G. Knotts, "Bound by the Spirit, Found on the Journey: The Methodist Women's Campaign for Southern Civil Rights, 1940–1968" (Ph.D. diss., Iliff School of Theology and the University of Denver, 1989), 29–39.

13. Robert Moats Miller, "Methodism and American Society, 1900–1939," in *The History of American Methodism,* ed. Emory Stevens Bucke (Nashville: Abingdon Press, 1964), 3:355.

14. Specific efforts to influence the South away from segregation remained a minority approach within the Methodist Episcopal Church. Such periodic efforts are highlighted in Miller, "Methodism," 367–68, citing *Evanston News-Index,* April 4, 1919, 1, and *Journal of the General Conference of the Methodist Episcopal Church,* 1924, 295.

15. Frederick A. Norwood, *The Story of American Methodism: A History of the United Methodists and Their Relations* (Nashville: Abingdon Press, 1974), 407–9.

16. W. Edward Orser, "Racial Attitudes in Wartime: The Protestant Churches during the Second World War," *Church History* 41 (March 1972): 337–53.

17. "Southern Methodist Women Ask Searching Question," *Christian Century* 54 (April 21, 1937): 509.

18. Orser, "Racial Attitudes," 345.

19. *Pittsburgh Courier,* December 21, 1940, quoted in Richard M. Dalfiume, "The 'Forgotten Years' of the Negro Revolution," *Journal of American History* 55 (June 1968): 91–94.

20. Orser, "Racial Attitudes," 351–52, citing *Zion's Herald,* July 8, 1942, 656.

21. "Address of the Council of Bishops," *Daily Christian Advocate,* April 27, 1944, 27, 28; Frank L. Robertson, "'White Supremacy'—'Master Race,'" *WCA,* February 14, 1947, 6.

22. *WCA,* October 28, 1948, 6.

23. *WCA,* August 19, 1948, 6–7.

24. Quoted in *Report of Interracial Leadership Conference,* Wesley Memorial Church, Atlanta, Georgia, January 28–29, 1957, 40–41.

25. Message on Race Relationships, Board of Social and Economic Relations of the Methodist Church, January 14, 1955, cited in *Report of Interracial Leadership Conference,* 1, 41.

26. Statement on Supreme Court ruling, June 13, 1954; and Janice Treadway to Bishop Arthur J. Moore, June 14, 1954, Arthur J. Moore Papers, Box 20, Robert W. Woodruff Library, Emory University, Atlanta, Georgia.

27. Episcopal Address to the 1956 General Conference and "The Methodist Church and Race," both quoted in *Report of Interracial Leadership Conference,* 43–47.

28. *WCA,* September 1, 1955, 8. See also the 1956 Episcopal Address of the Methodist College of Bishops, Southeastern Jurisdiction, *WCA,* July 26, 1956, 2–3, 11. The bishops' frank admission that many Methodists were not yet ready to follow Christian discipleship on the matter of ending segregation was at least an improvement over one Mississippi Presbyterian church, which in 1964 even more candidly confessed, "we know that this is not what Jesus Christ would do" before it proceeded to exclude African Americans from its worship. See Joel L. Alvis Jr., *Religion and Race: Southern Presbyterians, 1946–1983* (Tuscaloosa: University of Alabama Press, 1994), 97–98.

29. Copy of resolution in Arthur J. Moore Papers, Box 20.

30. Copy of telegram, W. B. Rouse to Chairman, Methodist Bishops, December 7, 1954, Arthur J. Moore Papers, Box 20.

31. Stanley Frazer, "The Methodist Church and Segregation," *WCA,* August 19, 1954, 3.

32. Meeting of the Association of Methodist Ministers and Laymen, December 14, 1954; see "Preservation of Central Jurisdiction to Be Discussed," *WCA,* December 2, 1954, 7; G. Stanley Frazer to Bishop Arthur J. Moore, January 24, 1955, Arthur J. Moore Papers, Box 20.

33. Donald Collins, *When the Church Bell Rang Racist* (Macon, Ga.: Mercer University Press, 1998), 19–20.

34. Resolution of the Lindale Methodist Church, February 4, 1952; Josie Lee Herrin to Arthur J. Moore, May 30, 1952. Both documents are found in the Arthur J. Moore Papers, Box 20.

35. Ellen D. Bunn to the Board of Missions of the Methodist Church, April 1, 1954, Arthur J. Moore Papers, Box 20.

36. Report of Workshop No. 3, *Report of Interracial Leadership Conference,* 95.

37. Letter from Mrs. E. C. Dowdell to Bishop James O. Andrew, 1861, cited by Knotts, "Bound by the Spirit," 6.

38. Knotts, "Bound by the Spirit," 40–45, citing *Thirteenth Annual Report of the Woman's Missionary Council,* 1923, 136; McDowell, *Social Gospel,* 109–11.

39. Knotts, "Bound by the Spirit," 142, 172; Thelma Stevens, "Advance in Human Rights," and "Advance—In Training, in Cooperation, and in Human Relations," *Methodist Woman,* September 1949, 19–20; *Journal of the Women's Division of the Board of Global Ministries,* Annual Report, January 17, 1953, 38. This latter source refers to the minutes of the Woman's Division of Christian Service of the Board of Missions of the Methodist Church. Each year's minutes bound together in one volume includes both the Annual Report and the Journal of the Executive Committee. Citations come from the quarterly "Report and Recommendations of the Department of Christian Social Relations and Local Church Activities to the Woman's Division of Christian Service of the Board of Missions of the Methodist Church." Since after 1968 all such volumes of the successor organization were entitled *Journal of the Women's Division of the Board of Global Ministries,* these annual volumes issued between 1940 and 1968 are also designated as *Journal* hereafter.

40. *Journal,* Annual Report of the Woman's Division, 1943–1944, 189.

41. "Christian Social Relations and Local Church Activities, a Program of Action for 1945," *Methodist Woman,* January 1945, 16.

42. Knotts, "Bound by the Spirit," 137–38 (citing *Journal,* Sixth Annual Meeting, November 27–December 3, 1945, 14), 141; *Journal of the General Conference of the Methodist Church,* 1948, 1093, 1096, 1099.

43. Knotts, "Bound by the Spirit," 184, 187, citing Thelma Stevens and Margaret R. Bender, "Information and Action," *Methodist Woman,* January 1954, 25.

44. *Journal,* Annual Report, January 16, 1954, 54; "Affirmations of the Assembly," *Methodist Woman,* July–August 1954, 43.

45. Knotts, "Bound by the Spirit," 190–91, citing *Journal,* Executive Committee Meeting, September 1954, 76–77; *Journal,* Executive Committee Meeting, September 1955, 29.

46. Marianne D. Fink, "The Methodist Church and Segregation: An Open Letter to the Wesleyan Christian Advocate," *WCA,* September 9, 1954, 11. Along with running Fink's rejoinder to Frazer, editor F. M. Gaines issued the cautious disclaimer that articles did not represent the views of the *WCA* or the Methodist church, adding: "The two articles published represent the two schools of thought on segregation. A continued discussion of the subject would probably result in more heat than light. So please let the *Advocate* sing the Amen and dismiss the subject."

47. *Eleventh Annual Report of the Woman's Missionary Society of the North Georgia Conference* (Gainesville, Ga.: 1921), 29; Tilly, "Leadership School," *WCA,* May 14, 1937; Ruth H. Collins, "We Are the Inheritors," *Response* 3 (July–August 1971): 31.

48. *Eleventh Annual Report,* 29; Knotts, "Bound by the Spirit," 164–65, citing Thelma Stevens, *Legacy for the Future: The History of Christian Social Relations in the Women's Division of Christian Service, 1940–1968* (Cincinnati: Women's Division, Board of Global Ministries, United Methodist Church, 1978), 48; Arndt, "Women's Crusade," n.p.; Smith, "Mrs. Tilly's Crusade," 66; Collins, "We Are the Inheritors," 31.

49. Tilly, "Leadership School."

50. Shankman, "Dorothy Tilly," 242–43; Ellis, "Commission on Interracial Cooperation," 178–89; memorandum on meeting of Tilly and Ellis Arnall, October 27, 1942, Box 35, Committee on Interracial Cooperation Papers, Atlanta University; Smith, "Mrs. Tilly's Crusade," 67.

51. See John E. Talmadge, *Rebecca Latimer Felton: Nine Stormy Decades* (Athens: University of Georgia Press, 1960), 36–45. On Felton's Holiness activities, see Briane Turley, *A Wheel Within a Wheel: Southern Methodism and the Georgia Holiness Association* (Macon, Ga.: Mercer University Press, 1999), 139, 172–73, 176–77.

52. *Atlanta Journal*, October 24, 1904; Rebecca Felton to *Atlanta Journal*, November 15, 1898.

53. *WCA*, September 27, 1940, 1, 13.

54. Knotts, "Bound by the Spirit," 158, citing unpublished material submitted to the *North Georgia Review* and a letter from Ames to Lillian Smith, December 30, 1941, Jesse Daniel Ames Papers, Southern Historical Collection, University of North Carolina Library, Chapel Hill.

55. Arndt, "Women's Crusade," n.p.

56. Collins, "We Are the Inheritors," 31; Shankman, "Dorothy Tilly," 243; Smith, "Mrs. Tilly's Crusade," 67; report of interview of Tilly with Governor Jim Nance McCord of Tennessee, March 6, 1946, Guy Johnson Papers, Southern Regional Council.

57. Ellis, "Commission on Interracial Cooperation," 86–87; Dorothy Tilly to "Dear Friend," August 19, 1942; "Interview between Ellis Arnall and Mrs. Tilly and Mrs. McDougald," August 1942, Committee on Interracial Cooperation Papers, Atlanta University, Box 22 ("Politics, Ellis Arnall"); Smith, "Mrs. Tilly's Crusade," 29.

58. Press release from Roosevelt's address, Lake Junaluska, North Carolina, July 25, 1944, Tilly Papers, Box 2, folder 1, Special Collections, Robert F. Woodruff Library, Emory University, Atlanta, Georgia.

59. Eleanor Roosevelt, *This I Remember* (1949; reprint, Westport, Conn.: Greenwood Press, 1975), 329–30.

60. Smith, "Mrs. Tilly's Crusade," 29, 66.

61. Shankman, "Dorothy Tilly," 243; transcripts of the President's Committee on Civil Rights, Tilly Papers, Box 4.

62. U.S. President's Committee on Civil Rights, *To Secure These Rights* (New York: Simon and Schuster, 1947), 151–73. For a brief summary of the report and Southern members' dissent, see John Egerton, *Speak Now against the Day: The Generation before the Civil Rights Movement in the South* (Chapel Hill: University of North Carolina Press, 1994), 415–16.

63. *Journal*, Eighth Annual Meeting, Women's Division of the Board of Missions, the Methodist Church, December 2–12, 1947, 15–16; Knotts, "Bound by the Spirit," 131; Rachelle McClure to Dorothy Tilly, November 11, 1947, Tilly Papers.

64. Smith, "Mrs. Tilly's Crusade," 66; Shankman, "Dorothy Tilly," 243; *Atlanta Constitution*, January 30, 1948, 23.

65. Egerton, *Speak Now*, 482–83.

66. *WCA*, July 29, 1948, 11; Smith, "Mrs. Tilly's Crusade," 66.

67. *Springfield Register*, February 14, 1949, clipping in Tilly Papers.

68. *Louisville Times*, February 14, 1950.

69. Tobias to Tilly, November 5, 1948, Tilly Papers.

70. *Journal*, Executive Committee Meeting, September 9, 1952, 36.

71. Tom C. Clark to Dorothy Tilly, October 28, 1947, Tilly Papers.

72. Smith, "Mrs. Tilly's Crusade," 67.

73. Tilly, "FOC," 8–9; Shankman, "Dorothy Tilly," 244; "Southern Church Women Draft Action Program," *New South* 4 (September 1949): 2–3; "Church and Con-

science in the South," *New South* 6 (February 1951): 1–4; *The Fellowship of the Concerned* (leaflet), n.p., n.n.

74. Smith, "Mrs. Tilly's Crusade," 29.

75. Shankman, "Dorothy Tilly," 245.

76. Arndt, "Women's Crusade," n.p.

77. Tilly, "FOC," 9; Arndt, "Women's Crusade," n.p.

78. Tilly, "FOC," 9.

79. Smith, "Mrs. Tilly's Crusade," 29.

80. Tilly to Mrs. C. A. [Esther] Meeker, June 11, 1956. Archives of the Southern Regional Council, Robert W. Woodruff Library, Atlanta University Center, Atlanta, Georgia.

81. Shankman, "Dorothy Tilly," 245.

82. Smith, "Mrs. Tilly's Crusade," 67.

83. Franklin Archer, "The New Attack," *Anderson (S.C.) Independent,* November 17, 1947.

84. Smith, "Mrs. Tilly's Crusade," 67.

85. "To the Two Southern Residents of the Civil Rights (?) Committee," anonymous letter to Tilly and Frank Graham, mailed to Tilly on February 8, 1948, copy in Tilly Papers.

86. Knotts, "Bound by the Spirit," 174; S. High, "Methodism's Pink Fringe," *Reader's Digest* 56 (February 1950): 134–38.

87. Shankman, "Dorothy Tilly," 246–47; Florence Robin, "Honeychile at the Barricades," *Harper's* 225 (October 1962): 174; Tilly to Dear Friends [in Alabama], December 17, 1958, Tilly Papers, SRC; Tilly to Bill Cleghorn, December 5, 1958, Tilly Papers, Southern Regional Council, Atlanta University.

88. Shankman, "Dorothy Tilly," 247; Tilly to Mrs. Page Wilson, April 10, 1964, Tilly Papers, Southern Regional Council, Atlanta University; Chester Davis, "Capturing the Strategic Foothills," *Winston-Salem Journal and Sentinel,* February 22, 1953; Ruth H. Collins, "We Are the Inheritors," 31.

89. Shankman, "Dorothy Tilly," 244; Smith, "Mrs. Tilly's Crusade," 67.

90. Tilly, "FOC," 9.

91. Smith, "Mrs. Tilly's Crusade," 29.

92. Tilly to Mrs. W. Murdock McLeod, August 6, 1956, Dorothy Tilly and the Fellowship of the Concerned Papers, Southern Regional Council, Atlanta University.

6

Billy Graham, Civil Rights, and the Changing Postwar South

Steven P. Miller

Billy Graham stands as one of the most recognizable religious figures in the United States and throughout much of the world. The remarkable duration of his tenure as an evangelist—which has lasted just over half a century—no doubt suggests something about both his consistency and flexibility. As Graham biographer William Martin noted, the evangelist has never lacked an understanding of the popular mind. As such, historians and other scholars of American religion have treated Graham as emblematic of, and contributing to, a number of national sociopolitical trends during the postwar era. Notable examples include a nationwide resurgence of interest and involvement in religion coinciding with Graham's rise as a public evangelist during the years after World War II, as well as the contemporaneous emergence of a "neoevangelical" community that distanced itself from the fundamentalist-modernist debates of previous decades.[1]

The far-reaching nature of the Graham ministry has led historians to overlook more discrete aspects of his personality and influence. Foremost among these neglected facets is Graham's relationship to his native U.S. South. Recently, a committee of historians, journalists, and public intellectuals rated Graham as the fourth most influential Southerner of the twentieth century, behind Martin Luther King Jr., William Faulkner, and Elvis Presley. Graham, a Charlotte native possessing an audible drawl, always embraced his status as a Southerner. Since the mid-1940s, he has resided in Montreat, North Carolina, even though his evangelistic organization has been headquartered in Minneapolis since its founding in 1950. Southerners have in turn embraced him as much, if not to a greater extent, than residents of other parts of the United States.[2]

Billy Graham, as both a product of his times and a public participant in them, similarly served to represent and influence the nature of sociopolitical change in his native South. As such, he exemplified American evangelicalism's particular relationship to evolving social and political currents: the manner in which revivalism and evangelical public theology, while embracing traditional forms of belief, also sanction new, modern expressions of these same values. Martin E. Marty has described evangelicalism as "the characteristic Protestant (and, eventually and by indirection, Christian) way of relating to modernity" in the United States.[3] Bearing in mind the symbiosis between evangelicalism and modernity, this chapter will explore Graham's relationship to sociopolitical change in the U.S. South by focusing on his behavior and rhetoric regarding the salient matters of race and politics. The principal years considered, 1950–1970, coincided with the civil rights movement and the beginning of political realignment in the South, a period when Graham maintained a vocal and visible presence in the region.

GRAHAM AS SOUTHERNER

Although Graham was raised within a conservative Reformed denomination, he embraced and voiced a theology aligned with the classic Southern evangelical theme of individual conversion. Graham continually evinced what historian Samuel Hill has termed the Southern revivalist focus on "the inauguration of the Christian life." The historical antecedents for Graham's type of evangelism transcended regional lines, however, and included the likes of Dwight Moody and Billy Sunday. Graham developed a national reputation as an evangelist only upon moving North, after briefly attending Bob Jones College (then located in Cleveland, Tennessee) and graduating from Florida Bible Institute, another fundamentalist school. In 1943, he received a bachelor's degree from a respected evangelical institution, Wheaton College, located in Evanston, Illinois. There, in the Chicago area, Graham developed a partnership with Torrey Johnson, founder of Youth for Christ (YFC) International, which coordinated youth-oriented evangelistic rallies throughout North America and the British Isles. Graham's career took off as YFC's flagship evangelist, and by 1947 he began leading his own revival services, eventually under the auspices of the Billy Graham Evangelistic Association (BGEA). He garnered national acclaim during his Christ for Greater Los Angeles meetings of 1949, when newspaper mogul William Randolph Hearst directed reporters to "puff Graham."[4]

The rise of Graham as a national figure by no means curtailed his willingness to embrace his Southern identity. To the contrary, Graham's Southern background might have contributed to his popularity as a polished, yet folksy and personal, evangelist. An early supporter described Graham as a "lank, handsome Southern lad." When in the South, of course, Graham did not hesitate to accentuate his Southern identity by using regional tropes. Speaking in his hometown of Charlotte, he jovially declared his pleasure upon returning to the "land of 'you all' and cornbread and grits." During the last sermon of the same crusade, after relaying anecdotes about his grandfathers, both of whom fought for the Confederacy, Graham emphatically declared, "I'm proud to be a Southerner and I'm proud to be a Carolinian." For less regionally specific audiences, Graham used his Southern background to affect a certain hardscrabble folksiness. During a speech in Los Angeles, Graham quoted Henry Grady's idyllic description of growing up in the mountains of North Carolina. In his autobiography, Graham again mentioned his Civil War heritage and likened his Depression-era upbringing on a farm near Charlotte to the experiences of the television family, the Waltons. (In actuality, the Grahams were members of the middle class.) Somewhat condescendingly, Graham also wrote of his admiration for Reese Brown, a black farmhand "with a tremendous capacity for working hard," and whose wife made "fabulous buttermilk biscuits."[5]

The South provided a strong base for many early Graham rallies and crusades, beginning with Charlotte (1947) and including Columbia, South Carolina (1950), Shreveport, Louisiana (1951), and Chattanooga, Tennessee (1953). These were among the many Southern cities during the postwar period that grew into Standard Metropolitan Statistical Areas with populations of at least 250,000. In 1953, even though he lived in North Carolina, Graham attained membership at First Baptist Church of Dallas, then the largest Southern Baptist congregation in the world. During the 1950s, the vast majority of Graham's crusades in the United States—and a substantial portion of his guest sermons and one-day rallies—took place in Southern cities. (The following decade saw more regional balance.) The BGEA maintained a branch office in Atlanta during the period considered, and it generally found crusades easier to organize in the South than elsewhere. Atlanta and Chattanooga were among the few cities to construct special tabernacles in which to hold crusade services. Graham's influence often extended beyond the sphere of tabernacles, of course. His 1950 address to a joint session of the Georgia legislature inspired the state senate to pass a prohibition law, which later died in the other chamber. Eight years later, by which time Graham was clearly associated with an integrationist position on civil rights, 13 percent of Southerners listed him as the man whom they most admired, compared with 2 percent of Northern residents. Graham had positioned himself to be characterized in the 1960s as "the South's folk preacher." [6]

Graham and Race

If Graham was indeed the folk preacher of the South, then the issue of race served to test this status. The emergence of the civil rights movement cast a spotlight on Graham's identity as a Southerner. National politicians, such as Dwight Eisenhower, and national publications, such as the liberal Protestant *Christian Century,* looked to Graham to exert regional leadership concerning integration and civil rights. That he would assume a public role in the area of race relations was far from inevitable. Graham wrote that growing up as a white Southerner, he "had adopted the attitudes of that region without much reflection." His education at Wheaton College, where he majored in anthropology and gained awareness of the cultural relativity of race, led him to question his racial assumptions. Still, during his first six years of holding solo revivals, he allowed for segregated seating arrangements in Southern cities. W. A. Criswell, pastor of the Dallas church to which Graham belonged (and future president of the Southern Baptist Convention), was a vocal defender of segregation. Nelson Bell, Graham's father-in-law and a member of the Presbyterian Church in the United States (that is, the Southern Presbyterian Church), perhaps also contributed to Graham's initial reluctance to thwart the racial status quo.[7]

Despite maintaining strong ties to such racial conservatives as Criswell and—into the 1950s—Bob Jones Sr. and Bob Jones Jr., Graham moved beyond his fundamentalist peers on the issue of race. Graham, as one historian has written, evolved during the 1950s from a "segregationist to [a] racial moderate." As early as 1949, Graham had received criticism in New England for tolerating segregation in Southern crusades. Particularly notable was a 1950 crusade in Columbia, South Carolina, where Graham stayed at the governor's mansion of former Dixiecrat presidential candidate Strom Thurmond. Criticism came from the South as well. A writer to the *Atlanta Constitution* chided Graham for holding segregated meetings in the city and asked, "Is he implying that God Almighty has room for segregation and discrimination in His work?" Graham himself grew concerned about lack of black attendance at crusades. His first public statement concerning segregation occurred during his 1952 crusade in Jackson, Mississippi, when he declared that church segregation had no biblical basis, and he added that "the audience might be segregated, but there is no segregation at this altar." Graham effectively retracted his statement the next day, positing that the Bible "has nothing to say about segregation or non-segregation."[8]

The next year in Chattanooga, Graham took a more forthright stand against segregation in religious settings. Before the start of the crusade, he personally removed the rope separating the black and white sections of the audience. The incident went unreported in Chattanooga's major dailies (which gave more attention to Graham's proficiency as a golfer), although Graham later claimed that his action "caused the head usher to resign in anger right on the spot (and raised some other hackles)." A photograph of the Chattanooga crusade, later used in a Graham promotional booklet, showed white and black audience members sitting together. Graham's initial foray into holding integrated services occurred during what historian Charles Eagles describes as a period of relative openness concerning race relations before and immediately after the Supreme Court's *Brown v. Board of Education* decision.[9]

As sentiments hardened in the years after *Brown,* Graham wavered in his willingness to continue standing up to local crusade committees regarding segregation. He largely avoided the Deep South during the mid- and late 1950s, but he conducted integrated crusades in such Upper South cities as Nashville (1954, several months after announcement of the *Brown* decision) and Richmond (1956). He would return to the Deep South during the particularly tense civil rights years of the mid-1960s. By 1964, Graham could publicly declare that he would not accept an invitation to hold a crusade in Atlanta without assurances of integrated seating. In first holding an integrated crusade in 1953, Graham was slightly ahead of his times in comparison with fellow evangelists and religious leaders in the South. The watershed *Brown* decision occurred one year later, and with it came a number of statements from Southern denominations, including one by the Southern Baptist Convention, in support of the decision. By the late 1950s, most mass evangelists in the South were conducting integrated services.[10]

Graham's public role regarding race matters extended well beyond the immediate realm of his crusade audiences. During the mid-1950s and continuing into the 1960s, he used national media outlets to communicate his views about integration and the civil rights movement. In 1956, Graham published a particularly telling article in *Life* magazine, in which he dismissed biblically based arguments supporting racial segregation and hierarchy, and called for the church to speak out in favor of racial tolerance. Although Graham endorsed basic legal remedies, he upheld individual conversion as a transformative factor in bettering race relations. He called for a national "baptism of love, tolerance and understanding" that "alone, in my opinion will solve our problems and ease our tensions."[11]

In staking out a moderate integrationist position centered on evangelistic priorities, Graham assumed authority not just as a renowned preacher, but also as a Southerner with particular knowledge about the region's populace, black and white. He had discussed the "[race] problem with leaders of all denominations and both colors in the South" and had concluded that "the vast majority of ministers in the South are not extremists on either side of the issue." As the civil rights movement gained momentum, Graham asymmetrically conflated militant segregationists and strident civil rights activists. Although his positions garnered the resistance of many segregationists, Graham also criticized the activist approach of Martin Luther King Jr. and the participants in Mississippi "Freedom Summer," even though the evangelist agreed with their integrationist sentiments. Graham shared this penchant for criticizing both activist integrationists and reactionary segregationists with the postwar white "progressives" and "moderates" whom historian William Chafe has described in Greensboro, North Carolina. In his *Life* article, Graham told of a white integrationist minister who became a racial moderate after moving to the South, and likewise chided an idealistic white Southern minister who foolishly invited an African American to deliver a guest sermon before ensuring that the congregation was prepared for such a drastic step. Graham seemed to extend the label of moderate to blacks in general, whom he claimed had attended his segregated Jackson crusade in much larger numbers than his integrated crusades in Nashville and elsewhere. Blacks, Graham declared, balked at legalized segregation, but often preferred to mingle among themselves. Four years later, writing in *Reader's Digest,* Graham questioned his own understanding of blacks, asking, "Even in the South . . . do we really know [the Negro]?" Although seemingly written for a white audience, the *Reader's Digest* piece was reprinted in the leading journal of the African Methodist Episcopal Church, alongside a photograph of Graham receiving an honor from the president of Liberia. In the article, Graham argued that segregation in American churches hindered evangelism abroad.[12]

Graham's presumed authority regarding race matters also allowed him to diagnose the race problem as transcending the South. "North and South alike," he wrote, are implicated in the tragic legacy of slavery, which extended back to the British and Dutch as well. The North, he noted, suffered from housing discrimination and slums. Graham, in providing historical and sociological balance, also conveyed a tone of regional defensiveness that would mark his rhetoric throughout the decades considered. "One of the most popular indoor sports of some Northerners these days is pointing out the faults of the South," he wrote. Although he defined racial prejudice as a transregional, national problem requiring national solutions (revival and obedience to the law), Graham upheld a distinctly Southern model for improving race relations, closing both the *Life* and *Reader's Digest* articles with the following story:

> Shortly after the close of the Civil War, a Negro entered a fashionable church in Richmond, Va., on Sunday morning while communion was being served. He went to the aisle and knelt at the altar. A rustle of shock and anger swept through the congregation. Sensing the situation, a distinguished layman stood up, stepped forward to the altar and knelt beside his black brother. Captured by his spirit, the congregation followed his tremendous example.

The layman who set the example was Robert E. Lee.[13]

If Graham served in part as a spokesperson for Southern moderates, he also played a vocal role within the region. In 1956, Alabama representative Frank W. Boykin recommended that President Eisenhower ask Graham to help facilitate a smooth transition toward integration. Eisenhower then wrote to Graham, who agreed to convene a meeting of Southern denominational heads. The meeting never occurred, but Graham did claim to meet individually with Southern religious leaders of both races, and he also discussed race matters with many Southern politicians. In 1957, a group of black North Carolina ministers asked Graham to lead an antisegregation crusade in his home state—a request he did not take up. Within the Southern Baptist Convention, as early as 1952, Graham spoke in favor of integrating Baptist colleges. In his crusade sermons, however, he remained less vocal about race— a pattern that would continue into the 1960s. During the integrated Nashville crusade of 1954, for example, Graham did not address race in his sermons. Four years later in Charlotte, Graham's comments about race consisted of occasional references to "racial problems," which he connected with individual sins. Still, the integrated Charlotte crusade garnered praise from the normally critical *Christian Century,* which noted reports of racially mixed seating patterns and a black minister counseling a white convert.[14]

Graham's actions and statements in support of improved race relations and integration, although cautious, garnered criticism from segregationists.

Notorious white supremacist John Kasper, who was active in the South during the civil rights era, branded Graham a "negro lover." In 1957, the Carolina Baptist Fellowship, a white ministerial group, criticized Graham's support for school integration. One year later, after the Charlotte crusade, Graham felt the wrath of South Carolina governor George Bell Timmerman, who refused to allow Graham to hold a rally in Columbia on the state house lawn, claiming that doing so would signify an endorsement of the evangelist's integrationist position. Timmerman implicitly characterized Graham as a traitor to the region. "As a widely known evangelist and native Southerner, his endorsement of racial mixing has done much harm," Timmerman stated. Instead, Graham held an integrated rally at a nearby army base. Graham later received criticism from two other South Carolinians, Greenville-based separatist fundamentalists Bob Jones Sr. and Bob Jones Jr., who opposed Graham's cooperation with liberal Protestants and involvement with civil rights issues.[15]

More dramatically, in the late 1950s, Graham began holding integrated services in Southern cities that had experienced outbreaks of racial violence. The first such service took place in Clinton, Tennessee, where segregationists had bombed the local high school in response to integration attempts. In 1958, Graham held a one-day rally in Clinton at the invitation of newspaper columnist Drew Pearson and Senator Estes Kefauver. Graham also worked with Americans Against Bigotry, an organization that raised funds to rebuild Clinton High School, although he declined an offer from Pearson to chair the group. Graham recalled strong opposition from the White Citizens' Council to his Clinton visit, which reportedly resulted in the conversion of a segregationist who had vowed to upset the meeting. The evangelist was also involved in the more publicized tensions in Little Rock, about which Graham claimed Eisenhower consulted him before sending in federal troops. Graham released a statement that "all thinking Southerners" were outraged by the violence in Little Rock. Although a group of Little Rock ministers requested that Graham come there in 1958, a large percentage of fundamentalists and a number of integrationist ministers objected to the idea, and Arkansas representative Brooks Hays purportedly cautioned Graham to delay his visit. Graham's eventual trip to Little Rock one year later, when he held two rallies, featured another conversion of a known segregationist, who renounced his militant activism, if not his preference for racial separation.[16]

As the civil rights movement drew more attention during its peak years in the early and mid-1960s, Graham followed in tow. In Alabama, site of Martin Luther King Jr.'s efforts in Birmingham and Selma, Graham held his

most publicized interracial rallies and crusades in the aftermath of demonstrations and race-related violence. In place of activism, Graham substituted
his brand of evangelical mediation of social change. Graham, ever a moderate, grew uncomfortable with the civil rights movement, which he continually worried might harbor politically subversive elements. This concern
probably influenced Graham's aforementioned tendency to criticize aggressive civil rights activists, as well as segregationists. The evangelist questioned
the civil rights movement despite his cordial and at times consultative (if
mostly private) relationship with King, who allowed Graham to call him
"Mike," a family nickname used mostly by King's black associates. In 1963,
during the height of the Birmingham demonstrations and amid controversies over the city's mayoral election, Graham urged his "good personal friend"
King to "put the brakes on a little bit." Graham doubted whether the black
community in Birmingham supported the sit-in movement. His words of
caution resembled a contemporaneous statement released by eight Birmingham religious leaders, to whom King responded with "Letter from Birmingham Jail," a work profoundly critical of white Southern moderates.[17]

Graham was not uninvolved in Birmingham matters, however. After
the September 1963 bombing of the Sixteenth Street Baptist Church by white
segregationists, he joined efforts to raise funds to rebuild the church. Graham had already put out feelers about holding a rally or crusade in Birmingham, which he insisted would need to be integrated. An opportunity
soon arrived several weeks before Easter 1964, when a group of Birmingham civic leaders and clergy invited Graham to hold an Easter rally in the
city's football stadium, situated at the foot of a black neighborhood nick-
named "Dynamite Hill." A member of the clergy had originally proposed
the idea the preceding autumn. Arthur P. Cook, a Birmingham newspaper
publisher, chaired the interracial sponsoring committee for the rally.[18]

An estimated 35,000 people, slightly more than half the stadium's capacity and including equal numbers of blacks and whites, attended the March
29 rally. The event featured an integrated choir and thoroughly mixed seating patterns amid heavy security after threats of violence. Birmingham mayor
Albert Boutwell and popular University of Alabama football coach Paul
"Bear" Bryant were among the guests of honor. A black member of the sponsoring committee, J. L. Ware, one of Birmingham's most visible black ministers and a moderate counterpart to the civil rights activist Fred Shuttlesworth,
gave the benediction. Despite public opposition to the rally by the Jefferson
County White Citizens' Council, no incidents of violence occurred. The
Sunday sermon, titled "The Easter Reconciliation," eschewed emotive refer-

ences to the city's racial tensions. In his only specific reference to racial violence, Graham cited bomb throwers as representatives of a "moral disease"
that "has blinded our minds, hardened our conscience, and confused our
judgment." Such a disease, he said, indicates "heart trouble," not social or
educational problems per se. Although he stuck to his trademark message
of individual confession and conversion, Graham also employed equally
common platitudes of revival-driven civic betterment: "This could be the
beginning of a new day in the great city of Birmingham that we all love so
well!" According to a United Press International story, the prepared text of
the sermon mentioned Birmingham's history of race problems several times.
In a nationally broadcasted radio address earlier in the day, Graham addressed the "racial problem" more specifically, but he stressed that it was a
world issue "not limited to Birmingham, Ala., or to the Southern part of the
United States."[19]

Between 3,000 and 4,000 audience members went forward during the
altar call—a significant percentage of the audience for any Graham service.
According to the dramatic, condescending front-page lead of one local newspaper, "The first to answer his call was a Negro woman," whose "hat was an
old black straw," but whose smile "was as new as the Easter Day." Other descriptions of the rally's impact were more reserved, but hardly less affirming. In handwritten messages left with Graham employees, Ware identified
the rally as a "turning point in changing the outlook and image of Birmingham into a city of peace and prosperity for all people"; Boutwell contended
that Graham had made the city "an improved and better place to live." A
variation on Boutwell's statement, in which he noted that extremists normally are "the only ones heard," appeared in an Associated Press story.[20]

The Graham rally was at least a momentary boon for the beleaguered
image of Birmingham, a fact that the *Birmingham News* did not hesitate to
establish. The rally, which was hailed in the national media as the largest
interracial gathering in Alabama history, received extensive newspaper coverage, including an affirming editorial from respected Raleigh newspaper
editor Jonathan Daniels. After soberly praising the Graham rally as an expression of common decency, a *Birmingham News* editorial noted that "the
city has been commended, widely, in the press," granting Birmingham an
opportunity to achieve a "harmonious condition of respect and mutual regard, one citizen for another." A planning committee member predicted that
the rally would be a "signal day in modern Birmingham." The *Birmingham
World,* an African American newspaper, was more circumspect in its analysis of the rally. An editorial suggested that "twenty-five Negro policeman on

duty [at the rally] would have been a better indicator of constructive [racial progress] in Birmingham than the seating arrangements." The Ministerial Association of Greater Birmingham, in which Ware served as an associate officer, felt differently and unsuccessfully petitioned Graham to hold a full crusade in Birmingham "at the earliest possible time." At this point, Graham was receiving many requests for appearances in other Southern cities.[21]

Graham's next visits to Alabama occurred one year later, in the aftermath of the much-publicized violence against civil rights demonstrators in Selma. In March 1965, Graham sent two associates to Alabama before, at the request of Alabamians, canceling a trip to England in order to visit the state. Graham held rallies in Dothan, Tuscaloosa, Auburn, and Tuskegee during April 24–27, then returned in June for a crusade in Montgomery. Before and during these visits, Graham spoke somewhat more explicitly about race and racial conciliation than he had in Birmingham. He overtly cast himself as a Southerner performing a mediating role. "As a Southerner," he told *Time*, "I may have a little more influence than a man with a Yankee accent." Similarly, he told a national newspaper that "at least for the time being I have a voice in the South and I will try to provide the leadership I can." At the same time, he told the Associated Press, "I'm not going to Alabama as a civil rights worker. I'm going as a preacher of the gospel." The simple act of holding integrated services "conveys enough on the subject of race," he added. Graham continually indicated that he was visiting Alabama at the invitation of local religious and civic leaders, black and white.[22]

Graham did keep his Alabama sermons focused on salvation, although behind the scenes and outside of the state, he spoke more candidly about civil rights. In Dothan, where his brother-in-law pastored a Presbyterian congregation, Graham spoke before an integrated audience of 5,500, including an integrated 450-person choir. The crowd was smaller than expected, perhaps because of fears of segregationist violence. (The vice president of the local Citizens' Council was quoted as calling the decision to invite Graham to Dothan "very unfortunate.") Afterward, Graham met with local black leaders. His nationally broadcasted radio address from Dothan bluntly prioritized spiritual over social issues: "The church today spends too much time answering questions nobody is asking." In Montgomery that same day, W. A. Criswell—no friend to the cause of integration—conducted a Sunday morning service that Graham missed only as a result of fatigue. Two days later, at Tuskegee Institute, Graham declared, "God is going to intervene in history before we blow ourselves up." Meanwhile, the Alabama House of Representatives killed, then belatedly passed a resolution to have Graham address a joint session of the legislature. Graham declined the invitation, citing previous commitments. (A year earlier, Graham had told a joint session of the Georgia legislature that he agreed with the essentials of Martin Luther King Jr.'s "dream" of integration.)[23]

Graham did hold a private "social visit" with Governor George Wallace during the June 1965 crusade in Montgomery. Graham's positive experiences in places such as Clinton and Birmingham might have influenced his willingness to hold his first fully integrated crusade in the Deep South. (It was also his first crusade held specifically in response to racial tensions.) Many newspaper photographs showed a thoroughly integrated choir in Montgomery. In addition, the crusade featured an introductory statement by a black minister, as well as a performance by Ethel Waters, a famous black vocalist who worked for BGEA. The crusade itself proceeded largely without incident, although several blacks were turned away from a white Presbyterian church when they attempted to attend a service conducted by Graham's brother-in-law, Leighton Ford, who became a well-known evangelical social activist. A Montgomery newspaper editorial labeled the crusade a success, although it alluded to "some opinions to the contrary." A white minister praised Graham's "willingness . . . to identify himself with our area at such a critical juncture. A Southerner himself, Billy Graham feels for us, for example, in the unfair treatment we have been given in the national news media."[24]

In his crusade sermons, Graham only indirectly addressed race, appealing to each audience member, "as one Southerner to another, [to] go out of your way to continue the spirit of unity and love that you have demonstrated this week." His public statements were slightly more forthcoming regarding race. Again positioning himself as a moderate, Graham urged "extremists" within both the Ku Klux Klan and civil rights movement to "quiet down" so Alabamians will have "time to digest the new civil rights laws." Graham had previously contended that civil rights demonstrations in Alabama served "to arouse the conscience of the people." In the case of Montgomery, though, he denied that his visit entailed a civil rights agenda, noting simply that his services were "open to those of all races to sit where they please . . . and listen to the gospel of Christ." As Graham reminded residents of Montgomery, he had already preached similar messages in other Southern cities. With characteristic hyperbole, he called Montgomery "the most rewarding and thrilling [crusade] of my ministry" and said black leaders were "literally shouting for joy over the new atmosphere that has been created." Graham apparently invested a great deal of energy in his visit to Montgomery, as he published a daily reflection piece in the *Montgomery Advertiser* immediately before and during the one-week crusade. Before the crusade, he wrote to the same paper to clarify remarks he had made about the state of Alabama. Soon afterward and in subsequent years, Graham complained about the lack of network news coverage of the integrated crusade.[25]

As the white Montgomery minister's perceptions of Graham suggested, linked with Graham's optimism was a continued defense of the South that at times translated into sympathy and even advocacy. Graham remained quick to point out that racial prejudice was not just a Southern problem. Turning Alabama into a "whipping boy," he said in a press statement released before his 1965 visits to the state, "often becomes just another diversion to direct attention from other areas where the problem is just as acute." After generalizing the race problem, he then proceeded to suggest a potential Southern advantage in the area of race relations. Graham repeatedly contrasted the South to the North, noting that the former had "a stronger religious foundation to build on," as well as "more personal friendships between the races—friendships that I find lacking in some Northern areas." He made similar comments to national, Southern, and Northern media outlets. Both white and black leaders in Alabama, he claimed, believe the state will solve the race problem before the North. Although he predicted "more Selmas," he stressed that "the friendships are closer [in the South], too, and we haven't reached the stage where we have ghettos."[26]

During the peak years of the civil rights movement, then, Graham adopted a strategy of arriving at Southern cities in the aftermath of racial tensions. "We try to get in there a little bit afterward to see if we can't bring the healing message of the Bible," he told the *New York Times*. In Alabama, he held publicized services that were often billed as the largest integrated meetings in either the state or locality. These services, as Graham admitted, represented his form of activism. Although civil rights supporters attempted to register black voters in Mississippi, Graham downplayed their efforts and cited his integrated services in Nashville, Clinton, and Birmingham as evidence of a spiritual solution to the race problem. "I have been holding demonstrations for 15 years," Graham declared during his visit to Montgomery, "but in a stadium where it is legal." Indeed, the interracial services were his alternatives to King's marches and strategies of civil disobedience, which, Graham feared, blurred the evangelical hierarchy of individual salvation over social change. Graham has since suggested that King advised him to stay away from demonstrations and to focus on the task of evangelism. This claim has never been corroborated.[27]

Graham's interracial gatherings served as legitimizing mechanisms for a certain style of Southern moderate politics. Thus, it is helpful to consider Graham in light of William Chafe's description of the post–World War II Southern "progressive mystique" with its aversion to conflict, latent paternalism, and overarching "commitment to civility." Regarding race relations, the role of Graham as a minister fell somewhere in between the civil rights activism of Will Campbell and the obstinate racial conservatism of Jackson, Mississippi, minister Douglas Hudgins, both fellow white Southern Baptists. Like progressives in Greensboro, Graham sought a middle ground between the "extremism" of the right and left, which he viewed as symmetrical. His visits inspired positive portrayals of Birmingham and Montgomery's better sides, and unlike King during his times in Alabama, Graham did not challenge or critique either city's white establishment. Similarly, Graham visited Clinton, Tennessee, in order to, in his words, "demonstrate to the world that Clinton is a Christian, law-abiding community—not one of violence and hate." Graham rallies and crusades provided public expressions of the evangelical decency affirmed by image-conscious officials in Clinton, Birmingham, and elsewhere.[28] These white Southern moderates, like Graham, appealed to law and order, but also to extrapolitical forms of personal relationships and spiritual piety.

The civility model, however, might unduly minimize Graham's simultaneously unique and circumscribed role as an evangelist who spoke to audiences not always linked with the world of chambers of commerce and op-ed pages. As suggested above, Graham sanctified the connection between civility and evangelical faith, at times incorporating moderate racial politics into his evangelistic messages. Yet he could do so only because his message primarily focused on salvation, not social issues. In the end, his integrated rallies and crusades functioned as performative confirmations of what historian Samuel Hill identified in the late 1960s as the "central theme" of Southern religion: individual conversion through the "regeneration of human hearts."[29] When supporting basic civil rights and holding integrated services, Graham never deviated from this central theme.

Graham and Politics

Although Graham facilitated theaters of racial reconciliation and evangelical decency through his crusades, he did not shy away from the less pious arena of politics. From the very beginning of his career, he linked the destiny of the United States and its leaders to the mission of his evangelism, particularly in relation to the cold war. His political connections and perceived political influence remained strongest in the South. There, Graham paralleled and sought to influence the currents of political change.[30]

In an insightful treatment of Graham and the politics of "Middle America," Lowell D. Streiker and Gerald S. Strober described a telling scene from the 1960 presidential campaign between Richard Nixon and John F. Kennedy. At a campaign rally in Columbia, South Carolina, Graham gave an invocation for his longtime friend, Nixon. Earlier, Nixon and Graham had appeared together on the state house steps (the same steps where, two years earlier, Graham was denied the right to lead an integrated crusade) beneath a Republican Party banner reading "Dixie Is No Longer in the Bag."[31] For the national Democratic Party during the decades after World War II, Dixie was ever in danger of falling out of the bag. Graham—who like most white Southerners was still a registered Democrat in 1960—was emblematic of the transitional status of many white Southerners, who began tilting toward Republicans in national elections. At times, as in Columbia, Graham sought to influence the direction of this transition.

During the late 1940s and through the 1950s, Graham evinced dual concerns for anticommunism and a strong public role for religion in politics—priorities that eventually found synergy in his relationship with President Dwight Eisenhower. In his crusades, when Graham advocated "Christ for This Crisis" (the title of his 1947 Charlotte revival), the crisis he spoke of entailed the specter of communism, as well as moral degeneration. His sermon titles—"The End of the World," "Will God Spare America?"—reflected an apocalyptic interpretation of the era. Graham at times aligned anticommunism with support for civil rights. In 1957, he wrote a supportive letter to a fifteen-year-old African American student who had experienced harassment when attempting to enter a previously all-white high school in Charlotte. "Democracy demands that you hold fast and carry on," Graham wrote, adding that "this is your one great chance to prove to Russia that democracy still prevails."[32]

At the same time, Graham yearned for moral leadership from national leaders. He seemed more than satisfied with the integrity of Eisenhower, whom he described to a Chattanooga journalist as "the most devout and deeply religious man we've had in the White House in many years." (Later during the same 1953 crusade, Graham strategically noted that liquor sales in Washington, D.C., declined after the new administration took power.) Eisenhower clearly recognized the political usefulness of Graham in the South, as their aforementioned communication regarding civil rights indicated. Graham's support for Eisenhower, although not uncommon among national evangelists, paralleled developments in Southern politics. In 1956, Eisenhower became the first Republican president in the twentieth century to win a plurality of Southern votes. Eisenhower received particularly strong support from affluent white residents of large and small Southern metropolitan areas (as well as some black residents of those areas), the types of growing cities that Graham frequented throughout the decade.[33]

As Graham grew in national stature, he interacted with a wide range of national politicians from both major parties. His connections, though, remained strongest with Southern Democrats, ranging from Tennessee governor Frank Clement to North Carolina senator Clyde Hoey and Texas governor John Connally. Graham regularly consulted with these and other Southern political figures. As early as 1950, he received publicized overtures to run for the U.S. Senate in North Carolina in a race that might have pitted him against a distant relative, the liberal Frank Porter Graham. Similar offers would follow throughout the decade. In 1964, the right-wing oil tycoon and Texan H. L. Hunt tried to convince Graham to run for the Republican presidential nomination—this, despite Graham's status as a registered Democrat. Graham recalled that other Republicans also approached him about running in 1964. After Walter Cronkite's premature announcement on the CBS *Nightly News* that the evangelist was considering running, Graham publicly denied any such intentions.[34]

Graham's Southern political connections assumed a particularly visible form during the 1950 Columbia crusade. In addition to staying in Governor Strom Thurmond's mansion, Graham inspired an outbreak of civil religion. Thurmond, more than a decade away from his trend-setting switch to the Republican Party, described religious revivals as "the hope for the world," officially declared the last day of the Graham crusade "South Carolina Revival Day," and called the crusade the "greatest religious gathering ever held in South Carolina—if not the South." Thurmond, his bitter political rival U.S. Senator Olin Johnson, and Graham posed around a Bible for a newspaper photograph. Graham also spoke before a joint session of the state legislature. During the Columbia Crusade, Graham met and befriended conservative *Time* magazine publisher Henry Luce, an encounter historian Numan Bartley has linked with the postwar "marriage of Southern fundamentalism and Northern anticommunism."[35]

Graham and another paradigmatic figure in the postwar South, Lyndon Johnson, had known each other since the 1950s. Their friendship grew, however, during Johnson's presidential term, when he frequently consulted with Graham. According to Johnson aide Bill Moyers, Graham and Johnson had an "almost visceral attraction for one another," due in part to their roots in Southern outposts, as well as their propensity for stoking each other's egos. Graham admired Johnson as a churchgoer with a Baptist background. His mother had been Baptist; he independently chose the Disciples of Christ. Graham also took pride in the fact that, while in Houston just one year after his election, LBJ had become the first sitting president to attend a Graham crusade. Johnson, according to Bill Moyers, also believed that receiving support from Graham on particular issues partially assured the backing of Graham's constituency. Indeed, Graham and Johnson were for the most part aligned on a number of issues, including civil rights and the Vietnam War. The evangelist went so far as to call for a global version of Johnson's War on Poverty. During a visit to Hawaii, Graham praised Johnson's congressional address in support of voting rights legislation as "the greatest speech on civil rights since Lincoln." Regarding civil rights, Graham assisted Johnson, whether consciously or not, by visiting Birmingham during Senate consideration of the 1964 Civil Rights Act and, partially at the request of Johnson, returning to Alabama months before passage of the Voting Rights Act. Historian Jerry Berl Hopkins has suggested a possible connection between Johnson's 1964 plea for Southern Baptists to support civil rights legislation and Graham's visit to Birmingham. Graham more overtly assisted Johnson's Office of Economic Opportunity (OEO) programs in Appalachia, touring the region by helicopter with Sargent Shriver in order to drum up support for the OEO. Graham also recorded a pro-OEO interview and helped to produce the antipoverty documentary *Beyond These Hills*. Both the interview and documentary were broadcast throughout the South.[36]

With the election of Johnson in 1964, Graham momentarily halted his support for Republican presidential candidates, which had continued through the 1960 election. Having turned down an offer to run for the Republican nomination, Graham experienced a moment of embarrassment during the campaign when one of his daughters publicly backed Barry Goldwater at a GOP rally in Greenville, South Carolina. Graham paralleled the portion of the Southern electorate that had voted for Eisenhower and Nixon in preceding elections, but that had pulled the lever for Johnson in 1964. As Hugh Graham and Numan V. Bartley have documented, for the first time since 1948, the Republicans failed in 1964 to garner support from the majority of Southern urban voters, particularly in border South cities.[37]

In the case of Quaker Richard Nixon, Graham clearly shifted from reflecting Southern political trends (as with Eisenhower) and supporting specific policies (as with Johnson) to attempting to influence the direction of

Southern (and national) politics. In doing so, Graham involved himself both implicitly and directly in the machinations of the Republican "Southern Strategy"—the GOP's attempt to win over Southern Democrats. Nixon and Graham first met around 1950 by way of North Carolina senator Clyde Hoey, although Graham had already met Nixon's mother at a crusade. More than with Johnson, Graham's relationship with Nixon at times assumed an explicitly strategic posture. During the months leading up to the presidential election of 1960, Graham wrote confidentially to Eisenhower urging the president to campaign in Southern states where he might "tip the scales" in Nixon's favor. This correspondence, when considered in light of Graham's aforementioned appearance with Nixon in South Carolina, suggested that Graham viewed the South as vital to the success of Nixon. Indeed, Nixon lost two Southern states, Johnson's Texas and heavily Catholic Louisiana, which Eisenhower had carried four years earlier. Still, the election continued a pattern of strong GOP presidential showings in the South.[38]

In the years after Nixon's delayed presidential victory in 1968, Graham became, in the words of one historian, "an unofficial Kitchen Cabinet member" of the Nixon administration. During the 1968 campaign itself, Graham used his personal connections in support of Nixon. According to the memoirs of Harry Dent, a major architect of Nixon's Southern Strategy, Graham claimed to have almost garnered Democrat John Connelly's support for Nixon in 1968, before successfully convincing the Texas governor (and future Nixon cabinet member) to back the administration three years later. Also in 1968, Graham privately encouraged Johnson not to actively campaign on behalf of Nixon's opponent, Hubert Humphrey. The evangelist later conferred with another Nixon threat, third-party candidate and former Alabama governor George Wallace, who held the electoral balance of power in the Deep South. Graham attempted to convince Wallace, with whom the evangelist had met during the 1965 Montgomery crusade, to withdraw from the race and support Nixon, a theme the evangelist reiterated in 1972, when Graham showed Wallace poll data revealing that most of the populist's supporters would back Nixon if George McGovern were the only other candidate. Indeed, during the 1972 election, with Wallace off the ballot, Nixon won over nearly all of the Southern voters who had backed Wallace in 1968.[39]

Graham's political influence, while not quantifiable, was deemed significant by Nixon and his staff. Nixon aide H. R. Haldeman wrote in 1970 that "it is important to start an early liaison with BG and his people. He was enormously helpful to us in the Border South in '68 and will continue to be in '72." Dent, who was also a Southern Baptist deacon and a former staff member for Strom Thurmond, told *Newsweek* that Graham had been "prepared" to endorse Nixon in 1968 "if necessary." Days before the 1968 election, Dent ran television advertisements noting that Graham had cast an absentee vote for Nixon.[40]

Most of Graham's efforts in support of Nixon took place behind the scenes, or at least well removed from crusade settings. A notable exception occurred in 1970 during a midterm campaign that represented a crucial test for Nixon's Southern Strategy. Nixon had focused much attention on a Senate race in the border state of Tennessee between incumbent Democrat Albert Gore Sr. and the leading Republican challenger, U.S. Representative Bill Brock. Gore, a critic of Nixon's Vietnam policy, was "nationally regarded as the number one target of the Nixon administration's Southern Strategy in 1970," in the words of two historians.[41]

In May 1970, Graham came to Knoxville to lead the East Tennessee Crusade, the product of seventeen years of planning by clergy and community leaders. The crusade, which Graham had announced would focus on youth, featured gestures in that direction through appearances by Johnny Cash, the Statler Brothers, and Carl Perkins. Graham's claim that he would "stay away from politics" during the crusade proved less tenable. Five days later, Knoxville papers reported that Nixon would visit Knoxville to take part in an upcoming service billed as "Youth Night." Although Nixon had attended Graham crusades before, this time, the president would take the unprecedented step of addressing the crusade audience. Nixon, who had last visited Knoxville during the 1968 campaign, expressed interest in connecting with college students, particularly in light of the recent shootings at Kent State University. Links between Nixon's appearance and the senatorial election were evident, however. The delegation traveling with Nixon from Washington, D.C., to Knoxville included Brock, Republican senator Howard Baker, several Tennessee Republicans running for office that year, and a Democrat whose congressional district included East Tennessee. Gore was not invited to join the party. (Neither Gore nor Brock hailed from the Knoxville area.) In Knoxville, Brock and Nixon stood beside each other during photographs of the delegation.[42]

An overflow crowd of 100,000—twice the size of the average crowd during the crusade—gathered inside and around the University of Tennessee's Neyland Stadium to hear Graham and Nixon speak. The service functioned as a performance of Nixon's so-called Silent Majority, a point which the conspicuously pro-Nixon *Knoxville Journal* celebrated. In introducing the president, Graham cast Nixon as a tireless, pious leader, "the President of the Democrats as well as the Republicans" and of "the blacks as well as the whites." Nixon's brief address echoed Graham's conciliatory tone, as the president praised the potential of college youth, most of whom did not "approve of violence," and called for a national spirituality that "cannot come from a man in government." During the service, around 300 protestors periodically chanted antiwar slogans. In response to them, Nixon acknowledged the legitimacy of dissent, but said he was "glad that there seems to be a rather solid majority on one side rather than the other side tonight." To the delight of the most of the audience, black vocalist Ethel Waters addressed the protestors with verve. "Now you children over there, listen to me," she was quoted as saying. "If I was over there close enough, I would smack you; but I love you, and I'd give you a big hug and kiss." Although the Nixon appearance occurred in largely Republican East Tennessee, rather than in a traditionally Democratic section of the South, the event received much regional and national attention and played out amid Nixon's obvious catering to the white Southern electorate. Whether helped or not by the Knoxville crusade, and although 1970 was not a propitious year for the Republican Southern Strategy, Brock would go on to defeat Gore in November.[43]

Graham, through his personal connections and popularity as a public figure, assisted the Southern Strategy of Richard Nixon. Graham did not contribute to what one historian has called "the Southernization of American politics"[44] so much as he facilitated a new type of Southern politics. For Graham (although not always for Nixon, and much less so for Vice President Spiro Agnew), influencing the course of Southern politics did not require revanchist appeals, à la George Wallace, to shibboleths of regional solidarity. Graham's discussions of the South often entailed more sanguine paeans to regional folkways, and his rhetoric about Southern race relations stressed the region's unique interracial intimacy. Graham behaved largely as a Southern moderate who supported integration, as well as Johnson's Great Society, at the same time that he evinced a preference for Republican presidential politics.

In light of many interpretations of the Southern Strategy, Graham's positions on race and politics might appear contradictory—or at least muddled. In aiding Nixon, the evangelist perhaps also abetted the forces of political reaction in the South. Certainly, many Southern politicians, such as Strom Thurmond, abandoned the Democratic Party largely over civil rights matters. This fact alone, of course, need not indict Graham as supporting Thurmond's brand of politics. Indeed, several scholars have recently shown that Nixon's appeals to Southern conservatives functioned more on the level of symbolism than policy. Even in the symbolic realm, Nixon largely referenced broad, traditional values—as during his visit to Knoxville—rather than specifically segregationist ones.[45] Nixon undoubtedly won the backing of many white racists in the South and at times used a coded language of race in doing so. Possibly, in Knoxville and elsewhere, Graham assisted Nixon in attracting these types of voters. In light of his long-standing policy of holding integrated services, however, Graham had by no means established a track record of garnering (or even seeking to garner) support from self-styled segregationists. More likely, then, Graham helped Nixon appeal to moderate evangelical Southerners, many of whom remained registered Democrats throughout the Nixon years.

Additionally, in the realm of policy, Nixon did not seek to turn back the clock on integration, as much as he resisted efforts (at least rhetorically) to broaden the purview of civil rights programs. Graham supported similar policies. The issue of school busing provides a fitting example. In 1970, at the request of Nixon, Graham produced five television spot announcements in which he urged white Southerners to "obey the law" and support public education amid school integration and court-ordered busing. According to Dent, the announcements received substantial airplay throughout most of the South. In the announcements, Graham acknowledged that many Southerners were "deeply disturbed" by busing changes—not because they opposed school integration, but because they objected to longer rides for their children. Graham later (and somewhat inaccurately) described the spot announcements as supporting "voluntary integration" in the South—a term that echoed Nixon's endorsement of "freedom of choice" plans for school integration.[46]

Ultimately, Graham's politics correlated with those of the South's growing metropolitan middle class, a group that increasingly leaned Republican. Numan Bartley has characterized this middle-class community as moderate on race, Republican in presidential politics, and supportive of economic development. Graham represented the values of this group. In his roles of renowned evangelist, peer of political leaders, and occasional regional spokesperson, Graham facilitated a type of postsegregation politics that was moderate at its core and ultimately correlative with party restructuring, as power shifted toward the metropolitan South. His evangelical language mediated and concomitantly limited the nature of Southern political change. To his audience members in the South, Graham combined awareness of the currents of modern life with evangelical reassurances that, in the words of one skeptical theologian in 1970, "the South of their childhoods—what they once knew and thought and counted on—is still to be believed in." These values appeared in the straightforward title of Graham's Memorial Day service in Knoxville: "God and Country Day."[47]

BILLY GRAHAM AS THE NATION'S MINISTER

As suggested by his involvement in a memorial service after the September 11, 2001, terrorist attacks, Billy Graham continues to proffer himself as the nation's minister as he attempts to provide a comforting message of individual salvation and civil religion. The national and international nature of his work, however, need not distract from his historical relationship with the U.S. South, particularly regarding the region's many social and political changes in the decade after World War II. Graham's connection to change within the region might initially seem incongruous, given that so many of his values correlate directly with the traditional values of white Southern evangelicalism. Indeed, after analyzing the 1970 Knoxville crusade, a group of sociologists labeled Graham crusades as representing "the dominant way of life, religiously, culturally and politically" in the South.[48] However, as a native son and a nationally recognized evangelist, Graham was in a unique position to influence his home region. His own life paralleled complex developments within the white South, as he moved toward an integrationist position and Republican politics. As a palpable Southerner, then, Graham both embodied and contributed to the evolution of Southern society and politics.

As more than another famous export of the South or a symbol of the nation's "Southernization," Graham sought to influence the region he called home. In his rhetoric about civil rights, and particularly in his integrated crusades in racially tense Alabama, Graham voiced positions somewhat, but not sharply to the left of many Southern politicians by favoring basic civil rights, gradual integration, and color-blind Christian fellowship. At the same time, he presented racism as a national problem, and he rather defensively contended that the South would solve its racial tensions faster than would the North. In the world of politics, Graham moved comfortably among Southern politicians. He parlayed these connections toward ends both benevolent (civil rights and Appalachian poverty work) and overtly political, in the case of supporting Richard Nixon. Graham also pointed toward the post–civil rights era emergence of yet another "new" South, this one aligned with middle-class values and Republican politics. Certainly, many of

Graham's biggest supporters were proponents of those characteristics. Evangelical moderates and development-minded civic leaders—not fundamentalists and political reactionaries—asked Graham to come south amid civil rights tensions.

Finally, Graham represents an intriguing window through which to consider the relationship between evangelical Christianity and sociopolitical change in the South. Graham's shifts toward earnest integration in his crusades and his identification with Republican politics manifested themselves most strikingly in the South, where they signified departures (if seemingly incongruous ones) from established patterns among whites. In no serious ways did these developments alter the basic premises of his evangelical theology, however. In his sermons, Graham continued to stress an individualistic grace theology and the conversion moment—a formula from which he has never seriously departed. Indeed, he posited the transformative effects of conversion, rather than activism and government policies, as the most effective means for ending racial prejudice and other social problems. Politicians from Eisenhower to Johnson and Nixon recognized the efficacy of Graham's evangelical mediation of race and politics in the South. In the 1970s, during the emergence of the Sunbelt, Jimmy Carter spoke a similar language when reflecting a thoroughly modern, yet enduringly pious image of the South. Graham and his style of evangelicalism became intrinsically linked with— rather than wholly oppositional to or in support of—the evolution of race relations and politics in the postwar South. Indeed, Graham suggests the peculiarly evangelical nature of the South's rapprochement with modernity.

Notes

1. William Martin, "Billy Graham," in *Varieties of Southern Evangelicalism*, ed. David Edwin Harrell (Macon, Ga.: Mercer University Press, 1981), 83. Martin's *A Prophet with Honor: The Billy Graham Story* (New York: William Morrow, 1991), provides the most thorough biography of Graham. See also Grant Wacker, "'Charles Atlas with a Halo': America's Billy Graham" (review of Martin's work), *Christian Century*, April 1, 1992, 336–41. Historian William McLoughlin situated Graham within what he termed the "fourth great awakening" in *Billy Graham: Revivalist in a Secular Age* (New York: Ronald Press, 1960). Joel Carpenter's *Revive Us Again: The Reawakening of American Fundamentalism* (New York: Oxford University Press, 1997) provides an incisive treatment of Graham and neoevangelicalism.

2. Ranking from John Shelton Reed, "The Twenty Most Influential Southerners of the Twentieth Century," *Southern Cultures* 7 (Spring 2001): 96–100. Historians of the South have understood Graham primarily in relation to two aspects of regional change: the postwar rise of metropolitan, entrepreneurial evangelicalism; and a general exportation of Southern culture to the nation. Examples of the former

include Numan Bartley, *The New South, 1945–1980* (Baton Rouge: Louisiana State University Press, 1995), 270–77; and Joe E. Barnhart, "Billy Graham," in *Encyclopedia of Southern Culture,* ed. Charles Reagan Wilson and William Ferris (Chapel Hill: University of North Carolina Press, 1989), 1319. Barnhart also embraced the latter interpretation, as did John Egerton in *The Americanization of Dixie: The Southernization of America* (New York: Harper's Magazine Press, 1974), 192–95. Two dissertations on the whole perceive Graham's sociopolitical behavior as reflective of his Southern identity, although the works do not relate Graham specifically to developments within the region. See Jerry Berl Hopkins, "Billy Graham and the Race Problem" (Ph.D. diss., University of Kentucky, 1986); and Eric J. Paddon, "Modern Mordecai: Billy Graham in the Political Arena, 1948–1980" (Ph.D. diss., Ohio University, 1999).

3. Martin E. Marty, "The Revival of Evangelicalism and Southern Religion," in Harrell, *Varieties of Southern Evangelicalism,* 9. Marty interpreted modernity in its postwar form as entailing questions about personal identity, as well as confusion about the correlation between personal agency and social change. In response to these modern developments, he contended, evangelical communities provided boundaries of identity and upheld the efficacy of personal religious experiences. As an evangelical, Graham readily related individual salvation to social change. As he wrote in 1965, "The greatest problem we face today is neither political nor social. It is the problem of man. When man gets right, the world will be right." See *Montgomery Advertiser,* June 7, 1965.

4. Samuel S. Hill Jr., *Southern Churches in Crisis Revisited* (Tuscaloosa: University of Alabama Press, 1999), 25. For a treatment of Graham and Southern revivalism, see Edward L. Moore, "Billy Graham and Martin Luther King, Jr.: An Inquiry into White and Black Rivalistic Traditions" (Ph.D. diss., Vanderbilt University, 1979). Martin, *Prophet with Honor,* 55–106. Martin argued that, particularly in terms of his cultivation of support from the professional community, Graham owed more to Northern than to Southern evangelistic traditions (Martin, "Billy Graham," 72).

5. "Southern lad" in Donald E. Hoke, "Harvesting at the Revival—In Columbia," in Billy Graham, *Revival in Our Time* (Wheaton, Ill.: Van Kampen Press, 1950), 21. Graham sermons, September 21 and November 25, 1958, Charlotte, North Carolina, available at www.wheaton.edu/bgc/archives/doc/bg-charlotte/charlotte/htm. Archives of the Billy Graham Center (hereafter BGC), Wheaton, Illinois. Graham also closed his Montgomery 1965 crusade with references to his Confederate heritage. See *Montgomery Advertiser,* June 21, 1965. Los Angeles sermon text in Graham, *Revival in Our Time,* 89. Billy Graham, *Just as I Am: The Autobiography of Billy Graham* (New York: Harper Collins, 1997), 3–12, 425–26, 714.

6. Metropolitan growth from Earl Black and Merle Black, *Politics and Society in the South* (Cambridge: Harvard University Press, 1987), 34–38. First Baptist Church from Martin, *Prophet with Honor,* 152. BGEA chronology, http://www.wheaton.edu/bgc/archives/bgeachro/bgeachron02.htm. Archives of BGC. Tabernacles in McLoughlin, *Billy Graham,* 163. Atlanta office in Bob Arnold, "Billy Graham: Superstar," *Southern Exposure* (Fall 1976): 81. "The Whiskey Rebellion," *Time,* February 22, 1950, 18. Poll in John Shelton Reed, *The Enduring South: Subcultural Persistence in Mass Society* (Lexington, Mass.: Lexington Books, 1972), 68. "Folk preacher" in Marshall Frady, "God and Man in the South," *Atlantic Monthly* (January 1967): 37–42.

7. "Billy Graham Sets the South an Example," *Christian Century,* November 19, 1958, 1358. The magazine suggested that Graham could "do much by example in the South to lessen the weight" of segregationists. Graham, *Just as I Am,* 425. Criswell in David L. Chappell, "Religious Ideas of the Segregationists," *Journal of American Studies* 32 (1998): 237–62. Bell's influence in Paddon, "Modern Mordecai," 120.

8. Hopkins, "Billy Graham and the Race Problem," 4, 33. Hopkins provides the most thorough overview of Graham's handling of race during the civil rights era. *Atlanta Constitution,* November 27, 1950. Jackson quotes from Hopkins, "Billy Graham and the Race Problem," 40–42.

9. Chattanooga quote from Graham, *Just as I Am,* 426. Press coverage from survey of *Chattanooga Times* and *Chattanooga News–Free Press,* March–April 1953. Photograph from *Billy Graham and the Black Community,* ed. Staff of *Decision* magazine (Minneapolis: World Wide Publications, 1973), 10. Eagles's analysis specifically concerns Mississippi. See Charles Eagles, "The Closing of Mississippi: Will Campbell, the $64,000 Question, and Religious Emphasis Week at the University of Mississippi," *Journal of Southern History* 67 (May 2001): 331–72.

10. Hopkins, "Billy Graham and the Race Problem," 56–61. *Atlanta Constitution,* January 14, 1964. Evangelists and integration in David Edwin Harrell Jr., "The South: Seedbed of Sectarianism," in Harrell, *Varieties of Southern Evangelicalism,* 53.

11. Billy Graham, "Billy Graham Makes Plea for an End to Intolerance," *Life,* October 1, 1956, 138–51; quote from 140. The article was accompanied by a published panel discussion among leading Southern clergy, including Nelson Bell, Graham's father-in-law.

12. Graham, "Billy Graham Makes Plea," 138, 140, 144. Graham, "Why Don't the Churches Practice the Brotherhood They Preach?" *Reader's Digest,* August 1960, 52–56; and the *AME Church Review* 78, no. 205 (July–September 1960): 52–56. On King, see *New York Times,* April 18, 1963. On Mississippi, see *Nashville Banner,* June 26, 1964. William H. Chafe, *Civilities and Civil Rights: Greensboro, North Carolina, and the Black Struggle for Freedom* (New York: Oxford University Press, 1980), 41–43.

13. Graham, "Billy Graham Makes Plea," 138, 146. Lee from Graham, "Billy Graham Makes Plea," 146; and "Brotherhood," 56. Historian Alan T. Nolan described the historical accuracy of this popular story about Lee as "highly unlikely." See Nolan, *Lee Considered: General Robert E. Lee and Civil War History* (Chapel Hill: University of North Carolina Press, 1991), 207.

14. The understanding of Southern moderates used here is drawn partially from both Chafe's description of white moderates/progressives ("who welcomed an atmosphere of tolerance but did not initiate or endorse change in the racial status quo") and Eagles's description of the "liberal" Raleigh newspaper editor Jonathan Daniels (who "advocated a cautious, compromising, prudent approach to change . . . counseling obedience to the law and gradual progress in racial matters"). See Chafe, *Civilities and Civil Rights,* 43; and Eagles, *Jonathan Daniels and Race Relations: The Evolution of a Southern Liberal* (Knoxville: University of Tennessee Press, 1982), 235. Boykin, Eisenhower, and meetings in Martin, *Prophet with Honor,* 201. Graham's claim from Graham, "Billy Graham Makes Plea," 138. North Carolina request and Baptist integration in Martin, *Prophet with Honor,* 234, 169. In 1952, Southern Baptist Seminary in Louisville, Kentucky, was already integrated. Survey of *Nashville Banner* and *Nashville Tennesseean,* August–September 1954. Charlotte sermons from

Archives of BGC, September 21–October 25, 1958. "Example," *Christian Century,*
November 19, 1958, 1358.

15. Kasper in Martin, *Prophet with Honor,* 234. Kasper was jeered when he disparaged Graham during a speech in Charlotte. See *Southern School News)* October
1958): 13. Baptist group in *Southern School News* (July 1957): 4. Timmerman quote
in Hopkins, "Billy Graham and the Race Problem," 89. Jones's opposition from "Boycotting Billy," *Time,* March 18, 1965, 103. Taylor Dalhouse, *An Island in the Lake of
Fire: Bob Jones University, Fundamentalism, and the Separatist Movement* (Athens:
University of Georgia Press, 1996), 2–3, 78–84.

16. Clinton visit and Little Rock consultation in Graham, *Just as I Am,* 201–2.
Clinton conversion in Hopkins, "Billy Graham and the Race Problem," 95. Organization in Drew Pearson, *Diaries: 1949–1959* (New York: Holt, 1974), 487–88. Quote
from Hopkins, "Billy Graham and the Race Problem," 80. Reaction of ministers
and Hays advice in Ernest Q. Campbell and Thomas F. Pettigrew, *Christians in
Racial Crisis: A Study of Little Rock's Ministry* (Washington, D.C.: Public Affairs
Press, 1959), 55, 82. According to Campbell and Pettigrew, Little Rock fundamentalists were opposed to involvement in race issues, whereas some prointegration
ministers thought a 1958 visit would come too soon after the tensions. "Little Rock's
Convert," *Time,* September 28, 1959, 42. President Bill Clinton later wrote that he had
been inspired as a child by an integrated Graham service in Little Rock. See Graham,
Just as I Am, 650.

17. "Mike" in Graham, *Just as I Am,* 360, as well as Taylor Branch, *Parting the
Waters: America in the King Years, 1954–1963* (New York: Touchstone, 1988), 227.
Branch contended that King borrowed from Graham's "revival-style format" when
organizing in cities (227). Graham quotes from *New York Times,* April 18, 1963. The
cautious sentiments of Graham and the Birmingham ministers were affirmed by
such national media outlets as *Time,* the *New York Times,* and the *Washington Post.*
See Terri Barr, "Rabbi Grafman and Birmingham's Civil Rights Era," in *The Quiet
Voices: Southern Rabbis and Black Civil Rights, 1880s to 1990s,* ed. Mark Bauman and
Berkley Kalin (Tuscaloosa: University of Alabama Press, 1997), 178.

18. Church rebuilding and feelers in Hopkins, "Billy Graham and the Race Problem," 116–17. "Dynamite Hill" from *New York Times,* March 30, 1964. Birmingham
invitation in *Birmingham News,* March 24 and 28, 1964.

19. Description of audience, J. L. Ware, Citizens' Council, and reference to bomb
throwers from *New York Times,* March 30, 1964. On Ware, see Andrew M. Manis, *A
Fire You Can't Put Out: The Civil Rights Life of Birmingham's Reverend Fred
Shuttlesworth* (Tuscaloosa: University of Alabama Press, 1999), 184–87, 260. Boutwell,
Bryant, and sermon quotes in *Birmingham News,* March 30, 1964. United Press In-
ternational story in *Nashville Banner,* March 30, 1964.

20. Response estimates and quotes from *Birmingham News,* March 30, 1964;
and Associated Press (AP) story, *Atlanta Constitution,* March 30, 1964. During crusades in Memphis (1951) and Greenville, South Carolina (1966), respondents numbered significantly less than 10 percent of the total audience. See Martin, *Prophet
with Honor,* 318; and Billy Graham, *America's Hour of Decision* (Wheaton, Ill.: Van
Kampen Press, 1951), 84–89.

21. Largest integrated service in *New York Times,* March 30, 1964; *Birmingham
News,* March 31 and April 5, 1964; Eagles, *Jonathan Daniels,* 227. "Signal day" in
Birmingham News, March 24, 1964; *Birmingham World,* April 4, 1964. Ministerial

Association of Birmingham petition, May 4, 1964, Protestant Pastors' Union Papers, File 911.2.30, Birmingham Public Library, Archives Department. Other requests in Hopkins, "Billy Graham and the Race Problem," 119.

22. Hopkins, "Billy Graham and the Race Problem," 128. "Billy Heads South," *Time,* April 30, 1965, 88–89. *New York Times,* April 17, 1965. AP story, *Montgomery Advertiser,* April 23, 1965.

23. "South," *Time,* April 30, 1965, 88–89. Crowd size and radio address quote from AP stories, *Montgomery Advertiser,* April 25 and 26, 1965. Citizens' Council quote in *Birmingham News,* May 9, 1965. In his *Atlantic Monthly* article, Frady cited Graham's "too much time" quote disparagingly (40). Criswell from *Montgomery Advertiser,* April 26, 1965. Tuskegee in *Montgomery Advertiser,* April 28, 1965. Alabama House in *Montgomery Advertiser,* May 1 and June 19, 1965. Georgia address in *Atlanta Constitution,* January 15, 1964.

24. Graham hinted that he and Wallace "did discuss" what a journalist termed "sociological matters." See *Montgomery Advertiser,* June 7, 1965. Previous experiences and church incident in Hopkins, "Billy Graham and the Race Problem," 131–33. Photographs, black minister, and Waters in *Montgomery Advertiser,* June 20, 1965, June 14, 1965, and June 18, 1965, respectively. Editorial and minister in *Montgomery Advertiser,* June 20, 1965, and June 10, 1965, respectively.

25. "One Southerner" in *Montgomery Advertiser,* June 21, 1965. "Extremists" in AP story, *New York Times,* June 21, 1965. "Conscience" in *Montgomery Advertiser,* April 27, 1965. "All races" in *Montgomery Advertiser,* June 7, 1965. Montgomery reflections in *New York Times,* June 20, 1965. Letter in *Montgomery Advertiser,* May 30, 1965. Network coverage in *Miami Herald,* June 25, 1965; and "The Hangover Syndrome," *Christian Century,* January 7, 1970, 31.

26. "Whipping boy" quoted in Hopkins, "Billy Graham and the Race Problem," 129. North-South quote in AP story, *Atlanta Constitution,* April 23, 1965. Alabama leaders in AP story, *Montgomery Advertiser,* April 25, 1965. "Selmas" in "South," *Time,* April 30, 1965, 88–89. Graham also gave the South a leg up on race relations during his address to the Georgia legislature. See *Atlanta Constitution,* January 15, 1964.

27. *New York Times,* April 17, 1965. Mississippi reference, *Nashville Banner,* June 26, 1964. "Demonstrations" quote in AP story, *Montgomery Advertiser,* April 27, 1965. In his autobiography, Graham attributed to King these rather succinct words of advice: "You stay in the stadium, because you have more impact on the white establishment there than you would if you march in the streets. Besides, you have a constituency that will listen to you, especially among white people, who will not listen so much to me" (*Just as I Am,* 426).

28. Chafe, *Civilities and Civil Rights,* 7–8. On Hudgins, see Charles Marsh, *God's Long Summer: Stories of Faith and Civil Rights* (Princeton: Princeton University Press, 1997), 82–115. Clinton quote in *Southern School News* (January 1959): 7.

29. Hill, *Southern Churches,* 73, 114. Hill quoted William McCullough's description of Graham as preferring "to make all social reform an appendage of revivalism and to subordinate all other activities to soul-winning" (114–15).

30. In the preface of his autobiography, Graham wrote, "The evangelist is not called to do everything in the church or in the world that God wants done" (*Just as I Am,* xi). Somewhat ironically, he framed the same preface around descriptions of visits with President Harry Truman (1950) and North Korean premier Kim Il Sung (1992). Paddon argued that Graham adopted a proactive, mostly

consistent approach of "this far only" in relation to the political arena. See Paddon, "Modern Mordecai."

31. Lowell D. Streiker and Gerald S. Strober, *Religion and the New Majority: Billy Graham, Middle America, and the Politics of the '70s* (New York: Association Press, 1972), 61.

32. Stephen J. Whitfield cast the rise of Graham as a cold war phenomenon in *The Culture of the Cold War,* 2nd ed. (Baltimore: Johns Hopkins University Press, 1996), 77–82. Graham's relationship with Truman never blossomed as a result of a combination of Truman's skepticism about evangelists and a protocol gaffe on the part of Graham. "Christ for This Crisis," November 1947 promotional poster, "Billy Graham Evangelistic Association Scrap Books: Book 1, YFC Rallies 1945–51 to Book 12, New England 1950," Microfilm Roll SB-360-1, Archives of BGC. Sermon titles from *Atlanta Constitution,* December 7, 1950, and *Chattanooga Times,* April 13, 1953. Charlotte letter quoted in Martin, *Prophet with Honor,* 245; and Peter Applebome, *Dixie Rising: How the South Is Shaping American Values, Politics, and Culture* (New York: Times Books, 1996), 171.

33. *Chattanooga Times,* March 15, 1953. *Chattanooga News–Free Press,* March 15, 1953. Election from Black and Black, *Politics and Society,* 34–49, 262. Hugh D. Graham and Numan Bartley documented the rise of urban Republicanism in *Southern Politics and the Second Reconstruction* (Baltimore: Johns Hopkins University Press, 1975), 81–110. The 1952 presidential election, they argued, "clearly established the G.O.P. as the respectable party of the urban and suburban affluent whites in the South's large and small cities" (86). Likewise, George Brown Tindall characterized the postwar rise of Republicanism as "an urban phenomenon." See Tindall, *The Disruption of the Solid South* (New York: Norton, 1972), 49–55. Samuel Lubell made a similar argument during the 1950s, contending that Southern support for the GOP varied between economic and racial motivations. See Lubell, *Revolt of the Moderates* (New York: Harpers and Brothers, 1956).

34. In his autobiography, Graham wrote that, into the late 1960s, "I had more friends in the Democratic party than I did in the Republican party; being a Southerner, I knew most of them" (*Just as I Am,* 448). Senate offer in *Atlanta Constitution,* November 28, 1950. Frank Porter Graham relation in Martin, *Prophet with Honor,* 66. Hunt proposal in Martin, *Prophet with Honor,* 300–301. Graham, *Just as I Am,* 410–11.

35. Thurmond quote, legislation, and picture from *Columbia State,* February 27, 1950; *Columbia Record,* March 10, 1950; and *Atlanta Journal,* February 28, 1950, respectively. Legislature from *Columbia Record,* March 1, 1950. Bartley, *New South,* 274.

36. Moyers's comments in Marshall Frady, *Billy Graham: Parable of American Righteousness* (Boston: Little, Brown, 1979), 260–65. Graham describes his relationship with Johnson in *Just as I Am,* 405–6. War on Poverty reference, *Nashville Tennessean,* May 25, 1964. Voting rights support in United Press International story, *Charlotte Observer,* March 17, 1965. Hopkins, "Billy Graham and the Race Problem," 120. Office of Economic Opportunity advocacy in Graham, *Just as I Am,* 397; and Martin, *Prophet with Honor,* 343. Although Graham never opposed the Vietnam War, his enthusiasm for U.S. involvement grew somewhat less strident during the latter years of the Johnson administration. See Martin, *Prophet with Honor,* 365–68.

37. Goldwater endorsement in Martin, *Prophet with Honor,* 407. Graham and

Bartley noted that Goldwater's opposition to civil rights legislation cost him the support of black voters in the urban South (*Southern Politics*, 107).

38. Nixon meeting in John Corry, "God, Country, and Billy Graham," *Harper's* (February 1969): 39; and Graham, *Just as I Am*, 440–41. 1960 Nixon campaign in Martin, *Prophet with Honor*, 273–280. Graham also contributed an article to the Luce-owned *Life* magazine in which he effectively endorsed Nixon. He eventually requested that the article not be published. Graham and Bartley, *Southern Politics*, 90–92.

39. Paddon, "Modern Mordecai," 11 ("Kitchen Cabinet"), 234 (Johnson meeting). Harry S. Dent, *The Prodigal South Returns to Power* (New York: Wiley, 1978), 269. Wallace meetings in Dan T. Carter, *The Politics of Rage: George Wallace, the Origins of the New Conservatism and the Transformation of American Politics*, 2nd ed. (Baton Rouge: Louisiana State University Press, 2000), 449. 1972 election results in Black and Black, *Politics and Society*, 263; and Graham and Bartley, *Southern Politics*, 173.

40. Haldeman quoted in Martin, *Prophet with Honor*, 391. "The Preaching and the Power," *Newsweek*, July 20, 1970, 54. Frady, *Billy Graham*, 450.

41. Graham and Bartley, *Southern Politics*, 157. During the 1968 campaign, Nixon made a publicized visit to Morrow Graham, the evangelist's mother. See Frady, *Billy Graham*, 447–49.

42. Planning in Randall E. King, "When Worlds Collide: Politics, Religion, and Media at the 1970 East Tennessee Billy Graham Crusade," *Journal of Church and State* 39 (Spring 1997): 277–78. Cash et al., *Knoxville Journal*, May 25, 1970. Graham quote in *Knoxville Journal*, May 22, 1970. "Youth Night" and Nixon comments in *Knoxville Journal*, May 27, 1970. Delegation description from *Knoxville News-Sentinel*, May 29, 1970.

43. Average crowd size in "The Presidency: In Praise of Youth," *Time*, June 8, 1970. Nixon "can now go about his challenging duties with the knowledge that America's heartland is with him," a *Knoxville Journal* editorial noted (May 30, 1970). Graham quote, service account, and Waters incident from *Knoxville News-Sentinel*, May 29, 1970. Nixon quotes from transcript of speech, *New York Times*, May 29, 1970. The event received front-page coverage in the May 29, 1970, editions of both major Nashville newspapers, as well as the *Atlanta Constitution*. Writing in 1971, two journalists connected the Nixon visit to his Southern Strategy. See Hal Gulliver and Reg Murphy, *The Southern Strategy* (New York: Scribner's, 1971), 122.

44. Carter, *Politics of Rage*, 324.

45. See Dean J. Kotlowski, "Nixon's Southern Strategy Revisited," *Journal of Policy History* 10 (1998): 207–27; Kotlowski, *Nixon's Civil Rights: Politics, Principle, and Policy* (Cambridge: Harvard University Press, 2001), 1–43; Lawrence J. McAndrews, "The Politics of Principle: Richard Nixon and School Desegregation," *Journal of Negro History* 83 (1998): 187–200; and Glen Moore, "Richard M. Nixon and the 1970 Midterm Elections in the South," *Southern Historian* 12 (1991): 60–71.

46. Kotlowski, "Nixon's Southern Strategy Revisited," 208. Dent, *Prodigal South*, 153–54. "Billy Graham Urges Compliance with School Integration Laws," *Christian Century*, September 23, 1970, 1115. Graham, *Just as I Am*, 452.

47. Bartley, *New South*, 277. Nixon and Southern middle class in Carter, *Politics of Rage*, 326; "The Preaching and the Power," *Newsweek*, July 20, 1970, 53; *Knoxville News-Sentinel*, May 29, 1970; and *Knoxville Journal*, May 30, 1970. Some scholars

have interpreted Graham's relationship with Nixon as establishing organizational and rhetorical groundwork for the subsequent rise of the Religious Right. Martin made this point, whereas Joe E. Barnhart viewed Graham's early rhetoric as fore-shadowing the language of Jerry Falwell et al. See William Martin, *With God on Our Side: The Rise of the Religious Right in America* (New York: Broadway, 1996); and Barnhart, "Billy Graham," 1319. Certainly, Graham, as a well-connected evangelist, influenced a Republican tendency toward seeking the support of evangelical leaders. To some extent, however, the Religious Right, with its strong appeals to family and gender norms, grew so quickly during the latter part of the 1970s precisely because established evangelicals, such as Graham, had not, for the most part, aggressively politicized divisive cultural issues. Graham has always maintained a substantial and critical distance from the Religious Right.

48. Donald Clelland et al., "In the Company of the Converted: Characteristics of a Billy Graham Crusade Audience," *Sociological Analysis* 35 (Spring 1974): 53.

Southern Baptist Clergy, the Christian Right, and Political Activism in the South

James L. Guth

Religion has always played a part in Southern politics, although that role has often been obscured. The leaders of institutional religion, the clergy, have often been deeply enmeshed in critical political developments in the region, though often while denying any such involvement. In this chapter, I consider the nature of contemporary political activity among an important Southern religious elite, the clergy of the Southern Baptist Convention (SBC), the region's "Established Church." The SBC is also the nation's largest Protestant denomination, with almost 16 million members in over 39,000 congregations located in every state. The SBC's membership growth, increasing conservatism, and growing activism have made it an important political force, especially in its native region.

In the following pages, I provide an overview and explanation of contemporary SBC clerical activism, drawing on a variety of sources. First, I sketch a brief historical picture of the denomination, pointing out characteristic political concerns and activities during its history. Then I consider the recent theological reorientation within the SBC, especially from 1980 to the present, which was accompanied by increasingly political conservatism and politicization of the denomination's elected leadership and clergy. Finally, I attempt to explain that activism by use of data from a 2000 survey of Southern Baptist ministers.

SBC HISTORY AND POLITICS

In some important ways, Southern Baptists have always been in politics. Colonial Baptists, who emerged from the Reformation's radical wing, faced widespread persecution from established churches and gladly joined Madison and Jefferson in their fight for separation of church and state. Baptist belief in adult baptism, individual competence to interpret Scripture, congregational autonomy, and a nonprofessional clergy were both shaped by and fostered American democratic culture.[1] In one sense, however, the SBC itself began in a less democratic vein, when Southern Baptists left the national movement in 1845 in a quarrel over slaveholding missionaries. This breach, which was a religious harbinger of the Civil War, has never been repaired, unlike the later schisms among Methodists and Presbyterians. During the war itself, Southern Baptist preachers emerged as some of the most vocal defenders of the Confederacy.[2]

After the Civil War, Southern Baptists began a steady expansion, despite the social and economic hardships of the Reconstruction era, and they overtook Methodists as the region's largest denomination. This growth revealed some of the limitations of the SBC's decentralized structure of mission agencies. During the 1920s, the SBC responded to these problems by creating the Cooperative Program, in which churches merged funds for mission agencies and seminaries. This program's rousing success simultaneously created a strong denominational identity and encouraged organizational isolation. Indeed, with few exceptions, Southern Baptists strenuously avoided ecumenical entanglements, even with other conservative Protestants, for most of the twentieth century.

During this expansionist era, Southern Baptist politics was usually muted. Although Baptist clergy played an especially prominent role in the development of the "religion of the Lost Cause," sacralizing the wartime sacrifices of white Southerners on the altar of the Confederacy,[3] broader clerical engagement was limited, for several reasons. Most SBC clergy were still blue-collar "called" ministers, limited politically by education and social class. Although most Baptists welcomed the return of Democratic Party hegemony, the development of the Solid Democratic South after 1896 also narrowed political options and opportunities—and not just for clergy. Many Baptist clergy also held strong attachments to church-state separationism and premillennialist theology, both of which encouraged political abstinence.

Above all, however, it was ministers' own understanding of their proper political role that limited clerical activism. As Rufus Spain has observed, Southern Baptists after the Civil War debated at length the appropriate degree and kinds of ministerial political involvement: "After years of disagreement they had fairly well agreed by 1900 that ministers had all the political rights of citizens, although the propriety of using those rights was questionable. Preachers should vote, but not seek political office; they should refrain from partisan politics; and they should preach on political questions only as those questions concerned public or private morals."[4] As a result of the last specification, ministers' political quietism sometimes gave way to sporadic activism on "moral" issues such as Prohibition, gambling, and evolution.[5]

Although by 1900 Southern Baptist clergy were increasingly calling on public authorities to enforce traditional morality, in this and other matters, Southern Baptist ideology was deeply conservative, usually buttressing the social, racial, and political status quo. Even during the Progressive Era, the Social Gospel made relatively few inroads among Southern Baptist ministers.[6] Indeed, these deeply traditionalist political tendencies persisted throughout the first half of the twentieth century. Although a few college professors and institutional leaders might agitate for a Southern Baptist version of the Social Gospel, clergy and laity alike rejected their efforts. Nowhere was this more evident than in the reaction of most Southern Baptist clergy to the emerging civil rights movement of the 1950s, which met widespread opposition within the denomination, despite the efforts of some leaders to set a more moderate course.[7]

By 1970, however, many SBC leaders were reconsidering the theological, ideological, and political commitments of the denomination. Seminary professors were beginning to break the theological isolation of the denomination, engaging wider currents of Christian theology, although usually within a conservative context. The controversies over segregation had caused many thoughtful Baptists to rethink the denomination's attachment to the racial status quo. At the same time, many denominational officials, especially in the SBC's Christian Life Commission and within the Baptist Joint Committee on Public Affairs, were both inching toward the political center and calling for more civic engagement, especially by the clergy and dedicated laity. These developments were epitomized by the election of Southern Baptist Sunday school teacher Jimmy Carter to the presidency in 1976.

This shift toward the theological and political center did not go unchallenged, however. Beginning in 1979, SBC conservatives or "fundamentalists" mounted a powerful campaign to eject its "moderate" leaders, charging that they had allowed infiltration of the denomination by theological and political "liberals." Although on the grand scale of Protestant theology the two sides might appear quite close, the internecine warfare was extremely fierce. After fifteen years of massive mobilization and razor-thin election margins at annual meetings, the conservatives were finally victorious, and they set about a systematic purge of their foes from SBC agencies and seminaries.[8] By 2000 this campaign was complete, and annual conventions settled into relatively routine events attended primarily by theological and political conservatives.

POLITICAL RUMBLINGS

Beyond the religious ramifications, this revolution fundamentally reshaped SBC politics. The leaders of the conservative mobilization were invariably either Christian Right notables or avid fellow travelers. During the SBC's hotly contested annual meetings in the 1980s, political controversies often garnered as much attention and controversy as the theological strife. By 1991, however, SBC convention resolutions were fully aligned with the Christian Right agenda on abortion, gay rights, school prayer, education vouchers, parental choice, and other matters. Prominent Republicans, including President George H. W. Bush, Vice President Dan Quayle, and Iran-Contra figure Oliver North, were often featured speakers at the annual meetings or at associated events.

The SBC's new conservative elite also restructured the denomination's social and political outreach. They first "defunded" the Baptist Joint Committee on Public Affairs, long the SBC's voice on religious liberty issues and a staunch defender of church-state separation. To compensate, they broadened the mandate of the Christian Life Commission, once the SBC's liberal social conscience but now veering right. During the 1990s, the Christian Life Commission was renamed the Ethics and Religious Liberty Commission (ERLC) and built a well-staffed Washington office, led by activist Richard Land. The ERLC quickly moved into a vigorous political role, occasionally on the liberal side (on racial bias and hunger), but most often in alliance with the Christian Right on abortion, gay rights, and other moral issues. Land also encouraged closer SBC cooperation with other orthodox Protestant groups, such as the National Association of Evangelicals—and even advocated political alliances with traditionalist Catholics.

During the presidential elections of 1992 and 1996, the SBC leadership's preferences were obvious. ERLC activities, such as the distribution of voter guides in Baptist churches, clearly favored the Republican ticket over fellow Southern Baptists Bill Clinton and Al Gore. Not surprisingly, denominational leaders provided little help for Clinton objectives while he was in office, despite initial promises of rapprochement. Clinton's early actions reversing Reagan-Bush abortion limitations, proposals on gays in the military, and nominations of social liberals to important posts quickly eliminated any possibility of cooperation. At the 1993 SBC convention, some twenty resolutions critical of Clinton policies were finally combined in an admonition to Clinton and Gore to "affirm biblical morality in exercising public office." An abortive effort was even made to "withdraw fellowship" from both men; representatives from Clinton's church in Little Rock were required to state their personal opposition to homosexuality before being seated. Ed Young, whose Second Baptist Church of Houston was famous for its extensive program of political activity, was reelected SBC president without opposition.

Throughout both Clinton administrations, SBC leaders remained fierce critics of Clinton social policies. During the Lewinsky scandal, they also condemned his personal behavior and vocally supported impeachment. By the end of the decade, then, SBC leaders were strongly aligned with the presidential wing of the Republican Party.[9] During the GOP presidential primary race in 2000, several SBC leaders advised Texas governor George W. Bush and, in the general election, Southern Baptist officials clearly favored Methodist Bush over fellow Southern Baptist Al Gore. Similarly, Southern Baptists in Congress were increasingly numerous and prominent on the GOP side of the aisle, including party leaders such as Newt Gingrich, Tom DeLay, and J. C. Watts in the House, and Trent Lott, the Senate majority whip and later the majority leader. Thus, the denomination has become a bulwark of the GOP's religious coalition.

PARTISANSHIP AND PRESIDENTIAL POLITICS

The trajectory of the SBC clergy's political migration from the traditional Democratic attachments of the old Solid South is evident in their political choices in the years since 1980. Table 7.1, which draws on surveys of SBC clergy in each presidential election year, lists the changes in partisan preference, presidential vote, and campaign activity over this period. In 1980, just as the SBC's fundamentalist movement was picking up steam, Democrats still made up almost half of the clergy, with another quarter claiming to be political independents. Only 27 percent identified as Republican. The traditional Solid South was somewhat attenuated, but Democrats were still the dominant political group among SBC ministers.

This changed rather dramatically in 1984 and the years thereafter. Beginning in 1984, the survey instrument used the standard National Election Studies seven-point party identification scale, rather than Gallup's three-point Democratic, Independent, or Republican item used in 1980. Although

Table 7.1

Partisanship, Presidential Vote, and Campaign Activism among
Southern Baptist Ministers, 1980–2000 (by percentage)

	1980	1984	1988	1992	1996	2000
Partisanship						
Strong GOP		28	24	30	41	50
Weak GOP	27	8	12	12	13	13
Lean GOP		30	31	31	26	18
Independent	28	9	10	8	7	6
Lean Democrat		8	8	6	6	3
Weak Democrat	45	9	8	7	4	5
Strong Democrat		8	7	6	3	5
Presidential Choice						
GOP	56	81	82	78	80	88
Democratic	42	16	17	18	14	12
Third Party	2	3	1	4	6	—
Proportion Active in Support of a Presidential Candidate						
GOP voters	—	—	40	65	46	63
Democratic voters	—	—	31	46	22	41
N	450	870	649	456	325	455

the data from 1980 and 1984 are not directly comparable, there is no doubt that Democratic identification suffered a huge drop between those elections. Even if independents who felt "closer to" the party are counted as Democrats, only 25 percent of the clergy still claimed some Democratic attachment in 1984. And although the total of "strong" and "weak" Republicans rises to 36 percent, this number is almost matched by independents who said that they were "closer to" the GOP. In fact, if all the independents are added together in 1984, they make up almost half of the clergy (47 percent), a much larger proportion than in 1980. Baptist ministers were obviously in political transition.

The story of the next two decades is very simple: continuing attenuation of any Democratic proclivities among the clergy, and movement of larger proportions into the "strong" Republican camp. Indeed, by the 2000 election, half the ministers claimed this title. Throughout the period, two factors contributed to this trend: conversion and selective recruitment. Many SBC clergy, especially older ministers, report moving toward the GOP over time, abandoning their previous Democratic attachments. At the same time, younger clergy have been disproportionately Republican from the start, especially those reaching maturity in the Reagan era and educated in the increasingly conservative environments of SBC seminaries and other evangelical institutions. Finally, the results may also be influenced by exit, as more theologically and politically liberal ministers have abandoned the SBC or have left the pulpit altogether.

These partisan changes are naturally reflected in the presidential choices of SBC ministers. Although I have no survey data for 1976, much evidence suggests that a solid majority of Southern Baptist ministers favored Jimmy Carter's candidacy, including—ironically—many who would lead the SBC phalanx in the Christian Right four years later. In 1980 many prominent SBC conservatives endorsed Ronald Reagan's candidacy. Grassroots sentiment among clergy moved in the same direction, giving him a solid majority over President Carter. As table 7.1 shows, in the presidential elections that followed, Republican nominees seldom slipped below four-fifths of the clergy vote, with George W. Bush peaking at almost nine out of ten ministers in 2000. Although some smaller evangelical denominations might exhibit even greater clerical uniformity, it is hard to imagine more political cohesion in a large national church such as the SBC.

Finally, I should note that Southern Baptist clergy had not only abandoned the Democratic Party, but had also rejected the old denominational consensus against ministerial involvement in partisan politics. Beginning in 1988, I sought to ascertain whether clergy were providing some sort of visible leadership for their congregation or even the larger community in presidential contests. Although I asked many questions on general political activism (which I shall use below), I addressed presidential campaign involvement explicitly. After inquiring about the minister's choice of presidential candidate, I added the following question: "Many people also work for a candidate by wearing campaign buttons, putting a sign in front of their house, attending rallies and speeches, etc. Beyond voting, did you actively support [your] candidate during the 2000 general election?" The ministers could choose "Yes" or "No" and then check whether they were "very," "somewhat," or "slightly" active.

In the final section of table 7.1, I report the percentage of Republican and Democratic voters who reported at least some activity on behalf of a presidential candidate. Although the percentages fluctuate from year to year, rising in the hot campaign years of 1992 and 2000, the level of activism is quite impressive for both Republicans and Democrats. In each year, however, the large Republican contingent reports substantially more activity than the faithful Democratic remnant does. This pattern is also reflected in general political activism: conservative and Republican ministers are more involved in a wide range of political actions than are their more liberal and Democratic colleagues.

To sum up, over the past two decades, the Southern Baptist clergy has become an important factor in the growing Republican strength in the formerly Democratic Solid South. They increasingly identify as Republicans, vote overwhelmingly for Republican presidential candidates, and work for Republican tickets, at least in presidential elections. And all the evidence suggests that their propensities increasingly affect "down ticket" races for the U.S. Senate and House, gubernatorial elections, and even state legislative seats. And clergy politics are also likely to involve a wide range of concerns in the local community, ranging from educational policies to zoning of adult entertainment facilities.

EXPLAINING CLERICAL ACTIVISM

How do I explain this rising clerical activism? To answer this query, I turn to an analysis of data from a survey of Southern Baptist clergy during the election of 2000.[10] First, I construct a measure of general political participation. Then I review relevant strands of political science theory on activism, drawn from both the literatures on mass public involvement and on ministerial politics. As I review each strand of theory, I report bivariate relationships, checking whether there is at least prima facie support for that perspective. Finally, I use a multivariate analysis of the competing perspectives to draw some conclusions about clerical political activity, making some comparisons with earlier studies of the SBC.

The political participation measure is an additive index of thirty-six acts, ranging from pulpit pronouncements to actual campaigning. Collectively, they produce a highly reliable index, ranging from 0 to 27, with a mean of 7.83 and a standard deviation of 6.33.[11] Even today, the index reveals, some Baptist ministers abstain from politics, whereas others are "complete activists." About 10 percent of preachers report no political actions in 2000, whereas an equal percentage claim 17 or more. The question is

obvious: why do some Baptist pastors join the political fray while others remain aloof?

Scholarly analysis of political participation has traditionally focused on
the mass public, with little attention to occupational groups, although Sidney
Verba, Kay Lehman Schlozman, and Henry E. Brady have noted that professional groups may display "different configurations of participatory factors
and levels of activity."[12] Taken together, however, the literatures on mass participation and on clerical politics offer four partially competing theories
explaining activism, emphasizing personal resources, professional ideology,
issue mobilization, and organizational activity. There are good reasons to
believe that each might play some role in the contemporary politicization of
the Baptist clergy. As I shall demonstrate, a first cut provides some support
for each view, but in the end, professional role orientation, ideology, and
organizational mobilization best account for clerical participation among
Southern Baptists.

Socioeconomic Status

The classic works on mass political participation emphasized the socioeconomic status model. This posits that political involvement was the product
of high social class origins, wealth, and advanced education, all of which
supply citizens with the personal resources for effective action.[13] Similarly,
most studies find that older citizens, who have more life experience, know
more about politics, and are more settled in their communities, evidence
higher activity levels.[14] Urban residence sometimes seems to facilitate participation, but in other studies, rural life encourages activity.[15]

Are Southern Baptist ministers affected by social status in the same way
as other citizens? At first glance, ministers might seem socially homogeneous,
as well-educated professionals with middle-class incomes. Indeed, most
scholars have made this assumption, and some conclude that such status
explains the clergy's characteristic high rates of participation.[16] Like many
other clergy in the evangelical tradition, however, Southern Baptists come
from almost every imaginable social class background (but primarily working class), have differing educational experiences, and enjoy a wide range of
incomes. This variation in personal status is reflected in the congregations
they serve: those with larger, middle-class congregations are not only
wealthier, but have at their disposal additional resources (and perhaps incentives) for political involvement.[17] In addition, as has been pointed out
elsewhere, differing kinds of educational experiences may have different
political effects.[18]

In another vein, age may also have a different impact among clergy. Generally, older citizens are more active. But in the 1960s, Harold E. Quinley found that younger clergy were most politically engaged, perhaps because of their extensive education, as a reaction to the political stimuli of the civil rights and Vietnam War era, or as a result of new role expectations inculcated in seminaries. In recent years, similar forces may well have shaped young conservatives: SBC ministers are increasingly well educated, grew up in the midst of protracted culture wars over abortion, gay rights, and sex education in the schools, and may be especially influenced by the new politicization of conservative Protestantism.

What did I find? Although I have fewer indicators of social status in the 2000 survey than in earlier studies, a quick review of table 7.2 shows that the link between personal status and political involvement is very weak. Surprisingly, age has virtually no relationship with participation, but length in time in the ministry does: those new to the profession are more active, as Quinley discovered in the late 1960s. Still, the correlation is weak. Nor does the size of the pastor's community have a statistically significant relationship to activism, although ministers in smaller communities tend to be a bit more active. And ministers in larger churches (with correspondingly larger salaries) are only a little more likely to be active, but again, the coefficient barely misses statistical significance.

More surprisingly, education seems to have little impact. The correlation for length of secular education with activism is positive, but small and statistically insignificant. Length of seminary education has virtually no influence. As has been argued elsewhere, however, the locus of education does make some difference, even within a single denomination.[19] Before the late 1980s, pastors educated in the two "liberal" SBC seminaries, Southern and Southeastern, tended to be most active, along with those from fundamentalist institutions outside the denomination. Pastors in other SBC seminaries fell in between. As the conservatives took over these institutions, however, their distinctiveness dwindled. Today graduates of all the historic SBC seminaries are less active than graduates of outside fundamentalist and evangelical schools, but the differences are small (data not shown).

Although these results are primarily negative, they do confirm that changes have occurred in the social location of SBC activism. During the 1970s and early 1980s, socially "advantaged" clergy dominated SBC politics: extensive education, higher social class origins, urban residence, and similar status measures all had strong positive correlations with participation, as did attendance at the more liberal SBC seminaries.[20] Although a 2000 study

Table 7.2

Personal Resources, Role Orientations, and Issue Mobilization as Influences on
Political Participation by Southern Baptist Convention Clergy

Characteristic	Pearson's r
Socioeconomic status	
Age	.00
Years in ministry	- .10*
Size of community	- .07
Size of church (pastoral income)	.08
Length of secular education	.08
Length of seminary education	.01
Psychological engagement	
Interest in 2000 campaign	.29**
Interest in politics	.28**
Political efficacy	.23**
Professional beliefs and role orientations	
Christian orthodoxy	.13*
Dispensationalism	.25**
Civic gospel	.24**
Civil religion	.15**
Separationism	- .39**
Approve ministerial activism	.46**
Approve denominational activism	.30**
Political beliefs encourage	.32**
Theological beliefs encourage	.27**
Pastoral duties require	.23**
Issue mobilization	
Strong Republican	.13*
Strong Democrat	- .14*
High moral reform agenda	.42**
High social reform agenda	- .20**
Strong issue conservatism	.34**
Strong issue liberalism	- .24**
Strong conservative identification	.24**
Strong liberal identification	- .03

* $p < .05$; ** $p < .001$

has fewer indicators of socioeconomic status, I can still say quite confidently that the influence of such factors has been erased, except for the marginal effects of education. Thus, I must look elsewhere to understand political activity by contemporary SBC clergy.

Psychological Engagement.

Many analysts argue that the most important personal resource is not status, but attitudes: strong political interest and a sense of political efficacy.[21] In the mass public, of course, such orientations often result from higher status and education, but among professional leaders, the continuing experience of conducting "public" activity may substitute in producing participatory attitudes. Indeed, if church membership produces civic skills and attitudes,[22] church leadership should have an even stronger effect.

In fact, for Baptist clergy, psychological engagement is a solid predictor of involvement. Participation is most strongly correlated with interest in the 2000 presidential campaign, general interest in politics, and confidence in a pastor's ability to influence the social and political views of the congregation, a vital type of professional efficacy. Although these coefficients are somewhat smaller than those reported in earlier iterations of this survey, this is largely the result of the increasingly uniform high levels of political interest, which has reduced the variation among SBC clergy.[23] In any case, ministerial activism is tied much more strongly to psychological engagement than to socioeconomic status, although comparison with past studies indicates that this is a recent development.

Professional Beliefs and Role Orientations

Theological Worldviews   Rather than focusing on social status or psychological engagement, as studies of the mass public do, most clergy studies have stressed theological beliefs that encourage this-worldly concerns, that foster approval of the church's political role, and that suggest that ministers should be politically active.[24] Indeed, it has been found previously that such theological and professional role orientations are powerful predictors of activism in many denominations.[25]

Competing theological perspectives have always been crucial to pastoral politics. Jeffrey K. Hadden and Harold E. Quinley found that "this-worldly" modernists, having abandoned supernatural Christian orthodoxy for a more liberal, naturalistic faith, outpoliticked "other-worldly" traditionalists.[26] Some scholars argued, however, that it was not orthodoxy that militated against political activity, but rather the dispensationalism that gripped many orthodox Protestants.[27] Dispensationalism emphasized the imminent Second Coming of Jesus, the end of this world, the priority of saving souls, and the futility of social and political reform—hardly a recipe for political activity.

There is massive evidence, however, that the relationship between theological perspectives and political activism has changed. Clergy who were not only orthodox but also dispensationalist fomented early Christian Right activism. Although some scholars have argued that such beliefs were downplayed to facilitate activism, there is little survey evidence to confirm this contention. Rather, dispensationalists modified their theories to accommodate a larger political role for Christians, including clergy, creating a new social theology I call the "civic gospel."[28] This perspective connects dispensationalism's characteristic pessimism about human history with the slide of American society away from its Christian origins toward a new, secular, and sinful identity. Unlike earlier versions of dispensationalist social theology, however, the civic gospel holds out some prospect for social reform if true Christians act. Just as the turn-of-the-century "Social Gospel" invited theological liberals into worldly politics, so the civic gospel calls for conservative activity. Thus, I might find the most orthodox and dispensational SBC clergy most active.[29]

I also expected that those ministers who have a basically positive assessment of the role religion plays in social and political life should be more active. If the arguments of social scientists such as Robert Putnam, Sidney Verba, and John DiIulio have led many intellectuals to reconsider the role of religion in American public life, clergy might also conclude that political involvement is a good thing, regardless of their theological stance. On the other hand, the revival of religious politics has also renewed separationist fervor, epitomized by groups such as Americans United for Separation of Church and State, the ACLU, and People for the American Way. Clergy adopting their perspective might limit their own activism, at least in religious venues.

To test all these possibilities, I calculated several theological measures. *Orthodoxy* is an additive index of items on the centrality of Jesus to salvation, the historicity of Adam and Eve, the Virgin Birth, the existence of the devil, and the Second Coming. *Dispensationalism* includes questions on biblical inerrancy, the special status of Israel in God's plan, the role of women in ministry, and two items on creation. The *civic gospel* measure incorporates six items: that the United States was founded as a Christian nation, that free enterprise is the only economic system truly compatible with Christian beliefs, that religious values are under attack in America, that government should protect the nation's religious heritage, that there is only one Christian view on most political issues, and that it is hard for political liberals to be true Christians. *Civil religion* comprises two items on whether religion has a salutary effect on social and political life. Finally, *separationism* includes four items stressing the necessity or desirability of churches and Christians staying out of politics.[30]

What did I find? First, SBC pastoral activism in 2000 is weakly correlated with Christian orthodoxy—not surprising given the lack of much variation in that measure—but is linked more strongly to dispensationalism, on which Baptist clergy differ more. Similarly, the civic gospel and civil religion variables are also positively associated with activism. Predictably, ministers scoring high on the separationism index were much more inactive. (As might be expected, dispensationalist ministers are indeed much more likely to score high on the civic gospel and, conversely, low on the separationism variable.) All these findings demonstrate that Southern Baptist activism is now the province of the most theologically conservative clergy, who have accepted a new rationale for political involvement.

Role Orientations   Although theological perspectives may influence ministers' views on the legitimacy of social and political activism, specific beliefs about such activity are likely to be embodied in stable role orientations about what clergy should or should not do, shared by those with similar theological views. In the 1960s heyday of the New Breed, modernist clergy approved far more forms of participation than did their orthodox brethren.[31] Even today, in mainline Protestant denominations, theologically liberal clergy are still somewhat more likely to approve activism, although the gap has certainly closed since the 1960s. But in some conservative denominations, including the SBC, the most orthodox actually have more positive attitudes.[32] In any event, I expect a strong link between role orientations and political activism, either because positive attitudes lead to greater activism or, as some argue, because activism produces more positive attitudes about involvement.

Not surprisingly, ministers' approval scores for *individual political activity* and for *denominational activism* exhibit strong links to involvement.[33] Thus, how ministers conceive of the appropriate political behavior for clergy—and the proper functions of denominational agencies—has a powerful relationship with what they actually do. In addition, I found that when ministers were directly asked what motivated their political involvement, the best bivariate predictors were, understandably, their own political and theological beliefs. Those ministers who saw political involvement resulting from "the duties of my position" were also much more active. Initially, at least, the size of these correlations suggests that professional beliefs incorporating political role orientations are likely to surpass the influence of socioeconomic status and even political engagement.

Issue Mobilization: Partisanship, Agenda, and Ideology

Analysts have also found that political attachments, beliefs, and issue concerns often elicit political activity. For example, political scientists have long noted that partisan and ideological affections often stimulate activism. Sometimes they assume that strength of partisan and ideological commitment is key, whatever its direction, but more often ideological and partisan "asymmetry" are found in activism, so that during particular eras either conservatives or liberals may dominate.[34] This phenomenon may be explained by Verba, Schlozman, and Brady's argument that citizens with strong sentiments on new issues such as abortion or the environment are activated by those feelings.[35] If the national agenda is not "balanced" in its ideological incentives, eras of advantage for one side or the other should naturally be expected.

To capture the impact of partisanship, I split the traditional seven-point party identification scale at the "pure independent" midpoint to create "strength of Republican" and "strength of Democratic" identification measures. (Thus, on the Republican measure, any kind of Democrat or pure independent was scored "0," an independent who leans Republican or a weak Republican "1," and a Strong Republican "2.") Indeed, the stronger the GOP attachment, the greater the activism, whereas strength of Democratic affiliation produces less involvement. Of course, among contemporary Baptist clergy Democratic partisans and "leaners" are very few (see table 7.1), and strong Republicans are dominant. But both measures do suggest that Republican loyalty is associated with activism in 2000, just as in the past, whereas Democratic ties seem to suppress involvement.[36]

This Republican advantage may stem from the emphasis put on "moral issues" in recent years, whether by party candidates or by associated Christian Right organizations. For at least two decades, issues such as abortion, gay rights, school prayer, and gambling have dominated the agendas of most SBC pastors, but a significant minority are more inclined to worry about social welfare policies, the environment, women's rights, and similar questions. Following the same procedure used in James L. Guth et al. (*The Bully*

Pulpit: The Politics of Protestant Preachers, 1997), I derived scores for the *moral reform* and *social justice* agendas.[37] Not surprisingly, preoccupation with the moral reform agenda is strongly correlated with activism, whereas concern for the social justice agenda is negatively associated in 2000.

Finally, ministers' ideological stances may influence their activity. Here two alternative operations produce almost identical conclusions. First, a *conservatism* score based on twenty policy items has a strong positive link to activism, but *liberalism* has a substantial negative one.[38] Confirming this finding, a second analysis using a bifurcated ideological self-identification scale reveals that conservatives are more active and liberals, less so. Quite clearly, the SBC clergy are a contemporary case of Verba and Nie's "hyperactive Republicans," mobilized by strong conservative beliefs.[39] To summarize: stronger GOP identification, moral issue concerns, and political conservatism are associated with greater activism. Strong Democratic and liberal commitments work against participation—at least in the SBC context during the 2000 election.

Organizational Mobilization

Activism also results from organizational mobilization. This may take the form of party efforts to increase turnout, interest groups seeking to elicit member activity, or other institutions attempting to activate citizens. Such mobilization should be especially pertinent to SBC clergy, enmeshed as they are in complex organizational networks.[40] They collaborate with other ministers in local Baptist associations, state conventions, and national bodies, whether the SBC itself, or its new competitor, the Cooperative Baptist Fellowship (CBF). They are employed by individual congregations (and dismissed by them with considerable regularity). And they join external organizations working for special causes, making them the target of communications from many sources, including the specialized religious media.

The Denominational Context   For Baptist clergy, intradenominational networks are crucial, given the SBC's long history of separatism, institutional self-sufficiency, and intensive internal politics. Denominational activity is a traditional outlet for clerical ambitions and may well influence political involvement. In 2000, fully 38 percent of pastors reported having attended five or more SBC national conventions. Although it is possible that heavy organizational involvement might preclude secular political activity, I suspect the opposite might be true. Because the SBC is now a fellow traveler of the Christian Right and its conventions have often resembled Republican rallies (especially in the years of presidential elections), frequent attendance might inspire clergy to greater political activity.

Table 7.3 shows that denominational activism has only a very modest spillover effect. Frequent attendance at SBC meetings has a weak positive association with political activity, but the coefficient is not quite statistically significant. Encouragement by other clergy is also correlated positively with activism, but again, the coefficient is weak and not quite statistically significant. More explicitly "political" SBC associations may have greater importance, however. As noted earlier, Richard Land, head of the Ethics and Religious Liberty Commission, has led conservative political interests within the denomination. Land, who has both a seminary degree and a doctorate in political science, was instrumental in establishing a Washington lobbying office and has led the drive for greater SBC activity in national politics. In 2000, he was a prominent religious adviser to George W. Bush and was subsequently appointed to Bush administration advisory positions.

On the other side, the CBF is a dissident group of "denominational loyalists" seeking alternative vehicles for mission projects, theological education, and other functions. Although CBF leaders are much more moderate politically (and more often Democratic) than the current SBC elite, they reject what they see as the "politicization" of religion. Insofar as they are involved with national affairs, many CBF leaders and affiliated churches work through the Baptist Joint Committee on Public Affairs, an old-line separationist organization made up of several Baptist denominations. Table 7.3 shows support for Land's ERLC is associated with greater activism, as expected, whereas backing for the CBF and Baptist Joint Committee on Public Affairs produces less political involvement.[41]

The Congregational Context   Do ministers' congregations influence their activity? The New Breed liberals of the 1960s were ultimately reined in by hostile parishioners, who not only rejected ministerial activism, but also favored more conservative politics.[42] Because clergy and laity are tightly linked in the Baptist congregational polity, which puts employment decisions solely with local churches, it might be expected that Baptist congregations are important potential constraints on ministerial activism. And although most surveys, including this one, find evangelical clergy much more in tune with their laity than are their mainline counterparts, some observers have seen a new gathering storm in these churches, as conservative activists antagonize a more moderate laity.[43]

Without any direct measures of congregational attitudes toward activ-

Table 7.3

Organizational Mobilization and General Political Participation
by Southern Baptist Convention (SBC) Clergy

Characteristic	Pearson's r
Denominational mobilization	
Support ERLC	.34**
Support CBF	- .22**
Support Baptist Joint Committee	- .17**
Attendance at SBC meetings	.08
Encouraged by other clergy	.06
Congregational context	
Church approves activism	.16**
More conservative than church	.11*
Laity contact	.09*
Length of tenure at church	- .03
Size of congregation	.08
National organization membership	
Belong to Christian Right group	.25**
Attended Christian Right meeting	.24**
Campaign mobilization	
Religious group contact	.16**
Party or candidate contact	.08
Interest group	.08
Denominational contacts	.03
Total contact index	.14*
Political information sources	
Religious magazines	.27**
Christian radio	.26**
Religious TV	.20*
Opinion magazines	.19**
Direct mail	.18**
Family and friends	.16**
News magazines	.13*
Commercial radio	.10*
Public radio	.05
Network TV	- .04
Newspapers	- .04
Public TV	- .06
Total "religious" sources	.34**

* p < .05; ** p < .001

ism or of congregational ideology, I must rely on ministers' own assessment. As Baptist pastors survive by reading the people in the pews, their judgments are probably not far out of line. In any event, pastors' actions are governed by their perceptions, not by reality. I asked ministers to what extent their congregations approved pastoral involvement, and I also incorporated two five-point scales on which ministers compared their political views to those of their members.[44] Finally, I tested the notion that ministers with longer tenure in their current posts might feel freer to participate politically, having built trust by extended pastoral service.

Given the typical high level of agreement between pastor and people, it is not surprising that congregational approval of ministerial activism has a solid but modest positive correlation with activism. And ideological differences also seem to have an effect, but not necessarily the expected one: clergy who perceive themselves more conservative than their congregations are more active, replicating earlier findings.[45] In addition, ministers who were contacted about political matters by laity during the 2000 campaign were slightly more active. On the other hand, I find little support for the "building credit" theory: clergy with long tenure in a church are actually a little less active, but the correlation is not significant. Nor does a larger church seem to encourage activism, although the coefficient has the correct sign and comes close to statistical significance.

National Political Organizations   Whatever denominational and congregational influences may affect SBC clergy, they are also the targets of outside mobilization. To tap such linkages, I first asked ministers whether they belonged to various religious interest groups. As I discovered in both 1992 and 1996, Baptist ministers join such groups in fairly large numbers. In 2000, the most popular was Dr. James Dobson's Focus on the Family, which claims 19 percent of SBC ministers, followed by Donald Wildmon's American Family Association (10 percent), and then the Christian Coalition (7 percent). Altogether, 27 percent of the clergy report membership in at least one conservative organization; 12 percent belong to two or more. Others do not join but "feel close" to these groups (for example, 73 percent to Focus, 45 percent to American Family, and 42 percent to the Christian Coalition). Very few SBC ministers join more liberal groups, such as Bread for the World and Americans United for Separation of Church and State (despite the prominent historical role Southern Baptist clergy played in each), but a significant minority feels close to these groups. Membership in the conservative religious interest groups correlates positively with political activity, with an additive index of group membership in table 7.3 having a healthy correlation. In the same vein, attendance at meetings of Christian Right groups also has a solid association with overall activism.

Campaign Mobilization: The Impact of Contacts and Communications
Political activism by clergy, especially during a presidential election year, may also be influenced by the mobilization efforts of political parties, candidate organizations, religious interest groups, and denominational officials. Similarly, the political information sources clergy use, especially the politics-laden religious TV and radio programs available to conservative Christians, might make a difference in clergy involvement.

Clergy are indeed popular folks during elections. Fifty-two percent report contacts from religious organizations attempting to influence their vote, 61 percent from party or candidate groups, 52 percent by national interest groups, and 12 percent by denominational sources. (Another 7 percent were contacted by laity from their church, as noted earlier.) Table 7.3 shows that all four types of outside contact are positively correlated with activity, but only those from religious organizations are statistically significant. An index of the total number of contacts is also correlated significantly with involvement. There is, then, some indication that outside mobilization efforts have impact, but contacts by religious interest groups understandably seem to have the most effect.

Ministers' favorite political information sources also have a significant bearing on activity. Use of religious periodicals, Christian radio, religious TV, opinion magazines, direct mail, and family and friends all have solid correlations with involvement, with nonreligious sources diminishing in importance. Thus, the clergy most integrated into communications networks dominated by conservative Christian activists are the most prone to political activity. Not surprisingly, they are also most likely to vote Republican; indeed, the vote for Bush among those most reliant on religious sources is almost unanimous.

A COMBINED MODEL OF CLERICAL ACTIVISM

To summarize the findings, table 7.4 presents a combined model explaining political activism among SBC pastors in 2000. To simplify the analysis, I ran a series of multiple regressions (Ordinary Least Squares with mean substitution for missing data) to discover which variables from the four theoretical perspectives demonstrated substantive influence. I then entered those in

Table 7.4

Determinants of Overall Pastoral Activism[a]

Characteristic	beta
Psychological engagement	
Interest in politics	.12**
Years in ministry	- .10**
Role orientations	
Approve political activity	.33***
Issue mobilization	
Moral agenda	.15**
Strong GOP	.10**
Conservatism	.10**
Organizational mobilization	
Attend Christian Right meetings	.16***
Support SBC ERLC	.10**
Attend SBC annual meetings	.09**
Religious group contact	.09**
Use Christian information sources	.07*
Adjusted R^2	.40

* $p < .10$; ** $p < .05$; *** $p < .001$.

[a] Multivariate (Ordinary Least Squares) analyses; final model. ERLC, Ethics and Religious Liberty Commission.

a final regression, eliminating those adding little power to the analysis. This process produced an elegant model with only eleven variables, which nevertheless explains a very respectable 40 percent of the variance.

First, only one social status variable survives the regression: years in the ministry, with those with less experience being more active politically. On the other hand, financial status (as measured by size of church) and educational attainments do nothing to explain activism once attitudinal variables are in the equation. The most important factor predicting activism, not surprisingly, is approval of clerical political activity; political interest, concern with moral issues, strength of conservative convictions, and strong Republican identification add explanatory power. In addition, organizational influences persist: those attending Christian Right meetings are significantly more involved in politics, as are those who support the SBC's political arm, the ERLC, attend SBC annual conventions, report campaign contacts from religious organizations, and rely on religious media. On the other hand, factors such as congregational context that were mildly important in earlier studies seem not to have had an independent effect in 2000, although their coefficients move in the right direction (data not shown).

Interestingly, the results do not change much if I omit the political-role orientations from the equation. Given the high correlation between approval of activism and activism itself, I reran the analysis without that variable. When the approval index is omitted, political interest, partisanship, ideology, and the moral agenda largely absorb its effects, becoming even more powerful as explanations for activism. And the reduced equation still explains 34 percent of the variance. Thus, although approval of activism makes a unique contribution to the equation, other variables have an important influence on participation.

What is noticeable in the final analysis, however specified, is the absence of theological variables. The failure of orthodoxy, dispensationalism, and the civic gospel to make the final equation may be puzzling because each had a solid bivariate correlation with activism. Their influence, however, is entirely captured by other variables in the analysis, which, of course, they influence, such role approval, ideology, and partisanship.[46] Once these latter factors are in the equation, theological orientations add no explanatory power. Their influence is entirely indirect: they play a critical role in producing the pastors' agendas, ideological stances, and partisanship, as well as determining whether or not they approve of activism. These factors in turn actually produce political activism.

POLITICAL ACTIVITY AMONG SOUTHERN BAPTIST PASTORS

This analysis allows us to bury for good some of the old conventional wisdom about political participation among SBC clergy. Political activity among Southern Baptist pastors is ultimately rooted in theologies long thought to discourage activism: otherworldly orthodoxy and, especially, dispensationalist beliefs. Adherents to these "conservative" perspectives have reoriented themselves to contemporary politics by adopting a new social theology, the civic gospel, that connects historic Baptist beliefs with the state of the contemporary world in a way that encourages activism. But theology and social theology operate indirectly through new attitudes toward political

activism, the mobilizing power of the moral reform agenda, and strong conservative ideological commitments, encapsulated in Republican partisanship. Indeed, these new attitudes and concerns are intense enough to prompt
much political involvement, reinforced by the activity of SBC agencies, Christian Right groups, and other supporting organizations and media.

What should be expected in the future? First, these results suggest that
SBC clergy are monotonously predictable in one respect: once again, in the
2000 election they voted overwhelmingly Republican and put their activity
where their hearts were (even if in most of the SBC's home territory Bush
needed little help). Fellow Southern Baptist Al Gore had no more luck in
attracting them back to their former Democratic home than he and Bill
Clinton had in the 1990s. And no doubt ministers' participation in the politics of their communities will remain at a higher plateau than that of a generation ago. The clergy's high level of political interest, sense of efficacy, and
approval of participation ensure that much. The fact that the most active
clergy are those who have recently entered the ministry suggests a secular
trend toward more involvement. And the infrastructure of Baptist associations, Christian political groups, and religious media may serve to sustain
or even bolster this new activism—or direct it toward special causes.

Having said this, I must be careful not to repeat Quinley's mistake in
assuming a permanent connection between a particular religious perspective and political activity.[47] The actual level of clergy participation at any
time, especially among theological conservatives, is indeterminate. Activism will reflect many external forces: the nature of the issues on the federal,
state, and local political agendas; the attractiveness of Republican candidates, and especially their commitment to conservative social values; the
activities of Christian Right organizations; and, perhaps, the encouragement
provided by denominational agencies and congregations.[48] Whatever the
future variations in these factors, however, Southern Baptist clergy have become a very important activist building block in the emerging Southern
(and national) GOP coalition.

Notes

1. Nathan O. Hatch, *The Democratization of American Protestantism* (New Haven: Yale University Press, 1989).

2. Rufus Spain, *At Ease in Zion: A Social History of Southern Baptists, 1865–
1900* (Nashville: Vanderbilt University Press, 1961).

3. Charles Reagan Wilson, *Baptized in Blood: The Religion of the Lost Cause*
(Athens: University of Georgia Press, 1980).

4. Spain, *At Ease in Zion,* 43.

5. Ibid.

6. James J. Thompson Jr., *Tried as by Fire: Southern Baptists and the Religious Controversies of the 1920s* (Macon, Ga.: Mercer University Press, 1982); Keith Harper, *The Quality of Mercy: Southern Baptists and Social Christianity, 1890–1920* (Tuscaloosa: University of Alabama Press, 1996).

7. John Lee Eighmy, *Churches in Cultural Captivity: A History of the Social Attitudes of Southern Baptists* (Knoxville: University of Tennessee Press, 1972); Thompson, *Tried as by Fire;* Andrew Michael Manis, *Southern Civil Religions in Conflict: Black and White Baptists and Civil Rights, 1947–1957* (Athens: University of Georgia Press, 1987).

8. Nancy Tatom Ammerman, *Baptist Battles* (New Brunswick, N.J.: Rutgers University Press, 1990); David T. Morgan, *The New Crusades, the New Holy Land: Conflict in the Southern Baptist Convention, 1969–1991* (Tuscaloosa: University of Alabama Press, 1996).

9. Oran P. Smith, *The Rise of Baptist Republicanism* (New York: New York University Press, 1997).

10. The ten-page survey was sent to 1,500 Southern Baptist clergy chosen randomly from "pastors" in the *Southern Baptist Convention Annual 2000.* After three mailings, the survey elicited 465 responses from ministers at 1,305 currently valid addresses, for a response rate of 37 percent. To check on possible response biases, I compared respondents to a profile of Southern Baptist clergy produced by the denomination. I discovered that respondents were slightly better educated than the clergy as a whole, but do not differ substantially in other ways. To check whether the respondents might more interested in politics than nonrespondents, I incorporated in the final model in Table 7.4 a variable measuring the rapidity with which respondents returned their questionnaires. The variable was not a predictor of general activism; ministers who responded quickly to the first letter were no more active than those responding tardily to the third letter requesting their participation. Nor did they exhibit any greater level of political interest—in fact, the correlation runs very weakly in the other direction. Thus, I think it unlikely than nonrespondents would be markedly different than those who participated in the survey.

11. The political participation items in this index are much more numerous than those in most studies of clergy politics, which tend to stress either political activity within the ministerial role or, alternatively, "citizen" acts. See Harold E. Quinley, *The Prophetic Clergy: Social Activism among Protestant Ministers* (New York: Wiley, 1974); Kathleen Beatty and Oliver Walter, "A Group Theory of Religion and Politics: The Clergy as Group Leaders," *Western Political Quarterly* 42 (1989): 129–58. The inventory includes the following: writing a letter to the editor, circulating a petition, contacting a public official, publicly endorsing a candidate, endorsing a candidate from the pulpit, taking a public stand on an issue, taking a pulpit stand on an issue, preaching an entire sermon on an issue, touching on an issue in a sermon, forming a church political action group, forming a church political study group, boycotting over an issue, urging parishioners to vote, distributing voter guides, campaigning for candidates (three variables), participating in a protest, committing civil disobedience, running for public office, giving money to a candidate, PAC, or party, joining a national political group, praying publicly for a candidate, praying publicly for a candidate or for an issue, attempting to persuade someone to vote for a par-

ticular candidate or party, joining a civic organization, joining a ministerial council, being appointed to office, or participating in several other types of in-church political activities. The alpha reliability coefficient for this index is .90.

12. Sidney Verba, Kay Lehman Schlozman, and Henry E. Brady, *Voice and Equality: Civic Voluntarism in American Society* (Cambridge: Harvard University Press, 1995), 414.

13. Sidney Verba and Norman H. Nie, *Participation in America* (Chicago: University of Chicago Press, 1972), 148; Verba, Schlozman, and Brady, *Voice and Equality.*

14. Steven J. Rosenstone and John Mark Hansen, *Mobilization, Participation, and Democracy in America* (New York: Macmillan, 1993), 136–41.

15. Verba and Nie, *Participation in America,* 229–47.

16. Quinley, *Prophetic Clergy;* Beatty and Walter, "Group Theory."

17. William D. Sapp, "Factors in the Involvement of Southern Baptist Pastors in Governmental Decision-Making" (Ph.D. diss., Southern Baptist Theological Seminary, 1975).

18. James L. Guth, "Reflections on the Status of Research on Clergy in Politics," in *Christian Clergy in American Politics,* ed. Sue E. S. Crawford and Laura R. Olson (Baltimore: Johns Hopkins University Press, 2001).

19. Ibid.

20. Sapp, "Factors"; James L. Guth, "Southern Baptists and the New Right," in *Religion in American Politics,* ed. Charles W. Dunn (Washington, D.C.: Congressional Quarterly Press, 1989).

21. Verba and Nie, *Participation in America;* Rosenstone and Hansen, *Mobilization.*

22. Verba, Schlozman, and Brady, *Voice and Equality.*

23. James L. Guth, "The Bully Pulpit: Southern Baptist Clergy and Political Activism, 1980–1992," in *Religion and the Culture Wars,* ed. John C. Green, James L. Guth, Corwin E. Smidt, and Lyman A. Kellstedt (Lanham, Md.: Rowman and Littlefield, 1996); and Guth, "The Mobilization of a Religious Elite: Political Activism among Southern Baptist Clergy in 1996," in Crawford and Olson, *Christian Clergy in American Politics.*

24. Jeffrey K. Hadden, *The Gathering Storm in the Churches* (Garden City, N.Y.: Doubleday, 1969); Quinley, *Prophetic Clergy.*

25. James L. Guth, John C. Green, Corwin E. Smidt, Lyman A. Kellstedt, and Margaret Poloma, *The Bully Pulpit: The Politics of Protestant Preachers* (Lawrence: University Press of Kansas, 1997).

26. Hadden, *Gathering Storm;* Quinley, *Prophetic Clergy.*

27. Paul Boyer, *When Time Shall Be No More: Prophecy Belief in Modern American Culture* (Cambridge: Harvard University Press, 1992); Clyde Wilcox, Sharon Linzey, and Ted G. Jelen, "Reluctant Warriors: Pre-Millennialism and Politics in the Moral Majority," *Journal for the Scientific Study of Religion* 30 (1991): 245–58.

28. Guth et al., *Bully Pulpit.*

29. Guth, "Bully Pulpit"; Guth, "Mobilization."

30. The alpha reliability coefficient for the orthodoxy index is .82, for the dispensationalism index, .79, for the civic gospel index, .82, for the civil religion index, .71, and for the separationism index, .63.

31. Quinley, *Prophetic Clergy.*

32. Guth et al., *Bully Pulpit.*

33. The political activity approval score is an additive index of responses to

questions on how strongly pastors approved or disapproved of clergy engaging in fifteen distinct political activities, ranging from preaching a sermon on a political issue to committing civil disobedience. The alpha reliability coefficient is .86.

34. David Nexon, "Asymmetry in the Political System: Occasional Activists in the Republican and Democratic Parties, 1956–1964," *American Political Science Review* 65 (1971): 716–30; Verba and Nie, *Participation in America.*

35. Verba, Schlozman, and Brady, *Voice and Equality,* 391–415.

36. Guth, "Mobilization."

37. The moral reform agenda and social justice agenda scores measure the attention paid by ministers to public issues. After an exploratory principal components analysis of twenty issues, I calculated a moral reform factor made up of items on abortion, pornography, prayer in schools, the death penalty, family issues ($n = 2$), domestic violence, gay rights, gambling, and alcohol (alpha = .89). The social justice factor consists of items on gender equity, civil rights, the economy, aging, and the environment (alpha = .81).

38. The *ideological liberalism* and *conservatism* measures were produced by a principal components analysis of twenty issues. The unrotated first component had an eigenvalue of 5.95, accounting for 30 percent of the total variance; all items had loadings of at least .40 on this component. Three other minor components each accounted for 10 percent or less of the variance. Thus, I used the unrotated first component as a measure of issue ideology. The theta reliability coefficient for this measure is .88. (The correlation with self-identified ideology is .69.) To allow for the possibility that ministers at both ends of the ideological spectrum might be more active, I bifurcated the score at its midpoint, producing the ideological conservatism and liberalism measures used in the text. I incorporated these measures in the multivariate analysis in preference to ideological self-identification because they have a greater range.

39. Verba and Nie, *Participation in America,* 224–28.

40. Ruy A. Teixeira, *The Disappearing American Voter* (Washington, D.C.: Brookings Institution, 1992); Rosenstone and Hansen, *Mobilization;* Verba, Schlozman, and Brady, *Voice and Equality.*

41. Guth, "Bully Pulpit"; Guth, "Mobilization."

42. Hadden, *Gathering Storm;* Quinley, *Prophetic Clergy;* and Randall Balmer, *Grant Us Courage* (New York: Oxford University Press, 1996).

43. Tony Campolo, *Can Mainline Denominations Make a Comeback?* (Valley Forge, Pa.: Judson Press, 1995).

44. This measure combines two items that asked pastors their relative ideological posture vis-à-vis their congregations on social issues and on economic issues (alpha = .77). Ministers tended to differ more in a conservative direction on the social issue item.

45. Guth, "Bully Pulpit"; Guth, "Mobilization."

46. Guth et al., *Bully Pulpit;* and Guth, "Mobilization."

47. Quinley, *Prophetic Clergy.*

48. That the level of clergy activism in any particular year is determined by a variety of factors is supported by another analysis not reported in table 7.4. I ran a similar regression on an index consisting of ministers' reports on the customary frequency with which they undertook various political acts. An equation that uses the same independent variables in table 7.4 shows that political interest and ap-

proval of activism largely determine "customary" activity. The short-term mobilization factors all drop out as predictors, suggesting that these may influence activity levels in particular election years, but that they do not appreciably influence long-term habitual behavior.

The Religious Right and Electoral Politics in the South

Charles S. Bullock III and Mark C. Smith

Perhaps no other topic surrounding religion and politics has received more attention of late than the role and activities of the Religious Right. In some quarters, it is generally assumed that the Religious Right has the political capital to run roughshod over virtually any opposition, within or without the Republican Party. However, a close examination of issues, constituencies, and electoral results in eleven Southern states between 1994 and 2000 suggests otherwise. The power of the Religious Right is not absolute or unfettered—although it is undeniably strong. This chapter will present a theory—"core constituency theory"—that seeks to shed light on the relationship between a party's most devout adherents and candidates for public office. What emerges is that the power of core constituencies, such as the Religious Right for the GOP, is real. Yet these constituencies and the candidates that appeal to them must maintain a delicate balancing act so as not to alienate general election voters with primary contests that indulge too overtly in the issues that move core constituents.

Survey data have long since confirmed the impression that the level of commitment to a political party greatly varies, even among voters who profess to be loyal supporters. Each party in the United States has a core group of supporters, and as one moves from the core supporters of one party toward the core of the other party, the intensity of support for the first party declines. After passing through a range of voters who are truly independent, one encounters voters with increasingly strong affinity for the opposition. Support for a party can be examined not only at the individual level but also at the group level. Discussions of realignment and dealignment invariably identify certain groups as being key components of each party. Thus the

New Deal Coalition is often defined as labor, Catholics, Jews, urbanites, minorities, and, at least until recently, Southerners.

The New Deal realignment largely bypassed the South, which had been the nation's most loyal Democratic region for decades.[1] White Southerners remained homogeneously Democratic through the mid-twentieth century.[2] In a region in which the face of the Democratic Party was Eugene and Herman Talmadge, Tom Heflin, Ben Tillman, Theodore Bilbo, and their political heirs, the few African Americans who could vote found little reason to forsake the party of Lincoln. Ironically, the extension of the suffrage to blacks in the South coincided with the Goldwater takeover of the GOP, which shifted Lincoln's party well to the right on a range of issues, including civil rights. Beginning about 1970, a new generation of Democratic leaders emerged who embraced moderate stands on school desegregation and minority voting rights—people such as Albert Gore Sr., Jimmy Carter, Albert Brewer, and Reuben Askew. This moderation resulted in a cementing of black support for the Democratic Party in the South well below the presidential level, where blacks had swung massively against Goldwater and to Lyndon Johnson. The search by Democratic candidates for black support at the primary and general election stages alienated conservative whites who shifted toward the newly respectable GOP.[3] With a growing black electorate taking the place of disaffected conservatives, Democratic Party nominees such as Hubert Humphrey and George McGovern supported more liberal policies, which alienated additional conservatives and which left the Democratic Party electorate still more liberal as the cycle repeated itself. In time, the partisan gap in the South came to resemble that in the rest of the nation, with the ranks of the GOP extending from the very conservative into the moderate range, whereas whites who remained loyal to the Democratic Party tended to be moderate to liberal. This sorting out of the electorate paralleled what was happening among public officials as the conservative Southern Democratic member of Congress became extinct, replaced by the conservative Republican.[4]

Once the Democratic Party became the party of the left in the South, its core constituency consisted of its most liberal voters. For that region as well as in the rest of the nation, the core support group was comprised of African American voters. Although blacks remain a minority within the Democratic Party and most jurisdictions, their cohesiveness, manifest in rates of support for Democratic candidates that often exceed 90 percent,[5] has made them the core constituency within the party. When the Democratic nominee is black, African Americans often provide near-unanimous support. White

Democrats typically get a slightly smaller share of the black vote, but except when running against well-established Republicans, they poll at least 85 percent of the black vote.

No set of Republican supporters matches the cohesion found among blacks. Evangelical Christians, particularly those with high commitment levels, have slowly realigned into the GOP, but they are by no means monolithic.[6] The closest approximation to black Democrats can be found with the Religious Right, a theoretical subset of evangelicals, which exit polls show often cast at least 70 percent of their votes for GOP nominees. Invariably the level of support given Republicans by voters who identified with the Religious Right far exceeds the share of the vote received from more secular white voters. Often the secular Religious Right is so great that although GOP nominees attract overwhelming support from Christian conservatives, many secular whites vote Democratic.

In this chapter, we examine the success of candidates identified with the Religious Right who have run for high political office in the eleven Southern states. The offices considered are governor, U.S. Senate, and U.S. House. The period covered is from 1994 through 2000. The emphasis here is on the South because it is in that region that the Religious Right has been particularly active and enjoyed some of its greatest successes.[7] Because of its activity in this region, we are more likely to have a sufficient number of cases to test the theoretical propositions.

THE CORE GROUP'S DILEMMA

Strong support from the core constituency is essential for the success of a party's nominee in competitive environments. Obviously in an area that is overwhelmingly made up of supporters for a party, hesitancy on the part of the core group will not be determinative. But in an environment in which the parties are evenly matched, lower turnout caused by the disaffection of the core constituency can defeat the party's candidates. Should some of the core constituency decide to "teach the party a lesson" and vote for the nominee of the opposition party in order to register disappointment with the choice of their own party, the result will almost certainly be victory for the opposition. A case in point is Senator Wyche Fowler's unsuccessful 1996 reelection bid as a Democratic incumbent, an election in which loyal, but not core, Democrats defected to open the way for a Republican upset while blacks remained steadfast in supporting Fowler.[8]

The cohesion of the core constituency provides a strong incentive for party activists eager to stimulate turnout among group members. Democrats, knowing that there is a .9 probability that each additional black voter who goes to the polls will vote for their ticket, concentrate get-out-the-vote resources on the minority community. Similarly, Republicans seek to encourage voting among Christian conservatives through use of targeted mail and telephone calls. Interest groups have also focused on parties' core constituencies. The Christian Coalition, although purporting to be nonpartisan, has distributed voting guides designed to make Republican candidates attractive to Religious Right fundamentalists at churches attended by Christian conservatives. The activities of figures such as Jerry Falwell, Pat Robertson, and James A. Dobson of Focus on the Family often parallel those of the Christian Coalition in this respect.[9]

On a number of dimensions, the members of the core constituency of a party have more extreme views than other partisans. Thus, African Americans are more enthusiastic in their support for affirmative action programs and are generally more liberal than many other Democrats. On the Republican side, the Religious Right is more conservative, especially on social issues such as access to an abortion, prayer in schools, and homosexual marriage than are other Republicans.[10] The continued enthusiasm of members of the core constituency comes at a price. As the most loyal partisans, the core group wants its preferences to be loudly and consistently articulated by the party's nominees and uncompromisingly set out in the party platform. To meet these expectations, the core group may recruit candidates. Even when they have not recruited a candidate, members of the core constituency often have a preference in the primary whom they support with money, volunteers, and get-out-the-vote efforts. To the extent that the core constituency supports a more extreme policy stance on highly salient issues, bidding for the support of the core constituency in a primary may result in the nominee being badly positioned for the general election. If a contested primary results in candidates vying to take more extreme stands in order to secure support from the core constituency, they may embrace positions unacceptable to the broader electorate whose support will be necessary in November.

Although nominating a candidate acceptable to the core constituency should ensure this group's enthusiastic support, it may diminish prospects for success in November. A nominee closely associated with the beliefs of the core constituency may be too extreme for independent voters or for those only loosely committed to supporting the party. Indeed, it is not only swing voters who may be turned off; internal battles between old-guard economic conservatives and social conservative converts of the Religious Right may keep the GOP from presenting a united front, as occurred in Virginia's Senate races of 1994 and 1996. In 1994, Republican senator John Warner refused to support Marine Colonel Oliver North's challenge to Democratic senator Charles Robb. North's role in Iran-Contra was a bigger factor in Warner's decision than issues of abortion or school choice, but it still divided the GOP and prompted the independent candidacy of Marshall Coleman, a Republican moderate. Although 54 percent of Virginia's electorate rejected the morally suspect incumbent, only 43 percent rallied to North. Two years later, when Warner faced reelection, many of North's most fervent allies backed James Miller's unsuccessful insurgency in the GOP primary.[11] In the narrow-partisan balance of today's competitive South, division in the ranks spells doom for November. [12] An electoral majority will require strong support from the core constituency, votes from other partisans, and in addition, a share of voters who are not affiliated with the party. As Earl Black and Merle Black demonstrate for the South, neither party can claim the loyalty of most of the region's voters.[13] The same is true in each of the region's states and in many congressional districts. A nominee who has fully embraced the policy preferences of the core constituency will be poorly positioned to appeal to the broader range of voters who are essential for victory. The party leadership therefore seeks to retain the enthusiasm of the core group, but without allowing them to determine the party's candidates.

Although the presence of a representative of the core constituency may turn off less rabid voters in a general election, even the unsuccessful candidacy of someone enthusiastically supported by the core constituency may spell trouble for the general election. In a contested primary in which one of the candidates is closely aligned with the core constituency's policy preferences, the other candidates may be pulled in the direction of the extremists. It is well known that primaries disproportionately attract strong partisans. In anticipation of this skewed primary electorate, moderate candidates may be pulled in the direction of the extremists, fearing that otherwise they will forgo support from voters who are especially likely to participate in the primary. As a consequence, even if the extreme candidate does not win the nomination, the nominee may have been pushed so far toward the core constituency's preferences that he or she will have become unacceptable to more moderate voters, especially swing independents.

In a competitive environment, the ideal situation for a party may be to have its nomination uncontested. In the absence of a primary contest, a nominee need not spell out positions on controversial issues. By keeping policy positions fuzzy, the nominee can retain the support of the party's core constituency while appearing to be reasonable to other members of the party and not alienate swing voters necessary for a November victory. If in the course of the general election campaign the nominee displays some deviation from the preferences of the core constituency, this may not prove fatal because in all likelihood the nominee, although not perfect for the core voters, will nonetheless be far more acceptable than the opponent.

Table 8.1 outlines the discussion of core constituency theory. It shows that a candidate who faces no primary competition on the way to nomination may have either adopted the positions of the secular or the core constituency. If the uncontested nomination goes to a secular candidate, then that individual can have adopted a set of mainstream policy stands that should be acceptable in the general election to all members of the party and that should position the nominee to make inroads among critical swing voters. An uncontested nominee who comes from the core constituency will bring a set of more extreme policy positions likely to appeal to the core constituency. If those positions have not been made too public, the uncontested nominee from the core constituency may still be able to attract enough secular support within the party and swing voters to secure victory in a competitive situation. Nominees who faced primary competition with individuals not associated with the core group will almost certainly have secular positions that should also place them in or close to the mainstream of the November electorate. These nominees may be less successful in uniting their fellow partisans as a result of criticisms directed at opponents during the primary. The degree to which the nominee can reunite the party may go a long way toward determining the outcome in November. Finally, candidates who have been opposed by core groups may have had to modify their positions, moving toward the extremes preferred by the core group. Under some circumstances, the winner may even appear to have close ties to the core group and have adopted a number of extreme positions. The nature of the general election coalition will depend on how far the candidate facing opposition from core group preferences has gone in trying to satisfy the core group.

In its early days as a competitive force, Republicans in the South had a weak candidate bench and often slated candidates with limited appeals for office. At times, any candidate who came forward and paid a filing fee would be the GOP nominee. Some of these early candidates were long on ideology but short on voter appeal, and they did little to alter the perception that the Republican Party in the region was filled with kooks. Aspirants who were

Table 8.1

Primary Competition and General Election Outcomes

Primary Competition	Winner	Policy Stands	General Election Strategy
None	Secular	Mainstream	All fellow partisans and swing core
	Core	Extreme	and some secular and few swing
Non-core group candidate	Secular	Mainstream	Most fellow partisans and swing
Core group candidate	Secular	Mainstream	May lose some core, secular, and swing
		Extreme	
	Core	Extreme	Core and some secular

more politically skilled and perceived to have serious electoral prospects continued to run the Democratic Party. The transformation of the GOP into the majority of the Southern congressional delegation in 1994 indicated that the party could now often provide voters with credible candidates.

THE DATA

This study focuses on candidates associated with the core constituency of the Republican Party. Reviewing copies of the *Southern Political Report*, edited by Hastings Wyman for election years 1994 to 2000, led to identification of candidates closely tied to the Religious Right. Although it is certainly possible that we missed some candidates with strong links to Christian conservatives, we believe that our approach turned up those who made the connection most explicit in their campaigns. We consider candidates for the offices of governor, U.S. senator, and U.S. representative. Because we focus on even-numbered election years, we exclude gubernatorial candidates from Louisiana, Mississippi, and Virginia, three states that elect their chief executives in odd-numbered years. Despite occasional references to Democratic candidates with strong ties to the Religious Right, we restrict our analysis to Republicans because it is in this party that the Christian conservatives constitute the core constituency.

Table 8.2

Distribution of Republican Candidates by Office, 1994–2000

	Governor	U.S. Senate	U.S. House	Total
Religious Right	8 (50%)	6 (21%)	27 (8%)	41 (8%)
Secular	8 (50%)	23 (79%)	427 (92%)	458 (92%)
Total	16 (100%)	29 (100%)	454 (100%)	499 (100%)

FINDINGS

Table 8.2 shows the distribution of Religious Right candidates for the three offices studied. Candidates identified with the Religious Right were most likely to seek the governorship. Half of the Republican candidates for governor in the study had ties to Christian conservatives. Among Republicans seeking a seat in the U.S. Senate, just over one-fifth were identified with the Religious Right. Candidates linked to Christian conservatism were least common among House nominees, where they comprised less than 10 percent.

Religious Right candidates are more commonly represented in statewide contests. A third of all Religious Right nominees have run for governor or senator. In terms of representation, the Religious Right, as a movement, is well represented in the Southern GOP at the state level but has been less successful in seeking House seats. The high incidence of Christian conservatives among gubernatorial nominees may reflect the greater openness in competition for that office. With Southern governors term limited except in Texas, there is more turnover in the office than in Congress. Open seat contests attract larger candidate pools, and it appears that the Religious Right is taking advantage of the opportunities offered by contests lacking incumbents.

In addition to the forty-one candidates linked to the Religious Right who appear in table 8.1, another eleven unsuccessfully sought the GOP nomination. Of these eleven candidates who lost in the Republican primary, four fell to other Religious Right candidates, and seven lost to more secular Republicans.

ELECTORAL SUCCESS

The 1990s, especially beginning with 1994, witnessed unparalleled levels of Republican success in the South.[14] As Earl and Merle Black detail in their comprehensive study, after close to a decade of Ronald Reagan in the White House, Southern Republicans finally came of age.[15] After decades of slow growth in contestation of offices below the presidential level, Republicans finally succeeded in getting conservative voters to bring their behavior for downticket offices in line with votes for the presidency.[16] The conversion of conservative white voters to full-fledged Republican loyalists, when accompanied by redistricting that separated black and white voters at levels heretofore not seen, increased the number of districts that Republicans could win with landslide support among whites, even if they were rejected overwhelmingly by black voters.

Overall, Religious Right Republicans enjoyed levels of success in general elections comparable to those of secular Republicans. Among the Religious Right candidates, 59 percent were elected, as were 62 percent of the secular Republicans. Although the general election success rates are similar, they mask differences that become apparent with a bit of probing.

When we compare the first and fourth rows of table 8.3, we find that 302 (66 percent) of 458 secular Republicans faced no opposition on their way to nomination. In contrast, only 17 (41 percent) of 41 of the Religious Right Republicans avoided primary competition. Even so, some of the primary opposition overcome by Religious Right candidates was minimal; nonetheless, as a whole, the group had to expend more resources on the way to nomination than did secular Republicans. Although much more research would be needed to substantiate the point, it may be that the secular wing of the GOP is reluctant to allow candidates of the Religious Right to secure nominations and therefore encourages challenges to candidates whom it perceives to be extremists and, consequently, unelectable.

Religious Right nominees who overcome secular opposition in the primary have success rates similar to those for Religious Right nominees who face no primary opposition. Both groups win general elections at least 60 percent of the time. The experience of secular Republicans who face primary opposition but not Christian conservatives is much less favorable; they win the general election only 37 percent of the time.

The impact of primary opposition from Religious Right candidates appears to have very different results depending on the nature of the primary winner. Contrary to expectations, there is no evidence that when a secular Republican defeats a candidate associated with the Religious Right in the primary that the victory is Pyrrhic, because all seven secular Republicans who triumphed over Religious Right favorites won general elections. Again, keeping in mind that the number of cases is quite small, only one of four

Table 8.3

General Election Results for Secular Republican Candidates, 1994–2000
(Governor, U.S. Senate, and U.S. House)[a]

Candidate	Victory	Defeat
Secular candidates		
Nominee with no primary oppostion	223 (74%)	79 (26%)
Nominee with primary oppostion non-RR	55 (37%)	94 (63%)
Nominee defeats RR candidate in primary	7 (100%)	0 (0%)
Total	285 (62%)	173 (38%)
RR candidates		
RR nominee with no primary opposition	11 (65%)	6 (35%)
RR nominee with primary opposition	12 (60%)	8 (40%)
RR nominee defeats RR RR candidate in primary	1 (25%)	3 (75%)
Total	24 (59%)	17 (41%)

[a] RR, Religious Right. Figures do not include forty-six races in which the GOP did not field a general election candidate.

Religious Right primary winners who defeated another Religious Right candidate managed victory in November. We find no evidence for the proposition that fending off a Christian conservative in the primary will force a more secular Republican to take positions unacceptable to the bulk of the electorate. It may be, however, that a contest between two Christian conservatives may prompt the winner to take such extreme positions that essential swing voters are alienated.

Table 8.4 presents an analysis similar to that in table 8.3 but is restricted to incumbents. The first thing to note is that most of the secular Republicans are incumbents, whereas most of the Religious Right–affiliated candidates were not. Although the numbers of cases were small, Religious Right nominees were more likely to face opposition than were secular nominees. Eight (44 percent) of 18 of the Religious Right nominees had a primary opponent, compared with only 31 (13 percent) of 246 of the secular nominees. Having a primary opponent did not result in a higher rate of defeat for the secular Republicans. In contrast, three of eight Religious Right nominees who overcame a primary opponent lost the general election. A possible explanation for this difference would be if secular voters were less likely to rally to the side of an incumbent identified with the Religious Right. Black and Black present a number of examples in which positions embraced by Christian conservatives turned off critical shares of the electorate needed to attain the landslides among white votes that Republicans often need to win in the South.[17]

Table 8.4

General Election Results for Southern Republican Incumbents, 1994–2000 (Governor, U.S. Senate, and U.S. House)[a]

Candidate	Victory	Defeat
Secular candidates		
Nominee with no primary opposition	212 (99%)	3 (1%)
Nominee with primary opposition non-RR	29 (97%)	1 (3%)
Nominee defeats RR candidate in primary	1 (100%)	0 (0%)
Total	242 (98%)	4 (2%)
RR candidates		
RR nominee with no primary opposition	9 (90%)	1 (10%)
RR nominee with primary opposition	5 (63%)	1 (10%)
RR nominee defeats RR candidate in primary	0 (0%)	0 (0%)
Total	14 (78%)	4 (22%)

[a] RR, Religious Right.

The recent experiences of two Republican governors who failed in re-election bids illustrate how a Christian conservative may adopt stands out of step with the bulk of the electorate. In Alabama, Fob James ran for reelection in 1998 by opposing the teaching of evolution in schools and supporting Etowah County circuit judge Roy Moore, who wanted to post the Ten Commandments in a courthouse despite clear indications that the latter action violated the First Amendment of the U.S. Constitution. The positions sparked a major challenge in the primary from old-guard business conservative and mining magnate Winton Blount. James narrowly prevailed. Even more damaging to James, though, was his opposition to a proposal to emulate Georgia's institution of a lottery to fund education programs. Although the Georgia experience (the brainchild of Democratic strategist James Carville) has become widely popular, especially for the use of funding college scholarships—and there were clear indications that Alabamians crossed the state line to buy tickets in Georgia's and Florida's lotteries, and to gamble in Mississippi's casinos—Governor James stood firm in his opposition. He lost by a 58–42 margin to Democrat Don Siegelman, who vowed to institute a lottery for education purposes as soon as he was elected—a promise that he failed to keep, thanks to a massive mobilization of the state's Christian Coalition against the referendum.[18]

The education lottery also played a role in David Beasley's unsuccessful quest for a second term as South Carolina's governor. Beasley also opposed instituting a lottery with proceeds earmarked for education. Democrat Jim Hodges, his general election opponent, used a clever television ad in which an actor representing a convenience store owner operating just across the Georgia state line thanked South Carolinians for buying tickets that helped pay for Georgia students' college educations. Perhaps even more damaging to Beasley was his opposition to video poker, which stimulated convenience store operators to display materials and contribute to the campaign treasury of the Democratic challenger. Ultimately, Beasley came up short in a 53-to-45 contest.[19]

Table 8.5 presents results for Republicans in open seat elections. Among these candidates, secular Republicans did much better than those with ties to the Christian right. Secular candidates were successful by more than a two-to-one margin, compared with only 40 percent of the Religious Right nominees. Among candidates who faced primary opposition but not from Religious Right opponents, secular nominations won general elections 59 percent of the time. In contrast, Religious Right nominees who faced primary opposition succeeded in November only 40 percent of the time. Table

Table 8.5

General Election Results for Southern Republican in Open Seat
Elections, 1994–2000 (Governor, U.S. Senate, and U.S. House)[a]

Candidate	Victory	Defeat
Secular candidates		
Nominee with no primary opposition	6 (75%)	2 (25%)
Nominee with primary opposition non-RR	19 (59%)	13 (41%)
Nominee defeats RR candidate in primary	6 (100%)	0 (0%)
Total	31 (67%)	15 (33%)
RR candidates		
RR nominee with no primary opposton	1 (33%)	2 (25%)
RR nominee with primary opposton	4 (40%)	6 (60%)
RR nominee defeats RR candidate in primary	1 (50%)	1 (50%)
Total	6 (40%)	9 (60%)

[a] RR, Religious Right.

8.5 presents further evidence that secular candidates who defeat opponents affiliated with the Religious Right in a primary are not handicapped in the general election: all six in this category won. Thus the speculation offered earlier that the presence of a candidate close to the Christian right would induce other candidates to move in that direction and potentially forfeit widespread support in the general election is not substantiated by the research here.[20]

THE RELIGIOUS RIGHT AND REPUBLICANS

Candidates who clearly identified with the Religious Right constitute about 10 percent of the Republicans who competed for high office from 1994 through 2000 in the South. Although we do not have comparable data on other regions, our expectation is that the presence of Religious Right candidates in the GOP is higher in the South than elsewhere. Although we cannot discount the plausibility of "stealth" candidates whose close ties to the Religious Right escaped our efforts at detection, the evidence does not support contentions that Christian conservatives have taken over candidate recruitment in the GOP across the South. Perhaps the attention accorded the Religious Right results from their greater presence among Republican nominees for high statewide offices.

Data for the South bear out parts of the core constituency theory outlined here. Among incumbents, secular Republicans won reelection, with rare exceptions. The success rate for secular incumbents stood at 98 percent. In contrast, even though most Religious Right Republicans also achieved additional terms, their success rate fell below 80 percent. These differences become starker in statewide contests. Secular incumbents won 94 percent of these races, whereas Religious Right candidates succeeded only 25 percent of the time. Again, the number of cases is small (only four Religious Right incumbents sought reelection to statewide office from 1994 to 2000), but the inability to exploit the natural advantages of incumbency might severely limit the Religious Right's influence in the South and in the Republican Party.

An even greater disparity exists between secular and Religious Right Republicans who sought open seats. The secular Republicans did not enjoy the immunity from defeat of incumbents, but they did manage to win two-thirds of the time. Among Religious Right contests for open seats, only 40 percent succeeded, providing further evidence that candidates closely linked to the GOP core constituency may be less electable than those not so tied to the more extreme positions of the core partisans.

The second aspect of the core constituency theory suggested that even secular Republicans who survive primary challenges from candidates supported by the Religious Right would face greater electoral difficulties than secular candidates who did not confront this kind of challenge. Although the numbers of cases are small, no secular Republican lost in November after defeating a candidate linked to Christian conservatives in the primary. If anything, then, there is some evidence to suggest that GOP secular nominees who faced a primary challenge but not from the Religious Right emerged as less electable. Thus we do not find evidence to suggest that a challenge from a candidate of the core constituency will induce competitors to adopt issue stands so extreme as to impede general election success.

NOTES

1. David W. Brady, *Critical Elections and Congressional Policy Making* (Stanford: Stanford University Press, 1988).

2. Earl Black and Merle Black, *Rise of Southern Republicans* (Cambridge: Belknap, Harvard University Press, 2002).

3. Stanley P. Berard, *Southern Democrats in the U.S. House of Representatives* (Norman: University of Oklahoma Press, 2001); Black and Black, *Rise of Southern Republicans*.

4. Black and Black, *Rise of Southern Republicans*.

5. Charles S. Bullock III and Richard E. Dunn, "The Demise of Racial Districting and the Future of Black Representation," *Emory Law Journal* 48 (Fall 1999): 1209–53.

6. John C Green, Lyman A. Kellstedt, Corwin E. Smidt, and James L. Guth, "The Soul of the South," in *The New Politics of the Old South: An Introduction to Southern Politics*, ed. Charles S. Bullock III and Mark J. Rozell (Lanham, Md.: Rowman and Littlefield, 1998).

7. Clyde Wilcox, *Onward Christian Soldiers? The Religious Right in American Politics* (Boulder, Colo.: Westview Press, 2000); Mark J. Rozell and Clyde Wilcox, *Second Coming: The New Christian Right in Virginia Politics* (Baltimore: Johns Hopkins University Press, 1996).

8. Charles S. Bullock III and Paul P. Furr, "Race, Turnout, Runoff and Election Outcomes: The Defeat of Wyche Fowler," *Congress and the Presidency* 24 (Spring 1997): 1–16.

9. Charles S. Bullock III and John Christopher Grant, "Georgia: The Christian Right and Grassroots Power," in *God at the Grassroots: The Christian Right and the 1994 Elections,* ed. Mark J. Rozell and Clyde Wilcox (Lanham, Md.: Rowman and Littlefield, 1995).

10. Black and Black, *Rise of Southern Republicans*.

11. Hastings Wyman Jr. identifies Virginia as one of the states in which the Religious Right and the old-guard intramural battles have been most open. See "Southern GOP Grapples with Christian Mainstream Tensions," *Southern Political Report*, September 30, 1997.

12. See discussions in Black and Black, *Rise of Southern Republicans*.

13. Black and Black, *Rise of Southern Republicans*.

14. Berard, *Southern Democrats*.

15. Black and Black, *Rise of Southern Republicans*.

16. Charles S. Bullock, R. K. Gaddie, and D. R. Hoffman, "Regional Realignment Revisited" (paper presented at the Annual Meeting of the American Political Science Association, Washington, D.C., August 31–September 3, 2000).

17. Black and Black, *Rise of Southern Republicans*.

18. The lottery referendum's failure suggests that James was not entirely out of touch with public preferences in his state. However, the referendum attracted fewer participants than the general election for governor.

19. The support lavished on Democratic Jim Hodges by the video poker industry proved misplaced as the new governor quickly drove this activity out of his state. Hodges proved more successful than Siegelman in getting the necessary changes made, and South Carolina now has a lottery in place.

20. Election returns used in this chapter are from several sources. See Richard M. Scammon and Alice V. McGillivray, *America Votes: A Handbook of Contemporary American Election Statistics* (Washington, D.C.: Congressional Quarterly, 1995); Richard M. Scammon, Alice V. McGillivray, and Rhodes Cook, *America Votes: A Hand-*

book of Contemporary American Election Statistics 22 (Washington, D.C.: Congressional Quarterly, 1998); 1998 U.S. House and Senate Races at http://www.fec.gov/pubrec/fe98/cover.htm; 1998 Gubernatorial Races from Michael Barone and Grant Ujifusa, *The Almanac of American Politics* (Washington, D.C.: National Journal, 1998); 2000 U.S. House and Senate Races at http://www.fec.gov/pubrec/fe2000/cover.htm; 2000 North Carolina Gubernatorial Race at http://www.sboe.state.nc.us/voterweb/elections.htm.

Donald Wildmon, the American Family Association, and the Theology of Media Activism

Ted Ownby

In December 1976, Donald Wildmon had what he describes as a life-changing experience. Frustrated and long enraged by things that offended his sensibilities, the Methodist preacher at a church in northern Mississippi launched a religious campaign, willing to work out a strategy as he went along. He rejected a religion that concentrates on saving souls, instead calling for church members, and especially church leaders, to give up their concerns for comfort, respectability, and fund-raising and urging Christians to join him in what he calls a "confrontational ministry." That ministry demands frequent—even daily—activism, personal sacrifice, and the willingness to face scorn and ridicule. Wildmon has consistently said he does not know if his ministry can succeed, but he stresses that in his understanding of Christian life, the goal should be holiness, not success.

Wildmon and his organizations have taken on corporate America in a direct way, naming what he sees as the worst offenders, researching and publicizing the interconnectedness of the corporate world, and shaming public companies with publicity most of them fear. In the late 1970s, Donald Wildmon organized the National Federation of Decency, which in 1988 changed its name to the American Family Association (AFA). Through these organizations, he has aggressively protested overt sexuality and anti-Christian sentiments in television and other media and has challenged the easy availability of pornographic magazines and movies. Wildmon and his groups have kept up some of most sustained examples of Christian consumer reform in American history.

This chapter investigates the theology behind Wildmon's activism. How does he understand religion and its relationship to public action? How does religion change for evangelical Christians who had once been reluctant to address public issues when they become conservative activists? A final question is broader. How have American religious organizations dealt with the fun industries—movies, television, sports, recorded music, and the rest—that have come to dominate so much of everyday American life, and where do Wildmon's efforts fit in that story?

Few white evangelical church leaders and church organizations in the South had been involved directly in public affairs until the mid-twentieth century, when the civil rights movement and the issues around it forced so many religious folks to take stands. The leading scholar of that tradition, Samuel S. Hill Jr., argued in several important works that white Sourtherners' evangelicalism, from the early nineteenth century through most of the twentieth century, concentrated so much on the central theme of converting the unconverted that they viewed most forms of political action and virtually all discussion of systems of legal, economic, or racial power as irrelevant to more important issues—or, in fact, the only important issue of people's eternal souls. Hill's description always characterized Baptists more accurately than Methodists, whose Wesleyan background had long encouraged serious, if sporadic, social activism in issues such as opposition to alcohol, some forms of violence, and child labor. Nonetheless, Hill's critique is broadly accurate in pointing out the limited range of much of white Southerners' religion, in which activism on any public issue tended—until recently—to be only occasional and clearly secondary to the larger issue of saving the souls of the unconverted.[1]

Like many figures in what came to be known as the Religious Right, Donald Wildmon started addressing public issues in an aggressive way only in the late 1970s. Unlike so many evangelical activists, he has not spent much time addressing the political world, instead concentrating on the issue that drove him into public life in the first place.

He likes to tell the story of his life-changing experience (almost a second conversion). His 1990 autobiography, *Don Wildmon: The Man the Networks Love to Hate,* describes how he sat down to watch television with his wife and four children on a December evening in 1976. His description seems awfully defensive, as if he needed to apologize for even watching television. He mentions that they hardly ever turned on the television when school was in session, but it seemed a relaxing way to spend some time during Christmas vacation. His beginning, "when Tim first suggested that we watch TV," makes the point that the idea came from his oldest son, suggesting that Wildmon himself might not have turned on the television. "I had thought my family might laugh together or that we might all hold our breath in suspense." He stresses the communal side of the experience; he was watching not for his own enjoyment but for the company of his family. "Ideally, I had hoped to find a program that would teach us something positive about the fascinating and complex world we live in—a program that would mix some kind of mind-stretching nourishment into the entertainment." The language here sounds too idealistic to be true; he hoped television would be educational and entertaining in ways that all members of his family would enjoy. Wildmon had liked television sometimes, he wrote, citing children's programs and coverage of space travel and the Montreal Olympics. But on this night, the first show the family settled in to watch involved married people having affairs. Tim changed the channel to a show with "an outburst of offensive expletives." The third and last option was a mystery in which one character killed another with a hammer. The three choices, then, were sex, profanity, or violence.[2] On that December night in 1976, Wildmon decided to do something. "That's it, I thought. I would take action. I would preach a sermon on television and challenge my church members to be better viewers."[3] This decision to "challenge my church members to be better viewers" helped establish Wildmon as a consumer activist.

The vignette of the violation of a relaxing evening with family in front of the television is especially revealing because it suggests the vision the founder of the AFA had of the ideal family life. "Family" has meant many things in American life, and at least three of those meanings are especially important for people in the twentieth-century South. One is the agricultural family—extended to include numerous close and distant relatives, working and producing, coping with a range of problems. A second is the evangelical definition of church group as family—a body of people who know each other and share the central goal of helping inspire new births into the familylike congregation. Wildmon has shown relatively little interest in either. Instead, he has worked from a third definition, a Victorian image of the family as a small unit of Christian parents teaching Christian children, united in their separation from a more sinful world outside the home.

Wildmon's upbringing offers clues about his decision to become a Christian consumer activist. Born in 1938, Donald Wildmon grew up in Ripley in northeastern Mississippi, where his father worked for the Mississippi Health

Department and his mother taught in public schools. His parents taught Sunday school in the Methodist church, where Don had his conversion experience at age nine. His parents were solidly nonagricultural small-town folks, which is what Wildmon himself became. He went to Mississippi State University for a while, then to Millsaps College, the Methodist college in Jackson that is certainly Mississippi's best liberal arts institution. As a teenager in 1957, he received a license to preach, which he said had been his goal since early childhood,[4] and went to divinity school at Emory, the best spot for a bright young Southern Methodist to get a degree. He returned to northern Mississippi as a minister, first in Tupelo in the late 1960s, then closer to Memphis in Southaven, before moving back to Tupelo in the late 1970s.

The Tupelo years may suggest something about Wildmon's distinctiveness within the tradition of Southern evangelism. He came from nonfarming people and spent much of his adult life in Tupelo as it was becoming distinctive within the Deep South. Tupelo emerged at midcentury as a fairly prosperous small city where wages were fairly high and old historical burdens were not particularly troubling. At first a center for garment factories that paid typically low wages to young white women (such as Elvis Presley's mother Gladys), Tupelo began to change in the postwar years by developing a furniture industry that paid decent wages.[5] As the son of salaried people, and as an adult in a rare part of Mississippi that paid reasonable wages, Wildmon did not have the farm native's inherited fear of consumer culture. Wildmon had long been especially interested and active in the media. He wrote newspaper sports stories and columns for his high school newspaper, for Millsaps College's *Purple and White,* and for the *Tupelo Journal.*[6] In the late 1960s, he founded his own publishing house, Five Star Publishers, to print Christian material, and he wrote religious columns for newspapers. In the 1970s, the church he pastored was Tupelo's first to offer a telephone devotional, where anyone could call to hear a recorded message. He was part of the media culture, and then he turned on it.

Practical Help for Daily Living

Before his life-changing moment in 1976, Wildmon had shown little interest in activism. We can learn a great deal about Wildmon's religious thought before his career as a protest leader. In the early 1970s, he wrote several short books of Christian advice and encouragement that allow considerable insight into his theology and ethics. The books all look alike, sound alike, and follow the same pattern. The chapters, which originated as short pieces for newspapers, consist of two- to three-page lessons that try to teach positive lessons. The intriguing thing is that he showed little of the anger and political focus—and none of the interest in corporate America—that have since dominated his religious thought and activism.

In his advice books in the early 1970s, Wildmon did not present himself as a systematic thinker or skillful theologian. "For the average fellow theology can sometimes get to be a very confusing and difficult subject to understand. . . . Even after seven years of higher education dealing specifically with that subject, I often find myself over my head in the subject." He rejects the idea that anyone "has claim on all the truth" and worried especially that theological differences often caused too much division. Ultimately, Wildmon decided, he could always return to "some basic fundamentals of which I am certain," and he is "thankful that the basic necessities are so simple even a little child can understand."[7] It is important that Wildmon does not list those fundamentals; as on many topics, the things that are right do not need to be spelled out.

His advice books offer accessible encouragement from a Christian perspective. Perhaps the theme of those books is clearest in the title of a 1972 volume, *Practical Help for Daily Living.* It begins with an essay on kindness, followed by "Some Words to Live By," an essay urging humor, friendly appreciation, encouragement, and forgiveness. As how-to books for Christian living, Wildmon's volumes frequently offered examples of the ways history's great men upheld particular virtues. In his 1970 volume *Nuggets of Gold,* Wildmon detailed the individual virtues of heroes, often saving their names as surprise conclusions. There once was a man who struggled toward his dream with great determination. . . . His name was Walt Disney. Another man showed courage that inspired people to overcome great obstacles. . . . His name was George Washington. Albert Schweitzer was an example of compassion, Abraham Lincoln understood and acted on what was truly important, William Seward exemplified self-discipline. Alfred Nobel showed a willingness to change, and William Waldorf Astor exemplified persistence and hard work. Antonio Stradivari discovered his true talents and put them to good use.[8] Other examples quoted Thomas Jefferson, Edgar A. Guest, Mahatma Ghandi, popular polls and popular magazines, and numerous ministers of great or little renown. When Wildmon's books mentioned Jesus, they typically referred to him as "the Nazarene carpenter" or "the Galilean," stressing the everyday character of Jesus' humanity. In Wildmon's books, Jesus provides good examples, especially the example of being willing to make sacrifices.

The emphasis on real-life examples from history gives many of

Wildmon's essays from the early 1970s a somewhat bland Christianity and American patriotism that stressed individual achievement. Live a good life, with good examples, determination, kindness, patience, and some humility, and God will likely bless you with a happy life. Many of the essays stress that doing good yields rewards. Kindness, for example, has two rewards. It "wins the heart of the recipient" and it "makes life enjoyable." People who seek the Kingdom of God have found the way "of matching happiness and holiness."[9] He consistently reassured readers that good times follow bad, that problems and depression do not last, that things are not as bad as they often seem. "When frustrations come, cool down and think things over. A period where you can just be alone for a few minutes and talk it over with God helps. Remember, also, that not everything is wrong. Most things are still right. Remember that God is still the same God, still present and wanting to help."[10] In a book of short addresses to graduates, he offered the blandest of all calls to resilience: "When life hands you a lemon, the thing to do is to make lemonade."[11]

From reading Wildmon's Christian advice books from the late 1960s and early 1970s, one would not likely imagine he would turn out to be an activist with a "confrontational ministry." In fact, he even offered one essay in 1973 urging people not to criticize or to assume too much self-righteousness. "When you look at yourself first—really look at yourself—you find it hard to throw a stone at someone else. . . . I'm afraid that several times our message has been too much condemnation and too little redemption."[12] For the most part, he seems in these books a kindly uncle with advice that is sincere, friendly, predictable, and forgettable.

Only occasionally did those books reveal the sentiments that have fueled his later activism. Only occasionally did he display an angry side that condemned the deteriorating morals of his day, or a pessimistic side that stressed not patience for better things but a belief that human beings are bad and not likely to get better. In one essay, he upheld the virtues of "righteous indignation—holy anger," observing that "what many folks call tolerance others call cowardice. . . . Wrong wouldn't stand much of a chance in our world" if more Christians got angry and did something about it.[13] In another, he mocked conventional notions of "progress," denouncing the growing acceptance of abortion in the name of women's freedom to control their own bodies, the coddling of criminals in the name of rehabilitation, and the acceptance of "legalized pornography on the newsstand and in the movie while outlawing prayer and Bible reading in public schools!"[14] Later in the same volume of short essays, he worried that the concept of sin is in decline. "It isn't sin anymore, it is situational ethics."[15] And in one rare essay, he snapped at liberal theology, including the Death of God theology popularized by Thomas J. J. Altizer, who taught at Emory while Wildmon was a student. "Yes, I'm tired. Tired of all the people who say God is dead who never knew He was alive. They live in palaces behind the sacred walls of education and spin out fancy theories about the nothingness of God."[16]

One rare example of the sentiments from the preactivist Wildmon that came to be common for the activist Wildmon is especially clear. Writing far more darkly than in most of his short columns, Wildmon stressed in a 1970 essay called "His Is a Great Love" that Christians faced ridicule from an American culture that was not merely sinful but that actually treated religion with scorn. American culture, he feared, taught the lesson that "You can't get ahead in life by practicing His [Jesus'] principles, so we are told and we must all get ahead. We take followers of His and make them sissies in our movies. We show them as weak, insecure, unstable people. Most of the time we picture them as some sort of holier-than-thou hypocrite." But one of the revealing points about such a combative piece is Wildmon's conclusion. Rather than urging organized action, he reassured Christians that Jesus loves them even when it seems few people do.[17]

Beginning in the 1970s, Wildmon, like many American Christians, turned to conservative activism. The list of events and issues is well known—Supreme Court decisions about organized prayer in schools in 1962 and abortion in 1973, the numerous protest movements and experimental lifestyles that conservatives interpreted as disorder and moral decline, conservatives' effort to uphold what they saw as moral absolutes in the face of turmoil, the movement from Silent Majority to Moral Majority, and the rise of Reagan Republicanism.[18] Wildmon shared much with the turn to conservative activism, but he has diverged from it as well, turning not to organized politics but to protests against the media. Wildmon continues the concentration on the morality of the individual as the central test of the worth of the Christian life, and, in the tradition of white Southern evangelicals, he hardly ever mentions justice or equality as Christian virtues. But he has leapt headfirst into public activism as crucial to his understanding of religious commitment, and he has set a new course by addressing what he sees as the systematic problems behind sinfulness in American life.

THE APATHY OF THE INSTITUTIONAL CHURCH

Like the religious thinking in his advice books, Wildmon's theology of activism is not particularly complicated, but he has developed it from his considerable experience as an activist. His theology shows most often in his monthly columns in the *American Family Association Journal.* His columns are short, personally revealing sermons that try to rally the troops to more effective activism. Three points characterize his theological perspective.

First, he criticizes churches, church members, and especially preachers and denominational leaders for being comfortable with the world as it is, or for retreating into the church. Much of his harshest language hits at the complacency of organized religion. His greatest criticisms, except possibly for those he aims at television executives and their corporate sponsors, mention the inactivity of comfortable Christians. He offers a point surprising only in that he feels he needs to make it. "I certainly don't have any complaint about a church helping people find Christ. I thank God for them." That is about as far as Wildmon cares to go on that topic. He continues, "But once an individual accepts Christ, what then? Is that it? Is that the sum total reason for the existence of the Church?" Wildmon concludes, in a critique of Southern evangelicalism shared by Samuel Hill and many others, that far too many churches "reduce Christianity to the act of being saved."[19]

Wildmon's ministry, both in writing his devotional books and in fighting overt sexuality and anti-Christian sentiment in the media, does not deal with issues of personal conversion. In his advice books and his pieces for the *American Family Association Journal,* Wildmon has never tried to convert unsaved people to Christianity. He has not written about his own conversion experience, and none of his hundreds of short columns have called for people to examine their souls and have life-changing experiences. Heaven hardly ever seems a concern. At one point, Wildmon said he believed in an afterlife but had no idea what it might be like.[20] (In fact, hell seems more real than heaven, because the existence of hell was necessary to prove a foundation for Wildmon to argue that there is, ultimately, evil, and that evil will ultimately be punished.)

Although Wildmon's activities are clearly focused on the evils of mass entertainment and consumption culture instead of conversion, his goal is to change society by "Christianizing" its institutions, "thereby pressuring the ungodly to live like saints." In his work, Wildmon has sought and received the support of many diverse religious groups, even those with more traditionally otherworldly concerns. In 1993 Wildmon claimed that the AFA was endorsed by over 200 top Christian leaders—including 81 Roman Catholics, 11 Episcopalians, 19 Southern Baptists, 16 United Methodists, 4 Greek Orthodox, and 3 American Baptists. Among those who have endorsed Wildmon's group are Catholic John Cardinal O'Conner, Catholic sympathizer Chuck Colson, Focus on the Family's James A. Dobson, and the Reverend D. James Kennedy of Coral Ridge Presbyterian Church in Fort Lauderdale. Wildmon himself has served on the Reverend Sun Myung Moon's Coalition for Religious Freedom, along with *Left Behind* author Tim LaHaye and televangelist Jimmy Swaggart.[21]

Wildmon, sounding like many preacher-activists who want to inspire Christians to more action outside their congregations, has combined two of the main critiques of a Christianity concerned primarily with saving souls. Like many preachers, he argues that an orientation toward salvation and the next life tends to ignore problems and possibilities in the world. For Wildmon, those problems involve an acceptance of sin in society, and the possibilities involve combating those sins. A bit more uniquely, he suggests that churches that are only concerned with saving souls risk becoming too concerned with numbers—with doing whatever it takes to bring new people into the pews and keep them there. Thus, the goal of converting the unconverted has too often turned into a kind of church boosterism complete with the reassurance that, at least within the church, everything is basically okay. Thus, he argues that a conservatism rooted in apolitical interest in saving souls becomes a conservatism rooted in acceptance of church life as it is. In 1999, Wildmon's column listed a number of news items that he found morally troubling, and it concluded, "Now to the important church news. Our church supper is scheduled for next Tuesday. Attendance was good even though it was down slightly last Sunday. The preacher delivered a good message about loving the earth. Our building fund is still growing. We need volunteers to help with the nursery next week. And our committee will meet on Thursday to decide the color of paint to be used in the youth Sunday School room."[22]

In a 1994 column, Wildmon ripped the mainstream churches in language one expects of an activist. "Our society is so saturated with this 'winning' attitude that we have forgotten what gives meaning and substance to life. You don't fight battles because you are guaranteed victory. You fight battles because it is the right thing to do—regardless of the outcome. . . . This 'health and wealth' attitude has been adopted by our society. Unfortunately, and at a loss of authenticity, this 'peace and prosperity' gospel has been preached by some of the best known ministers in America." His concluding sentence was particularly biting for a critic of American popular culture and its advertisers. "And millions of Americans have bought into it."[23] He made the same comparison between marketing and American Christianity in the harsh conclusion of his autobiography. "We have packaged

Christianity similar to a social club and often judged it by the same standard the world uses to judge—size, power and riches."[24]

This repeated critique seems especially revealing because it differs so much from his earlier writing. In an article the *Mississippi United Methodist Advocate* published a month before his life-changing television experience in1976, Wildmon praised "The Influence of the Church on America" as the story of one success after another, starting with Columbus coming to America on the *Santa Maria,* to the Anglican priests in Jamestown, to the religious ideals of the Puritans, through numerous recent examples of churches supporting education, building hospitals, and caring for the poor. He concluded, "I feel comfortably within the mark when I say that no other institution has influenced our country for good in anywhere near the proportion which the Christian church has."[25] Donald Wildmon would likely not reject the idea that Christian churches have influenced America for the good. More importantly, however, since he has become an activist, he has never made that point. He concentrates instead on the ways churches have failed America, especially in a society overwhelmed by entertainment media. In 1996, he concluded that "those who should be your greatest allies ignore the battle. The greatest disappointment I've had in this battle has been the apathy of the institutional church."[26]

As a definer of family, Wildmon has thus rejected one of the traditional evangelical definitions: that the church congregation has a parental role of encouraging new births, and that the congregation serves as a kind of parent teaching the newly birthed Christian the basics of religious life. It might be possible to argue that fighting pornography is part of the effort to evangelize the world and therefore to argue that Wildmon's efforts are ultimately about saving souls. Perhaps if there are opportunities for sin, sin everywhere, sin that is widely accepted, sin not condemned, then potential Christians, both old and especially young, will never have life-changing conversion experiences. But that is clearly not what Wildmon thinks about his ministry.

SEX AND SECULARISM

The second feature of Wildmon's theology as an activist surprised him. He began his activism simply to change the content of television shows. As he understood it, he was fighting forms of sinfulness that resulted from market forces, and he was especially protesting the decisions of irresponsible corporate leaders who were getting rich by offering consumers something he believed approached a publicly accepted pornography. Sexual content on television, he believed at first, came from network decisions to attract viewers with images that were immediately compelling. As he put it simply, "The hard truth is that sex and violence appeal to the base instinct in man. It's easy to get a crowd."[27] The marketplace, Wildmon believed, had the potential to be morally neutral, and he wanted to use the influence of large numbers of Christians to change it.

As he got deeper into his campaign, however, he came to believe that forces more powerful than the market were at work. In his autobiography he described how he was skeptical when other religious leaders began denouncing secular humanism as the root of America's moral decline. After considerable thought, he came to believe that the problem lay in an anti-Christian conspiracy. Displaying as much sexual content as possible seemed to Wildmon to go hand in hand with ignoring or ridiculing Christianity. Television, he decided, was the "unrecognized foe of the Christian faith and its values" because it glorifies immediate pleasure, upholds a relativistic understanding of the world, and does not take religion seriously. Taking on the mantle of the hated and misunderstood martyr, Wildmon decided to make his position clear in a speech to a group of television executives in 1981. He criticized the lack of religious characters and respect for Christianity, and said that all sorts of smaller groups receive treatment from television that is more frequent and more favorable. He detailed "how network television has taken many Judeo-Christian religious values (i.e., marital and pre-marital fidelity, honesty and integrity in dealing with others, a helpful or service-minded attitude, stewardship, forgiveness, etc.) and ridiculed, belittled or basically ignored them." Finally, he attacked networks for portraying Christians as "non-people."[28] (The seeds of this understanding of the world were there from the beginning of his activism. In an interview in 1979, Wildmon awkwardly made the same points. "Nothing on television is unintentional. These people want to sell their values through the best medium available. . . . These people want all America to end up like they are. They are from different backgrounds than we are. They have different lifestyles. They are very successful, usually from the East and basically Jewish. Don't get me wrong. I'm not anti-Semitic. I have a Jewish brother-in-law."[29]) Wildmon seemed more certain in the first lines of his 1986 book *The Case against Pornography:* "There is a great spiritual war being waged. An intentional effort is being made to change the very foundation on which Western civilization is built, to replace the Christian concept of man with a secular and humanist concept."[30]

It seems fair to judge that much of Wildmon's argument that current

television intentionally rejects positive values is blatant overstatement. Forgiveness, kindness, and helpfulness are enormously popular on television
programs. Honesty often wins the day, although television characters consistently try big or small lies first before they learn their lessons. Television
dramas frequently offer heroes whose jobs or passions inspire them to heroic work in the interest of law and public good. But is he completely wrong
about his larger point? Despite his overstatement, it seems fair to say he
accurately assessed at least three primary points about television programming. First, American popular culture, especially popular music and television programs, concentrates to an extraordinary degree on love and especially
sex between attractive young people. Other things matter sometimes, but
not nearly as much. In an extraordinary number of television programs and
movies, sex as desire, pursuit, culmination, pleasure, joke, basic reality, whatever, is indeed at the center, and often at the margins as well. Second, American popular culture tends to be wary of any assertion of moral virtues other
than the virtue of tolerance and respect for all people. Kindness is fine, but
the greatest kindness often comes in overcoming intolerance. The best people
are those who do not judge others. And third, most American television
programs, movies, and popular music have little positive to say about religious life. Much of that popular culture does indeed tend to stress Christians' intolerance toward non-Christians, although it avoids religion more
often than ridiculing it. Although Wildmon is certainly wrong to suggest
that television executives represent a conspiracy of secular humanists scheming together to portray Christians in a negative light, it is certainly possible
to suggest that calling many television programmers secular humanists is in
fact a great compliment.[31]

Wildmon has never accepted a primary tenet of popular culture—that
it demands novelty, and that some of the most novel and exciting sides of
that culture come by pushing beyond the boundaries of what is widely acceptable and respectable. He rejects the common notion that good art—art
that is cutting edge and provocative—should surprise and will often shock.
In fact, the tendency of television and the movies to go as close to the line of
what is acceptable, to make jokes about the sacred, to use sexual puns to say
things shows could not say more directly, all seem especially offensive. Media makers' attempts to push every rule to its brink, and the fact that the
very pushing to the brink was part of the entertainment, has suggested to
Wildmon that all popular culture is about disobedience. The television com-
edy episode that was about masturbation without mentioning masturbation, the talk show guests whose language is bleeped to the amusement of

the audience, the actress whose award-show dress really should fall off but doesn't, the shampoo commercial in which a woman is so happy with her hair that she sounds as if she is having an orgasm—all these are about going as far as the lines of acceptable conduct allow, and then daring to step beyond those lines. The question of what is acceptable for network television at some times but not at others, the questions of what is acceptable on cable television but not on network television and what is acceptable on some cable stations but not others, the question of what "partial nudity" really means—all these questions suggest that the issue of standards for different times and stations and shows is not really about standards at all; this is all just a complicated and cynical game. This sense of a culture of breaking rules to offer more sex and violence makes Wildmon angry. In a 1996 column called "Please Pray for Steven Bochco," Wildmon bemoaned the television producer's boast that he was "going to push the limits of television as far as I can push them." What Bochco saw as pushing limits, in shows such as *Hill Street Blues, Public Morals, NYPD Blue,* and *Philly,* Wildmon interpreted as efforts "to see how much trash he can put on television."[32]

The group that preceded Wildmon's National Federation of Decency was the Catholic League of Decency, which operated in 1934 until the 1960s. The League of Decency did not just play the game; it helped create the game of setting standards of acceptable conduct to show in motion pictures. The motion picture industry had grown up early in the twentieth century by appealing to an audience of urban immigrants, many of them Catholic, and it had no intention of losing Catholic viewers. The various boards the motion picture industry created to set and enforce standards of moral conduct tried hard to satisfy the League of Decency, and the system produced a generally friendly back-and-forth process, in which moviemakers received the stamp of approval for their movies by cutting a little profanity here and a lot of adultery there, staying clear of any evidence of homosexuality, and suggesting that good almost always triumphed over bad. By midcentury, directors and writers were writing against the production code, trying to make art that was provocative by breaking the rules, with sexual double entendres and plenty of violence that had either to be punished or had to serve a good cause.[33]

Sometimes the AFA seems to be playing the same game, publicizing examples of television shows that cheat and reminding broadcasters to play by the rules. As Wildmon remembered in his autobiography, he was troubled by fact that they were all disobeying authority and getting away with it. More importantly, it is clear that Wildmon believes the whole game of setting standards so the networks and studios he views as secular pornographers can find ways to violate them is so corrupt that he wants to get outside it. In rejecting—even condemning—the race for novelty and the sense that art comes from breaking rules and the open-ended openness to different experiences, he has turned against basic elements of American popular culture, and really the central elements of American consumer culture.

We should consider Wildmon a kind of antimedia fundamentalist. He rejects the term, and he told a reporter in 1983, "If you find me one United Methodist minister in the United States who's a fundamentalist, I'll give you 50,000 bucks."[34] But along with the fundamentalists, he rejects cultural optimism, keeps up a sense of angry defensiveness toward American culture, and upholds the importance of biblical inerrancy. Religious historians have noted that fundamentalism, as an organized movement of self-identifying Protestants, was slow—perhaps surprisingly slow—to get started in the American South.[35] As William Glass has argued, Southern fundamentalism developed in the early twentieth-century South not among the large and established denominations but in newly established Bible institutes and conferences outside existing centers of denominational organization. As Glass suggests, Methodists, Baptists, and Presbyterians in the region did not join a self-conscious movement of fundamentalists because the South did not have an organized modernist movement for them to reject. In the early twentieth century, because not many people in the evangelical-dominated South believed the modernist credos that human knowledge was expanding, that human beings know more, can do more, can help other people more than they could in the past, evangelicals did not see much reason to fight that perspective.[36]

But by the late twentieth century, those ideas were all around, often mixed with other ideas, less optimistic about the future of the world but full of a kind of confidence in human potential. As a Methodist, Wildmon has been spared much of the fundamentalist-moderate turmoil of the Southern Baptist Convention. The idea that the Bible is the only source of truth is not something he would reject, but his Christian advice books showed that Wildmon believes people could learn a lot from other people and their examples. Mississippi's United Methodists have not spent time and energy debating biblical inerrancy, and they certainly hold no suspicions that social activism reflects doubts about the Bible. Wildmon has not railed against liberals and modernists within the United Methodist Church. Although he says he was disappointed when ministers in the North Mississippi association of his church considered but did not support his early boycotts of television networks, and he was angry and aghast when some of the same ministers supported homosexual marriage,[37] he has generally considered churches irrelevant to the issues he cares about.

For Wildmon, the most troubling and especially the most pervasive face of a generally modernist perspective came through entertainment media. His narrative of recent history is one of steep decline brought on by television, and people in churches did not really notice while the agents of an insidious form of modernism more or less took over. In a 1993 column, he recalled a bucolic small-town childhood, with orderly communities based on religious principles. Back then—and this would have been Mississippi in the 1940s and early 1950s—"Society as a whole viewed moral behavior as being an important element in life. The combined pressures from society's institutions managed to keep the publicly accepted morality based on Judeo-Christian values. . . . Back in those days our streets were safer, our homes and families more solid, our crime less violent and our moral standards higher. Sure there were wrongs. But there was also a norm which could be used to address these wrongs." Wildmon continued by stressing television as the culprit, devious, relentless, and pernicious. "Then came television—and, unfortunately, a change in the attitude and values of those in the entertainment media. The old prohibitions were removed. The Playboy philosophy came to be the norm in Hollywood and at the network headquarters in New York." The crisis continued. "Before long those who held contempt for the old values gained new friends. . . . in education, the media, the legal system, and other areas of influence."[38]

The demand for entertainment, especially the need for novelty, could lead to challenges to the Bible. Occasionally, Wildmon refers to the Bible as literal truth in ways that show his similarities to fundamentalists. In condemning a television movie about the life of Jesus in 1980, Wildmon spoke up for inerrancy. A CBS movie that was trying to be sympathetic to Jesus' story made several creative changes to the Bible, and Wildmon took offense. "This may seem like an insignificant issue. . . . But you walk a mile by going the first half-inch. If you take the liberty to contradict the Biblical account with even a little sentence, it could very well be that 10 years from now, you could take liberty to rewrite an entire Biblical episode."[39] Eight years later, that prophecy seemed to come true with the filming of *The Last Temptation of Christ*. Like many Christians, Wildmon was troubled with that film for a scene in which Jesus dreams about having sex. He was concerned as well about the film's tone, which portrayed Jesus as a tormented soul worrying about his own sins, lies, and desires. In the end,

Wildmon and many other viewers decided, the film suggested Jesus was put on the cross not for humanity's sins, but for his own, and he was not resurrected. The specific misrepresentations of Jesus were troubling enough, but Wildmon offered a fundamentalist's interpretation of what was most offensive about the film. "The big problem with *The Last Temptation of Christ* is this: It intentionally lies about the One whom Christians hold precious and dear. Indeed, as Christians we owe everything to Jesus Christ. For someone (or some $3.5 billion company) to lie about him on purpose is offensive."[40]

The broader way Wildmon identifies with a fundamentalist perspective lies in his rejection of the optimism and human-centered nature of entertainment media. The innovations in technology that television and the movies rely on seem to Wildmon simply to bring more experiences into people's lives. He rejects any ideas that human beings are making intellectual or moral progress, and his language condemning popular media sounds very much like fundamentalism in its call for basic, unchanging Christian principles. Near the end of his autobiography he clarified his understanding of the relationship between entertainment and religious crisis. He said too many Christians believe they can separate themselves from unwanted forces, "But like a cancer spreading slowly through a body, the moral decay does not stop at the superficial wall we have established. It touches us and ours. . . . We have accepted, nearly without question, the creed of the secularist that freedom is free—a license; that left to himself man will naturally progress to his highest."[41]

CONFRONTATIONAL MINISTRY

Wildmon's third theological point stresses that confrontation is essential to Christian life. Perhaps his most important theological belief is that Christians should be active. Reviewing the success his and other organizations had in limiting the theatrical release of *The Last Temptation of Christ*, Wildmon said the thing that cheered him most was the simple fact that so many Christians got involved. "I believe our side won because multitudes of Christians decided they would no longer passively sit back and watch the entertainment industry's assault on their faith and values. Though many did no more than sign their names on a petition, that was more than they had done in the past."[42] The *American Family Association Journal* encourages a kind of full-tilt activism: keep your eyes open for things that are particularly offensive, and write your congressman, write the networks, write the sponsors of television programs, speak out, boycott, picket, be vigilant. The valleys we walk through get darker all the time. Fear no evil; fight it.

Wildmon's movement from a consoling message to a confrontational ministry shows especially clearly in his willingness to go public in condemning things he finds offensive. The issue of manners and protest is significant, in part because of the Deep South setting in which protest was so clearly linked to civil rights activism and in part because of a broader sense that protesting was bad manners. Protesting means saying one is superior to somebody else, and it means bothering people. Before he became an activist, Wildmon wrote in one of his religious advice books that if people with power would only listen, most protest would be unnecessary. In 1971 he offered a parable of a child whose parents only noticed him when he yelled, "Pass the butter!" No one had noticed when the child had softly asked for the butter, but when he yelled, he was punished. Wildmon concluded, "If we would have listened to the pleading of the colored man years ago perhaps our problems in race relations wouldn't be as great today. And if we had listened to the common man, perhaps the unions would be controlled by a different breed of men today."[43] After becoming a protester, Wildmon still occasionally said that he feared becoming too aggressive or self-righteous, or at least that he felt uncomfortable taking on the tools of secular protesters. As he recalled in his autobiography, "At first I felt very strange carrying a placard which screamed, 'Boycott Sears' in big, bold, black magic marker letters. When I had watched civil rights and Viet Nam war demonstrations on television I had never envisioned that I would one day be doing the same thing. In my mind, carrying a sign conjured up images of rebellion, disrespect for authority and even violence. That's something good Christians just didn't do."[44] A National Federation for Decency protester made the point even more directly as she explained why—and how—she was picketing an ABC television station for showing episodes of *Soap* in 1978. "You can turn it into a bad thing—picketing and all this—because it seems to have a bad connotation in Mississippi. . . . We're trying to do it in a nice way."[45]

Wildmon, who quickly overcame any worries that nice people don't picket, developed a taste for confrontation. At the scene of his first picket and boycott, in Chicago at Sears's headquarters, he and other members of the National Federation for Decency cut up Sears credit cards as journalists watched.[46] He learned that insulting language drew attention. In 1979, for example, he called ABC "the prostitute network," and later called R. J. Reynolds the "number one 'Porno Pushing Advertiser.'"[47] While picketing ABC headquarters in New York, he tried to deliver a funeral wreath with the words "The death of constructive programming on ABC" to network execu-tives.[48] Wildmon was proud when the ACLU named him Arts Censor of the Year, and even the title of his autobiography, *Don Wildmon: The Man the Networks Love to Hate,* celebrates the fact that people hate him. In 1993, he wrote of earning "the privilege of being persecuted" and asked what he thought about it. "I praise God for it! I consider their condemnation to be a high honor. It means I'm doing my job right."[49]

For Wildmon, the life of Jesus provides the theological justification for naming sinners and taking the wrath of critics. Since the late 1970s, he has consistently said that confrontation and sacrifice are the essential elements of Christian life. He takes satisfaction in being hated, being frustrated for a cause, being persecuted, because that tells him he is following Jesus' example. "The cross is a symbol of suffering and shame, hurt, rejection, humiliation, pain, sacrifice, even death." He urges more churches to call their members "to sacrifice—real sacrifice. I don't hear many calls for people to suffer for Christ, forget all else and press on toward that high calling."[50] Wildmon is especially frustrated by people who tell him that Jesus was a nice fellow who did not criticize or condemn people or that Jesus stood above all for toler-ance and kindness. No, he replies, Jesus stood for righteousness. He con-demned the moneychangers, idolaters, and government officials who called on religion to support their authority, and he suffered and died for it.[51]

In 1991, a group of ministers asked him if he thought his effort to re-form television could ever be successful. "My response to that question was the same as it has always been. God did not call me to be successful, only faithful."[52] More frequently, Wildmon has stressed, "The goal in life is not happiness, as many seem to think. The goal in life is holiness. Living your life in the will of God. Investing your life in something which will outlive you. Contributing to those who have preceded and those who will follow you."[53] This is the theme Wildmon repeats most frequently in his columns, certainly to inspire readers and possibly to reassure himself. In 1996, for example, he responded to a rhetorical question with this certainty: "No, my life was not wasted. When one seeks a high goal, pursues it with all the strength and ability he has, then that life is never wasted. . . . I have lived long enough to learn that God doesn't call us to be successful. . . . God does, however, call each of us to be faithful. And that, we can do."[54]

This understanding of holiness is a tragic if commonsensical idea of doing the best one can, even if that means unhappiness, exhaustion, and persecution. Perfection is not possible, success is not likely, and total devo-tion to making the world a better place is the only real Christian life. Wildmon quoted Dietrich Bonhoeffer, without attribution, that there is no such thing as cheap grace, and he has consistently stressed the price of Christian activism.

Wildmon's continuing religious assault on the entertainment industry has such a tragic and exhaustive sense because the entertainment industries create such a total experience. Many people who hear Wildmon's story about the three television channels in 1976 laugh because today's television offers so many more options. If television is all about sinfulness, more sin comes with more channels. The mass nature of mass culture is central to Wildmon's belief that Christians should fight back as consumer activists. He had heard and generally if uncomfortably believed that we should have the freedom to choose or not to choose movies, television programs, and the like, because that choice is a basic feature of our market society. And the range of choices available, he had heard and generally believed, reflected the openness and diversity of American culture. But as he heard, again and again, just turn it off, *you* don't have to watch that show or buy that magazine or rent that movie, he turned his anger toward the people who were surrounding everyone with those choices, in television, at the movies, on the radio, in easily available magazines, on the Internet. Popular culture is always there, and fighting it means always fighting.

This sense that Christian life should mean the life of an outsider sounds familiar. The search for outsider status sometimes reaches a kind of chicness in Christian thinking, as in many forms of contemporary culture, as people interpreting and applying their theologies often claim that their understanding of Christianity holds the truest way to escape the expectations and power relations of society as it exists. The intriguing (though certainly not entirely unique) things about Donald Wildmon's claims to outsider status are, first, that he defines the center of American culture as television and a broader perspective it seems to embody. Second, he is a conservative who often sounds like Christians on the left, condemning do-nothing churches and the insidious effects of corporate power.

So what should Christians do? They should fight the power of corporate America with an onslaught of boycotts and letters to advertisers, television stations, production companies, and government officials. They should patronize only the businesses that do not offend them. They should learn about connections among corporations, who knows whom, who partners with whom, and they should hold those corporations accountable for the actions of all of their partners and subsidiaries. To read the *American Family Association Journal* is to wallow in the association's understanding of sinful-

ness. On a multipage spread in every issue, the association's television viewers, apparently clenching their teeth, shaking their heads in disgust, rolling
their eyes with near disbelief, list the problems with specific episodes of television shows. Long lists of plot summaries detail which shows featured which
types of sex jokes, which shows portrayed extramarital sex—heterosexual
and homosexual—as an acceptable option, which shows upheld dishonesty
as an apparent virtue, which shows glorified violence, and which shows
mocked Christianity. As a page one story began in 1999, "So, what's on the
tube tonight? Let's see, the new fall season is underway, and featured on
prime-time network television are . . . bestiality, adultery, fornication, homosexuality, and pedophilia. There are endless jokes about all sorts of sexual
situations and perversions. What's going on?"[55] Each issue of the *Journal*
lists the writers, producers, and advertisers of each show, often in stories
with unflattering headlines like "Sara Lee supports teen sex theme in ABC's
'Doogie Howser'" or "Ford, Sony ads on NBC pro-homosexual show."[56]

Other AFA initiatives have never strayed far from keeping up steady
opposition to mass culture. Not surprisingly, as television has expanded, the
AFA has expanded its watch to target MTV, movie services such as HBO and
Showtime, and worst of all, the Playboy Channel. It encourages local communities to fight the expansion of such services in their towns and cities.
Sustained boycotts, with occasional pickets, of bookstores and convenience
stores that sold pornographic magazines produced some successes when
some stores, and eventually some corporations, got out of the business. Boycotting Holiday Inns for having in-room access to pornographic films had
similar characteristics: seeing, publicizing, and fighting evil in a local, familiar company people knew and considered safe and comfortable. Increasingly in the 1990s, Wildmon and his organization thought and fought more
broadly. The AFA led protests against Time-Warner for publishing Madonna's
book *Sex,* and against Pepsi Cola for supporting a Madonna tour and video.
In 1993, the AFA published *The Fight Back Book,* a short publication that
listed all television stations and pornographic magazines and all of their
advertisers, with their addresses and telephone numbers. In 1996, about
twenty-five years after Wildmon identified Walt Disney as someone with
virtues Christians should emulate, the AFA targeted the ever-expanding
Disney corporation as a source of particular concern, for its movies and
television programs and its "Gay Day" at Disney World in Orlando. When
Disney formed a partnership with McDonald's, the AFA condemned it as
well.

It may come as a surprise that Wildmon offers little sense of an ethical theory. He does not explain proper moral behavior or proper family behavior; he assumes his readers already know that. His job, as he defines it, is to inspire them to fight immorality as part of their understanding of Christian life. From what he says is wrong, it is not difficult to deduce what Wildmon thinks is right: a heterosexual relationship between adults, who become parents of children they treat with love and kindness, teaching them Christian beliefs and protecting them from the harmful effects of a sinful mass culture. The striking thing is that Wildmon hardly ever makes those points. Instead, he concentrates on the difficulty—maybe bordering on the impossibility—of living out his understanding of Christian family life, and thus the need to fight.

Wildmon differs from most figures on the Religious Right in that he does not refer to or rely on a stated eschatology. In 1978, Sacvan Bercovitch theorized that Americans since the Puritans have tended to offer jeremiads that, while sounding angry and countercultural, are in fact full of confidence that the future will bear out their ultimate righteousness. Writing broadly, Bercovitch concludes, "Only in the United States has nationalism carried with it the Christian meaning of the sacred. Only America, of all national designations, has assumed the combined force of eschatology and chauvinism. . . . Of all symbols of identity, only *America* has united nationality and universality, civic and spiritual selfhood, secular and redemptive history, the country's past and paradise to be, in a single synthetic idea."[57] Wildmon is interesting in part because, unlike most figures on the Religious Right,[58] he does not fit Bercovitch's model. He does not suggest things are moving toward the final days. If he believes Jesus is coming soon, he has never mentioned it in print. Nor does he believe Americans, or more particularly American Christians, are pressing on toward a better, more Christian society. Things are not getting better, not from a Christian perspective, and not as part of an American narrative of progress. He has repeatedly said with considerable sadness that his goal is to do what he can to keep things from getting much worse. The world is in rough shape, and it is our job to fight it.

Wildmon's religious outlook, at least as he expresses it in public, is nearly joyless. Christians should look into religious radio, music, entertainment, Internet services and the rest, without ever thinking they will be isolated from sinful forces. The most joyful noise produced by the AFA, certainly, is the expanding American Family Radio network, which combines Christian music with Christian talk shows. But although Wildmon works hard to build up that network, he hardly ever celebrates or even mentions it in his ever-combative columns. In fact, the *AFA Journal* publishes a special report on its radio network in every issue, but that report lies outside the rest of the journal, on a different grade of paper, as if to symbolize that the upbeat, building elements of the AFA do not fit comfortably inside the angry, fighting side.

Instead, Wildmon consistently stresses that confronting everyday forms of sinfulness in everyday ways is painful. Early in his activist days, he said, "What I'm doing is constant confrontation. Day in and day out. That gets to be old hat after awhile." More sadly, he summarized the course of his ministry by stressing its consequences: "the past 15 years have not been easy, and rarely enjoyable. They have taken their toll on me, my wife and my children. I have paid a price, and so has my family."[59] Family, for Wildmon, has thus become less the Victorian refuge from sinfulness that helped begin his activism, and more a rallying cry for more activism. One cannot stay inside the Christian home separate from the forces that violate his understanding of home life, any more than one can stay inside the church. Instead, the only Christian thing he sees to do is to search for more and better forms of activism, and keep up the fight.

NOTES

1. Samuel S. Hill Jr., *Southern Churches in Crisis* (New York: Holt, Rinehart, and Winston, 1967); Hill et al., *Religion and the Solid South* (Nashville: Abingdon Press, 1972); Hill, *The South and the North in American Religion* (Athens: University of Georgia Press, 1980).

2. Donald E. Wildmon with Randall Nulton, *Don Wildmon: The Man the Networks Love to Hate* (Wilmore, Ky.: Bristol Books, 1990), 28.

3. Wildmon, *Don Wildmon*, 31–32.

4. *Mississippi United Methodist Advocate,* May 8, 1957, 5.

5. See Vaughn L. Grisham Jr. with a foreword by William F. Winter, *Tupelo: The Evolution of a Community* (Dayton, Ohio: Kettering Foundation, 1999).

6. *Mississippi United Methodist Advocate,* May 8, 1957, 5; *Purple and White,* sports stories and columns, 1958.

7. Donald Wildmon, *Living Thoughts* (1971; reprint, Tupelo, Miss.: Five Star Publishers, 1973), 13–14.

8. Donald Wildmon, *Nuggets of Gold* (1970; reprint, Tupelo, Miss.: American Family Association, 2000), 11–32; Wildmon, *Pebbles in the Sand* (Tupelo, Miss.: Five Star Publishers, 1970), 22–24.

9. Wildmon, *Practical Help for Daily Living* (Tupelo, Miss.: Five Star Publishers, 1972), 5, 15.

10. Ibid., 24.

11. Wildmon, *A Gift for the Graduate* (1968; reprint, Tupelo, Miss.: Five Star Publishers, 1973), 59.

12. Wildmon, *Windows to Life* (Tupelo, Miss.: Five Star Publishers, 1973), 52.

13. Wildmon, *Practical Help*, 32–33.

14. Wildmon, *Pebbles in the Sand* (Tupelo: Five Star Publishers, 1970), 19.

15. Ibid., 80.

16. Ibid., 104–5.

17. Ibid., 96.

18. For a narrative, see William Martin, *With God on Our Side: The Rise of the Religious Right in America* (New York: Broadway Books, 1996).

19. Wildmon, *American Family Association Journal* (hereafter *AFA Journal*), November–December 1990, 29.

20. Ibid., April 1994, 2.

21. "Donald Wildmon" entry, Council for National Policy Web site information, http://www.seekgod.ca/toast.htm, November 22, 2004 (quotations).

22. Wildmon, *AFA Journal*, January 1999, 2.

23. Ibid., January 1994, 2.

24. Wildmon, *Don Wildmon*, 211.

25. Wildmon, "The Influence of the Church on America," *Mississippi United Methodist Advocate*, November 10, 1976, 6.

26. Wildmon, *AFA Journal*, February 1996, 2.

27. *Jackson Clarion Ledger*, April 8, 1981, 12A.

28. Wildmon, *Don Wildmon*, 124, 126.

29. *Jackson Clarion Ledger*, October 14, 1979, 1E.

30. Wildmon, *The Case against Pornography* (Wheaton, Ill.: Victor Books, 1986), 7.

31. Historian Timothy Smith made this point in a graduate seminar in the early 1980s.

32. Wildmon, *AFA Journal*, September 1996, 2.

33. Gregory D. Black, *The Catholic Crusade against the Movies, 1940–1975* (Cambridge: Cambridge University Press, 1997); Black, *Hollywood Censored: Morality Codes, Catholics, and the Movies* (Cambridge: Cambridge University Press, 1994); Frank Walsh, *Sin and Censorship: The Catholic Church and the Motion Picture Industry* (New Haven: Yale University Press, 1996); Frank Miller, *Censored Hollywood: Sex, Sin, and Violence on Screen* (Atlanta: Turner Publishing, 1994).

34. *Jackson Clarion Ledger*, January 20, 1983, 1F.

35. This characterization of fundamentalism comes primarily from George Marsden, *Fundamentalism and American Culture: The Shaping of Twentieth-Century Evangelicalism, 1870–1925* (New York: Oxford University Press, 1980); Marsden, *Understanding Evangelicalism and Fundamentalism* (Grand Rapids, Mich.: Eerdmans, 1991); James J. Thompson Jr., *Tried as by Fire: Southern Baptists and the Religious Controversies of the 1920s* (Macon, Ga.: Mercer University Press, 1982); and in its emphasis on the rejection of progress, James Turner, *Without God, Without Creed: The Origins of Unbelief in America* (Baltimore: Johns Hopkins University Press, 1985).

36. William R. Glass, *Strangers in Zion: Fundamentalists in the South, 1900–1950* (Macon, Ga.: Mercer University Press, 2001).

37. On the North Mississippi Annual Conference, *Jackson Clarion-Ledger*, July 5, 1981. On some United Methodist ministers in California supporting gay marriage, Wildmon, *AFA Journal*, January 1999, 2.

38. Wildmon, *AFA Journal*, April 1993, 2.

39. *Jackson Daily News*, March 19, 1980, 7E.

40. Wildmon, *Don Wildmon,* 201.

41. Ibid., 215.

42. Ibid., 207–8.

43. Wildmon, *Living Thoughts,* 38–39.

44. Wildmon, *Don Wildmon,* 51.

45. *Jackson Daily News,* November 1, 1978, 4B.

46. *Jackson Daily News,* June 17, 1978, 1B.

47. *Jackson Daily News,* January 6, 1979, 1B; *Mississippi United Methodist Advocate,* May 14, 1980, 3.

48. Wildmon, *Don Wildmon,* 56.

49. Wildmon, *AFA Journal,* December 1993, 2.

50. Ibid., August 1991, 2.

51. See especially Wildmon, *AFA Journal,* September 1993, 2.

52. Wildmon, *AFA Journal,* April 1991, 2.

53. Ibid., February 1993, 2.

54. Wildmon, in *AFA Journal,* February 1996, 2.

55. *AFA Journal,* November–December 1999, 1.

56. These quotes appeared in the *AFA Journal,* January 1993, 7, but similar stories appear in every issue.

57. Sacvan Bercovitch, *The American Jeremiad* (Madison: University of Wisconsin Press, 1978), 176.

58. Sara Diamond, *Not by Politics Alone: The Enduring Influence of the Christian Right* (New York: Guilford, 1998); Michael Lienesch, *Redeeming America: Piety and Politics in the New Christian Right* (Chapel Hill: University of North Carolina Press, 1993); Martin, *With God on Our Side.*

59. *Jackson Clarion-Ledger,* January 20, 1983, 1F; Wildmon, *AFA Journal,* February 1993, 2.

10

The Christian Right
in Virginia Politics

Mark J. Rozell and Clyde Wilcox

In Virginia, the Christian Right has evolved from a marginal player in the state's once small Republican Party to a major faction in a party that now has firm control of the state legislature and has largely dominated statewide elections since the 1990s. The movement has developed from a small cadre of uncompromising activists into a strong but deeply divisive faction in the Republican Party, and finally into a skilled and successful partner in the GOP coalition. The Christian Right clearly played an important role in the rapid growth of the GOP in the state.

In many ways, Virginia is the birthplace of the Christian Right movement. In the late 1970s Jerry Falwell built the Moral Majority on the foundation of a successful evangelical mobilization against paramutual betting, and Pat Robertson's Christian Coalition was initially headquartered in Virginia as well. Other prominent figures in and around the movement live in Virginia, including fund-raiser Richard Vigurie, Morton Blackwell, Paul Weyrich, Michael Farris, and Cal Thomas, and the Christian Coalition's Ralph Reed made the state his home during his years at the Christian Coalition. Yet despite the movement's long history in the state and the large pool of leaders and supporters, and despite the importance of the movement in the electoral success of the Republican Party, the policy successes of the Christian Right in Virginia remain modest.

THE CONTEXT

In his seminal *Southern Politics in State and Nation* in 1949, V. O. Key Jr. described Virginia as a "political museum piece." He wrote: "Of all the American states, Virginia can lay claim to the most thorough control by an oligarchy."[1] Daniel J. Elazar later echoed this sentiment when he described Virginia's political culture as "traditionalistic," in the sense that there was a strong impetus toward hierarchy, tradition, and authority. Elazar described the Northern Virginia suburbs as more "individualist" and less moralistic than other parts of the state, and that sentiment would certainly be even more true today than when he penned his classic study of federalism.[2]

For decades, the Democratic political machine of Harry F. Byrd dominated Virginia politics. Byrd served as governor from 1926 to 1930 and as U.S. senator from 1933 until he retired in 1965. He assembled his machine from the county courthouse organizations of the landed gentry, who preferred stability to economic growth and were fiercely committed to racial segregation. This elite sought to limit political participation by holding its gubernatorial and other statewide elections in odd-numbered years, a practice that continues to this day. This has allowed the Christian Right (and other highly mobilized groups) to play a disproportionately active role in statewide elections.

Another remnant of the Byrd machine is the system of no formal party registration. This restriction suited the Byrd machine's objectives during the era of single-party dominance of state politics. Today, it means that in those rare cases in which Republicans nominate their candidates by political primaries, all registered voters may participate. The Republicans have more frequently nominated their statewide ticket at large, statewide conventions that allowed any citizen to participate who was willing to pledge to support the party nominees. Although these conventions were often huge events—in 2001 more than 10,000 delegates attended the convention—this system made it especially easy for the Christian Right to exert intraparty influence because a few thousand delegates could easily tip the balance. Ralph Reed said that "the caucus-convention nominating process in the [Virginia] Republican Party is unusual in that it does tend to give [our] grassroots activists a greater voice than they have in primaries."[3] Yet the Christian Right has also sometimes prevailed in party primaries. In 1989, the GOP gubernatorial primary favored the most conservative candidate, who won with less than 37 percent of the low-turnout vote in a three-way race. In 1997, a Christian conservative candidate won nomination for attorney general in a very low turnout, multicandidate race.

The evidence is nonetheless clear that Christian Right influence on Republican nomination politics has often hurt the party in general elections. The urban corridor that includes the Washington, D.C., suburbs has a majority of the state's population, and the Northern Virginia suburbs in particular are distinctive in their affluence, their high levels of education, their relatively low levels of religious involvement, their social liberalism, and in their many Republican voters. Many of these Republican voters are unwilling to support candidates strongly identified with the Christian Right, and they have defected in large numbers to moderate Democrats and even to an independent candidate in some recent elections.

Virginia is a heavily Protestant state, full of Baptist and Methodist churches, and in much of Virginia, these Protestant churches are theologically conservative regardless of denomination. Surveys show that nearly half of the state's residents profess an affiliation with an evangelical denomination and that more than 10 percent identify as fundamentalists. More than 40 percent of likely voters indicate that they believe that the Bible is literally true. The Northern Virginia area has a sizable number of Catholics in what is perhaps the most conservative diocese in the country, and it also has a growing number of non–Judeo-Christian immigrants. Overall, white evangelical Protestants, the core constituency of the Christian Right, comprise about 25 percent of the Virginia population. White mainline Protestants comprise 18 percent, black Protestants 18 percent, seculars 17 percent, and Catholics 14 percent. Various other religious affiliations, including Jews and Muslims, comprise the remaining 8 percent of the Virginia population.[4] In 2000, 17 percent of the Virginia electorate were "white Religious Right" voters, and 82 percent of them supported George W. Bush for president. Not surprisingly, these voters also heavily identified with the Republican Party (62 percent).[5]

During the 1970s and early 1980s, Virginia was home to the Moral Majority, a Christian Right organization based in the Bible Baptist Fellowship that was centered mainly in the fundamentalist right. Reverend Jerry Falwell, former head of the Moral Majority, lives in Lynchburg, and his huge congregation is a major institution in that region of the state. The Moral Majority was more active in Virginia than in most other states, and its presence was visible at state nominating conventions. The group was also somewhat involved in policy advocacy, although its statewide lobbying effort was never very sophisticated and faced a large Democratic majority in the legislature.

In 1989, Marion G. (Pat) Robertson built the Christian Coalition from his failed presidential campaign. Robertson and Falwell were longtime rivals in religion and in politics, and many of the fundamentalists of the former Moral Majority did not become involved in the more Pentecostal-oriented Christian Coalition. The Christian Coalition focused its efforts primarily

on electoral politics, where it could count on the votes, if not the membership of Falwell's fundamentalist supporters. As is true elsewhere, the Christian Coalition in Virginia declined rapidly in the latter half of the 1990s.
Where once there were active county chapters throughout the state, in recent years, the group has struggled to retain a state chair, a position that has
turned over frequently. But as elsewhere, the organization continues to distribute voter guides through its network of activists, although in reduced
numbers.

The most active and effective group in policy advocacy has been the
Family Foundation, which affiliated itself with James Dobson's Focus on
the Family. The organization has retained at least one statewide lobbyist for
more than fifteen years, and several of its leaders have served in Republican
gubernatorial administrations. The organization is involved in elections and
has produced both voter guides and incumbent scorecards, but its distinctive niche has been its statewide lobbying.

Among the other social conservative groups that have been active in the
state are Concerned Women for America, the Virginia Society for Human
Life, and the Madison Project. Home-schooling advocacy groups have also
been active parts of coalitions of conservative groups on a variety of social
issues. Leaders of the various social conservative organizations in the state
confer frequently and have effective means for reaching their many group
members on matters of policy interest or to help mobilize potential voters.

These groups operate in an ecology that includes few strong opposition
groups. Unions are weak in Virginia: unlike neighboring West Virginia, many
of the state's coal miners work in nonunion mines, and those who do belong to the union are generally socially conservative. Although the high levels of education in the Northern Virginia suburbs creates support for gender
equality and abortion rights, feminist groups also are not strong in the state.
The state has a sizable African American population, although not as large
as other Southern states, which reliably supports Democratic candidates. In
general, liberal interest groups have very little presence or influence in Virginia politics. By contrast, Virginia is one of the states defined in *Campaigns
and Elections* as having a "strong" Christian Right influence.[6]

The state is also a stronghold of the National Rifle Association. Many
Virginians are hunters, and even in the state's Northern suburbs, many citizens have lined up to apply for permits to carry concealed weapons. The
power of the NRA is evidenced both in the policy debates that sometimes
occur (whether concealed weapons can be carried into bars and public recreation centers), as well as in policy (the state's law banning carrying guns

near school property allows for an exception for hunters). In most but not all cases, the NRA and the Christian Right have worked in tandem to help GOP candidates. Indeed, Chuck Cunningham was first an NRA electoral activist, then head of the Christian Coalition voter guide efforts, and is now back at the NRA working on legislative affairs. Yet the libertarian bent of some NRA members produces some policy divisions, especially on abortion.[7]

MODERN VIRGINIA ELECTIONS AND THE CHRISTIAN RIGHT

The Christian Right has been active in Virginia elections since the late 1970s, with increasing sophistication over time. In 1978, conservative Christians attended the state Democratic nominating convention to support G. Conoly Phillips, a Virginia Beach car dealer who said that God had called him to run for the U.S. Senate. Phillips expressed surprise that the call had even specified the Democratic Party, for he would have preferred to run as an independent. Campaign mentor Pat Robertson, the son of a former Democratic U.S. senator, also urged that choice. Phillips called his campaign "a ministry unto the Lord" and called his campaign headquarters a "prayer room."[8] His strength in a losing cause surprised many observers, and presumably helped alert elites to the potential power of evangelical voters. A smaller number of Christian conservatives participated in the GOP nominating convention, backing the eventual nominee, former state party chair Richard Obenshain. Conservative Christians rallied to Obenshain's campaign until he died in a plane crash. The party selected John Warner as a replacement candidate, and he won and remains in the Senate today.

The Republican realignment took on metaphysical overtones in the 1980s as the Christian Right moved into the GOP. In 1981 the Moral Majority helped to mobilize some 700 delegates to the state GOP nominating convention, primarily to support lieutenant governor candidate Guy Farley, a former Byrd Democrat turned born-again Republican. Farley lost a bitter nomination fight in which opponents characterized him as a Christian Right extremist. But Jerry Falwell openly endorsed the Republican ticket, headed by Attorney General J. Marshall Coleman, and this endorsement became the centerpiece of the Democratic campaign. In what was to become the standard Democratic tactic for many years, moderate Democratic candidate Charles S. Robb attacked the GOP ticket as being too closely linked with the unpopular Falwell. The Democrats swept all three statewide races.

In 1985, Christian conservatives mobilized behind the gubernatorial candidacy of Wyatt B. Durette, a pro-life leader who advocated a constitutional amendment to ban abortion, even in cases of rape and incest, and a constitutional amendment to allow spoken nondenominational prayers in the classroom. Christian Right supporters pressed Durette even further to the right, and he eventually advocated the mandatory teaching of creationism in public schools. Falwell again endorsed the GOP ticket, the Democrats again made this a central issue in the campaign, and the Democrats again swept all three statewide offices.

In 1988, Pat Robertson's presidential campaign did poorly in the state primary but well in the local and congressional caucuses that selected delegates to the national convention. Because the state party central committee is selected out of those caucuses and the resultant state convention, Christian conservatives gained a strong foothold in the party apparatus and helped select a Christian conservative as party chair.

In 1989, the GOP experimented with a party primary, its first since 1949. Former attorney general Coleman ran as the most conservative candidate on abortion and won the gubernatorial nomination in a close three-way contest. The Supreme Court handed down the *Webster* decision after the primary, which rallied pro-choice voters, and Coleman scrambled toward the middle on abortion in a general election race that centered on that issue.[9] Many moderate Republicans defected to support Democratic nominee L. Douglas Wilder, who became the nation's first elected black governor.

By 1993 Christian conservatives had a strong foothold in the party. The state GOP chair, Patrick McSweeney, had won office by appealing to the Christian Right, and our survey of the state central committee showed that about one-third of its members were strong supporters of Christian Right organizations and issues.[10] The statewide nominating convention selected Michael Farris, a former Washington state Moral Majority executive director, a former attorney for Concerned Women for America, and current head of a legal defense organization for home-schooling families as GOP candidate for lieutenant governor. At the top of the ticket was former U.S. Representative George Allen, who appealed to Christian Right activists with promises to push hard for parental notification on abortion, support for charter schools, and rollbacks in the state's Family Life Education program.

Yet unlike Republican nominees in earlier contests, Allen did not stress his socially conservative views in the general election campaign. Rather, his campaign centered on traditional GOP issues such as tax cuts and crime, and he sought to portray himself as a moderate on abortion. By 1993, more pragmatic activists such as Ralph Reed of the Christian Coalition and Walter

Barbee of the Family Foundation were leading the movement, and they worked hard to keep their followers from demanding that Allen move right on abortion. Farris's controversial pronouncements on public schools, public inoculation programs, and other topics dominated the statewide media, allowing Allen to appear quite moderate compared with his running mate. Allen won in a landslide, as did the GOP attorney general candidate James Gilmore, but Farris lost, running an extraordinary twelve percentage points behind the top of his ticket. In a major switch in movement tactics, the Christian Right (especially the Christian Coalition) was more supportive of Allen and Gilmore than of Farris. The movement was self-consciously focusing on working for candidates who could actually win an election and who would appear nonthreatening. The 1993 elections marked another departure: although the Democratic candidates again campaigned by linking the GOP ticket to Falwell and Robertson, this tactic was successful only against Farris because of his past record of Christian Right leadership and some controversial writings and statements in speeches.

In what was to signal a bitter intraparty feud, incumbent GOP senator John Warner refused to endorse Farris, although he campaigned for the rest of the GOP ticket. In 1994, this split widened as Warner not only refused to endorse GOP nominee Oliver North, but also recruited former GOP candidate Marshall Coleman (now running as a social moderate) to run against North as an independent. North had long been a popular speaker and effective fund-raiser for the Christian Right in Virginia, and he had the enthusiastic support of the Christian Coalition, which reportedly coordinated their voter guide with the campaign and allowed the campaign to use their membership and activist lists. North defeated conservative Jim Miller for the nomination in a convention with strong Christian Right participation. Despite this strong movement support, and despite a nationwide tidal wave for the GOP, North lost to a weak incumbent who was tainted with a sex scandal. As before, the Democratic candidate linked North to Falwell and Robertson, but many Republicans also opposed North because of his role in the Iran-Contra scandal.

By now the state GOP was deeply divided. Our surveys of delegates to GOP statewide nominating conventions showed moderates rating North and Farris quite poorly, and Christian conservatives equally negative toward Warner—indeed, many found that a score of zero degrees on a feeling thermometer was insufficiently low and penciled in negative numbers. The state party chair, a Christian conservative, unsuccessfully lobbied Senate GOP party leaders to strip Warner of his membership on the Defense Committee, a major source of jobs and pork for Virginia. Jim Miller, who in 1994 had been the candidate of the moderates against North and then in 1996 decided to run as the candidate of the Christian Right, challenged Warner for renomination. Had Warner been forced to run in a party convention, he would clearly have lost, but state law allowed him to choose a primary. The Virginia GOP challenged the constitutionality of the state law in federal court, but a federal judge tossed out the case. Ten days before the primary, the state GOP held its convention and endorsed Miller by a 3–1 margin in a straw poll and elected a Christian conservative as state party chair. The most dramatic moment of the convention came when Oliver North addressed the delegates and urged them to get behind the candidacy of his former opponent. He asked that each delegate pledge $20 to Miller's campaign and actively work to identify and urge similar help from every 1994 North supporter. North mailed a plea to 16,500 supporters asking for their assistance for Miller's campaign. But Warner won the primary handily with 66 percent of the vote, in part because of crossover voting from Democrats and independents. Perhaps the most apt comment after the primary came from former state GOP spokesman Mike Salster, who said that the Christian Right had been "spoiling for this fight for three years . . . Now they have found their base, and it is 34 percent, not 50.1 percent."[11]

In a remarkable display of pragmatism, Christian conservatives then rallied behind Warner in a tough general election fight against Mark Warner (no relation). The 1996 exit polls showed that the Christian Right turned out, that they overwhelmingly voted for John Warner, and that they contributed 30 percent of his overall vote. Most telling of this pragmatism was the activity of the Christian Coalition. Although a January 1996 Christian Coalition scorecard gave the senator a 100 percent voting record for 1995, in June 1996 during the GOP primary, the group's voter guide gave him a 20 percent rating (Miller received 100 percent). But then after the primary, a new Coalition guide gave the senator an 83 percent rating. The organization used different issues for its primary election and general election voter guides for the Senate race, allowing it to portray Warner first negatively and then positively. In the statewide congressional races, the Coalition used the same issues for both elections.

An Associated Press survey of the Virginia delegates to the Republican National Convention in 1996 showed the continued strength of the Christian Right in the state party. Of the 52 delegates, 48 responded to the survey. Among those, 21 responded that they considered themselves a part of the Christian social conservative movement, 19 said "no," and 8 chose "no answer." Among those who chose "no answer" were delegates Pat Robertson and Ralph Reed.[12] The delegation also included Farris, former National Right to Life spokesperson Kay Coles James, antiabortion leader Anne Kincaid, and Family Foundation (of the Focus on the Family) head Walter Barbee.

By the latter half of the 1990s, the division between the Christian conservatives and moderates began to heal, primarily because the Christian Right worked to support conservative candidates who staked more moderate stances on social issues. In 1997, the movement supported the nomination and election of Jim Gilmore, then attorney general, to the governorship. Gilmore was clearly more conservative than his Democratic rival, but his campaign centered on a promise to end the personal property tax (commonly called the car tax), not on abortion or other social issues. Democratic candidate Don Beyer, who had defeated Michael Farris for lieutenant governor in 1993, sought to link Gilmore with Falwell and Robertson, but this worked even less well than it had against Allen in 1993. The candidate for lieutenant governor, John Hager, also won election, despite his pugnacious character, a penchant for embarrassing remarks, and strong pro-tobacco stands.

The only contested race for the Republicans was for attorney general, and a Christian conservative who had support from many labor and African American leaders won. Mark Earley, a state legislator who had promoted Christian Right positions and who was an able politician, defeated three candidates in a primary that attracted only 6 percent of eligible Republican voters, because the other two statewide offices were uncontested. Pro-life activist and former Family Foundation head Anne Kincaid managed Earley's primary campaign as Earley focused his resources on Christian radio and targeted mailings. Although the other three candidates attacked each other in mass media ads, the Earley campaign sought to stay below the radar and mobilize its base.

Although Earley ran as the social conservative candidate in the party primary, he did a masterful job of presenting himself to the general electorate as a mainstream conservative. In truth, his views on the social issues were not easily distinguishable from the views of Michael Farris and Oliver North. Earley opposes abortion, even in the cases of rape and incest, a position to the right of the vast majority of Virginia voters. Yet Democrats found the electorate reluctant to accept a depiction of Earley as a pawn of Robertson and Falwell. Unlike Farris, Earley had not been active in a Christian Right organization, and unlike North, he lacked any elements of public scandal. Where Farris had been the Christian Right attorney in the "Scopes II" trial,

Earley had served as a missionary in Manilla. And unlike either Farris or North, he had a record as a successful state legislator who was clearly willing to compromise on issues. Earley's pragmatism even earned him the general election endorsement of the *Washington Post*.

Although Earley opposed most abortions, his campaign focused on parental notification and consent, a ban on partial-birth abortions, and denial of public funding for abortions. Although Virginia is a pro-choice state, these positions were popular. And unlike the 1989 election, when pro-choice moderates were frightened that the GOP candidate might truly take away their abortion rights, Earley could point to his ten years of activity in the state legislature, where he was one of the most active supporters of parental notification, but had never introduced legislation to ban abortions. When asked about his views on the procedure generally, Earley merely responded that he respected current constitutional interpretation and had no plans as attorney general to challenge federal law in that area.

The failure of Democratic candidate Bill Dolan to successfully link Earley to the Christian Right is telling, because on its merits, it was an easy case. In part, Dolan's attacks on Earley—for making a speech at a "Field of Blood" pro-life rally which featured hundreds of crosses displayed on a hillside to mourn fetal deaths, and for accepting $35,000 from Pat Robertson—seemed too negative. The *Washington Post* in endorsing Earley criticized the tone of the Dolan campaign. Perhaps a more subtle campaign would have gained some traction, but it seems likely that after nearly twenty years, this campaign theme had gone stale. Ultimately Earley won a landslide, and he even carried 40 percent of pro-choice voters.

Earley's success suggests that Christian Right candidates need not be social moderates so long as they focus on popular social positions and have a record of public service that is seen by voters as evidence of an ability to compromise. A Christian Right nominee also is electable statewide if he or she can credibly campaign as a broad-based coalitional candidate with appeal beyond more typical ideological boundaries. Earley is unique among the Christian Right candidates we have encountered in our studies of the movement in Virginia Republican politics. He joined the NAACP in 1982, supported a state bill to mandate multicultural education in the public schools, and supported a "fair share" bill to require nonunion employees to pay union dues in unionized work settings or be fired. He attracted the endorsements of the state firefighters' union and of the immediate past president of the NAACP.

In 2001 Earley lost his bid for the governorship. The GOP nomination was a contest between Earley and Lieutenant Governor John Hager, and although Hager had little chance of victory, he contested the nomination to the end. Hager focused his campaign on the contrast between his package of economic conservatism and social moderation with Earley's economic moderation and social conservatism. Although Earley won the convention easily, the charge of social extremism from a very conservative Republican damaged his public image of moderation. He faced a Democratic Party desperate to win the governorship, and a multimillionaire opponent, Mark Warner, who had run a credible campaign for the U.S. Senate in 1996 against incumbent John Warner. Mark Warner also positioned himself as a social moderate, and he vigorously (but unsuccessfully) sought the endorsement of the NRA.

Earley tried to convince Republican donors to try to match Warner's millions, and this task was made far more difficult by the terrorist attacks of September 11, 2001, which essentially froze the campaign for weeks and made fund-raising events seem divisive. George W. Bush canceled planned appearances for Earley as he sought to maintain bipartisan support for his foreign policy. Earley was also hurt that the Republicans had squabbled openly and awkwardly over budget issues for the past year, that Gilmore had not ended the car tax as promised, and that the state faced a huge revenue shortfall. With a big lead to start the campaign, Warner did not attack Earley on the social issues or for his ties to Pat Robertson or Jerry Falwell. Interestingly, it was Earley who raised the issue in a last, desperate effort to mobilize his base. Earley ran a radio ad that quoted Warner out of context criticizing the Christian Right in the GOP, and he charged that Warner was hostile to "people of faith." This echoed a theme of the Farris campaign in 1993, but it was widely seen as an unfair and negative attack, and Warner won easily.

Earley's defeat was a disappointment to the Christian Right and a relief to critics who saw him as the movement's Trojan horse. Yet in defeat, the movement and the GOP as well had much to celebrate. In 1999 the GOP achieved control of both houses of the state legislature, making Virginia the first state of the old Confederacy to have Republican control of all statewide elected state offices and both houses of the legislature. In 2000, former governor George Allen defeated incumbent senator Chuck Robb, also giving the party both U.S. Senate seats. And in 2001, despite losing the governorship, the GOP won the attorney general race and picked up a remarkable twelve seats in the House of Delegates, giving the party control of two-thirds of the seats of the lower house.

Perhaps one of the best examples of the movement's electoral success in recent years was in the 2000 GOP presidential primary in Virginia. The Christian Right was largely united in its opposition to the candidacy of Arizona senator John McCain and supported Texas governor George W. Bush. McCain made a controversial speech in Pat Robertson's hometown of Virginia Beach to denounce the Christian Right leader and Jerry Falwell for what McCain considered their deceitful electoral activities. McCain's speech emphasized what he saw as the negative impact of various Christian Right leaders' activities on the Republican Party. Although many party moderates applauded McCain's speech, Christian Right activists turned out in large numbers against him. Exit polls revealed that McCain had won the votes of moderate Republicans and non-Republicans voting in the open GOP primary. But Christian Right opposition to him was intense and united. McCain's defeat in Virginia marked the practical end of his presidential aspirations.[13]

THE EVOLUTION OF THE CHRISTIAN RIGHT

In the 1980s the Christian Right in Virginia was primarily a cadre of intolerant political novices who helped nominate politically extreme candidates and pushed them to take unpopular stands on social issues. In the 1990s the movement entered the political mainstream of Virginia, a major influence not only on GOP nominations and platforms but on general elections as well. In the new century, now twenty-five years after the movement first emerged on the scene in state politics, Christian Right organizations are less visible, but activists are firmly ensconced in the Republican Party, and its supporters are habitual voters.

The Christian Right in Virginia learned the art of electoral politics. In part this was a result of new leadership in the 1990s, which stressed the importance of pragmatism and winning over ideological purism and likely defeat. It could also be attributed to certain longtime leaders having learned from past mistakes. These arguments for movement pragmatism were bolstered by data from exit and tracking polls that showed that moderate Northern Virginia voters would reject any candidate who took socially extreme positions, and would mobilize against any highly visible movement efforts. They were also aided by the taste of political victory in 1993, when moderate rhetoric helped elect a social conservative as governor. The Christian Right may have learned the art of electoral politics partially by necessity as well. In the 1990s the GOP became a competitive party, thereby attracting better candidates and more diverse coalition elements. Today the GOP is a far bigger tent than before, and thus it is harder for the Christian Right to fully dominate party nominations.

Virginia has experienced successive waves of Christian Right mobilization, which have brought different types of activists into politics. Falwell's Moral Majority brought Baptist fundamentalists into politics, and Robertson's Christian Coalition mobilized Pentecostals. Farris brought in home-school advocates, and North drew strong support from charismatics. The fundamentalists of Falwell and the home schoolers for Farris were often unsophisticated political ideologues, and many of them are no longer active in politics. Those that remain are more pragmatic, both because they learned the value of compromise and because those who were unwilling to compromise dropped out. But many activists in the movement have been around for twenty years or more, and they have learned valuable lessons.

As a result, the Christian Right no longer arouses so much fear in the electorate, at least so long as it supports pragmatic candidates. Although Robertson and Falwell are unpopular in the state, the intensity of this opposition has declined. As the movement has become more strategic in its use of campaign appeals and issue positions, the public perceives less of a threat from GOP candidates who have some association with the Christian Right. It is telling that in 2001, the Virginia Democratic gubernatorial candidate determined that a key to election was to avoid talking about the GOP candidate's social issue positions. He correctly understood that the days of being able to run Democratic campaigns by simply declaring the GOP nominees as social extremists were over—assuming, of course, that the GOP does not again some day nominate a Farris or North for statewide office. If the Christian Right continues to back mainstream conservatives with broad-based electoral appeal, it will remain an important part of the successful GOP coalition in Virginia.

The Christian Right also has succeeded in state politics by more closely aligning its policy positions with the preferences of significant portions of the public. Earlier appeals to outlaw abortion rights frightened the electorate, but parental notification is as popular in Virginia as elsewhere, and it does not mobilize pro-choice opposition. Today the movement is much more likely to be involved in a debate over allowing public school students to say prayers during a moment of silence than to advocate the mandatory teaching of creationism.

The evolution of the state electorate has had some advantages for the movement as well. In recent years the suburbs have experienced phenomenal population growth. Given the tendency of suburbia to vote Republican, this change has helped the movement increase its fortunes, as the state has become dominated by the GOP. In the 2001 elections, most of the newly elected state legislators hailed from GOP-leaning suburban districts on the farther outskirts of the central urban areas. Although in the past suburbia led the way in Virginia in defeating Christian Right candidates for state office, today the growing suburbs are leading the way toward a Republican-dominated state. As long as the Christian Right works within the GOP and avoids the mistakes of the past—such as pushing for the nominations of extreme candidates and taking extreme issue positions—the movement appears poised to continue to be part of winning GOP coalitions.

THE PAYOFFS OF CHRISTIAN RIGHT ACTIVISM

For many Christian Right activists, elections are now exciting enterprises that are worthwhile in their own right. For others, voting has become a habit, and even without a strong Christian Right get-out-the-vote drive, evangelicals are likely to be a major element of the electorate. Yet after nearly twenty-five years of electoral activity, the policy achievements of the movement remain modest. It is possible that this will soon change, for the large GOP legislative majority, if coupled by a Republican governor in 2006, could enact policy with little input from Democrats.

Yet it is also instructive to consider the policy victories of the movement after some twenty-five years of activity. Although most Christian Right activists would prefer to ban most abortions, the only victory to date has been the passage of parental notification and a ban on certain late-term abortions. Although these are highly symbolic victories, some activists privately complain that it is not evident that these policies have prevented *any* abortions in Virginia. Most Christian Right activists would like to see prayer in schools, religion as a natural part of the curriculum, and evolution replaced by (or at least supplemented by) creationism in the classroom. The most visible victory to date is a mandatory moment of silence, during which very few public schoolchildren pray. The Christian Right has also succeeded in limiting the scope of sex education in the classroom to a certain extent, although most social conservative activists want it eliminated altogether.

Most movement activists prefer that mothers remain in the home with their children, and they oppose policies that make it easier for them to work outside the home. In this area, the movement has clearly lost ground, for localities increasingly offer after-school care with public subsidies to meet the demands by two-income families. Indeed, a majority of evangelical mothers of school-aged children work outside the home. The movement is divided in its preferences on gay rights, but at a minimum, activists would like to see all discussion of homosexuality taken out of the classroom, and they want no laws providing benefits or protections to gays and lesbians. Here the movement has succeeded in stopping various policies that might expand gay rights, but public attitudes are clearly changing rapidly on this issue, even in Virginia.

The Allen administration, from 1994 to 1998, was the most favorable to the Christian Right of any in contemporary history, so it is worthwhile to consider what payoffs Allen provided to one of his most loyal constituency groups. Christian Right leaders lobbied hard for the state to refuse public funding for the Goals 2000 program, which they feared would mandate weak national learning standards and would incorporate values they opposed into the curriculum. Allen refused federal funds from 1994 through 1996, and then bowed to public pressure to accept the funds after negotiating some exceptions for Virginia. The governor launched a $300,000 "traditional values"–based series of advertisements to extol the importance of fatherhood. The initiative, called the Virginia Fatherhood Campaign, was an outgrowth of the gubernatorial Commission on Citizen Empowerment. Allen also supported initiatives in the state legislature to mandate parental notification on abortion for underage girls and to establish a new criminal category of "feticide" to declare the act of killing a fetus a murder. The former eventually gained approval during the Gilmore administration. The latter failed. Allen made other gestures in the area of charter schools that were also unsuccessful.

These efforts represented partial victories for the movement, and they provided activists with some evidence that winning elections actually mattered. But the movement's gains remain limited to secondary issues. In 2002 the effort to pass a parental consent bill stalled in the state legislature. Legislative initiatives to post the Ten Commandments in public school rooms and to incorporate values-based teaching in the curriculum also failed. The legislature did pass a bill to post the motto "In God We Trust" in the public schools, and at this writing, the governor has not signaled his intention to sign it. Even if the governor consents, the major policy victory of the latest legislative session is a largely symbolic measure, even though the GOP has considerable strength in the two chambers. The movement has had some successes defending against initiatives supported by social libertarians. In one case, the movement lobbied successfully against a bill that would have allowed emergency contraceptives to be available to women over the counter at pharmacies.

It is likely that the movement will have more policy successes in the future as long as it is focused on defensive actions and on promoting secondary policy gains. But more than a quarter-century of activism has not yielded a major change in the state public's attitudes toward social issues, and policy gains of the movement have been limited in character. Even in this GOP-dominated, conservative Southern state, the Christian Right is limited in the degree to which it can achieve its foremost policy goals.

NOTES

1. V. O. Key Jr., *Southern Politics in State and Nation* (New York: Alfred A. Knopf, 1949), 19.

2. Daniel J. Elazar, *American Federalism: A View from the States* (New York: Thomas Y. Crowell, 1972), 1178.

3. Ralph Reed, oral interview conducted by Mark J. Rozell, Washington, D.C., September 29, 1994. In possession of the authors.

4. These percentages are figured from studies by the Ray Bliss Center of Applied Politics at the University of Akron as well as Barry A. Kosmin, Egon Meyer, and Ariela Keyser, American Religious Identification Survey, 2001 (New York: Graduate Center of the City University of New York, 2001).

5. From 2000 exit polling data.

6. Kimberly Conger and John C. Green, "Spreading Out and Digging In: Christian Conservatives and State Republican Parties," *Campaigns and Elections* 2 (February 2002): 58–65.

7. Mark J. Rozell and Clyde Wilcox, *Second Coming: The New Christian Right in Virginia Politics* (Baltimore: Johns Hopkins University Press, 1996).

8. Ibid.

9. Elizabeth Adell Cook, Ted G. Jelen, and Clyde Wilcox, "Issue Voting in Gubernatorial Elections: Abortion in Post-*Webster* Politics," *Journal of Politics* 56 (1994): 187–99.

10. Rozell and Wilcox, *Second Coming.*

11. Mark J. Rozell and Clyde Wilcox, "Virginia: When the Music Stops, Choose Your Faction," in *God at the Grass Roots, 1996: The Christian Right in American Elections,* ed. Mark J. Rozell and Clyde Wilcox (Lanham, Md.: Rowman and Littlefield, 1997), 99–114.

12. Ibid.

13. Mark J. Rozell, "The Christian Right in the 2000 GOP Presidential Campaign," in *Piety, Politics, and Pluralism: Religion in the Courts and the 2000 Election,* ed. Mary Segers (Lanham, Md.: Rowman and Littlefield, 2002), 57–74.

11

The Mercedes and the Pine Tree

Modernism and Traditionalism in Alabama

Natalie M. Davis

Over the past several years, literature has emerged to tackle the issue of transformations in the contemporary world. Basic to these transformations is the tension between modernism and traditionalism. Modernism is linked to secularism, rationalism, new technologies, globalism, tolerance, change, and a belief in the future. In contrast, traditionalism is defined by religiosity, faith, hierarchy, particularism, fundamentalism, experience, and recourse to the past. Modernists embrace change and the future; traditionalists are skeptical of both. Given the opportunities as well as dislocations associated with globalism and technological change, many see modernism and traditionalism in constant conflict.[1]

In assessing the impact of globalization on culture, politics, and economics, questions arise about change in an increasingly high-tech, high-growth, information-driven world. Who gets left behind? Why? And will those left behind challenge in a serious, even violent way, modernity? For a while, these questions were mainly the stuff of academic discourse. But the terrorist attack of September 11, 2001, forced a wider consideration of the modernist-traditionalist discussion. The question posed by September 11 was, to use Benjamin Barber's terms, whether "jihad" could inflict real damage on "McWorld." If jihad succeeds, democracy and civil society collapse. Barber is an optimist who believes that McWorld—a place of computers, cell phones, fax machines, the Internet, and fast food—will triumph in the end.[2]

Samuel Huntington is not so sure. Huntington's "clash of civilizations" is just that: the potential for violence in the world is a result of cultural conflict as western Enlightenment encounters Eastern fundamentalism. Huntington believes cultural differences—especially religious differences—will be the driving forces. Although civilizations may be defined by a number of variables, including history, language, and culture, the most important is religion.[3]

Thomas Friedman shares intellectual space with Barber. He uses the luxury car brand Lexus and the olive tree as metaphors for modernism and traditionalism:

> The Lexus and the olive tree were actually pretty good symbols of this post–Cold War era. Half the world seemed to be emerging from the Cold War intent on building a better Lexus dedicated to modernizing, streamlining and privatizing their economies in order to thrive in the system of globalization. And half the world—sometimes half the same country, sometimes half the same person—was still caught up in the fight on who owns which olive tree.
>
> Olive trees are important. They represent everything that roots us, anchors us, identifies us and locates us in the world—whether it be belonging to a family, a community, a tribe, a nation, a religion, or most of all, a place called home.[4]

What none of these books do, because they take up globalism, is look at the applications of these concepts to domestic politics. James Davison Hunter, in *Culture Wars*, examines domestic politics as an arena for conflict between modernism and traditionalism.[5] His book provides a solid grounding in the historical forces that have shaped American political ideology, beginning with eighteenth-century Europe and the Enlightenment and going to nineteenth- and twentieth-century reactions to it, including papal condemnation of modernism.[6] He argues that with the exception of the *Scopes* trial in 1925, American Protestantism was essentially progressive during the first half of the twentieth century. Meanwhile, setting aside Vatican II, American Catholicism has remained a force for conservatism for most of the century.[7] The conflict between religious fundamentalism and mainline Protestantism is not new. It does not simply date to the Moral Majority of the late 1970s but has been a part of American culture for a long time. What is new is that fundamentalist strains as recourse to traditionalism have become potent forces in American politics in general and Southern politics in particular.

If Friedman were writing about Alabama, he might very well title his book *The Mercedes and the Pine Tree.* In Alabama, the Mercedes culture is

synonymous with modernism. The establishment of a Mercedes plant in
Vance, Alabama, symbolizes globalism. On the heels of Daimler-Chrysler
and Mercedes, Honda, Toyota, and Hyundai have also come into the state in
recent years. Along with these plants, it is important to note what has happened to urban life. In the last twenty-five years, Birmingham has traded
steel for service. The largest employer in Birmingham is an urban university. In contrast, pine tree culture represents a culture indigenous to the soil,
where agriculture, timber, and cotton shared a base for an economy that
still lags far behind most states. The red clay of Alabama is a powerful
political symbol in the state. Nearly every biographical campaign commercial—whether touting a trucking entrepreneur, a poultry-raising
planter, a sporting goods equipment tycoon, or a mining and mineral magnate—emphasizes the candidate's rural roots and the traditional "Alabama
values" that go along with them in much of the state's consciousness. Politicians remind voters that they are no more than one generation removed
from the farm.

To what extent do these cultures drive Alabama politics, and in what
ways does one prevail over the other? Given Alabama's pattern of voting for
Republican candidates for president, it is not surprising that George W. Bush
overwhelmingly defeated Al Gore in the 2000 presidential election, 57 to 41
percent. Postelection analysis, however, is revealing on what actually happened below these top-line numbers. According to the exit polls, 23 percent
of Alabama's voters called themselves members of the Religious Right; 77
percent did not. Within that 77 percent, Gore edged Bush 52 to 48. Among
the 23 percent who identified themselves with the Religious Right, Bush
swamped Gore 78 to 20. Thus, the Religious Right really made it possible for
Bush to beat Gore badly in Alabama in 2000. In that same election, Alabamians faced a referendum on whether to remove the state's constitutional ban
on interracial marriage. Although the ban had been ignored for many years,
it was thought appropriate to actually remove it from the 1901 Alabama
constitution. The amendment passed 60 to 40. However, regression analysis
demonstrates that a majority of Alabama whites actually voted to keep the
antimiscegenation language in the century-old constitution. Statewide, only
44 percent of white voters supported removal of the ban, with the question
failing worst in the white rural counties—the same places where George W.
Bush enjoyed his strongest support.[8] Where race and culture intersect, the
tension between the Mercedes and the pine tree can be found.

Hunter's definition of two polarizing impulses aptly describes Alabama.
He divides American political culture into two groups—orthodox and pro-

gressive—and the culture war is characterized by this cleavage: "the impulse toward orthodoxy and the impulse toward progressivism." Orthodoxy is defined as "the commitment on the part of adherents to an external, definable, and transcendent authority . . . it tells us what is good, what is true, how we should live, and who we are. It is an authority that is sufficient for all time."[9] In contrast, progressivism does not rely upon a transcendent authority, but rather a "moral authority . . . defined by the spirit of modern age, a spirit of rationalism and subjectivism . . . truth tends to be viewed as a process, as a reality that's ever unfolding."[10] Here, Hunter sets the terms of the debate: progressives (modernists) adapt beliefs to contemporary life. Those who practice orthodoxy (traditionalists) cling to steadfastly held beliefs. For the most part, orthodox beliefs are rooted in Scripture.

With few exceptions, those who have done the most extensive work on secularism within modern Protestantism agree. Peter Berger suggests that the distinction between modernism and traditionalism may be reduced to a tendency toward either accommodation to a situation, a pluralism, or a refusal to accommodate, with individuals maintaining entrenched attachment to specific elements of religious faith.[11] Robert Wuthnow, a New Right scholar, accepts Hunter's distinction. He tends to defend orthodoxy, arguing that there is a certain "truth" to the position of fundamentalists because they are "bearers of tradition."[12] Wuthnow disagrees with those who believe that fundamentalists are essentially defensive, that they are fighting off the imperatives of modernity and are simply retreating to simpler times. In fact, he claims just the opposite to be true—that fundamentalists believe the past should define the future. Progressives are viewed derisively as moral relativists.[13] Kenneth Wald concludes that religious influence and economic growth are incompatible: "According to the classical modernization perspective, the hold of traditional religious values is challenged by industrialization, mass education, technological sophistication, population mobility, rapid urbanization, and the proliferation of complex forms of social organization. These developments undercut religion by rendering its theological claims less plausible by restricting its moral impact to the realm of privately held values and orientations."[14]

J. D. Hunter and others contend that party identification is no longer the key to understanding political differences. Instead, they argue that the real division in politics is along the two lines of modernism and traditionalism. Modernists have a different worldview. It is based on adaptation of and a willingness to embrace change, both seen as necessary and even desirable responses to contemporary life. Traditionalists cling to fundamentalist religious values. They see the past as prologue. They claim a certainty about their beliefs that is based on moral authority.

There is at least one dissent. In *One Nation After All,* Alan Wolfe posits that the cultural war tendered by Hunter is overstated. His view is that although elites may be in cultural conflict, most Americans are not.[15] Hunter sees the relationship between modernism and traditionalism as dichotomous, whereas Wolfe proffers a more complex explanation: "The two sides presumed to be fighting the cultural war do not so much represent a divide between one group of Americans and another as a divide between sets of values important to everyone." He claims that it is possible to classify people as "modern traditionalists" or "traditional modernist." People who adhere to such traditional values as belief in God, strong families, patriotism, and civic and neighborly loyalty do so because, in most cases, they choose to do so; they are best described as modern traditionalists. And people who insist on the importance of their own conceptions of God, who value women's autonomy, and who select their friends and neighbors on the basis of personal taste believe strongly in the importance of religion, family, neighborhood. They can best be viewed as traditional modernists. For Wolfe, it is a basic truth of American society that no one is a traditionalist or a modernist, but that everyone lives with varying degrees of both.[16]

Although traditional voting behavior emphasizes party identification as the principal driver in elections, the real division in politics may be between modernism and traditionalism. This distinction has yielded a number of specific findings. First, it is possible to identify religious variables that define modernism and traditionalism. James L. Guth and John C. Green point out in *The Bible and the Ballot Box* that religion has always played a prominent role in American politics in at least three important ways—religious leadership, religious organizations, and religious identification—with the result being that religion offers information and guidance about political matters.[17] Moreover, religious leadership has been particularly important in translating articles of faith into contemporary approaches to the solution of problems associated with modernity.[18] In analysis of three election cycles, G. Layman and E. Carmines find that religious traditionalism had a stronger effect than any other value priority on political choices.[19] Green and Guth also find that among political activists, "traditional religious activists are moving toward the political right and less traditional activists are moving left."[20] Other groupings have also concluded that traditionalism exerts an independent effect on political behavior. P. H. Ray divided Americans into three groupings—traditionalists, modernists, and cultural creatives; cultural creatives have much in common with the postmaterialists of Ronald Inglehart. In Ray's study, traditionalists make up 29 percent of Americans; 47 percent are modernists; and 24 percent can be placed in the category of cultural creatives. Among the traditionalists, 70 percent are also members of the Religious Right as compared with 26 percent of modernists and 31 percent of cultural creatives. Fifty-five percent of modernists say they are not members of the Religious Right. Overall, traditionalists are older and less educated than modernists or cultural creatives.[21]

In an empirical test of Hunter's cultural war thesis, Dale McConkey makes use of the 1988 and 1998 General Social Survey databases. He looked at four variables and constructed a religious conservatism scale. These variables focused on the experience of being born again, on believing that the Bible is the literal word of God, on encouraging someone to believe in Jesus Christ, and on belonging to an evangelical denomination. On the basis of the distribution of these responses in the 1998 data set, 12 percent of respondents were classified as evangelical, 65 percent as moderate, and 23 percent as progressive. On virtually all items related to issue positions—from homosexuality to abortion to suicide and euthanasia—evangelicals were significantly more likely to be conservative.[22] Similar conclusions were drawn by Layman and Carmines when it came to issues of partisanship and voting preferences, where, in their schema, religious traditionalists tended to be more at home in the Republican Party and more likely to vote for conservative candidates.[23]

To test the relationship between religious values, modernism and traditionalism, and political preferences, I used survey data collected in Alabama in 2002. This statewide telephone survey (of 450 registered voters) included many items that allowed me to create measures of religiosity, modernism and traditionalism, and political preferences. There is consistency in the view that the modernist-traditionalist distinction has consequences for American politics. Can such effects be found in Alabama politics? Do modernism and traditionalism affect the distribution of political attitudes and voting preferences within the state? Where do these attitudes come from? The thrust of the analysis is to test this model:

Religious Values →   Modernism   → Political Preferences
                         Traditionalism

Religious values are seen as preceding the development of a modernist or traditionalist orientation. In combination, these variables affect the distribution of social and political preferences.

Table 11.1

Traditionalism and Modernism in Alabama

Item	Whites	Blacks	All Respondents
The world is always changing and we should adjust our view of what is right or wrong to these changes.[a]			
Strongly agree	10.1	27.5	13.6
Agree	33.2	44.0	35.3
Neutral	3.8	5.5	4.2
Disagree	24.9	14.3	22.8
Strongly disagree	27.9	8.8	24.1
Which comes closest to your view? [b]			
Experience and tradition are our best teachers. Reliance on faith and values prepares us well for the future. Keeping faith with the past is the best way to make the world a better place.	45.0	31.2	—
or			
The best way to plan for the future is to be open to change. The world is constantly changing, and to make progress we must be willing to break with the past. Making the world a better place means being flexible and open to change.	55.0	68.8	—

[a] Gamma = - .48; $p < .01$.
[b] Gamma = - .28; $p < .01$.

In table 11.1, I examine the distribution of traditionalism and modernism in terms of two survey items. The first asked respondents whether they agreed or disagreed with the statement, "The world is always changing and we should adjust our view of what is right or wrong to those changes." Among all respondents, approximately 49 percent agreed and 47 percent disagreed. The second item asked voters to indicate which of two philosophies represented or came closest to their view. The first dealt with the importance of

Table 11.2

Modernism and Traditionalism by Religious Values

Item	All Respondents	Modernists	Neither	Traditionalists
In thinking about the Bible[a]				
"The Bible is a book written by men and is not the word of God"	1.1	1.2	1.9	—
"The Bible was written by men inspired by God, but it contains some human errors"	23.5	33.3	21.4	13.4
"The Bible is the word of God but not everything in it should be taken literally word for word"	22.0	22.4	18.8	25.2
"The Bible is the actual word of God and is to be taken literally, word for word"	52.5	41.5	57.1	61.4
Most important way to know God's will [b]				
From church teachings	12.6	11.6	14.8	11.0
From the Bible	33.9	28.3	31.0	50.4
Through human reason	6.7	11.0	6.5	1.6
Through the Holy Spirit	17.3	14.0	17.4	21.3
You just know it in your heart	26.9	36.6	27.1	14.2
Church attendance[c]				
Mean number of times per month	4.15	3.29	4.29	5.08

[a] Gamma = .28; $p < .001$.
[b] Gamma = .24; $p < .001$.
[c] Eta = .24; $p < .05$.

"experience and tradition," and the second emphasized the "future and an openness to change." On that item, change won out over tradition 58 to 42 percent. Table 11.1 also looks at the differences between whites and blacks on those items. For both questions, blacks were much more likely to embrace change and the future, whereas whites were more likely to rely on tradition and reject change.

Table 11.3

Associations between the Modernism-Traditionalism Variable
and Political Preference

Variable	Modernist (%)	Neither (%)	Traditionalist (%)	Total (%)
Political ideology[a]				
Very conservative	9.3	14.9	20.5	14.4
Somewhat conservative	33.3	43.5	42.5	39.5
Middle of the road	33.3	26.0	28.3	29.3
Somewhat liberal	18.5	11.0	7.9	12.9
Very liberal	5.6	4.5	0.8	3.8
Party identification[b]				
Democrat	41.9	31.3	27.4	34.1
Lean Democrat	5.6	7.3	4.8	6.0
Strictly independent	13.8	15.3	10.5	13.4
Lean Republican	5.0	8.0	8.9	7.1
Republican	33.8	38.0	48.4	39.4
2002 Gubernatorial choice[c]				
Riley (R)	51.0	59.2	74.5	60.2
Siegelman (D)	49.0	40.8	25.5	39.8

[a] Gamma = - .25; p < .003.
[b] Gamma = .18; p < .001.
[c] Gamma = - .32; p < .001.

Both survey items were combined into one measure of modernism-traditionalism, and my sample was divided into three groups: traditionalists, who responded to both questions with the "traditional" answers; modernists, who answered with the "modern" responses; and those who were not consistent. A total of 36.7 percent are modernists (32.2 percent of whites, 54.4 percent of blacks); 28.6 percent can be classified as traditionalists (32.8 percent of whites, 12.2 percent of blacks); and 34.7 percent comprise the "neither" category (35.0 percent of whites, 33.3 percent of blacks). Again, whites and blacks were decidedly different. Whites were more likely to be traditionalists than were blacks.

Table 11.2 takes up questions of religious values. The first item is an

Table 11.4

Modernism and Traditionalism by Selected Issues[a]

Item	All Respondents	Modernists	Neither	Traditionalists	p Value
Judge Roy Moore thermometer	61.2	51.3	63.6	71.1	.001
Feminists thermometer	42.1	51.6	6.4	32.4	.001
Homosexuals thermometer	27.2	34.6	23.4	20.6	.001
Can usually trust the federal government	2.95	3.12	2.82	2.83	.080
Need to support increases in property taxes for education	3.05	3.33	3.09	2.65	.001
Genetic engineering can be used to save life of unborn	3.58	3.87	3.57	3.20	.001
Voting makes a difference	4.29	4.25	4.50	4.17	.022
OK for two people of different races to marry	3.21	3.45	3.12	2.97	.009
OK for homosexuals to adopt children	2.26	2.76	2.13	1.70	.001
How informed are you? (self-rating)	6.42	6.58	6.42	6.21	.283
Free trade or protectionist?	1.93	1.89	1.81	2.07	.241
Abortion OK if teen is not capable of taking care of child	1.86	1.75	1.92	1.94	.340
Abortion OK if child is likely to be born with birth defect	1.79	1.63	2.00	1.85	.171
How literally to treat the Bible	3.25	3.06	3.27	3.48	.001

[a] The scores are means. The first three items are ratings that range from 1 to 100; the remaining are Likert scale items with mean scores ranging from 1 to 5 (the higher the score, the more likely respondents were to agree with the statement).

ordinal question on whether the Bible should be taken literally. Traditionalists are more likely to take the Bible more literally than are the modernists. The pattern is similar when "the most important way to know God's will" is looked at. Traditionalists are more likely to place their faith in the Bible. Not

Table 11.5

Impact of Selected Variables on Modernism and Traditionalism[a]

Variable	B	SE	Standardized Coefficient Beta	p Value
Church attendance	9.796E-02	.028	.172	.001
Literal treatment of the Bible	.284	.103	.143	.006
Religious denomination	.204	.090	.110	.025
The most important way to know God's will	- .405	.163	- .118	.013
Age	4.227E-02	.053	.038	.419
Race	1.153	.204	.272	.001
Rural-urban	- .268	.226	- .055	.235
Sex	- 5.168E-02	.164	- .015	.753
Education	.200	.178	.057	.261
Income	.104	.064	.084	.103

[a] R^2 = .20.

surprisingly, traditionalists are more likely to attend church more often than are modernists.

Modernism and traditionalism also predict political attitudes (table 11.3 and table 11.4). For example, when it comes to Chief Justice Roy Moore, the difference between traditionalists and modernists could not be clearer.[24] Thermometer ratings are significantly higher on Roy Moore among traditionalists than they are among modernists.[25] In the case of feminists and homosexuals, the reverse is true. Modernists are also more likely than are traditionalists to support increases in property taxes for education, to embrace genetic engineering, and to approve of interracial marriage. On all but a few items that were included in the survey, the distinctions between modernists and traditionalists are statistically significant.

When a regression analysis is performed where the dependent variable, modernism-traditionalism, is regressed by a number of religious independent variables, of the four independent variables tested, three are significant: (1) church attendance (B = .104, SE = .027, p = .001), (2) a variable where respondents are asked "the most important way to know God's will" (B = -.525, SE = 158, p = .001), and (3) belief that the Bible is the actual

Table 11.6

Regression for Modernism-Traditionalism and Political Variables

Variable	B	SE	Standardized Coefficient Beta	p Value
Party identification (R^2 = .04)	.201	.049	.193	.001
Political ideology (R^2 = .07)	- .155	.028	- .258	.001
2002 gubernatorial choice (R^2 = .07)	- 6.508E02	.014	- .229	.001

word of God, to be taken literally (B = .209, SE .102, p = .040).The fourth variable, religious denomination, was not statistically significant (B = 5.264E-02, SE = .087, p = .544) (for all, R^2 = .10).

Without question, there is a connection between religious fundamentalism and traditionalism. In expanding the model, I entered race as well as other demographic indicators. The results are presented in table 11.5. Race is the most significant predictor. Other variables, including sex, whether the community was rural or not, income, education, and age, provide only minimum contributions in explaining modernism and traditionalism.

In examining the association between the modernism-traditionalism variable and political preferences, it is clear that political ideology, party identification, and gubernatorial choice are statistically related (table 11.6). Gubernatorial choice is most affected by modernism and traditionalism, with modernists more likely to support the 2002 Democratic candidate, Don Siegelman; traditionalists were more likely to say they would vote for Bob Riley, the Republican candidate, who eventually won by a margin of less than 1 percent. Those who identify themselves as Democrats are more likely than Republicans to be classified as modernists. The reverse is also true. Traditionalists are more likely to be Republican. Political ideology is also a function of the modernism-traditionalism variable. On this self-placement scale, from very conservative to very liberal, the latter are more likely to be modernist. Conservatives fall mostly into the traditionalist grouping.

In table 11.7, I regress modernism-traditionalism on these political variables. Treating the same three political variables as dependent, I created another model that included the religious values questions, education, place of residence, and modernism-traditionalism. In other attempts to build a model, I included race. Race is a predictor but tends to overwhelm the analysis, accounting for about 15 percent of the variance. I did not include race in

Table 11.7

Multiple Regression for Modernism-Traditionalism

Variable	B	SE	Standarized Coefficient Beta	p Value
Gubernatorial choice (R^2 = .07)				
Constant	1.588	.101		.001
Rural-urban	2.414E-02	.070	.017	.731
Education	- 4.237E-02	.052	- .042	.413
Modernism-Traditionalism	- 6.127E-02	.015	- .216	.001
Church attendance	- 2.366E-03	.009	- .015	.788
Literal treatment of the Bible	- 9.195E-03	.056	- .009	.869
The most important way to know God's will	8.657E-02	.052	.088	.096
Religious denomination	9.152E-02	.058	.089	.101
Party identification (R^2 = .06)				
Constant	2.238	.342		.001
Rural-urban	- .362	.239	- .072	.131
Education	.200	.174	.056	.251
Modernism-Traditionalism	.218	.052	.209	.001
Church attendance	- 4.082E-02	.029	- .071	.166
Literal treatment of the Bible	.218	.187	.062	.244
The most important way to know God's will	- .177	.172	- .050	.305
Religious denomination	5.691E-02	.193	.015	.768
Political ideology (R^2 = .11)				
Constant	3.079	.190	—	.001
Rural-urban	- .135	.133	- .046	.312
Education	8.624E-03	.097	.004	.929
Modernism-Traditionalism	- .115	.029	- .191	.001
Church attendance	- 3.630E-02	.016	- .108	.028
Literal treatment of the Bible	.209	.104	.103	.046
The most important way to kow God's will	.173	.096	.085	.072
Religious denomination	- 6.955E-02	.108	- .032	.518

Table 11.8

Regressions Comparing Moderism-Traditionalism, Race,
and Political Predispositions

Characteristic	B	SE	Standardized Coefficient Beta	p Value
2002 Gubernatorial choice (R^2 = .20)				
Constant	1.925	.069	—	.000
Modernism-Traditionalism	- 2.819E-02	.014	- .099	.043
Race	- .500	.060	- .407	.000
Party identification (R^2 = .09)				
Constant	1.260	.235	—	.000
Moderism-Traditionalism	7.458E-02	.046	.072	.108
Race	1.918	.194	.440	.000
Political ideology (R^2 = .09)				
Constant	3.415	.146	—	.000
Modernism-Traditionalism	- .133	.028	- .221	.000
Race	- .354	.120	- .140	.003

this equation because I was interested in understanding the relative impact
of modernism-traditionalism when combined with the religion variables.
Modernism-traditionalism remains a robust predictor. In fact, of the seven
variables entered, only modernism-traditionalism was significant (table
11.7). Modernism-traditionalism does drive political preferences. Party identification is less a function of modernism than are either political ideology
or candidate choice, a finding that is consistent with the literature. Moreover, the religious variables are unrelated to political preferences as long as
modernism-traditionalism remains in the equation.

Table 11.8 reintroduces race. It is clear from the regressions that race
continues to be the most significant predictor of politics and political predispositions. When it comes to clearly partisan variables, such as gubernatorial choice and party identification, race is extremely robust, although
modernism-traditionalism is still statistically significant. However, when I
look at political ideology apart from partisan considerations, modernism-
traditionalism gains potency and is a stronger predictor than race.

My model can be confirmed, at least for Alabama. It suggests an important addition to my ideas about the relationship between religion and politics in the South. Religion affects whether one is a modernist or a traditionalist, and these views in turn predict political preferences.

There is a Mercedes and a pine tree culture in Alabama. It divides politics. It affects whether one is liberal or conservative, whether one votes Democratic or Republican, whether one agrees that interracial marriage is okay. In reviewing findings for fourteen social, economic, and political variables, modernism-traditionalism was a strong predictor in all but four. What does that mean for Alabama and for the South? It suggests a fault line very consistent with the one offered by Hunter. This fault line has consequences for a state like Alabama, where economic growth and educational achievement lag. The Mercedes culture and the pine tree culture simply do not "truck together"—they do not communicate. The painful result is lack of progress.

Politicians are not unmindful of this. George Wallace and others have demonstrated that playing one culture against the other can advance political careers. The Mercedes culture does not need the pine tree culture as much as the pine tree culture needs the Mercedes culture. The culture war is subtle— sometimes overshadowed by race, but nonetheless present. This culture war has consequences. The most likely for Alabama is that in the end, both cultures will lose.

NOTES

1. Thomas L. Friedman, *The Lexus and the Olive Tree* (New York: Farrar, Strauss, and Giroux, 1999); Samuel Huntington, "The Clash of Civilizations?," *Foreign Affairs* 72 (1993): 22–49; Samuel Huntington, *The Clash of Civilizations and the Remaking of World Order* (New York: Simon and Schuster, 1996); and Benjamin Barber, *Jihad vs. McWorld: How Globalism and Tribalism Are Reshaping the World* (New York: Ballantine Books, 1996).

2. Barber, *Jihad vs. McWorld,* 299.

3. Huntington, "Clash of Civilizations," 30, 40.

4. Friedman, *The Lexus and the Olive Tree,* 25.

5. James Davison Hunter, *Culture Wars: The Struggle to Redefine America* (New York: Basic Books, 1991). See also by Hunter, *Before the Shooting Begins: Searching for Democracy in America's Culture War* (New York: Free Press, 1994); and Hunter with S. Ainlay, eds., *Making Sense of Modern Times* (New York: Routledge and Kegan Paul, 1986).

6. Hunter, *Culture Wars,* 83.

7. Ibid. On the question of evolution, Hunter cites a number of Protestant antievolution responses to the *Scopes* trial. Here is one: "I regard evolution to be the greatest menace to civilization in the world today. It goes hand and hand with modernism; makes Jesus Christ a faker; robs the Christian of his hope and undermines the foundation of our 'government of the people, for the people and by the people.'

People are free in this country to worship God as they please but they are not free to do everything that the Devil wants done" (139).

8. Natalie M. Davis, "Mercedes, Pine Tree Reveal Much about State," *Birmingham News,* November 26, 2000, C1.

9. Hunter, *Culture Wars,* 44.

10. Ibid.

11. There is a large body of literature that deals directly with the evolution of modern Protestantism. See, for example, Peter L. Berger, *Facing Up to Modernity* (New York: Basic Books, 1977); and Peter L. Berger, B. Berger, and H. Kellner, *The Homeless Mind: Modernization and Consciousness* (New York: Vintage Books, 1973).

12. Robert Wuthnow, *Christianity in the Twenty-first Century: Reflections on the Challenges Ahead* (New York: Oxford University Press, 1993), 127.

13. Ibid.

14. Kenneth Wald, "Assessing the Religious Factor in Electoral Behavior," in *Religion in American Politics,* ed. C. Dunn (Washington, D.C.: *Congressional Quarterly,* 1989), 105–21; quotation on 106.

15. Alan Wolfe, *One Nation After All: What Middle-Class Americans Really Think about God, Country, Family, Racism, Welfare, Immigration, Homosexuality, Work, the Right, the Left, and Each Other* (New York: Viking, 1998).

16. Ibid., 279.

17. James L. Guth and John C. Green, eds., *The Bible and the Ballot Box* (San Francisco: Westview Press, 1991), 208.

18. Ibid., 210.

19. G. Layman and E. Carmines, "Cultural Conflict in American Politics: Religious Traditionalism, Postmaterialism, and U.S. Political Behavior," *Journal of Politics* 59 (1997): 751–77, quotation on 759.

20. John C. Green and James L. Guth, "A Look at the Invisible Army: Pat Robertson's 1988 Activist Corps," *Religion and the Culture Wars,* ed. Lyman A. Kellstedt, John C. Green, James L. Guth, and Corwin E. Smidt (Lanham, Md.: Rowman and Littlefield, 1996), 137.

21. P. H. Ray, "The Emerging Culture," *American Demographics* 19 (1997): 28–34.

22. D. McConkey, "Wither Hunter's Culture War? Shifts in Evangelical Morality, 1988–1998," *Sociology of Religion* 62 (2001): 149–74.

23. G. Layman and E. Carmines, "'Cultural Wars' in the American Party System: Religious and Cultural Change among Partisan Activists since 1972," *American Politics Quarterly* 27 (1999): 89–121.

24. Judge Roy Moore is the controversial Alabama judge who, as a circuit court judge, hung wooden plaques of the Ten Commandments in his courtroom, and then, as chief justice of the Alabama Supreme Court, erected a granite monument engraved with the Ten Commandments and had it placed in the lobby of the Alabama Supreme Court building.

25. Thermometer ratings ask respondents to offer ratings from 1 to 100 in terms of how "cold" or "warm" they feel toward the person or group. The higher the ratings, the warmer or more positive they feel.

The Status Quo Society, the Rope of Religion, and the New Racism

Glenn Feldman

The history of the South is, in many respects, the story of an ongoing clash—a centuries-old conflict now, between progress and tradition, change and continuity, reform opposed to reaction. In this way, and in many others, the South serves as a subset—albeit the most intense and concentrated subset—of the greater nation of which it is a part. A variety of our most insightful and revered American and Southern historians, over a long period of time, have written their histories of the South and understood the region from such a tableau. C. Vann Woodward made the change/continuity question a hallmark of his work on the South. Dewey Grantham cast his classic study of Southern progressivism in terms of the clash and reconciliation of progress and tradition. George Brown Tindall also wrestled with the notion of change versus stasis, preferring to emphasize a dialectic of conflict, in which a new synthesis repeatedly emerged over time. Countless others have followed their lead.[1]

And they were right about this, of course. The history of the South has been, most fundamentally, the story of the struggle between liberalism and conservatism in a variety of venues and in a spectrum of areas. Politics is history, and history is politics. Whether it is the story of women's suffrage, trade unionism, Native Americans, civil rights, educational spending and policy, environmental studies, class, gender, race and "whiteness," poor whites, literature, the degree of compliance and involvement of the German people in Hitler's holocaust, or virtually any other topic of historical inquiry, it is at its most basic level about politics. The choice of the subject, the narrowing of topic, the selection of evidence, the perspective of the researcher—all include, no matter how mightily we might strive for the value-free objectivity of the "scientist," the assumptions, biases, whims, predispositions, goals, beliefs, and ideology of the researcher and, just as importantly, of the *researched*. More, at some utterly reducible level, the topics themselves involve questions of "who gets what, when, and how?"—perhaps the most basic definition of politics of all.

It almost goes without saying that in this overarching struggle between liberalism and conservatism, the latter won out—repeatedly. The South is still the most conservative region of the country. Scholars from a variety of disciplines—in spite of the volumes written about the "Americanization of Dixie" and the "Southernization of America"—are in agreement about that. In virtually every way that conservatism can be measured—political, social, cultural, religious, patriotism, militarism, church attendance, voting, manners—the South still clearly and consistently measures as *the* most conservative section in the nation. Within that, the Deep South states of Alabama, Mississippi, Georgia, South Carolina, and Louisiana comprise an ultraconservative belt—the most conservative part of the most conservative region in America.[2]

There are exceptions, to be sure. Not all is stagnancy, conservatism, stasis, and continuity in the Southern past. Countless examples of progress, reform, liberalism, change, and vitality can readily and easily be found in virtually any facet of the Southern experience. The story of religion in the American South is not merely, solely, or purely one of conservatism. As an enduring paradox to this dominant story—one that has refused to die off thus far—faith serves as the engine for a not insignificant amount of progressivism, when and where it can be found below the Mason-Dixon Line. In fact, throughout its history, religion and spirituality have driven some of the most committed types of Southern progressivism: abolitionism, the Social Gospel, prison reform, child labor reform, Christian Socialism, civil rights. Conservatism, even that very potent type driven by religion, has its limits—even in the American South.[3] Still, when dealing with the "soft" science of historical inquiry, allowance for human exception must be made in the equation of evaluation. History—which, after all may be defined as the study of the actions of human beings in the past—must acknowledge that the lack of absolute, unqualified, laws without exception is the stuff of other academic disciplines, most notably those in the "hard" sciences. In those modes of inquiry, it is also a fact that a single exception to the general rule—any exception—must be treated as the most serious challenge to the validity of that law, perhaps to its very survival. If one apple refuses to fall to the ground after detaching from a tree, the law of gravity is in serious peril. If the earth were to decide one day to exercise free will and stop revolving around the sun, astronomy—not to mention virtually every other field of scientific inquiry—would find itself in an immediate state of crisis.[4] Not so in the humanities or social sciences. The weight, the preponderance—not necessarily the unanimity—of historical evidence is what compels. In fact, it is what is to be realistically expected in a humanistic inquiry. It is an altogether different kind of beast.

In the final analysis, even with all of the exceptions, and qualifications, and historical evidence that does not fit, it is clear that this liberal tradition—this stream of toleration, progressivism, inclusiveness, openness to new ideas, receptivity to change, self-criticism, a commitment to liberty balanced by an insistence on equality, valuation of the collective whole and the public good in addition to individual rights and private interest—has been, and still is, a distinctly minority current in the South. Perhaps nowhere is this more apparent than in the critical intersection between politics and religion.

Despite the many exceptions that may be found, religion in the South has, far more often than not, been a force for convention, tradition, continuity, the status quo: in a word, conservatism. Leading religious historian John B. Boles, concurring with the work of Samuel S. Hill Jr. on this topic, wrote that the "individualistic, conversion-centered focus" of the dominant Southern religious denominations has made them "de facto defenders of the status quo, even though—and in part because—their theology [is] otherworldly." Ted Ownby, among other scholars, has also validated this trend.[5] To be sure, religion in this regard has not acted as an immutable, unchanging concept, nor has it functioned as a completely independent variable, unattached to the culture or other pillars of the society in which it is found. Nor has it been immune to being affected itself by the deep-seated and ingrained conservatism of the region. "Religion" in this regard does not refer to the totality of religious experience in the region, only the theology and practice of the most dominant—numerically, racially, socially, economically, politically. Change, when and where it has come in the region, has, almost without exception, been principally the product of "outsiders": nosey Yankee abolitionists, immigrant, Jewish, and Northern "agitators," the "outside agitators" of civil rights and labor union fame, and "native outsiders"—people who resided physically in the South (maybe even Southern by birth) but only on the periphery of mainstream society—ethnic, racial, religious, and cultural minorities, seldom accepted as "true Southerners" or "of the South" in any elemental sense. In this way, Reconstruction has enjoyed a kind of immortality in the South. Those who would dare to bring liberal change to the South are still "carpetbaggers" and "scalawags" of one sort or another—meddling Yankees, agents of an overreaching and intrusive federal government, or disloyal, treasonous natives who, their detractors insist, do not represent the "true South." And, on some level, a kind of macro level, they do not.[6]

Most religious-based social reformers in the South—and they have existed, as is clear by the readings in this book—have usually swum against a current that was too strong to effect permanent or internal-based change. Even on the race issue, arguably the most important defining moral issue of the twentieth century, change came from Northern "do-gooders," a "grasping" central government, "disloyal" white Southerners, and "uppity" blacks— outsiders all to the dominant Southern political, social, and economic paradigm. In such a society, change came only slowly and incompletely, when at all. Even the changes that were effected—integration of public education and accommodations, viable black voter registration, the election of African American officeholders—have done little to alter deep-rooted and long-held patterns of white privilege and residential and educational segregation by custom; nor has it changed the still-yawning chasms in wealth accumulation and the availability of economic opportunities. What is more, for a distressing number of Southern whites, change imposed from without and from a minority within has left a strong residue of hollow acceptance, bitter quiescence, and legal compliance with the letter, but not the spirit, of the law. Compliance with court-ordered change has, so often in the region's history, meant little more than lip service, window dressing, or purely pragmatic coping in order to avoid the monetary and national penalties associated with a continued pattern of defiance.[7] A strong aftertaste of bitter resentment has nourished lasting political cleavages in a region already compelled by a "politics of emotion" that runs the gamut of passions from fear to rage, envy to insecurity, hate to anxiety, disgust and loathing, to helplessness to smug superiority. Resentment over government "giving away" everything to blacks has led to anger among many Southern whites and a general feeling that African Americans should quit dredging up the "exaggerated" racial injustices of the past and just "get over it."[8] Such lingering resentments are mass political power waiting to be tapped by those cynical elite strategists who recognize it as such. And they have.

Historian Dan T. Carter focused on rage and anger in his prize-winning and masterful biography of George C. Wallace, but the "politics of emotion" as understood here includes a broader gallery of emotions. Note the potent mixture of fear, envy, disgust, resentment, and other types of emotion on display in a white Georgia supporter of Ronald Reagan's interviewed at a 1980 Atlanta speech of J. B. Stoner, the militant racist leader of the National States' Rights Party: "I'm not a member of the Klan . . . but some of the things that Mr. Stoner says, I know are right." "I don't consider myself a racist. I'm for black people having their rights . . . but I'm also for white people having a few rights too. . . . Black people are getting more rights than the white people. . . . they get more welfare, food stamps, and the law's on their side. . . . you see 'em riding down the road in a Cadillac full of children and you know they're going to pick up their welfare check, and you know it isn't right. It just isn't right." "The Democratic government of Lyndon Johnson and Jimmy Carter turned everything over to the blacks, they spend my tax money for welfare and food stamps. . . . Well, I'm sick of all that. Back in the sixties and early seventies I voted for George Wallace for president whenever I had the chance. . . . I'll vote for Ronald Reagan for president because I think he wants to . . . give some of the government back to the white people. I guess it's just about that simple." The racial rationale for voting Republican has not subsided in the modern South in the last two decades, only settled at a seething place just beneath the surface of polite conversation. A white working-class Republican north of Birmingham, for example, noted that he had completely bought into the recent GOP strategy to depict itself as the friends of average Americans. He voiced resentment of the Democratic Party advertising itself as the party of the working class when "every time I go to the grocery store, as I am waiting in line wearing my Wal-Mart jeans, I . . . stand behind someone in designer clothes, with three or four kids, who pays for groceries with food stamps" and then "[I] watch the same people . . . put their groceries into a new car. . . . The Democratic Party is not for the working class, but for those too lazy to be in the working class."[9]

Such an acute racialization of Southern politics has clearly kept pace with the strides of the modern-day civil rights movement. It manifests itself in the ascendance of a once-odious Republican Party in the South whose popularity has run a rough parallel to Southern white disgust with the steadily increasing racial liberalism of the national Democratic Party since the New Deal.[10] In terms of white politics, the Solid Democratic South—a Jim Crow, segregated South—has been replaced by the Solid Republican South that is desegregated and forcibly "reformed" on race. No accident here. From time to time, as made so apparent by the recent trials of Mississippi senator Trent Lott, even polite, self-conscious, learned, politically correct water cooler conversation can, in a moment of reckless candor, give way to the enunciation of the most unreconstructed racial views and desires. That particular incident created a crisis in which a nationally ascendant GOP flailed about, trying to put the tarp back over the racial engine that has powered that party's steady rise in Dixie ever since Strom Thurmond left the Democratic Party. Do not pay attention to the man behind the curtain. Yet systematic voter suppression of minorities and ritualistic pilgrimage to South Carolina's Bob Jones University, a bastion of hostility to racial progress and religious inclusiveness, are hallmarks of the modern Southern Republican experience. And a refusal to fly the Confederate flag can still get an incumbent governor unseated in Georgia—as long as the candidacy of the flag-friendly Republican challenger is accompanied by the almost manic campaigning of a sitting U.S. president.[11]

The Status Quo Society

In all of this, the Deep South states of Alabama, Mississippi, Georgia, South Carolina, and Louisiana furnish the purest examples of a "status quo society" (SQS) that the United States has to offer. The SQS may be defined as an extremely conservative kind of society that, on a continuum of five American society types, occupies the furthermost slot on the right: radical left, liberal/progressive, moderate, conservative, and hard right (or status quo). The Outer South states of Tennessee, Florida, Arkansas, Texas, North Carolina, Virginia, Kentucky—and even significant portions of Missouri, Oklahoma, West Virginia and, increasingly, sections of the Midwest and the Great Plains—may also be currently grouped as status quo societies, only of a somewhat less absolute strain than the Deep South variety.

The realization that the white South is a kind of society intrinsically wedded to conservatism goes a long way toward explaining why the "Solid Democratic South" has, in recent decades, apparently changed to become the "Solid Republican South." Is there a New South in a political sense for the white inhabitants of the region? Has there ever been? Has the South ever really changed? In the realm of politics, which is, after all, arguably the very essence of society, is the history of the South generally one of continuity or one of change?

Obviously, classifying the South as a status quo society does little to conjure images of regional change. In actuality, the white South has never really changed politically, and in the way that politics is a reflection of society, it has not changed fundamentally either. Despite the volumes written about a New South, a Sunbelt South, a modern South, a postmodern South, the region, as measured by perhaps its most defining element, has moved very little, if at all. The political parties that have been willing to cater to the white South's ingrained, seemingly endemic, and largely immutable conservatism (its worship and protection of the status quo) have, turn by turn, "won" the South. But in reality, the South has never really been *won* in terms of being conquered by a particular political party. The South, and especially the Deep South states, has, generally speaking, simply chosen the party that, at the time, most closely mirrors its essential political, racial, class, gender, ethnic, and religious conservatism. Before and after the Civil War, this party was the Whig Party and then the Conservative Democrats (also known as the Bourbons or Redeemers). In 1928, the region split over the question of method, not aim, as it divided its vote between Hoovercrat and Loyalist Democrat, a split that largely fell along Deep South and Outer South lines. In 1948, the Deep South went with the Dixiecrats in revolt against the Democratic Party's growing racial liberalism and affinity for civil rights. In 1964, it was Goldwater Republicanism. In 1968, it was the George Wallace Independent movement—all way stations on the road to the recent, modern, solid GOP ascendance in national elections as made manifest by the Southern successes of Eisenhower, Goldwater, Nixon, Reagan, Bush the Elder, Dole, and Bush the Younger. Alabama, for example, once the staunchest of Solid Democratic states, has voted for a Democratic candidate only one time in the last twelve presidential elections—almost a half-century's worth. That was in 1976, when Georgia neighbor Jimmy Carter took Alabama over Gerald Ford, and even with the regional pride factor, it was fairly close. Moreover, the racial split in Alabama has only become more pronounced in recent years, with the Democratic Party being understood by the man and woman on the street as the "black party" and the Republican Party as the "white party." In the 2000 presidential election, 80 percent of Alabama's whites voted for Republican George W. Bush, while an almost mind-boggling 98 percent of the state's African Americans cast their ballots for Democrat Al Gore. The 2004 contest, with John Kerry replacing Gore, replicated these results, with Bush gaining 82 percent of the white male Alabama vote and 95 percent of its white conservative Protestants.[12]

But the ultimate lesson is that the South's *partisan* allegiances are transitory, whereas its fundamental *political* allegiance is unchanging. It is a tableau that still constitutes—despite occasional breakthroughs of progressivism here and there, even religious-based progressivism—a general fealty to the preservation of the region's essential and enduring conservative self.[13]

More than that, though, conceiving of a SQS is a way of gaining some understanding of the bigger picture of what goes on in an extremely conservative society such as the states that make up the Deep South—how and why they are the way they are, and how interrelationships work on a number of different levels and in a number of different fields. The goals of an SQS are threefold and related: the maintenance, preservation, perpetuation, and conservation of rigid societal hierarchies; privilege associated with the system of social hierarchy; and order as defined by those currently in power, the status quo elites. The SQS rests on five main pillars that can be referred to as the five prime factors of history, society, and politics. Other factors do arise and can be important, but so far, these five have proved dominant: race, class, gender, ethnicity, and religion. All five of the pillars touch and overlap with one another. Symbiotic and mutually reinforcing relationships with and among each other are discernible in the past—a phenomenon that may be referred to as the "interlocking thesis."

It is tempting, although difficult and largely self-defeating, to try to pick out one of the five, or some other, as the central theme of our politics, history, and society. In attempting this, the historian forcefully rips apart in the here and now what was joined together so closely in the past. This ripping apart can be so sudden and so arbitrary that it leaves us with jagged, artificial, and incomplete constructs. Tearing apart concepts that were joined in the past, merely for the sake of present-day clarity and simplicity in analysis, violates the integrity of the concepts, indicates a lack of respect for their historical interplay and symbiosis, and results in the construction of artificial concepts that might be easier to work with in the present, but that likely bear little, if any, resemblance to the concepts as they once existed and interacted in the past. Such an approach misses the important story of how the various factors of historical causality worked together, fed from each other, supported one another, and were shaped by society's architects to provide the foundation and support for the society under examination—to be, in fact, the pillars of a society based most fundamentally on preserving the status quo.

There is an unmistakable and important interlocking nature to the five prime factors of historical causality that is obvious in the historical record, yet that is sometimes lost when scholars force them apart in the present for the sake of constructing neater analytical compartments. There is a kind of "Three Musketeers" or NATO quality to the interaction of the factors, wherein a threat to one was treated as a threat to all, or an injury to one was seen as an injury to all, capable of bringing down the whole interrelated system like a house of cards. For example, a threat to the economic status quo, such as a strike, was often portrayed and understood in the white South as far more than just a threat to class relationships. This was also a threat to race relations through the biracial membership of the union, to white womanhood and sexual purity, to traditional religion that frowned on challenges to earthly masters in the form of bosses and men and whites, and to regional and ethnic homogeneity through the importation of dangerous foreign and outside ideas.

Such an example was furnished by the 1908 Alabama coal strike, one of the most notable Southern industrial conflicts of its period. Because two-thirds of the miners' union was black, the strike took on much more than just questions of capital and labor. Interrelated race, religious, gender, and ethnic considerations were vital as well. The United Mine Workers (UMW) practice of housing striking black and white families under its tents became a major issue in the strike. White journalists nursed Alabama's fear of what it called the "social equality horror" by alleging that striking blacks had raped two white women near the tent camp; Governor Braxton Bragg Comer, a leading progressive of the time, publicly agreed that the existence of idle blacks in the tent camps posed a sexual threat to white women and the "integrity of our civilization" that was "too dangerous to contemplate." Dolly Dalrymple, a leading women's editor, fairly quaked with fear and rage at the strike's racial threat: "White women and black women meeting on the basis of 'Social equality' indeed! White men holding umbrellas over negro speakers! Black men addressing white men as 'brother!' . . . White miners eating side by side with black men. . . . It is monstrous!" "My heart swells to the bursting point," she wrote. "The recent distressing conditions, existing in this district from the strike . . . ha[ve] caused the women to shudder, at the very thought . . . [of] this unspeakable crime."[14]

In real terms, the ringing of the racial tocsin communicated that race-war tactics should be applied against the biracial union until the crisis passed; that whites should participate in, support, or ignore the means used, however ugly or violent they became. But dissent on behalf of racial treason would not be tolerated.[15] Various whites, mostly in the employ of the upper classes, called for violent suppression of the strike and for support for the repression from the community. A Birmingham columnist, also in the employ of the coal company owners, led the way by urging whites to avoid revisiting the nightmare of social equality of "the late [18]60s and 70s, when political carpetbaggers . . . [and] agitators . . . came among us." "I am sure," he wrote, "the Caucasian blood of this state would rebel against such des- ecration of the home fireside. . . . Lynch law seldom oppresses an innocent victim." The *Birmingham Age-Herald* termed the "miscegenation" that was obviously going on in the UMW tent camps "repulsive" and "damnable." Suppose blacks in South Alabama should "leave the farms and pitch tents close by" to white families, another columnist stoked the community flames. "How long would the planters of Alabama permit that condition to exist?" Were the racial and sexual barrier "to be broken down," another editor as- serted, a "silent tragedy, more terrible than that of the torch and sword, would fill our fair Southland . . . the decay and obliteration of our white civiliza- tion." Some responded by agreeing that the time for talk had "past; the time for action is at hand. . . . Let's start things up!"[16] Appeals from Southern dam- sels in distress carried special potency: society columnist Dolly Dalrymple called for a "manful stand against th[e] unspeakable crime" of social equal- ity and asked point-blank whether white men would rise to the occasion, thus equating opposition to the strike with proper masculinity: "Men of our glorious Southland, will you stand idly by and see these infamies committed? Has the pursuit of money so tarnished your chivalry that you are willing to see such conditions go unpunished? Or is it that you are simply biding your time, to show the world that in your veins still runs the blood that for generations has had no peer?"[17]

In order to till the soil of Alabama's conscience in regard to the use of violence, the white press instinctively demonized and dehumanized the black and white targets of community wrath. Violence, of course, was much easier to support, overlook, or participate in if it were performed against individu- als that were not really human. The *Age-Herald* ran a piece that specifically used religious imagery to conjure this effect: "Today in this district we be- hold pluralism in the sex of devils, embodied in male and female," its author wrote. "Who instilled that spirit of the devil? . . . Whose voice of disruption, agitation and misguidance is responsible? Who are the emissaries of the devil, the very incarnation of the evil spirit? . . . Milton pictured Satan as an arch- angel . . . but . . . plainer devils have come to this district."[18] Of course, the principal sin of these "devils" was to inspire racial unrest: "the cunning, the avarice, the wickedness, the chicanery of devils in disguise who are mislead- ing not only viciously inclined white men, but ignorant members of Booker T. Washington's race" are shocking. The situation required an immediate solution, one that every reasonable and moral man and woman in Alabama could support.

These devils have sought to teach the negro that he should affiliate socially with white men and with white women . . . [and] encouraged negro miners . . . that they were as good as white men. . . . These hellions have poisoned the minds of ignorant blacks to be fired up against law and order and peace; to apply dynamite to peaceful shelters; to crouch and cower in ambush and draw the murderous trigger against innocent men and helpless women. Led into temptation by vain promises given by this satanic spirit, ignorant whites and blacks alike have been idling away. . . . It has caused the burning of bridges, the slaughter of innocents, and the shedding of blood. . . . A continuation of this unholy warfare can only bring more sorrow, more tears, more cost of money and of blood. . . . There is a daily prayer for peace, and for order ascending to heaven from every righteous man and woman in Alabama. . . . Soon the light will break forth and the clouds of darkness pass away . . . and industrial and social peace shall reign again.[19]

Bolstered by business, press, and political alarm, the coercive machinery of white supremacy swung into action. White deputies broke up meetings, arrested strikers without warrants, and at times even tried to instigate violent reactions. Deputies broke up one union meeting by arresting thirteen blacks and one white; they shot two blacks in the process. At another, two company guards shot a black Baptist preacher and union chaplain through the neck for "refusing to surrender" his rifle. Deputies shot and killed a black unionist in front of a courthouse for allegedly trying to escape; he was found still in his handcuffs. Company guards in St. Clair County killed a black striker, and at Brighton, two deputies hanged one. A thousand people from the surrounding community came by to gape at the corpse. Such violence was not surprising considering the arrangement at Dora where coal operator Walter Moore served as judge, jury, police magistrate, and commander of a small army of eighty coal company guards. In the end, though, Governor Comer provided the coup de grace by ordering the state militia to strike down the tents of 40,000 striking miners and their families by first, citing sanitation issues and then admitting the racial rationale behind his action. "There are a great many negroes being gotten together and . . . being madly advised . . . by carpetbagger and scalawag," Comer declared. "The state could not allow it" during Reconstruction "and will not allow it now. . . . You know what it means to have eight or nine thousand niggers idle in the State of Alabama, and I am not going to stand for it."[20]

Nor did the religious aspects of the societal threat represented by aggressive organized labor action diminish over time. During the Great Depression, the North Carolina Piedmont found itself roiling in textile strikes, put down brutally by a white populace aroused by religious charges that the textile union was a "hellish serpent . . . creeping into the Garden of Eden" to bring only "bloodshed and death." A Gastonia, North Carolina, newspaper encouraged community hysteria that led to massive violence against the striking textile workers and their organizers by charging that the strike meant "world revolution, irreligion, racial mixing, and free love" and the "overthrowing of this government."[21] Such emotional language and imagery was a notable part of the community backlash among thousands of ordinary whites during the 1965 Selma March and other events of the civil rights period.[22] Late in the twentieth century, religious televangelists such as the Virginia-based Jerry Falwell and Pat Robertson could still motivate many in the South by damning union challenges to the authority of secular bosses as a surefire way to get oneself to Hell. Nor were such sermons reserved for the unsophisticated, the poor, or the fundamentalist in the New South. At a just slightly more sophisticated level, the "better sorts" hear the same thing. In the year 2002, privileged white Catholics in an affluent section of Birmingham could hear their priest instruct them from the pulpit that God's plan for eternal happiness was simple. It merely consisted of unquestioning obedience to the earthly representatives of His authority: priests, teachers, and *employers*. Deviation from the plan invited unhappiness and jeopardized one's chances of salvation. "Labor unions should study and read the Bible instead of asking for more money," according to the Moral Majority's Jerry Falwell. "When people get right with God, they are better workers. . . . I think we should take the shackles off business and get rid of outfits like OSHA." The political training manual of the Christian Coalition, founded by the 700 Club's Pat Robertson, put it this way: "Christians have a responsibility to submit to the authority of their employers since they are designated as part of God's plan for the exercise of authority on the earth by man."[23]

Threats to Jim Crow, disfranchisement, and other staples of the racial status quo of white supremacy for so long transcended mere risks to race relations. On many occasions, changes in race relations portended a shakeup of the class structure that has been viewed by conservatives as dangerous to the very order and stability of society. For example, the World War II–era creation of the Fair Employment Practices Committee (FEPC) met with huge resistance throughout the Southern states. Mark Ethridge, the otherwise liberal editor of the *Louisville Courier-Journal,* famously warned that "there is no power in the world—not even in all the mechanized armies of the earth, Allied and Axis—which could now force the Southern white people to the abandonment of the principle of social segregation."[24] In Congress, the "conservative coalition" of Northern and Western Republicans and Democrats from the South, such as the gentlemanly Richard B. Russell of Georgia, the intemperate Theodore "The Man" Bilbo of Mississippi, and the immensely powerful Harry F. Byrd of Virginia, killed off the FEPC in 1946. First, they slowly strangled it by cutting its funding, then openly damned it with racial, class, and religious invective as a federal agency that was "following the Communists' lead" and "going against God's law" by "creating a mongrel race" and turning the country to a "communistic state" and the "damnable philosophy of communism."[25] Extreme reading now, perhaps, but this was strong stuff in the post–World War II South and—evidently—the Great Plains. Along the South's Gulf coast, shipyards broke out in bloody confrontation between pipe-wielding white unionists and a handful of black workers promoted to welder, while white management incompetence exacerbated the racial tensions.[26] The FEPC, like other racial changes instituted from outside the region, threatened to upset the apple cart of white economic privilege—the material benefits of being classed "white" in the South. It also revived the almost ever-present worry about the threat to white womanhood represented by black advancement of any kind—and the threat to ethnic homogeneity and conventional notions of patriotism represented by the importation of dangerous Yankee ideas and the "meddling" of an all-intrusive federal government.

THE NEW RACISM

Although the five prime factors of historical causality may be considered coequal in terms of importance, race and religion do stand out as being somewhat different from the other three pillars of conservative Southern society—not necessarily more important per se, but more versatile from the standpoint of language, emotion, and rhetorical power. Because of the South's deep-seated conservatism and emotional makeup, racial and religious imagery have been the easiest and most efficacious of the various pillars to use in addressing a mass audience in the region. Conservatives have long used racial and religious orthodoxy with much success to cast issues in the most emotional of terms in order to achieve a desired response from the bulk of the South's white populace. The use of race and religion to press societal hot buttons has proven itself in a variety of Southern time and places as an effective way for Southern elites to curry mass support for elements of their agenda that the people might otherwise not support. This "politics of emotion," which primarily uses race and religion, has worked for a variety of party labels, yet all are predicated on the common denominator of conservatism.

Such appeals wedded together whites of varying classes to bring about the demise of Reconstruction, to put down the independent political revolts of the Greenbackers and Populists in the 1880s and 1890s, to sell the various disfranchising schemes that swept the region near the turn of the century, to combat organized labor on repeated fronts, and to oppose national assaults on segregation, poll taxes, and other ramparts of white supremacy throughout the twentieth century.

More recently, the founders and architects of the wildly successful Religious Right—usually Southerners or people with strong ties to the South—have not been at all shy about acknowledging the emotionally distractive nature of their strategy and tactics. Paul Weyrich, charter member of the Virginia-based Moral Majority, admitted during the 1980s that "we can't win by defending Reagonomics. We can only win by pushing those populist/conservative anti-elitist themes which real people support." "I am not going to try to explain trickle down to an unemployed steelworker in Birmingham," he admitted. "But that same steelworker if asked to choose between our desire to see hardened criminals punished and the liberals' defense of soft-headed judges, will be with us. That's where it's at." Real people, especially middle- and working-class white Southerners, Weyrich maintained, care about "emotional issues"—issues like "gun control, taxes and crime" that beat "talking about capital formation" any day of the week. For most average Southerners, Weyrich explained, particular, single, morality-based, emotional issues overrode any notion of "party preference." Most effective of all have been "Right-to-Life, Right-to-Work, and Gun Control." For a former director of the National Rifle Association, the gun issue is "the one thing that will spin the blue-collar union member away from his union."[27] Abortion and issues of gay rights do not hurt the cause either.

Nor is this solely a Southern thing. Ever since the 1964 capture of the GOP by the party's Southern conservative wing, Dixie's conservative social predilections have been almost as big an export as cotton once was. "Don't let your labor union, don't let the teachers groups . . . tell you how to vote," the Republican pastor of the 5,000-member First Baptist Church in Arnold, Missouri, implored his congregation before the 2004 presidential election. "You vote the way the word of God tells you to vote." A sixty-six-year-old

United Auto Workers member in rural Ohio reconciles his intense lobbying for the reelection of George W. Bush this way: "I say [to friends], 'I put moral and Christian values ahead of union values.'"[28] And of course, this is exactly the way Paul Weyrich and company drew it up.

On the other side of the political fence, labor union leaders in the South, responsible for the political mobilization of their members, were in sad concurrence. One Southern union leader admitted that his efforts to talk to the rank-and-file membership in Alabama about Al Gore's 2000 presidential candidacy had been repeatedly and solidly thwarted by "the three G's," all insurmountable negatives for the Democratic Party: "God, Guns, and Gays."[29] Ralph Reed, the former executive director of the Christian Coalition, longtime political advisor to Republicans such as Georgia's Newt Gingrich, North Carolina's Jesse Helms, and Texas's George W. Bush, recently assumed the chairmanship of the Georgia Republican Party and coordinated Bush's 2004 reelection campaign in the South. Reed lauded the utility that issues like school prayer and abortion have in tapping into a mass white vote that might not be especially sympathetic to elitist economic policies. Such issues were the "bridge that gets you to constituencies that aren't with you on the economic issues."[30]

In the 2002 midterm elections, Reed's Georgia Republican Party unseated a popular Democratic U.S. senator, largely by running television ads that pictured him alongside photos of Saddam Hussein and Osama bin Laden. The voice-over intimated that Max Cleland was a coward who could not stand up to America's enemies because he had opposed the fast passage of a Homeland Security Bill as a pork-laden measure designed to benefit the Republican allies of President Bush. A massive turnout among white, rural Georgia voters led to Republican Saxby Chambliss's upset win, despite the fact that the candidate hand-picked by President Bush and his closest advisers had never worn the uniform of his country. Cleland had left three limbs in Vietnam.[31]

Nor is the phenomenon of using emotion-laden strategy reliant on themes like patriotism and religion isolated or accidental. "This alliance between religion and politics didn't just happen," Paul Weyrich explained. "I've been dreaming and working on this for years."[32] Indeed, a moment of indisputable import was Barry Goldwater's 1964 campaign, when the conservative wing of the Republican Party seized power from old-guard liberal Republicans the stripe of Nelson Rockefeller, George Romney, and Everett Dirksen, and waged a presidential campaign that netted just six states. In addition to Goldwater's home state of Arizona, they were the former Dixiecrat states (Alabama, Mississippi, South Carolina, and Louisiana) plus Georgia. George Wallace would take the same exact states in 1968, minus Arizona. In the wake of the Goldwater defeat, Republican operative Richard Viguerie volunteered to raise funds for the Wallace presidential campaign with the proviso that he get to keep the governor's contributors list of urban ethnics, blue-collar workers, and Southern Democrats alienated by their national party's leftward drift on racial questions. Thus was born the vaunted direct-mail operation of Viguerie. After an ill-fated attempt to take over Wallace's American Independent Party, the Religious Right set its sights on the capture of one of the two major political parties. They chose the GOP and sealed the decision with a formal 1979 summit that merged Viguerie's organization with the other Religious Right forces represented by Jerry Falwell, Howard Phillips, and Paul Weyrich.[33]

For decades, race was the most reliable fodder of a politics that ran on emotion. In the Jim Crow South, even through the 1960s, it was perfectly acceptable, even admirable, for the region's political figures to race-bait opponents openly and directly. With federal intervention in the area of voting rights, a growing black electorate, and the maturation of a post-*Brown* generation of white Southerners who reject segregation—at least in public and in principle—it is no longer socially acceptable to do this. More subtle race appeals still exist, of course, clever and thinly disguised references to "law and order," welfare, quotas, taxes for "social programs," food stamps, "states' rights and local government," urban decay, "big government," crime, and "personal responsibility." But conventional race baiting has largely been supplanted and supplemented by what may be termed the "new racism": a type of religious-morality baiting of political opponents on the basis of "character," "values," and the like. It is no longer socially acceptable in the South to call a political opponent a "nigger lover." It is acceptable, even commonplace and shrewd, to paint political opponents as moral reprobates, of flawed character, inferior values, suspect religious orientation, and questionable integrity—basically, of being morally and religiously inferior human beings.

The result is, essentially, the same as the old racism. That is, in a South once compelled by notions of racial orthodoxy and now equally as compelled by conceptions of moral and religious orthodoxy, political figures can gain ground by questioning an opponent's moral fiber in much the same way they once did by impugning a person's commitment to white supremacy. Waged in this way, elite politics can tap into mass support for an economic agenda of low taxation, corporate welfare, antiunionism, gutted social services, fiscal retrenchment, inadequate funding of public education, decreased

worker safety, lower environmental pollution standards, and the like by using morality in the same way that they once race-baited. And in the most
private councils of conservative religious strategists, there is euphoria over
their ability to tap into a Southern white conservative base in this way. "We
can elect Mickey Mouse to the Senate," the late Terry Dolan, head of the
National Conservative Political Action Committee, boasted back in 1982.
"People will vote against the liberal candidate and not remember why." The
key to raising funds from Christian conservatives, Dolan lectured, was to
"make them angry and stir up hostilities. The shriller you are, the easier it is
to raise funds. That's the nature of the beast." Paul Weyrich agreed. "In the
past we conservatives paraded all those Chamber of Commerce candidates
with Mobil Oil strapped to their backs. It doesn't work." There are "rural
people in West Virginia who don't understand Reaganomics and who are
being hurt by Reaganomics and who wouldn't like it if they did understand
it." The way to reach that mass of people is through emotional issues like
"the issue of prayer in the schools."[34]

More troubling, the ascendance of the new racism has made hate respectable again. One of the most important casualties of the modern civil
rights movement was the death of hate as a socially acceptable form of political discourse, both in the South and in the nation at large. For a century,
the very lifeblood of Southern politics—race hatred and prejudice—became,
almost at once, un-American and politically incorrect, rejected in public
even by those who continued to practice it in private. The double-speak of
the 1960s Republican "Southern Strategy" was an artful personification of
this duality in the racial realm. But the Southern Strategy does not even
begin to approach the sophistication of a "compassionate conservatism" that
reassures conservative white Southerners (even the old racial type) while
simultaneously calming national Republicans and young urban Republicans who do not consider themselves racists—and, in fact, are in denial or
blissful ignorance of the white supremacist roots of the Southern bedrock
of the Grand Old Party. It is no accident that South Carolina's religious fundamentalist Harry Dent, the primary architect of Richard Nixon's Southern
Strategy, also coined the term and created the concept of "compassionate
conservatism" in order to make the national Republican image kindler and
gentler. It took Dent and other GOP strategists two decades to find the perfect candidate to articulate the creed, but it finally happened in the 2000
election.[35]

The new racism has done much to bring hatred and, even more specifically, feelings of prejudice and innate superiority back into vogue in poli-

tics—especially politics in the South and, increasingly, in the Great Plains and the Rocky Mountain West. Only now, it is based more on moral, religious, and affiliated sexual differences where it was once based on racial ones. Moral chauvinism, even "moral authoritarianism" and autarchy, have largely filled the void left by the delegitimization of white supremacy as a vehicle of respectable politics. Unfortunately, this is a debauched substitution that gratifies something in the older and darker part of the Southern political psyche while providing a moral scapegoat for society's problems. It appeals to a tragic strain of addiction in the Southern makeup to disliking others for their moral differences—real and perceived—where once a racial scapegoat proved so useful. Public denouncements of "niggers" and "nigger lovers" have largely been replaced by public denouncements of atheists, "queers," moral degenerates, and the godless ACLU: the "Anti-Christian Liberties Union."[36]

The political party that associates itself with liberalism thus becomes in the SQS South all that is bad—religiously, morally, sexually, culturally. It is the party of she-men, of "girlie men," as Arnold Schwarzenegger famously put it at the 2004 Republican convention; the party of liberal "bed-wetters" whose "soft whiny teeth" need to be kicked in by manly Republicans.[37] In short, "Republicans are real men. Democrats are gay." They are "wusses."[38] Nor, in the ideologically conservative South, does this stop at the door of partisan politics. Anything less than lockstep allegiance to extreme conservatism is increasingly viewed as collaboration with the enemy—and it can reach truly alarming extremes. One of many angry religious conservatives in Alabama canceled his subscription to the devoutly conservative *Birmingham News* because the paper refused to endorse a state supreme court justice's defiance of two federal court orders to remove a 5,300-pound granite monument of the Ten Commandments that he had surreptitiously placed in the rotunda of the state judicial building. The *News*'s "politically correct slip" was showing in its "leftward drift" of editorial opinion, the reader raged. "You are dedicated lefties and anti-Christian bigots. There aren't as yet enough homosexuals . . . and self-righteous atheists to sustain your rag."[39]

A noxious mixture of conspicuous piety, narrow-minded intolerance, and vicarious machismo is capable of reaching the level of the absurd in that curious twilight where Roman Catholicism meets Southern culture. Although George W. Bush became the first president in history who was too busy to appear at the annual convention of the NAACP for four years running, he did find time during his 2004 reelection bid to speak to the national conference of the Knights of Columbus. The Knights, the world's largest male Catholic lay organization at 1.6 million members, is well known as a bastion of traditionalism and has many within its ranks who like to think of themselves as the front line of defense of the faith. The group is comprised solely of adult men who perform acts of community service, but whose leaders also enjoy dressing up in brightly colored feathers, plumes, capes, and helmets, brandishing gold-hilted sabers, and leading public marches through town streets on Church feast days—kind of a Catholic version of the Society for Creative Anachronism. Although it is ostensibly a nonpartisan group, the 2,500 Knights at the national convention in Dallas, Texas, greeted Bush's appearance with something close to religious ecstasy, repeatedly chanting, "Four more years! Four more years!" Its leader welcomed the president to the stage by thanking him for the opportunity to say "Thank you for restoring moral integrity to the office of the presidency," a not-so-subtle slam of his Democratic predecessor Bill Clinton.[40] The president did not disappoint. Although he did not explicitly say that he agreed with common evangelical positions that the Bible is inerrant, abortion is murder, creationism is more accurate than evolution, salvation is for Christians only, and the Iraq war is part of God's plan, Bush cleverly took the advice of the Knights' grand leader Carl A. Anderson and invoked the powerful code phrase "culture of life" on at least three different occasions. The president also stroked the group's pseudo-militaristic conception of their patriotic and religious manhood by praising them as essential "foot soldiers" in an epic war of cultures.[41]

Historians of religious clashes in Europe have theorized that the French people were able to butcher each other for hundreds of years in the name of Catholicism and Protestantism as the one true religion because they dehumanized their adversaries before disemboweling them. Five hundred years later, the religiously proscriptive impulse to dehumanize before brutalizing is alive and well—perhaps to the largest degree in this country's experience since Salem. When *Sojourners* magazine editor David Batstone recently questioned the wisdom and validity of the Iraq war along religious lines, an angry Christian responded with a profanity-laced e-mail asking how Batstone could call himself a Christian and criticize the president. When Batstone wrote back, asking how his insulter could consider himself a Christian and still write such a violently profane note, the response was illuminating: "I can write to you as I like, for you are not a human being. You have forfeited that right; you are nothing but pond scum."[42]

Those who depart from 100 percent religious and political conservatism in the South all too commonly find themselves on the receiving end of the pejorative label "godless." In fact, the characterization of the ACLU as anti-Christian is a garden-variety white conservative sentiment in the South and can be found in Alabama almost as commonly as the kudzu that grows wild there. It has gained especially frequent airing in the last several years in response to a successful ACLU and Southern Poverty Law Center lawsuit in the state's recent Ten Commandments imbroglio—the same issue that so exercised the *Birmingham News* reader who canceled his subscription. The suit, which was filed in federal court and received international attention, sought to compel Alabama Supreme Court Chief Justice Roy Moore to re-move a giant granite monument of the Ten Commandments that he had placed in the rotunda of the state judicial building under cover of night. Moore, who had been an obscure Etowah County jurist just a few years be-fore, catapulted to the chief justice's seat on the state's highest tribunal by running as a conservative Republican on the sole issue of his desire to keep displayed a plaque of the Ten Commandments on the wall of his courtroom and his custom of having litigants join him in a prayer of his choice before hearing their cases. The initial plaque cause célèbre gained added attention when right-wing Christian Republican governor Fob James threatened to call out the state's national guard to protect Moore from an anticipated fed-eral court order to remove it—shades of George Wallace. After taking his seat on the court, Moore gained additional publicity by issuing a bizarre and extraordinarily long opinion declaring homosexuality an "inherent evil" and setting down in detail his reasons for opposing the right of homosexual parents of either sex from retaining custody of their children.[43]

The meteoric rise in popularity of a hate–talk radio industry that rou-tinely peddles addictive and highly stimulating "political pornography" with-out regard to the fairness doctrine in the public airwaves has worked hand in glove with the entry of the Religious Right in politics.[44] Increasingly, po-litical differences have been defined in stark millennial terms of good and evil, right and wrong, godless and faithful, Christians and heathens. Defin-ing politics in such an emotional and religious way has also endowed mod-ern politics with a moral urgency once reserved for religious crusades and jeremiads, and a willingness for many of the principals to do or say anything in defense of the "true religion," in order to achieve the greater good of vic-tory in a holy war.[45] Nor have these developments, which have drastically improved the fortunes of the Republican Party in the South, been at all acci-dental or simply inevitable. At the height of the race-based Southern Strat-egy, used by Republicans to win in the white South, Kevin Phillips, perhaps the leading architect of the strategy, let slip what modern Republican politi-cal ascendance was based on, especially in the region: "Who hates whom?

That is the secret." Gay-bashing and feminist-bashing conservative Catholic activist Terry Dolan said much the same thing: making people angry and stirring up their hatreds was the name of the game in Republican fund-raising. "We are *trying* to be divisive," Dolan admitted [italics mine].[46] These are as open avowals as it is possible to find of how the "politics of emotion," especially hate, has been manipulated. With it, the modern Republican Party was working to capture the white South from the Solid Democratic column and turn it into a bastion of support from which to launch a national ascendance. Phillips saw the candidacy of George Wallace and his race politics as merely the way station for disenchanted Southern Democrats in transit to a more permanent home in the Republican Party.[47] Harry Dent, the South Carolina protégé of Strom Thurmond and himself an architect of Richard Nixon's successful Southern Strategy, agreed with Phillips. But Dent also cautioned that for national political consumption, the racial messages had to be coded and then denied in public.[48]

Creeping into the race-based strategy during the 1960s, precisely the time when overt race baiting was giving way to more subtle varieties, were also notions of patriotism, national fidelity, and proper religion and morality. These were emotional "God and country" issues tied to the civil rights and Vietnam era that played especially well in the South. Defending the GOP's often simplistic appeal to such issues, Phillips explained that John Wayne "might sound bad to people in New York." "But he sounds great to the schmucks we're trying to reach through John Wayne. The people down there along the Yahoo Belt" in rural America.[49]

Perhaps no one realized the potential of emotional issues predicated on moral chauvinism for modern Republican fortunes in the South more than Lee Atwater, the most influential Republican strategist in the modern era (until perhaps Karl Rove). Atwater was the South Carolina pupil of Harry Dent and Strom Thurmond and would raise emotional politics to an art form for Republican presidents Ronald Reagan and George H. W. Bush. Throughout his brief but glory-filled career, Atwater worked closely with Roger Ailes, a leading adviser to Presidents Nixon, Reagan, and Bush I, and later the head of the Fox News ("fair and balanced") cable news network. As chairman of the Republican National Committee, Atwater schooled an entire generation of Republican political operatives including Karl Rove, Mary Matalin, and Tucker Eskew. Atwater, a native Southerner, knew well that "Republicans in the South could not win elections by talking about issues"— that the party's bread-and-butter economic insulation of the privileged classes held little intrinsic appeal for the common Southerner. Character assassination on racial, moral, and religious grounds was the key. "You had to make the case that the other candidate was a bad guy."[50]

Issues were not important for this newer "politics of emotion"; vague perception of especially religious and moral character was. Atwater took pride in not knowing the ins and outs of actual political issues. "I don't know 'em. I don't want to know 'em." Instead, he viewed himself as a "Machiavellian political warrior," especially adept at using "ad hominem strategies characterized by personal attacks, dirty tricks, and accentuating the negative."[51] Atwater specialized at implanting negative emotional images in the minds of voters so powerful that the perception could not be "busted up" even with the reality of the candidates' stands on different issues. The average voter, according to Atwater, was "kind of slow. . . . You could throw fact after fact at a voter . . . who might never be able to connect the dots"— an opinion not unlike that of the GOP's other modern wunderkind, Kevin Phillips. For these voters, the mass of average voters, perception was greater than reality. In fact, perception *was* reality. According to his biographer, Atwater saw his job as tapping into the voters' "emotions instead of their brains," finding the one specific example, the one "outrageous abuse, the easy-to-digest tale that made listeners *feel*—usually repulsion—rather than think."[52]

Along with Phillips, Lee Atwater tapped into Southern conservative religious symbols and black/white images to lay the groundwork for the transition of emotional politics from overt race baiting to a combination of subtle racism and explicit moral chauvinism. While Atwater lay on his deathbed apologizing for his infamous Willie Horton ad that was used so successfully on behalf of George H. W. Bush in 1988, another Southerner, a congressman from Georgia, was overseeing the full transition of this politics to conservative morality and religion. Newt Gingrich, who in 1994 would spearhead the capture of both houses of Congress, a feat last accomplished in 1947, talked about welfare and subtle race messages—but he perfected the art of the new racism. Central to his strategy was exploiting the deep religiosity of Southerners, especially white Southerners, to brand partisan differences based on perception and religious/moral messages deep into the psyches of millions of voters. His project, Gingrich privately told a gathering of Republican lobbyists just a week before the historic 1994 congressional elections, was to paint Democrats as the enemy of "normal Americans" and the proponents of "Stalinist" policies. To this end, Gingrich ruthlessly created perception based on notions of traditional morality and conservative religion. He sought, with wild success, to fully transform the political landscape into a religious "battleground" between the Republican Party as the party of God on the one hand and the "secular anti-religious view of the left" on the other. Democrats were not simply wrong, he announced. "These people are sick." To provide uniformity, concerted action, and consistency of message that has since become legend, the House Speaker distributed a vocabulary list to be strictly adhered to by Republicans when talking to any member of the press about any Democrat—words that would allow the poison of emotional politics to seep into the very consciousness of voters and take root there: "sick, traitors, corrupt, bizarre, cheat, steal, devour, self-serving, and criminal rights." The strategy itself knew no moral or ethical bounds because the ends justified the means, as in any holy war. Just two days before the 1994 election, Gingrich tried to exploit a tragic South Carolina incident in which a mentally deranged young mother named Susan Smith drowned two of her children in a car. Pouncing on the event, Gingrich laid the incident directly at the doorstep of Bill Clinton and the Democratic Party— despite the fact that Smith's father was himself a member of the Religious Right. The double-child murder "vividly reminds every American how sick their society is getting and how much we have to change." The "only way you get change," Gingrich went on, "is to vote Republican." Religious Right fund-raiser and strategist Paul Weyrich beamed about Gingrich that he was "the first conservative I have ever known who knows how to use power."[53]

The use of a new politics based on moral and religious venom, divisiveness, and the darker angels of human nature to build the Republican Party in the South is not unlike the old race-based strategy of white supremacy used so long by the conservative Democratic Party to control the Solid South. In this important way, the modern Republican legacy in the South is essentially equivalent to its old George Wallace–Dixiecrat legacy—a reality that made Trent Lott's racial gaffe particularly embarrassing and potentially damaging on the national level. The essential kinship between the old racist politics of the Southern Democrats and the moral and religious bigotry of the new Republican politics was not lost on one of the region's most astute political observers: Wallace himself. "It sounds to me like when I hear all this talk," Wallace said in surveying the 1990s political landscape, "that the Republicans have stolen a lot of their thoughts and words and principles from old George Wallace." "You know I should have copyrighted all of my speeches," Wallace said wistfully. "If I had, the Republicans in Alabama, throughout the South, and all over the nation would be paying me hundreds of thousands of dollars. They owe everything to my kind of Democratic thinking."[54]

Emotional politics is so powerful in the South because white Southerners have felt so passionately about what they value, good or bad, be it slavery, states' rights, segregation, white supremacy, Confederate heritage and symbols, prayer in public settings, patriotism, national loyalty and national defense, religion and a belief in God, college football, or a myriad of other issues. To a large extent, this emotionalism, augmented by the power of religious appeals, has left many Southerners open to being manipulated politically. For masses of plain-white voters, a powerful "principle of moral reflection" is at work when they go to the polls. In such a society, voting is not merely a political act; it is a statement, a public testament, a witness and pronouncement of what kind of neighbor, what kind of citizen, and ultimately what kind of human being an individual is. Supporting a Republican Party that professes to represent God, family, and traditional values translates in the conservative South to proclaiming oneself to one's neighbors as a reliable, virtuous, solid patriot and citizen in the same way that voting for the conservative Democratic Party of white supremacy once did in days gone by. Although the South was once defined by a "race-based conformist politics," that has now given way to more subtle and understood coded messages on white supremacy combined with an overt, articulated, and socially acceptable "morality-based conformist politics"; religious orthodoxy has played a central role in each.

People on different sides of the political fence in the South know that these ground rules exist and live their lives by them. A middle-aged member of the Alabama Transportation Workers Union, despondently weighing the Republican sweep of the 2002 midterm elections, bitterly concluded that, "All you got to do to be elected in this state is pin an elephant to your chest and say you're a Christian. It doesn't matter if you aren't." As if by cue, a twenty-two-year-old white man from Tuscaloosa named Jared called into a local radio show to confirm the belief. Jared, informing the host that he "hasn't been in politics very long" but that he studies the issues, said he was a Christian, and he prayed to God for guidance on how to vote. Jared noted that he votes Republican in elections because, to him, the Republican Party is "more Christian" than the Democratic Party. When informed by the talk show host that there are Christians in both parties, Jared replied with silence. Later he said that, as an example, he votes for GOP candidates because of their opposition to abortion. Jared added that he realizes that a candidate's promise to "vote against abortion" is no guarantee that she will, if the issue actually comes up. But Jared concluded that, for him, it is enough that Republican candidates *say* that they will vote against abortion, even if they do not actually do so when given the chance.[55]

THE ROPE OF RELIGION

Race was once the rope that tied the other pillars of Southern society together, the central beam that connected the buttresses of a whole "Southern
way of life" referred to so often whenever the custom of white supremacy
seemed in peril.[56] Now, religion and morality, character, and values comprise the rope that ties together the other pillars of the SQS. Race and religion are especially important factors and may be seen as horizontal buttresses
that connect and support the vertical pillars of class, gender, and ethnic/
patriotic/militaristic orthodoxy. Although it is not acceptable any longer in
polite Southern company to disparage a political foe as a "race mixer," it is
perfectly acceptable to cast aspersions on the character or morals of candidates and what they stand for, and even to paint them as the worst kind of
regional traitor, moral degenerate, or religious heretic because of it.

Nor is this the province only of fundamentalist or fringe evangelical
sects. It is intimately wound up with mainline Protestantism, and increasingly since the 1973 *Roe v. Wade* decision, with Roman Catholicism as well.
Below the Mason-Dixon Line, the Catholic faith once largely stood apart as
progressive and liberal, especially on matters of race and social justice. This
stance owed a great deal to the Catholic theological emphasis on good works
as the ticket to salvation, as opposed to the Protestant concentration on faith
and the Calvinist stress on an "elect" discernible from the damned by out-
ward signs of piety. It also owed something to the ethnic makeup of the
Catholic Church—largely Irish, Italian, and Lebanese in the South—"foreigners" culturally and socially for so many years in an overwhelmingly homogeneous white Anglo-Saxon Protestant region. The Calvinist theology,
so central to the dominant conservative Baptist, Methodist, and Presbyterian Church in America (PCA) denominations in the South (what some
historians have dubbed the South's official religion) did much to encourage
a narrow judgmentalism that sometimes found expression in the moral
authoritarianism of groups such as the Ku Klux Klan—and not inconse-
quently included periodic denunciations of Catholicism as a "cult" or alien
Roman popery.[57] No more. Since the prominence of the abortion issue, it
has become increasingly difficult to tell Protestants and Catholics apart in
the South on social issues—much less on politics. Yet the overlap has not
been because white Protestant churches have moved leftward. On the contrary, white Catholics have moved to the right. And the newfound cross-
denominational cooperation and apparent toleration for Catholicism is not
unlike the Left Behind version of the Religious Right's embrace of Judaism

and the State of Israel. Its goals are exceedingly conservative—even reactionary.[58] It is a kind of newfound "ecumenical conservatism."

Although the tax-exempt status of churches is technically dependent on a legal prohibition against their endorsement of political parties and candidates, many Protestant and Catholic pastors abide by the letter of that law while routinely violating its spirit. Some are in the habit of giving sermons on the Sunday before election Tuesday in which not voting is defined as a sin and a serious transgression against God, and abortion is repeatedly emphasized as the central or even sole issue upon which the faithful should cast their ballots.[59] In the 1996 election that sent Democrat Mary Landrieu to the U.S. Senate, Louisiana Archbishop Phillip Hannan bluntly informed his heavily Catholic state that its faithful could not vote for a Democratic candidate like Landrieu without committing a serious sin. In the hotly contested 2002 midterm elections, Republican operatives left recorded messages on the answering machines of Pelican State voters describing incumbent Landrieu as a heretic, hopelessly fallen away from her church, "'pro-abortion' and otherwise a bad person," and the "most lapsed of all lapsed Catholics."[60]

Section 501c(4) of the U.S. tax code grants tax-exempt status to a nonpartisan Christian organization, including churches and groups such as the Christian Coalition, that routinely prepare voter guides that they claim are not endorsing particular candidates or parties, yet have a direct and vital impact on determining how Christians in the South (that is, most Southerners), vote. Such groups claim particular effectiveness in moving the votes of white women (who vote Democratic more often than white men) over to the Republican column. For example, in 2002, the Alabama branch of the Christian Coalition claimed sole credit for electing Republican gubernatorial challenger Bob Riley by using the voter guides to change the votes of white female swing voters. Riley himself went to great pains to link his candidacy with the Christian Right by plastering his campaign publications with material that stressed religion and morality instead of substantive policy issues. "As our governor, Bob Riley will end the corruption and restore honor, and integrity, and trust to state government. In Congress, Bob Riley has been one of our nation's strongest defenders of faith, freedom and family. That's why the National Christian Coalition has honored him with their 'Friend of the Family Award.' Bob Riley has a 100 percent lifetime voting record with the National Right to Life Committee and has consistently fought to protect life and our values in Congress . . . and will fight to prevent the destruction of Alabama families caused by gambling. A committed Christian, Bob Riley understands the importance of God in our daily lives and opposes efforts to ban religious expressions from the public arena." "I . . . will be guided," Riley promised "by my faith in God and my trust in the people of Alabama."[61]

The Catholic version of the marriage between the Church and the GOP has centered on opposition to abortion as the party's dowry—a purse that has gained the party unstinting and unquestioning support from many Catholics for a whole range of its economic, material, environmental, and foreign policies. In fact, in the past few years, the easy majority of public statements from various American bishops has amounted to the most thinly veiled of directives to vote for Republicans—or at the very least, not vote for Democrats. Many of the statements have come in the midst of closely fought campaigns between Republicans and Democrats. Although it would be comforting to regard men of the cloth as above partisan politics, the rampant freelancing among American bishops has made clear that some are little more than party hacks masquerading as priests. Shortly before the 2000 presidential election, Archbishop Elden Curtiss of Omaha, Nebraska, gained massive support in Southern and midwestern Catholic circles by declaring that the Democratic Party was antilife and "therefore anti-Catholic," and instructing the faithful not to vote for its candidates. During a 2002 runoff election, Louisiana Archbishop Phillip Hannan announced that if someone "actually believes in Catholic doctrine, then I don't see how they can vote for" a pro-choice Democrat "without a feeling of sin." A year later, during California's special gubernatorial recall election, Sacramento bishop William Weigand, said, "I am saying you can't be a Catholic in good standing" and be pro-choice. "People need to understand that you cannot call yourself a Catholic in good standing and at the same time publicly hold views that are contradictory to the Catholic faith." He then barred sitting Democratic governor Gray Davis from receiving communion because his pro-choice position was "in very great error," put his "soul at risk," and meant that he was not "in good standing with the church." During the 2004 presidential campaign, Archbishop Raymond L. Burke of St. Louis declared it a sin to vote for pro-choice candidates, including John Kerry, and an area priest, Fr. John J. Ghio, told reporters, "I don't know how a Catholic in good conscience could vote for a candidate who was pro-abortion."[62] Even when the highly conservative German cardinal Josef Ratzinger—arbiter of doctrinal orthodoxy and considered by many to be the number two at the Vatican—gave public leeway to Catholics to vote for pro-choice candidates if, after proper reflection, they felt that there were "proportionate reasons" to do so, conservative American bishops and theologians remained unrepentant. They also remained seemingly deaf, dumb, and blind.[63]

Despite the obviously partisan political nature of these utterances, it is thus little wonder that abortion has increasingly taken on the status of an automatic default, or the "eclipse issue," for many Catholics in the South. Bumper stickers are ever more common, echoing in various ways the declarations of certain bishops that one cannot be both a Catholic *and* a Democrat, or "You Can't Be Both Catholic *and* Pro-Abortion." More direct versions in Catholic parking lots simply declare "Pro-Choice is Pro-Murder."[64] The raising of the abortion issue to one of singular political determination has led to a situation in which many of the Catholic faithful allow abortion to block out any other issue that might possibly make up their minds on politics. Because they are wedded to the Republican position on abortion, many also find themselves reflexively voicing support for the most conservative economic policies of the GOP as a matter of course. And, of course, for Republican operatives, this is precisely the idea. For many Catholic lay folks, it is a package deal, because for them, the GOP is, first and foremost, the defender of innocent life from Democratic "baby killers." This conjunction has led to the curious, almost schizophrenic, condition of Southern Catholic clerics and newspapers printing articles that support the Church's social service and humanitarian tradition—going slow on war as a tool of diplomacy in the Middle East, concern for the despoliation of the environment, feeding the hungry, and caring for the poor—with relentless hammering of the abortion issue.[65]

This hammering from the Catholic pulpit is often accompanied by a selective invocation of papal authority as—ipso facto—a directive to "vote life," or, in other words, to vote Republican. Catholics in the Deep South think nothing now of littering their churches and perpetual adoration chapels with literature from antiabortion groups that prepare voter materials to instruct the faithful on how to clear all other issues from their conscience save abortion when going to the polls. The popular flyer "It's Time to Elect Candidates Who Will Protect Life!," distributed by Priests for Life for the 2004 elections, provides a blueprint on how to vote for Republican candidates without jeopardizing the group's 501c(4) tax-exempt status by actually mentioning the party by name. First the flyer quotes the United States Bishops' "Living the Gospel of Life": "Every voice matters in the public forum. Every vote counts . . . We encourage all citizens, particularly Catholics, to embrace their citizenship not merely as a duty and privilege, but as an opportunity meaningfully to participate in building the culture of life." Then the flyer informs the Catholic faithful that "As we approach our national elections, Priests for Life has prepared resources to help you to carry out your civic responsibilities . . . in the light of moral law." What is more, these "resources will help you" learn to put abortion above and beyond any other possible competing issue and to "Understand why the Right to Life is the primary election issue." Once the faithful Catholic has put abortion at the pinnacle of her list on how to vote, she may indeed feel free to remove all other competing issues from her conscience because she has done her duty as a good Catholic. The flyer closes by inserting a quote from Pope John Paul II's 1988 encyclical, *Christifideles Laici,* chosen for its supposedly crystalline precision in clearing the conscience of Catholics to use abortion as the sole criterion of their civic lives: "The common outcry, which is justly made on behalf of human rights—for example, the right to health, to home, to work, to family, to culture—is false and illusory if the right to life, the most basic and fundamental right . . . is not defended with maximum determination."[66] If that isn't clear enough, Catholic leaders such as Bishop David E. Foley of Alabama put their interpretation in simple terms that the lay folk can understand and have it printed on the front page of the diocesan newspaper so that no one can miss it: "One cannot support abortion or the right to choose an abortion and be a Catholic." Not even a Catholic who is sinning—a *Catholic,* period.[67]

Clearly, though, the mandate to vote a certain way solely on the issue of abortion is an artificial and human construct that is flawed—or at the very least highly contradictory to the Church's own teachings. Official church teaching is rife with mandates to the Catholic faithful (some over a century old now) to place issues of poverty, race, social and economic justice, war, and workers' rights and protections at the very pinnacle of their concerns when involving themselves in the lives of the polities in which they live. As the Religious Right has made inroads in American politics, such troublesome teachings have been increasingly pushed to the margins of a Catholic concern that has sprung dramatically closer to the Republican Party.[68]

In fact, the powerful desire to serve the master of partisan allegiance rather than the Teacher from Nazareth, or even simple logical consistency, has led to embarrassing gymnastics of illogic and excesses born of a slavish—even freakish—devotion to the GOP. Where the two competing versions of Catholic tradition—social justice and abortion-centric—have clashed, most obviously and dramatically with the Vatican's repeated condemnations of America's rush to war in Iraq, it has been, quite simply, breathtaking to observe how quickly the pope's moral authority has evaporated when placed against that of George W. Bush. From his perch at the Ethics and Public Policy Center in Washington—a religious-based conservative think tank bankrolled by the cash of Richard Mellon Scaife and visited regularly by Antonin Scalia, Richard Perle, and other luminaries of the far right— George Weigel has done perhaps as much as anyone alive to demonstrate the heretofore unknown elasticity of the papal word, as well as its innate inferiority when placed against the national interests of the United States as articulated by the neoconservative advisers to the Bush administration. For years, on almost a weekly basis, Catholics could read in Weigel's syndicated column, the "Catholic Difference," about his favorite topic: abortion and its centrality in Catholic life as the ultimate issue on which to vote. For his authority, Weigel drew unsparingly from papal enunciations, encyclicals, pastoral letters, and Vatican pronouncements—that is, right up until early 2003, when it became clear that the Republican administration was mobilizing for war in Iraq. Suddenly, the Weigel obsession with papal infallibility vanished, only to be replaced by a damning of Europe's weak-kneed and decadent Catholic clergy for their reticence in rubber-stamping the Bush adventure in Iraq. Overnight, it was "not at all clear" that the Vatican's insistence on peace between the United States and Iraq had anything "to do with" European protestations against the war. In fact, these calls for peace—aided by the Holy See's permanent observer at the United Nations, the Vatican's foreign minister, and John Paul II himself—were actually self-defeating, according to Weigel. In fact, they were feeding "anti–Anglo-American policy" and "undercutting the effort to disarm Iraq through diplomatic and political means."[69] When the bombs actually started flying and the limbs of Iraqi men, women, and children who took up arms against the "preemptive" American attack—as well as those who did not—were separated from their bodies, Weigel responded by arguing hotly in favor of the concept of a "just war" such as the one in Iraq. He expressed easy confidence that the "precision guided munitions ('smart bombs') make it . . . easier to observe the just war-conduct principles of proportionality (no more force than necessary . . .) and discrimination (noncombatant immunity) than in the past." "War can be less destructive," Weigel soberly informed his Catholic readers in his best imitation of Secretary of Defense Donald Rumsfeld, "and force more precisely focused on legitimate targets and combatants because of modern technology." So there was no need for worry; all would be well.[70]

For some Southern Catholics, though, there is the still the hard-to-shake feeling that something is wrong. A nagging suspicion lingers that there might be something to all of this talk about Republican greed and selfishness, of rapacity and the exploitation of workers, of un-Christian disregard for the poor that the Democrats keep harping about; a worry that unquestioned allegiance to the GOP might in some way contradict Jesus' teachings and desires for mankind—as the party's critics keep on insisting. If the critique were true, this would certainly constitute a serious challenge to the Christian of conscience. To relieve his sense of unease, one leading Southern apologetic (a conservative and public defender of the Catholic faith) took it upon himself to investigate the situation just a month away from the 2000 national elections. Only he did it with an obviously preordained mandate from above to deny any evidence he might come across that could be disquieting. As could be predicted, the results were comforting. In perhaps the most simple-minded exhibition of political investigation possible, the apologetic simply got himself a copy of the official Republican platform and began to read if it were true what the Democrats were saying—that the GOP was antiworker, antipoor, and probusiness to the point of societal neglect on issues such as health care, ecology, and housing. Try as he might, the Eternal World Television Network employee could not find a single sentence in the Republican platform stipulating that the party was antiworker or partial to the rich at the expense of the poor. Relieved, he reported his findings in the regional Catholic newspaper. "Nowhere . . . is there a plank which states that people should not receive fair wages. Nor is there a plank which states that people should not have access to adequate housing. Nor . . . a plank . . . which states that people should not receive health care." Satisfied that he had done his religious duty of adequately investigating the issues by consulting the official party platform, he breathed a little easier, relieved to learn that the Republican agenda posed no contradiction to the duty of Catholic social justice or to his own personal salvation. Thus encouraged, the apologetic took it one step further. So, he concluded, "The Republicans want fair and living wages for all. They want adequate housing for all. They want health care available to all."[71]

Contradictions between the New Testament message and present-day American economic and foreign policy realities were resolved by Catholic opinion makers like George Weigel through a decided clipping of the papal wings, and by others through a tortured and simplistic attempt to sort out the issues by consulting Republican campaign material. But for some Southern Catholics, it doesn't even get this far. For them, the obsession with abortion is a papal permission slip to be ignorant. It provides official absolution from having to worry about pesky and time-consuming things like actually having to pay attention to current events and policy issues in order to vote.

As one older Catholic put it in an e-mail broadside to his circle of friends and relatives throughout the South, the only issue in 2004 was, "Is John Kerry a Saint?"

> I WOULD NOT VOTE FOR HIM, AS HE IS OKING OBORTION, THO HE IS A CATHOLIC, BUT WE CATHOLIC WILL BE SINNING IF WE GO ALONG WITH OBORTION, THAT IS HOW HE IS GETTING MOST OF HIS VOTES, I WILL BACK UP OUR CHURCH RULES, YES I AM AGAINST OBORTION, AS THAT IS MURDER, OUR CHURCH TEACH US AGAINST OBORTION. SO KERRY WANT GET MY VOTE, TO BE A CATHOLIC, YOU MUST FOLLOW THE CHURCH RULES & KERRY IS NOT A TRUE CATHOLIC, SO DON'T VOTE FOR HIM, AS GOD IS AGAINST OBORTION, & SO R WE, I PRAY.[72]

Actually, this kind of thing has been more in keeping with the Religious Right tradition as personified by notables such as Jerry Falwell. Falwell, who still insisted on tax-exempt status for his Moral Majority mission, had no problem announcing that, despite what some people may think about Iraq, "God is pro-war." And actually, "It is the responsibility of every evangelical Christian, every pro-life Catholic, every traditional Jew . . . to get serious about re-electing President [George W.] Bush," no matter what "left-wing thugs" might want.[73] Reflecting on the lay Catholic e-mail and Falwell's exhortation to the faithful, one wonders what Adam Smith might have had to say. The eighteenth-century classical economist has had his works bastardized to the point of posthumous conscription to the cause of the present-day version of extreme economic conservatism. Yet it might surprise many to learn that the Scottish moral philosopher was actually a hearty and pioneering exponent of humanity toward labor and public education, principally because this would, in his view, help raise the toiling masses from the cultural and moral degradation that so often accompanies grinding poverty. Public education, for Smith, held the potential to liberate the masses from the "delusions of enthusiasm and superstition" and "hence to being stirred up by priests and preachers." Education and rational information about public issues was, for Smith, the very lifeblood of a healthy democracy. The more educated the masses were, Smith believed, the "more capable" common folk would be of rising above the cultural torpor of their existence to "see through" such emotional appeals to become better citizens.[74]

Conservative religion is not merely the product or result of what a conservative society wants in its religion as a buttress of that society. Over time, religion also takes on a life of its own. The answer to the chicken-and-egg question (which came first, the society or the religion?) is impossible to answer beyond doubt. But the question itself eventually becomes moot because of the symbiotic nature of the two. Society is created in the image of its dominant religion and creates the kind of religion it desires, which in turn buttresses the society that created it, and so on. Perhaps nowhere is this more clear than in the metamorphosis of the Catholic Church in the South over the last three decades. For so long, Catholicism was seen as a Northern, immigrant, ethnic (Italian, Irish, and Lebanese) import into the WASPish South. Up until 1973, Catholicism generally functioned as a "liberal" force in the South—it was for civil rights, against segregation, and concerned with issues of social and economic justice. Since that time, it has become an abortion-fixated religion that is highly conservative, scarcely distinguishable from evangelical Protestant sects in the South, which deemphasize good works, social service, and social justice in favor of toeing the conservative political line for the whole Republican platform because the GOP is seen as the "party of life" versus the Democratic Party of choice and "baby killing."[75]

Religion does more than just bolster and buttress spiritually, ideologically, and emotionally the status quo society. Conservative religion actually perpetuates the SQS and helps make it more solidly conservative and resistant to change. It feeds and shapes conservative societal opinions on race, class, and gender, as well as issues of ethnicity, patriotism, and nationalism. Religion doesn't just "cause" a culture to be the way it is, and a culture doesn't just "cause" a religion to be the way *it* is. Over time, the two interact and mutually support one another. Religion plays a big part in determining a culture's makeup, ethos, and basic personality. But religion is not independently deterministic. It is closely tied to the other four prime factors of historical causality: race, class, gender, and ethnicity/patriotism.

Religion—organized and folk—is also closely related to notions of self-interest, if not in theory then certainly in actual practice. Once it becomes tied to a specific culture, "religion" ceases to be some abstract universal concept. It becomes a human construct, susceptible to all the warts, whims, predilections, hubris, and shortcomings of its human architects. To a large extent, it becomes a tool—one that is used to preserve the status quo if one perceives of the status quo as a good thing, as well as one's membership in the status quo. Likewise, it can also be used as a tool to undermine the status quo if that status quo is understood as a bad thing, especially if one does not perceive oneself as a member of the status quo with a vested stake in its survival—a status quo that can be conceived of in terms of any one of the five prime factors of causality or some combination thereof.

In this way, the American South is both distinctive and similar to the rest of the country. It is similar in that in all times and all places and all cultures, the "status quo society" and the "rope of religion" theory is applicable to varying degrees, but still applicable and useful as a tool of analysis. It was present in Enlightenment France with its culture wars between the *philosophes* and the anti-*philosophes,* in a Renaissance Italy that had to confront the discoveries and implications of Nicholas Copernicus and Galileo Galilei, in a modern Middle East that struggles between the fundamentalist and the more cosmopolitan. But the American South is also distinctive in that its own history, accent, manners, experience with slavery, civil rights, and frequently adversarial relationship with the federal government make the Southern experience unique. It is not possible to understand the fetish that states' rights has become in the South unless one can adopt the mindset of a region and a people that actually felt themselves traditionally and habitually cast beyond the pale of representative national government for a hundred years. Faulty, flawed, fallacious, and hypocritical, to be sure—but the feeling itself was and still is real for many inhabitants of the white South. Only when that is understood can the region's persistent suspicion and hostility toward the federal government be fully engaged. The South's "Reconstruction syndrome," its susceptibility to "God and country" issues, and a "politics of emotion" render the region's SQS and rope of first race and then religion as qualitatively different in intensity, degree, and efficacy than anywhere else in the western world.[76]

INTERACTION AND THE FIVE PILLARS

The five pillars enumerated above undergird the status quo society in the American South, but they do not do so in a separate and completely independent manner. Race conservatism in the South has traditionally meant white supremacy. Over time, the racial status quo took various forms: slavery, the Confederacy, convict lease, segregation, disfranchisement, lynching, and "massive resistance." More recently, racial conservatism has appeared in the form of "institutionalized racism," enduring class prerogatives of whiteness, affinity for the Confederate flag, and white resistance to affirmative action, employment discrimination charges, taxation and social programs, and federally mandated economic opportunities. Class considerations have been amplified by ethnic issues both in relation to race. African Americans, after all, were the ultimate outsiders to native white society in the South for so long—aliens actually brought by force to the shores of the most homogeneous region of a new country. Efforts to improve their station—from the first Reconstruction to the second—have been identified with the efforts of "outside agitators." Much of the meat of white supremacy—slavery, the old Confederacy, Jim Crow, and "massive resistance"—was buttressed by appeals to orthodox and patriotic Southern religion, a perennially strong rationale in the region. While driving down the many "Martin Luther King Jr. Boulevards" in the South today, it is difficult to recall that a mere few decades earlier, when blacks could not vote freely in the South, King was widely and routinely deplored by white conservatives in explicitly religious and patriotic terms as "Martin Lucifer King," "Mahatma Martin," and a "false prophet in league with the devil" with his "un-American phony civil rights."[77]

Strong ties between orthodox religion, notions of standard patriotism, and the maintenance of white supremacy have been hallmarks of the white South for centuries. During the turn-of-the-twentieth-century controversy over disfranchisement, for instance, a Black Belt planter defended ballot-box fraud and manipulation as "a magnificent system that [unfortunately] cannot be ... perpetuated. It is Christianity, but not orthodox. ... It is wrong but right. . . . . It is life instead of death."[78] Nor did the rationale know the limits of class bounds. A leading tribune of the plain-white masses also invoked religion to echo the call for black disfranchisement. "I believe as truly as I believe that I am standing here, that God Almighty intended the Negro to be the servant of the white man."[79] During the late 1940s' and early 1950s' challenges to the system of Jim Crow that had been erected, many white Southerners responded with religious or patriotic justifications for the continuance of segregation, based on a kind of folk understanding of what constituted orthodox theology and good citizenship. Horace C. Wilkinson, a Baptist deacon for close to four decades and one of the South's Dixiecrat founders, explained that whites were the chosen race. "A just God would not favor one race so far above another if he did not recognize superiority in one above the other," the constitutional lawyer reasoned, and George Washington's troops would not have stayed at Valley Forge "fifteen minutes" for social equality. "I deny that Jesus Christ or the Apostle Paul ever subscribed to" racial equality, Wilkinson wrote. Blacks have "never given humanity a code of laws . . . flown a flag, sailed a ship, or offered the world a worthwhile religion. To that race, liberty is more or less synonymous with license. Its idea of religion is to be relieved of the necessity of earning a living by the sweat of its brow. . . . God made the [race] different and that is no part of a man's job to destroy a God designed difference. . . . Christ died . . . but [not to] blur the color line."[80]

Class conservatism has traditionally meant the preservation of a sharply stratified economic hierarchy in the South—one of rich over poor, employer over employee. It is a section of the country with strong elements of deference granted to society's economic "betters," a place where deference to one's "betters" still means something—something very difficult to separate from piety and even loyalty to God. It is a place where religious people can still hear their ministers exhort them to practice a blind obedience to their employers as part of God's plan for earthly order and human happiness—a wildly irresponsible mandate for submission that in many workplaces can result in the actual loss of life or limb if followed unquestioningly.[81] In this region, rebuilt after the Civil War on the promise of a New South constructed on the backs of cheap, plentiful, and docile workers, a favorable physical and political climate, low or nonexistent taxation, government aid and economic assistance to business, strong antiunionism, and the social portrayal of employers as community benefactors, class relations bleed over onto the other pillars of society. Unions were commonly, and in some places still are, cast as un-Christian and un-American. Union organizers were seen as "outside agitators" with "alien ideas" who were trying to stir up "contented Negroes and happy Darkies." Southerners commonly denounced them as godless, communistic, subversive, treasonous, unpatriotic, and un-American—ammunition to oppose the reconstruction of class relations that drew on very strong regional class, racial, ethnic, and religious sensibilities.[82]

It is a section of the country where notions of proper patriotism are hopelessly interwound with proper religion, a high-octane combination that does much to preserve a rigidly conservative status quo in nearly every area of life. As a Brownsville, Tennessee, member of the Daughters of the American Revolution put it a few years back, in the mind of much of the white South, the two sacred tenets are almost interchangeable. You just "don't find a real patriotic person who is not as well a religious person," she remarked. "Religious people are usually patriotic people." And it almost goes without saying that the combination is explosive in terms of whipping up mass emotions. A Methodist minister in Haywood County, Tennessee, implicitly concurred, noting about his neighbors that there is still the tendency in the rural South for people to "take their religious faith and their love of country, and they are almost synonymous—connected, tied together . . . almost like a religious commitment. . . . It has created some problems at times." One such recent problem that can be pointed to with some abundance of surety is the Roy Moore controversy over his two-and-a-half-ton granite monument of the Ten Commandments. It speaks volumes that, in the summer of 2004, the ousted state supreme court justice plotted a comeback by entrusting his monument to be driven to "God Bless America" rallies around the country by a group that perfectly fused the religious-patriotic combination, the American Veterans Standing for God and Country.[83] The Catholic version is no less intense or emotional. At the national convention of the Knights of Columbus in Dallas, Texas, the group's common fusing of theological conservatism, traditional family and gender roles, and a kind of pseudomilitaristic patriotism, complete with saber rattling, was on conspicuous display.[84]

The South has long been a bastion of patriarchy—white male control of households and society resources, and white male loci of power. Sex, gender, and family relations have been principally defined in the region in the most narrow and male-dominated terms. Conservative orthodoxy in this realm meant that women who worked or lived outside the home, outside of the supervision of a male authority figure, threatened the very biblically mandated foundation of society based on male domination as found in a selective reading of the letters of Saint Paul. Per a corporatist view of society, women who threatened the traditional lines of patriarchy also threatened the foundation of society itself. Interracial sex, in particular, was a bogey that threatened the mongrelization and the very survival of the white race. Despite much ado about Alabama's having thrown off the old shackles of race, in November 2000, a majority of the state's whites voted *against* expunging a century-old law against miscegenation still on the books.[85] The Klan, in various manifestations during the twentieth century, targeted such women for brutal repression as the most dangerous threats to the Southern way of life. Women who cross the bounds of racial and economic orthodoxy in the South have, for a long time, been cast as ethnic rebels, aliens to traditional family values, and the importers of dangerous foreign ideas about the home and family.[86]

More recently, preservation of the family and conventional gender roles has meant an aversion to—in addition to abortion—the "homosexual agenda" tied to the Democratic Party. In the South, toleration for, and defense of, the civil liberties of homosexuals is routinely assaulted from the right as the advent of the decline of western civilization and the family as an institution, equivalent to mandating homosexual marriage for all. In the Deep South, conservative talk show hosts who advocate the broadest and deepest possible types of economic and racial conservatism can still be heard publicly advising listeners on Christian radio stations "not to drop your soap" around people they perceive to be homosexuals.[87]

In the South, ethnicity has been closely connected to notions of sectionalism, nationalism, and good patriotism, depending on the period under question. On many occasions, actual nativism, jingoism, and xenophobia have been present in the Southern orthodoxy on ethnicity. Blacks, obviously, were considered by many as the ultimate outsiders. But labor unions and "unruly women" have also been tarred as dangerously foreign, godless, communistic, and threatening to the prevailing status quo. In the Jim Crow South, good citizenship was inextricably wound up with fealty to white supremacy.[88] In more recent years, this race-based notion of solid citizenship has given way to one based on a conventional understanding of orthodox religion and morality.

Of course, religion relates to all of the other four pillars of conservative Southern society. Although strains of progressive theology have punctured the South's traditional religious ramparts, they have, in the main, been exceptions rather than the rule. A progressive religion based on social service, good works, and the like has appeared across the Southern landscape, like bright lights, at different times and places throughout the region's history. Some of the essays in this very book—most notably those by Andrew Manis, Steven Miller, and Mark Bauman—make this point. But for the most part, the picture has been much more bleak: the predominance of a conservative religion based on faith instead of works, and emphasizing personal conversion, salvation, and competitive moral superiority as opposed to social justice.[89] This "old-time religion" provided, in turn, biblical justifications for slavery, the Confederacy, the "lost cause" as God's cause, lynching, disfranchisement, segregation, and the Ku Klux Klan, and, once threatened, it provided grounds for "massive resistance."[90] Conservative religion adhered itself well to the other buttresses of conservative Southern society: race, class, gender, and ethnicity. In the proper God-ordained order, a special place was designed for all: whites over blacks, men over women, employers over employees, natives over "outsiders." Moreover, tampering with this status quo meant tampering with nature and the ultimate author of nature: God.[91]

The religious language used to uphold the status quo was usually very simple, easy to parrot, and highly emotional, with black-and-white divisions between good and evil. Individuals who challenged the religious status quo or the social status quo buttressed by religion were heretics and sinners of the worst sort who threatened the very salvation of the communal whole.[92] The conservative religious underpinning and moral chauvinism that drove, along with racial and ethnic proscription, the 1920s and 1940s Ku Klux Klans was evident again later in the twentieth century. A powerful strain of "neo-Kluxism" bonded with a "neo-Bourbonism" (economic conservatism) to birth the Southern Republican ascendance into existence. From time to time, spokesmen for the Religious Right such as Jerry Falwell let slip the conservative Christian parameters of their definition of "religion." Even more telling, the most powerful national politicians associated with the Christian Right have made plain their understanding of an exclusive, exclusionary, Truth that solely consists of conservative Christian theology. Not all Republicans feel this way, of course, but all of these exclusionary political figures are strongly identified with modern (usually Southern) Republicanism.[93]

Such strong and overlapping ties among the factors over the length and breadth of the South's experiences make it very difficult, if not downright impossible, to locate the central theme of Southern history in only one single factor. Yet attempts to do so are well known, and historians continue to try. U. B. Phillips thought the "central theme" of Southern history was race—white supremacy, to be exact. Kenneth Stampp chose class, George Tindall ethnicity, W. J. Cash humidity and violence, and C. Vann Woodward the burden of guilt over slavery and military defeat; more recently, Charles Marsh opted for religion and Sheldon Hackney for ambivalence. Other examples abound.[94]

Having said that, at the risk of making the same mistake I have just pointed out, the essence of Southern distinctiveness may very well lie not in one central theme, but in a tendency that has run the length of regional history, one that ties together a number of factors. In a series of intelligent commentaries, Robert B. Reich, the Rhodes scholar who served as President Clinton's labor secretary, has made it clear that as a people, Americans retain the almost innate impulse to vote their pocketbooks.[95] Perhaps. But Southerners most assuredly do not—not in any large sense. Instead, they have shown a distressing predilection for letting emotion overwhelm rationality in a variety of forms: racism, uber-patriotism, militarism, moral and religious chauvinism, and so on. The tendency shows no sign of abetting, only of substituting new subjects that generate emotional fuel.

In addition to the symbiotic ties among the various factors of Southern history, it is virtually impossible to pinpoint one central theme because it is difficult to even identify or quarantine a single theme, completely unconnected from the others. The interlocking nature of the main factors makes it impossible for historians to rip the variables apart in the present without producing jagged and artificial constructs. More, the importance of the factors—even prime factors—changes over time and place, even within the South. For example, for so many years, race was the ultimate glue that bound the other prime factors of the status quo, until the recent ascendance of religion and a narrow conception of what constitutes moral behavior.

THE CONSERVATIVE PARAMETERS THESIS

Politics in a status quo society takes place within what may be called "conservative parameters." That is, the conventional continuum of political possibilities—from radical left, liberal/progressive, moderate, conservative, and radical right—does not apply. Instead, politics is conducted within a set of narrowly skewed conservative boundaries. The use of such parameters shifts political possibilities a whole degree to the left. Thus, in the political continuum that exists in a SQS, the classic #2 (liberal or progressive) position becomes generally defined as a #1 (radical leftist) position. The #3 (moderate) position is understood as conventional "liberalism," although it is, in actuality, moderation. The #4 (conservative) position becomes defined as "moderation," or the median political position of the possible political continuum. And in such a society, the #5 (radical right) position morphs into mainstream "conservatism."

These parameters are amply present in the modern South's recent political vacillations. The extremism once connected to the Dixiecrat or States' Rights Party of 1948, and later linked to the extreme candidacies of Barry Goldwater and George Wallace, have almost, without change, found a home in today's respectable and modern Republican Party in the South. Present is the same language accusing liberals and Democrats of being socialists and communists, traitors, moral degenerates, and godless atheists. Nor is this the province only of the South's lower classes. On the contrary, one finds the same sentiments emanating from the "better classes," only with a self-conscious and often affected "aristocratic drawl." In 2004 a visitor to Birmingham, Alabama, can still find one of the city's most prominent, Harvard-educated attorneys denigrating the "People's Republic of Cambridge" and admitting that, deep down, "I . . . really cannot shake the view that people who support the national Democratic candidate, whether through ignorance or malice, are fostering beliefs and policies that can be fairly characterized as socialistic and unpatriotic."[96] The racial rhetoric is muted and more subtle now, but it still represents exclusivity and white supremacy. Oh, it is still possible to hear the occasional slip from the Republican neighbor down the street who, mistaking one for a kindred spirit, casually refers to the danger of "Africanoes" moving into the neighborhood and destroying it all. Or the campaign chairman for a Deep South Republican governor who confides to you at a church bazaar that a black woman told him on the campaign trail that, really, blacks had it pretty good during slavery—a sentiment he heartily agreed with but could not voice publicly.[97]

But the real extreme rhetoric is not on race now; it is on morality and "values." And it *is* okay to say that out loud—the louder the better down South. Considered extreme rhetoric just a generation ago, the revolution in media—Internet, cable television, and talk radio—has, through ceaseless repetition of the extreme, numbed our collective sensibilities to it. It has also lent legitimacy to what was previously understood to be extreme propaganda, because there is a public, published, repetitive outlet for it while providing a 24/7 diet of uninterrupted, unchallenged "news" from news/talk AM radio and Internet Web sites. Such sentiments, given almost daily articulation by Rush Limbaugh, Sean Hannity, Jerry Falwell, and a legion of local imitators, is treated as respectable Republican politics, even "news," by an alarming and growing number of average Southern, and non-Southern, whites—even though Fox News and other "fair and balanced" outlets have been repeatedly exposed as little more than right-wing propaganda machines.[98]

What is perhaps most alarming is the contemporaneous emasculation of the mainstream media; its loss of the ability to inform readers and viewers that black is black, and up is not down. It is a paralysis made evident by even a casual viewing of the news as presented by the mainstream media's army of milquetoast anchors—people such as Wolf Blitzer, Aaron Brown, Jeff Greenfield, and Judy Woodruff, who apparently would rather avoid informing than give offense, to anyone. It is a petrified state that is the product of a direct fear of having right-wing commentators such as Rush Limbaugh out the network—in this case CNN—with the kiss of death as the "liberal media." The movement toward vanilla reporting in the mainstream media has grown so obvious in recent years that the outgoing head of the National Association of Hispanic Journalists was able to observe, with a good deal of truth, "If [an administration official] said the world was flat, today's corporate media would dutifully report, 'Breaking News: There Appear to be Differing Views on The World's Shape.'"[99]

Several things result from the full shift toward extremism, which may be subsumed under the term the "principle of constrained choices." First, and most obviously, there is no real radical left possibility in such a society. But perhaps more importantly, liberalism or traditional progressivism becomes very difficult to effect, and almost impossible to sustain, because it is widely understood as extremism. Barring outside intervention, stasis is the almost inevitable result in such a society. In the status quo society, trade unions and racially liberal policies such as civil rights and school integration, when introduced, are commonly equated with communism, tyranny, and other sorts of extremism, customarily reserved for identification with the radical left position in a conventional political model. This results in a discrediting process of mainstream progressivism and traditional liberal possibilities as extreme, dangerous, communist, subversive, tyrannical, and the like, and limits the effectiveness and societal attractiveness of such movements.

Other skewed results follow. Moderate positions are fallaciously celebrated by contemporary members of such societies (and thus often by scholars working with the sources left behind by these individuals) as examples of liberalism, enlightenment, and progressivism when they are, in fact, rather mild examples of moderate political behavior. Thus, in the SQS that was the Deep South of the 1960s, as historian C. Vann Woodward recognized, moderates were viewed as "liberals" and integrationists were considered "radicals."[100] In another observation bearing out the same point, Hodding Carter Jr., the Pulitzer prize–winning editor of the Greenville (Miss.) *Delta-Democrat*, recognized that the South was "the only place in the western world where a man could become a liberal simply by urging obedience to the law."[101] Swedish sociologist Gunnar Myrdal, in *An American Dilemma*, his famous 1944 study of the South and race relations, essentially made the same point: "In the South . . . a person may be ranked as liberal . . . merely by insisting that the law shall be adhered to in practice."[102]

In this society, genuinely conservative positions are seen as little more than mainstream common sense and moderation, thereby gaining enormous, self-perpetuating inertia among the mass of population. Thus, many of the battles between "liberalism" and "conservatism" in this political and social system are actually waged between various types of conservatism. They are better described as fratricidal conflicts between different kinds of conservatism rather than genuine contests between liberal and conservative alternatives. In such a system, there is no long-lasting, viable liberal alternative. Thus, in a society like Alabama, the 1998 Republican gubernatorial primary was waged between the business conservatism of Winton Blount and the religious/moral values conservatism of Fob James. The fight to replace the state's 100-year-old constitution occurred, to a large extent, between similar forces: Religious Right conservatives from the Association for Judeo-Christian Ethics (who opposed it) and business conservatives, passing as progressives, such as Republicans Steve Windom and Jim Bennett, who backed a new constitution because they thought it would boost outside investment in the state. During the 1990s, the battle between Democrat Jim Folsom Jr. and Republican Jeremiah Denton was actually billed as the "battle of the conservatives."[103] In the 1960s and 1970s, political battles raged between Republicans and "Alabama" Democrats, both of whom claimed no connection to the national Democratic Party, integration, Vietnam protest, or political liberalism. (Variations on that theme still occur today.) In 1948, Dixiecrat bolters and Democratic loyalists agreed on the fundamental repulsiveness of civil rights legislation but disagreed on economic policies and, more importantly, on whether federal government intervention would be more fruitfully opposed from inside or outside the Democratic Party. During the Depression, an Alabama dairy farmer said much in confiding to novelist John Dos Passos: "Well, around here communism's anything we don't like. Isn't it that way everywhere else?"[104] The vaunted Southern bolt during the 1928 presidential election was war in Alabama, a bitter battle waged between two different types of racial conservatives. On the one hand stood the regular Democratic establishment, which backed national Democratic nominee Al Smith, despite his odious Catholicism and Yankee/Irish pedigree, because the establishment believed allegiance to the national Democratic Party held the best chance for the South to retain regional control over race relations and white supremacy. On the other hand stood a KKK/prohibitionist/nativist/moral values group (the Hoovercrats) that opposed Smith and bolted from the Democratic Party to support Republican Herbert Hoover because they believed that the New York governor personified impure ethnic blood, Roman popery, and, worst of all, liberalism on the race issue. During the decade of the 1920s, the battle between pro- and anti-Klan forces was one between supporters of the sheeted order and "pragmatic" opponents who were just as conservative on race, religion, ethnicity, morality, and the place of women in society. A principle-based opposition did not develop until decades later. Just a decade earlier, though, progressivism was for whites only—the only question was which whites would benefit from governmental activism.[105] Around 1900, disfranchisement was legally enacted with a new constitution and an all-white primary. All but the rarest of whites agreed that blacks should lose the franchise. The real disagreement occurred over the question of methods—whether the mechanisms of disfranchisement that were used would also entrap poor whites along with blacks.

Today, the SQS is increasingly evident on a national stage. The presidency of George W. Bush is seen by many as the second coming of Ronald Reagan, when in fact it may be more accurately described as the revenge of

Barry Goldwater, replete with the proposition of nuclear weapons being used. During Goldwater's time, this was a scenario that even George Wallace was moved to distance himself from as extreme. In Bush the Younger's administration, tax cuts and preemptive wars that Goldwater could only dream about have become reality, and the extremism that netted the Arizonan just six states in 1964 is now largely accepted as mainstream conservatism. Indeed, in the current administration, the Ralph Reeds, Paul Weyrichs, Paul Wolfowitzes, Jerry Falwells, John Ashcrofts, and Grover Norquists are in the saddle. Norquist has regular access to the president—the same person who called bipartisanship "another term for date rape" and declared that he didn't want to just reduce the level of government, he wanted to shrink it to the size where "I can drag it into the bathroom and drown it in the bathtub." Indeed, we seem to be headed toward the looking glass as Federal Reserve chairman Alan Greenspan recently gave credence to what many liberals had hoped was paranoia on their part: the "starve the beast" theory of intentionally running deficits so large that government programs around since the New Deal would have to be axed. The Fed chairman spoke out loud of cutting Social Security and Medicare payments as a method of retrenching the historic deficit caused by tax cuts for America's wealthiest and by spending in the war in Iraq. Liberals around the country look back at Richard Nixon now and find themselves appalled that they consider him a liberal by today's standards. The 1960s and early 1970s GOP wunderkind Kevin Phillips became so disgusted by the extremism of the new GOP that he left the party, as did members of the Eisenhower family. Phillips became an independent and wrote articles and books that savaged the Reagan and Bush presidencies.[106]

In such a skewed political system, where ultraconservative notions of conventional religion and racial beliefs both intertwine with notions of what constitutes good patriotism, red baiting takes on a power not found in other, less extreme political climes.[107] Liberalism becomes, in the minds of many, the rough moral equivalent of communism. Although this has been a highly effective tactic for the forces of conservatism in the status quo society, the tactic is not purely cynical or disingenuous. People in an SQS are not working with a classic political continuum. They are working with a worldview and political continuum that has been shifted so that, for many of them at least, liberal activity really is tantamount to "radical," "dangerous," "subversive," "godless," and "communist" behavior. It is revolutionary by nature because it threatens to subvert the status quo. Conservatives in an SQS do not merely call Democrats "communists" for political gain—although this does occur as well. Many actually *believe* that liberal Democrats are the same thing as communists. The threat to home, hearth, religion, law, and order is the same. At the turn of the century, populists found themselves denounced by some conservative Democrats as communists. The same thing awaited 1920s-era textile strikers.[108] At the turn of the next century, even some white Southern unionists fell prey to the skewed nature of the larger political system in which they lived. There is an explanation, although it would be a stretch to call it rational, why in 1999 a flight-baggage handler in a CIO union in North Carolina could denounce Bill Clinton as a "draft-dodging, pot-smoking, Communist"—and really mean it.[109]

But why is it, exactly, that so many ordinary people in the South have supported so intensely a status quo that does not serve their interests in an economic sense? First, and perhaps most obvious, is the reality that many average Southerners are not aware that many parts of the status quo do not serve their economic interests. In this sense, Southerners are not unlike many of their brethren elsewhere in the country. Perhaps the only difference here is one of degree rather than kind. But beyond that, the majority strain of Southern culture throughout its history has been conservative; the minority strain, liberal. Religion, in an intensely religious section such as the American South, can be used by either side—and has been to great effect. It figured prominently in the arguments of both prosegregationists and integrationists during the height of the civil rights movement. But merely in terms of numbers, conservatism has been the majority strain in all five main areas of historical causation. Many people who should, by all accounts, locate themselves in the minority have convinced themselves that they are part of the majority and thus have a vested interest in maintaining and preserving that majority—and hence the broken-down pickup truck with the busted-out windows on the back roads of the South sporting a "Vote Republican" bumper sticker.

There are a number of other reasons for this kind of phenomenon. Many people simply want to be on the winning side. There is a strong psychological component of wanting to belong that is at work here. Recognizing that conservatism has been, is, and probably will be in the saddle in the South, many ordinary Southerners simply climb on board the bandwagon. Moreover, emotion has had a special resonance for the voters of the South. W. J. Cash famously wrote that Southerners "felt"; they did not "think."[110] Regardless, if one would take the argument to that degree, there is little question that Southerners are, and always have been, emotional people. Whether it is because of an anti-intellectual strain that continues to permit subpar spending for education, or because of an emotional religion, or just because it is in the water and the air and the people, passion is a basic part of Southern politics and Southern life. People tend to lose sight of issues that have a relevance for their day-to-day lives in the rush to feel part of a majority that carries with it a sense of emotional well-being, even superiority. For so long in the South, that issue was race and white supremacy. Now, it is increasingly morality and religion, accompanied by a sense of moral superiority and righteousness. But it is still very strong, and the politics of many Southerners reflects their desire to feel a part of some majority—the white majority, the Christian, God-loving majority, the patriotic American majority, the heterosexual majority. Born and bred on the emotionalism of white supremacy, illiberalism, antifederalism, and xenophobia so closely tied to the Reconstruction past, newer generations of white Southerners have a deep-seated tradition of politics that is conducive to the waging of a politics based on passion.

It is not news in the study of human behavior to recognize that if individuals perceive of themselves as part of a status quo (in any of the five prime factor areas)—no matter how faulty that perception might be in reality—then they have a strong incentive to work to ensure its preservation. By the same token, there is a logic to the corollary. Persons, even in a status quo society, who do not perceive of themselves as part of the status quo will have a strong impetus to work to undermine that status quo. In a society like the South, compelled by faith, religion can work as a rope to strengthen the status quo or a solvent to dissolve the bonds that hold that status quo together.[111]

In a real way, though, economic elites are the most psychologically and emotionally secure of all conservatives in such a society because they have a real, tangible, rational reason to be conservatives: the status quo serves them, and its preservation keeps them ensconced in the top ranks of society. So it is that economically privileged conservatives often display a far less stringent affection for actually acting out issues of cultural and religious conservatism than conservatives of more modest means. In Alabama, for example, the enthusiasm of a Winton Blount, a Bob Riley, or even a Bill Pryor for actually going beyond lip service on issues such as public display of the Ten Commandments was always far less than that of their fellow Republican rivals, Fob James and Judge Roy Moore. Although Riley and Pryor, for example, praised the idea enthusiastically in public, when push came to shove and Fob James threatened to call out the National Guard, George Wallace–style, and Chief Justice Moore filed suit against the federal government, privileged conservatives ran for the hills in embarrassment, leaving Republicans of modest means to support the fanatical and futile defiance. Such temerity has its price, as when Roy Moore called Gorman Houston (a fellow Republican and acting Alabama chief justice who presided over Moore's expulsion from the bench for defying a federal court order to remove the monument) and informed him that he had knowledge Houston was going to burn in hell for "covering God" and that there was nothing he could do about it.[112] Such emotional issues—school prayer, gay rights, display of the Confederate flag—allow poor and plain-white conservatives to feel good about their conservatism even in the face of a harsh economic reality. It is a back door to psychological supremacy that economic elites like Winton Blount and Bob Riley do not need to take. They are already home.

Obviously, if the society (in this case, the South) goes with the majority strain, the result, politically and religiously and culturally, will be conservative. If the society goes with the minority strain, the result will be liberal. So far, the liberal surprises in the Southern experience have been few, fleeting, and, compared with the deep and enduring conservatism of the region, relatively shallow.

Perhaps one of the most telling examples of this observation's veracity occurred recently in Alabama. It may be recalled from earlier in this chapter that Republican U.S congressman Bob Riley won the 2002 governor's race in the Heart of Dixie by appealing heavily to the Christian Right—so heavily, in fact, that the Alabama branch of the Christian Coalition claimed sole responsibility for moving enough swing voters to secure his election. Although Riley had performed as a model Reagan-Bush Republican in Congress for three terms—opposing every tax measure imaginable, invoking God at nearly every juncture, and making antipathy to the federal government a staple—once elected governor, Riley went off the reservation . . . way off. Whether it was the cold water of actually having to fund government programs as a chief executive, or a genuine religious epiphany as a result of reading a divinity student's master's thesis on the godliness of accepting taxation as a social responsibility—or both—Riley drew up a historic $1.2 billion tax hike and proposed its passage through state referendum. If it passed, the unprecedented reform package would have more fairly distributed the tax burden in a state routinely recognized as having the most malformed tax system in America and provided badly needed monies to reform perhaps the most consistently pitifully performing state education system in the country. More, Riley campaigned vigorously for the plan as a religious and moral duty to "the least of those among us," angering many Republicans who had voted him into office largely on the basis of religion, morality, and character.

"I've spent a lot of time studying the New Testament," Riley told a state whose people pride themselves on their religiosity, "and it has three philosophies: love God, love each other, and take care of the least among you. I don't think anyone can justify putting an income tax on someone who makes $4600 a year."[113]

Riley's plan targeted Alabama's woefully undertaxed corporations, utilities, and large landholding farm and timber interests while lessening the burden on lower and working-class families. Yet the package triggered a highly emotional backlash that focused on interpretations of religion, and these interpretations had a definite racial subtext to them. Riley soon found himself bitterly opposed by the Republicans who had put him in office as a Southern Judas Iscariot. Republicans fondly recalled Riley's Christian Right days as congressman, but they were repulsed by the new Governor Riley with his liberal theology of feeding the poor and hungry, invoking the Beatitudes and Acts of the Apostles, and the other stuff of Christ's radical New Testament gospel. The Christian Coalition of Alabama publicly denounced him, although they did it in the curiously Christian way that finds its most perfect enunciation in the Deep South. "We applaud tax relief for the poor," state Coalition director John Giles claimed, although the group had never done so publicly before. "You'll find most Alabamians have got a charitable heart; they want to do that," Giles explained. "They just don't want it coming out of their pocket." State GOP chief Marty Connors came out hard against Riley, lining up the state Republican executive committee as well as county executive committees to deplore the governor's package. "We've got a *conservative, evangelical Christian, Republican* governor," Connors said in obvious wonderment, "trying to get a massive turnout of *black* voters to pass a *tax increase* so he can raise taxes on Republican constituents." "Alabama needs to raise some revenue; there's no question about that," Connors continued. "But this is a . . . massive redistribution of wealth. We are the *Republican* Party—of *Alabama!* If a Democrat had proposed this, we would be burning down cities" [emphasis in original]. Marty Connors, a curious bird, even for Alabama, was the kind of state Republican chairman who actually took pride in articulating what were once the most sacred tenets of the Confederate-Reconstruction brand of conservative Democratic hostility toward anything having to do with the federal government other than state, disaster, and corporate relief checks. Two of Riley's Republican cabinet members resigned in protest to the plan, a former state GOP chair led rowdy antitax rallies, and SouthTrust bank executive Wallace Malone, the Republican son of a leading Wiregrass Dixiecrat, trotted out the old, discredited bogey that the tax increase would result in the state's losing 30,000 jobs. Malone's involvement was perhaps the cruelest joke of all since he stood close to retiring with a $30.3 million golden parachute, in addition to his regular $9.4 million annual compensation, as soon as Wachovia Financial bought out his bank and laid off hundreds of his employees. Conservative talk show hosts Russ and Dee Fine damned Riley as a traitor to Republicanism and suggested that he be expelled from the party. Close Bush administration adviser Grover Norquist vowed to make Riley "the poster child for Republicans who go bad." "I want every Republican elected official in the United States to watch Bob Riley lose," Norquist instructed, "and learn from it." Around the state disgruntled Republicans sported politicoreligious bumper stickers asserting "Bush Giveth, Riley Taketh Away." Marty Connors and the state GOP even imported Bush ally and former House power Dick Armey of Texas to stump against the plan.[114]

Riley faced his most serious opposition from the well-heeled corporate and megafarm and timber interests that had bankrolled his rise to the governorship just one year before. The state's largest bank, county farmers' associations under the parent group, the Alabama Farm Bureau Administration (ALFA), and two timber and paper companies footed the bill for radio spots on black radio stations, featuring a voice with poor diction warning listeners that white lawmakers had been "ignorin' us for years" but now the Riley plan could result in black property taxes going up "as much as fo' hundred percent." The spots were aimed, ironically, at black mistrust of white power in Alabama, long consistent with Riley's conservative planter-industrialist opposition and their penchant for using emotional issues to cloud the vision of poor voters, both black and white.[115] Riley, who had become accustomed to having the Republican media and spin machine work to his benefit through four elections, was flummoxed by the misrepresentations and distortions of his tax plan that he faced from former supporters. Confronted by one antitax pamphlet that opponents distributed throughout the state, Riley said, "I told Patsy [his wife] that I am amazed. There is nothing in this . . . that even comes close to talking about the plan I helped develop."[116]

In the end, Alabama's electorate crushed the package 68 to 32 percent in a vote that had clear racial meaning. Riley's plan prevailed in only thirteen of Alabama's sixty-seven counties, all of them in the heavily African-American Black Belt. Perhaps most telling, though, the referendum went down to flaming defeat, receiving support only in the black counties and getting most hammered in the poor-white and hill counties, where the heavily rural white populations had just one year before given Riley his largest margins of victory. Results confirmed election-eve polls that had consistently located the seat of the plan's strongest opposition in the quarter of the Alabama electorate making less than $30,000 annually—precisely the voters who stood to benefit most from the package. What is more, within moments after watching his referendum go down to defeat, Governor Riley, chastened by the enduring realities of Alabama's racial and religious conservatism, dutifully returned to the GOP reservation: he prepared to cope with defeat by proposing to keep taxes low and slashing badly needed public services and programs for the poor.[117]

Notes

1. C. Vann Woodward, *Origins of the New South, 1877–1913* (Baton Rouge: Louisiana State University Press, 1951); Dewey W. Grantham, *Southern Progressivism: The Reconciliation of Progress and Tradition* (Knoxville: University of Tennessee Press, 1983); George Brown Tindall, *The Persistent Tradition in New South Politics* (Baton Rouge: Louisiana State University Press, 1975).

2. Scholars and observers as diverse as George Mowry, Dewey Grantham, Lewis Rubin, Frank Friedel, C. Vann Woodward, V. O. Key Jr., and W. J. Cash are in agreement that the South has been the most conservative region in the United States. See, for example, George Mowry, *Another Look at the Twentieth-century South* (Baton Rouge: Louisiana State University Press, 1973), 33–34; V. O. Key Jr., *Southern Politics in State and Nation* (1949. Reprint. Knoxville: University of Tennessee Press, 1984), 8–9; W. J. Cash, *The Mind of the South* (New York: Alfred A. Knopf, 1941), 421. See also David Herbert Donald, "The Southernization of America," *New York Times,* August 30, 1976. See also John Egerton, *The Americanization of Dixie* (New York: HarperCollins, 1974).

3. Some of the most intriguing examples of the religious sources of Southern progressivism and the limits to religiously inspired political conservatism in the South may, fittingly enough, be found within this volume. For examples of religiously based progressivism in the Southern experience, see particularly the chapters by Mark Bauman, Steven P. Miller, and Andrew M. Manis. For the political limits to religious conservatism, see the chapters by Mark J. Rozell and Clyde Wilcox and that by Charles Bullock III and Mark C. Smith. Of course, the present volume also contains a good deal of material to support the view that religion has played, principally, a conservative role in the Southern polity. Here, see especially the chapters by Fred Arthur Bailey, Paul Harvey, James L. Guth, Ted Ownby, and Natalie M. Davis.

4. R. G. Collingwood's classic *The Idea of History* (Oxford: Clarendon Press, 1946) addressed these very ideas. Various studies continue to address the interplay between politics and religion at different times, some focusing on the South. See, for example, Gaines M. Foster, *Moral Reconstruction: Christian Lobbyists and the Federal Legislation of Morality, 1865–1920* (Chapel Hill: University of North Carolina Press, 2002); Terrie Dopp Aamodt, *Righteous Armies, Holy Cause: Apocalyptic Imagery and the Civil War* (Macon, Ga.: Mercer University Press, 2002); Michael Barkun, *Religion and the Racist Right* (Chapel Hill: University of North Carolina Press, 1994); and

Michael Lienesch, *Redeeming America: Piety and Politics in the New Christian Right* (Chapel Hill: University of North Carolina, 1993).

5. Scholars of Southern religion have, with very few exceptions, agreed that dominant religion in the region has been conservative. See the voluminous work of Samuel S. Hill Jr., especially *Southern Churches in Crisis* (New York: Holt, Rinehart and Winston, 1966); and Hill, ed., *Religion and the Solid South* (Nashville: Abingdon Press, 1972). Wayne Flynt has been perhaps the most notable dissenter on this subject, but the essential validity of Hill's thesis is still accepted by scholars such as John B. Boles. See Boles's discussion of Hill, Flynt, and others in "The Discovery of Southern Religious History," in *Interpreting Southern History: Historiographical Essays in Honor of Sanford W. Higginbotham,* ed. John B. Boles and Evelyn Thomas Nolen (Baton Rouge: Louisiana State University Press, 1987), 512–15 and 542–43, 512–13 (quoted). See also Ted Ownby, "'Ethos Without Ethic': Samuel S. Hill and Southern Religious History," in *Reading Southern History: Essays on Interpreters and Interpretations,* ed. Glenn Feldman (Tuscaloosa: University of Alabama Press, 2001), 247–60.

6. For example, "Where the Confederate nostalgia does get suspect is when white Southerners make the assumption that their South is *the* South—that it's somehow un-Southern, for example, to think the battle flag, a symbol as offensive to many blacks as the swastika is to Jews, doesn't belong at the heart of the Georgia state flag or flying above the state house in Columbia, S.C." Peter Applebome, *Dixie Rising: How the South Is Shaping American Values, Politics, and Culture* (New York: Harvest Books, 1997), quoted in Cynthia Tucker, "He's Surely Not Free to Dodge Flag Stance," *Atlanta Journal-Constitution,* November 10, 2002. David L. Chappell's work is a kind of counter to the main emphasis on "outside agitators." See *Inside Agitators: White Southerners in the Civil Rights Movement* (Baltimore: Johns Hopkins University Press, 1994).

7. Numan V. Bartley defined this kind of compliance, designed to avoid prison time and monetary fines, and to keep the region attractive as an area for outside investment, as "pocketbook ethics" in his classic book *The Rise of Massive Resistance: Race and Politics in the South during the 1950s* (Baton Rouge: Louisiana State University Press, 1969), 342–45.

8. Kay G. Wood, Hoover, Alabama, to Editor, *Birmingham News,* May 7, 2002, 8A (quoted). Similar language is common among white Southern Republicans. "Blacks need to let the past be the past and get on with the future. Abraham Lincoln set them free. The War Between the States sealed it. They are going to wake up one day and see how they have been used" by the Democrats. "I don't think U.S. Sen. Trent Lott said anything that is so bad." Charlie C. Davis Sr., Leeds, Alabama, to Editor, *Birmingham News,* December 19, 2002, 16A (quoted in note).

9. Dan T. Carter, *The Politics of Rage: George Wallace, the Origins of the New Conservatism, and the Transformation of American Politics* (New York: Simon and Schuster, 1995). Wayne Greenhaw's fascinating *Elephants in the Cottonfields: Ronald Reagan and the New Republican South* (New York: Macmillan, 1982), 187 (first quotation). Kevin Small, Fultondale, Alabama, to Editor, *Birmingham News,* April 19, 2002, 14A (second quotation).

10. For this topic explored in more detail, see Glenn Feldman, "Ugly Roots: Race, Emotion, and the Rise of the Modern Republican Party in Alabama and the South," in *Before Brown: Civil Rights and White Backlash in the Modern South,* ed. Glenn Feldman (Tuscaloosa: University of Alabama Press, 2004), 268–309.

11. On the Trent Lott furor, see the respective cover stories for *Newsweek* and *Time* magazines, December 23, 2002; and Paul Krugman, "All These Problems," *New York Times,* December 10, 2002. On the Trent Lott issue as related to the Confederate flag issue in the Roy Barnes–Sonny Perdue gubernatorial race and Republican presidential visits to Bob Jones University, see Cynthia Tucker, "GOP and Racists? Thick as Thieves," *Atlanta Constitution,* December 15, 2002; Maureen Dowd, "Of Ghosts and Mississippi," *New York Times,* December 18, 2002; and Bob Herbert, "Racism and the G.O.P.," *New York Times,* December 12, 2002. On the Republican use of the Confederate flag issue in the 2002 midterm elections, see Cynthia Tucker, "He's Surely Not Free to Dodge Flag Stance"; and Richard Whitt, "Confederate Flag Supporters to Next Governor," both in the *Atlanta Journal-Constitution,* November 10, 2002; and Jim Galloway, "Barnes Says He's Done with Politics," *Atlanta Journal-Constitution,* November 13, 2002. See also Richard Cook, Cumming, Georgia, and Nelson Jones, Panama City, Florida, both to Editor, *Atlanta Journal-Constitution,* November 11, 2002, A16. On continued voter suppression tactics used by Republicans to limit black voter turnout in Louisiana, Florida, and other places, see the article on Hillary Clinton in the *New Orleans Times-Picayune,* December 29, 2002; Bill Walsh, "Dirty Deeds Abounded in Elections," *New Orleans Times-Picayune,* December 12, 2002; and Greg Palast, "The Re-election of Jim Crow," *Southern Exposure* (October 29, 2002). This subject will be discussed in more detail below as relates to the antidemocratic and racist tendencies of the modern emergence of an extreme strain of conservatism as mainstream.

12. These election figures were supplied by Southern Opinion Research. My thanks to Professor Patrick J. Cotter, Department of Political Science, University of Alabama. In 2004, Bush again got 80 percent of Alabama's white vote, 82 percent among men and 79 percent among women, 95 percent of its white Protestant conservative vote, 88 percent of the states' white evangelical/born again vote, and 73 percent of mostly white North Alabama. As per nationally, Bush's percentage of the black vote rose some, from 2 percent to 6 percent. Population area also made a difference. Bush and Kerry split the state's smaller cities with 49 percent apiece; Bush barely took Jefferson County, where Birmingham is located, 50–49. But Bush won both the suburbs and rural areas with two-thirds of the vote. Exit polls, 2004 presidential election, http://www.cnn.com, November 3, 2004.

13. Here and in the preceding several paragraphs, by the "South" is meant the "white South," which still predominates in terms of numbers, money, and political power in the region. Even when race is obviously a strong factor, many voters still believe that the South has gone Republican merely because the region is more "conservative" in a generic, not a racial, sense. See, e.g., Reed Billman, Huntsville, Alabama, to Editor, (Birmingham) *One Voice,* September 29, 2000, 5. On the parties as bastions for each race in Alabama, Carol Ann Vaughn to author (e-mails), January 8 and 17, 2002; and NJW to author (e-mail), January 13, 2002, all three in possession of the author.

14. *Birmingham News,* August 25, 31, 1908; *Birmingham Age-Herald,* August 4, 7, 24, and 30, 1908; Wayne Flynt, *Poor but Proud: Alabama's Poor Whites* (Tuscaloosa: University of Alabama Press, 1989), 141.

15. Dissent in the South was often muted, especially when racial purity was involved. See the concept of the "savage ideal" in Cash, *The Mind of the South,* 137–41.

16. *Birmingham Age-Herald,* August 22, 24, 25, 1908; Carl V. Harris, *Political Power in Birmingham, 1877–1921* (Knoxville: University of Tennessee Press, 1977), 222. Whites in the Birmingham district had good reason to be confident that they could rally white solidarity from disparate whites against the UMW in 1908 on the basis of the threat the strike posed to race conditions. Race had long united poor, working-class, and privileged whites. John Witherspoon DuBose, a Birmingham booster, described white solidarity across class lines around the turn of the century: "The white laboring classes here are separated from the Negroes, working all day side by side with them, by an innate consciousness of race superiority. This sentiment dignifies the character of white labor. It excites a sentiment of sympathy and equality on their part with the classes above them, and in this way becomes a wholesome social leaven." See Horace Mann Bond, *Negro Education in Alabama: A Study in Cotton and Steel* (Tuscaloosa: University of Alabama Press, 1994, first published in 1939), 145. See also Allen to Editor, *Birmingham Age-Herald,* August 26, 1908.

17. *Birmingham Age-Herald,* August 30, 1908 (quoted).

18. Ibid., 22 and 25, 1908. This type of demonization and dehumanization as a prelude to community violence was a notable feature of conflicts such as the French wars of religion. See Barbara B. Diefendorf, *Beneath the Cross: Catholics and Huguenots in Sixteenth-century Paris* (New York: Oxford University Press, 1991), 145–58.

19. *Birmingham Age-Herald,* August 22 and 25, 1908 (quoted).

20. Frank Evans Pamphlet, Alabama Coal Operators' Records, Birmingham Public Library Archives, 34; (Indianapolis) *UMW Journal,* July 30, 1908, 2; August 15, 1908, 4; and September 5, 1908, 1; *Birmingham Age-Herald,* August 5, 1908; Richard A. Straw, "The Collapse of Biracial Unionism: The Alabama Coal Strike of 1908," *Alabama Historical Quarterly* 37 (Summer 1975): 96–97, 102, 104; Frank M. Duke, "The UMW in Alabama: Industrial Unionism and Reform Legislation, 1890–1911" (M.A. thesis, Auburn University, 1979), 84–85. On B. B. Comer quote, see the *Birmingham Labor Advocate,* August 7, 1908; *Birmingham Age-Herald,* August 5, 1908; and Philip H. Taft, *Organizing Dixie: Alabama Workers in the Industrial Era,* ed. Gary M. Fink (Westport, Conn.: Greenwood Press, 1981), 27 and 30 (quoted).

21. George Brown Tindall, *The Emergence of the New South, 1913–1945* (Baton Rouge: Louisiana State University Press, 1967); *Gastonia (N.C.) Gazette* quoted on 345 (second quotation); also see 347 (first quotation).

22. William L. Dickinson, a Republican congressman from Alabama, took a leading role on the national scene in trying to discredit the whole voting rights movement as immoral on the basis of the allegation that incidents of interracial sex took place around the march activities at Selma. See William L. Dickinson to Editor, *South: The News Magazine of Dixie,* March 1967, 4, and November 1969, 4.

23. Joanne Ricca, "The American Right," report delivered at the United Association of College and Labor Educators' Annual Meeting (Los Angeles, California, April 2002), 18–20 (Falwell and Robertson quoted). Also notes from the sermon of Father Michael J. Deering, ca. September 2002, Our Lady of Sorrows Catholic Church, Homewood, Alabama (notes in possession of the author). It is also worth noting that the new priest who gave this sermon became a member of the cloth only after a twenty-plus-year sales/management career with the Eastman-Kodak Company. After only two years in the priesthood, Deering had so ingratiated himself with the conservative Catholic hierarchy in Alabama that he was elevated to the position of

chancellor of the Birmingham Diocese, a lofty office just below that of bishop but above monsignor.

24. Louisville (Ky.) *Courier-Journal,* June 21, 1942 (Ethridge quoted).

25. Andrew Edmund Kersten, *Race, Jobs, and the War: The FEPC in the Midwest, 1941–46* (Urbana: University of Illinois Press, 2000), 129 (quotations). Acutely interesting is Kersten's account of how these conservative, antilabor forces at first sought to kill the committee slowly by strangling its funds, a strategy eerily reminiscent of the Reagan administration's attack on labor laws and agencies such as the NLRB and the Bush II administration's gutting of OSHA and the NLRB. Harry Byrd hyperbolically asked, "If we cannot manage John L. Lewis at home, how can we expect to protect ourselves against Joe Stalin abroad?" This and other Byrd gems of conservative malapropism earned him the sobriquet "Mr. Demopublican" by Harry Truman—and in fact Byrd continued to drift toward Dixiecrat revolt and then affinity for Republicans in national elections. See Ronald L. Heinemann, *Harry Byrd of Virginia* (Charlottesville: University Press of Virginia, 1996), 254 (first quotation in note), 255 (second quotation in note and quotation in text), 263, 368–69, and 412–13.

26. Ernest Obadele-Starks, *Black Unionism in the Industrial South* (College Station: Texas A&M University Press, 2000), 105–6.

27. Ricca, "American Right," 14 (Weyrich quoted) and 21 (NRA leader quoted). Paul Weyrich was one of the very few conservative voices to defend Trent Lott in the wake of the controversy over his remarks at Strom Thurmond's 100th birthday party that led to Lott's resignation as Senate majority leader. Weyrich dismissed the controversy as "political correctness" that "reared its ugly head again." Paul Weyrich, "Protecting Political Speech," http://www.freecongress.org (guest commentary), December 12, 2002.

28. David D. Kirkpatrick, "Churches See an Election Role and Spread the Word on Bush," *New York Times,* August 9, 2004 (first quotation); Jackie Calmes and John Harwood, "Bush's Big Priority: Energize Conservative Christian Base," *Wall Street Journal,* August 30, 2004 (second quotation).

29. Remark at Politics 2001 Workshop, Alabama AFL-CIO State Convention, Mobile, Alabama, October 30, 2001 (quoted).

30. Ricca, "American Right," 21 (Reed quoted).

31. On the disgraceful Max Cleland episode, David Gergen, a former Republican White House adviser, criticized the Georgia Republican tactics on MSNBC, November 6, 2002. See also Clarence Hobbs, Douglasville, Georgia, to Editor, and Peggy Davis, Atlanta, to Editor, *Atlanta Journal-Constitution,* November 11, 2002, A16. George W. Bush made five campaign visits to Georgia alone. See Jim Tharpe, "Zell Miller Criticizes Democrat Party Elite," *Atlanta Journal-Constitution,* November 9, 2002.

32. Ricca, "American Right," 15 (Weyrich quoted).

33. Ibid., 8–9. As one California Republican ally said confidently about Goldwater near the time of the 1964 purge of the progressive wing of the GOP, "the nigger issue will put him in the White House." Rick Perlstein, *Before the Storm: Barry Goldwater and the Unmaking of the American Consensus* (New York: Hill and Wang, 2001), 374 (quoted).

34. Ricca, "American Right," 11 (Dolan quotation) and 15 (Weyrich quotation). One of the tragic ironies of Dolan's life and his right-wing, homophobic brand of Christianity was that he died in 1984, of AIDS, as a closeted homosexual. See David

B. Smith, "You're Talking about Them, Not Me, Right God," *Voice of Prophecy,* http://www.vop.com, July 27, 2004 (second Dolan quotation). John Gallagher and Chris Bull, "Perfect Enemies: The Religious Right, the Gay Movement, and the Politics of the 1990s," *Washington Post,* ca. 1996 (second Dolan quotation repeated).

35. The term *compassionate conservatism* was first introduced and explained as a fail-safe strategy, in Harry S. Dent, *The Prodigal South Returns to Power* (New York: Wiley, 1978), 299 (quoted). For examples of its articulation, including on race, see "President Promotes Compassionate Conservatism," http://www.whitehouse.org, Parkside Hall, San Jose, California, April 2002; and George W. Bush, presidential proclamation, "Rededicating Ourselves to Dr. King's 'Dream,'" http://www.rnc.org, January 20, 2002. A representative, self-described "young urban Republican" from the Deep South explained recently that Trent Lott had to go—"The time had come. Enough's enough"—because he and others like him were "sick of having to explain that we aren't backward racists." Robert Lee Oldham, Southside Birmingham, Alabama, to Editor, *Birmingham News,* December 23, 2002, 10A (quoted). Although President Bush publicly maintained a hands-off policy on the Lott affair, his younger brother, Florida Governor Jeb Bush, top adviser Karl Rove, and conservatives such as black pundit Thomas Sowell of the Hoover Institution called for Lott's resignation as Senate majority leader—not because of what the statements represented, but largely because his continued presence "hurts [the] GOP" and its ability to make "inroads into the Democrats' virtual monopoly of minority votes in the years ahead," including the large Latino vote. Thomas Sowell, "Lott's Failure to Resign Post Hurts GOP," *Birmingham News,* December 19, 2002, 17A (quoted), 8A. Also see the *New York Times* and the *Atlanta Journal-Constitution,* both December 16, 2002. Conservative business Republican newspapers in the South, such as the *Birmingham News,* revealed much in their call for Lott to step aside, not because of any intrinsic offense ("It's not as if . . . Lott has committed the unpardonable sin"), but because his continued leadership, especially on the GOP's racial conservatism, had been compromised. "The question isn't one of forgiveness, but of Lott's ability to lead. And on that point, he is hopelessly compromised . . . with downright groveling, with Lott declaring support for affirmative action and . . . legislation to 'make amends.' Lott? A new shepherd of civil rights causes? . . . That doesn't make Lott a fitting leader for his own party." *Birmingham News,* December 19, 2002, 16A (quoted).

36. The ACLU charge was phoned into a conservative/libertarian radio talk show and heartily agreed with by the host. Caller to the conservative/libertarian "Richard Dixon Show," on WAPI 1070 AM, Birmingham, November 20, 2002 (quoted).

37. Amy Fagan, "Schwarzenegger Stands By 'Girlie Men' Comment," *Washington Times,* July 20, 2004 (first quotation); "Dems Arttack Schwarzenegger's 'Girlie Men' Comment," http://www.FOXNews.com, July 19, 2004 (first quotation); Tom McNamee, "Tell Arnold to Stop By Here," *Chicago Sun-Times,* September 6, 2004 (first quotation repeated at national GOP convention); Jeff Walker to Editor, Athens (Ga.) *Banner-Herald,* September 3, 2004, A10 (second quotation). George Allen has also referred to IRS agents as "buzzards gathering 'death taxes'" and the federal government as a "'grimy boot' trampling the rights of the people." See Michael Leahy, "A Player Who Doesn't Play It Safe: Impulsive George Allen Goes After Goals," *Washington Post,* October 3, 2000 (third quotation and quotations in note).

38. Kathy Pollitt, "The Girlie Vote," *The Nation,* September 14, 2004 (first quotation); Mara Liason, "Democrats Seek to Fire Up 'NASCAR Dads' Vote," on *Morning Edition,* http://www.npr.org, September 19, 2003 (second quotation).

39. Lionel Ledbetter, Adamsville, Alabama, to Editor, *Birmingham News,* April 14, 2002, 2C (quoted).

40. Alan Cooperman, "Bush Tells Catholic Group He Will Tackle Its Issues," *Washington Post,* August 3, 2004 (first quotation); Bill Howard, "President Bush Addresses Knights at Annual Convention," Catholic News Service, http://www.Catholic Herald.com, August 5, 2004 (second quotation).

41. The phrase "culture of life" is, of course, closely connected with Pope John Paul II's concentration on the subject of abortion. Cooperman, "Bush Tells Catholic Group" (second quotation); Alan Cooperman, "Openly Religious, to a Point," *Washington Post,* September 15, 2004 (first quotation).

42. Diefendorf, *Beneath the Cross;* David Batstone, "Jimmy Swaggart Tells Congregation He'd Kill Gays," *Sojourners Magazine,* http://www.sojo.net, September 22, 2004 (quotation).

43. *Ex parte H.H.,* supreme court of Alabama, February 15, 2003 (quotation). In the opinion, Moore went on at length that homosexual conduct was "abhorrent, immoral, detestable, a crime against nature, and a violation of the laws of nature and of nature's God upon which this Nation and our laws are predicated . . . and is destructive to a basic building block of society—the family." State Republican chairman Marty Connors did little to dispel the impression that the GOP was intolerant. Connors said, "In this age of political correctness, some people are going to condemn his outspokenness, but I'm certainly not. I think he's right." "Poll: Majority Oppose Gay Marriages, Less Approve of Moore's View," *Associated Press,* February 24, 2002 (Connors quotation). On Roy Moore's career, see Malcolm Cutchins, "Reagan, Bush, Justice Moore and the Walls," *Opelika-Auburn News,* February 27, 2002; Wendi Cermak, Irondale, Alabama, and Barry L. Mullins, Tuscaloosa, Alabama, to Editor, *Birmingham News,* both in March 4, 2002, 6A. Mullins's letter objects to an editorial cartoon depicting Moore as a "hate" monger; Elaine Witt, "Dispute Was Always about Judge Moore, Not God," *Birmingham Post-Herald,* November 19, 2002. Fob James lost his reelection bid in 1998 to Democrat Don Seigelman, not so much because of his erratic behavior, but more as a result of a viciously divisive Republican primary against economic conservative Winton Blount and his opposition to Seigelman's plan to finance public education through a state lottery. It is significant that Morris Dees's Southern Poverty Law Center, most frequently associated in the public mind with civil rights and antirace hate causes, was involved against Moore— evidence of moral chauvinism as the new racism.

44. On the 1987 demise of the Fairness Doctrine as part of FCC policy, see Bridget Gibson, "The New Un-Fairness Doctrine: What's That Smell?," *Baltimore Chronicle and Sentinel,* January 23, 2001; and "Broadcasting Fairness Doctrine Promised Balanced Coverage," July 25, 1997, the Wisdom Fund, http://www.twf.org. Predictably, the fastest and most vociferous defenders of the demise of the FCC's Fairness Doctrine have been people associated with the far right: Rush Limbaugh, Bill O'Reilly, and the Heritage Foundation. Judges Antonin Scalia and Robert Bork were part of the Washington, D.C., majority on the federal appeals court that overturned the law in a 1987 case. See Jeff Cohen, "The 'Hush Rush' Hoax," http://www.fair.org, November–December 1994; Bill O'Reilly, "The Fairness Doctrine," http://www.worldnetdaily.

org, January 17, 2002; and Adam Thierer, "Why the Fairness Doctrine Is Anything But," http://www.heritage.org, October 29, 1993.

45. At times, the word "crusade" is actually used. The extreme right-wing Catholic group, the America Life League, entitled its project to pressure American bishops to deny pro-choice politicians the Eucharist the "Crusade for the Defense of Our Catholic Church." See Jodi Enda, "The Politics of Communion," *Conscience* 25 (Summer/ Autumn 2004): 12–16, 14 (quotation). George W. Bush also invoked the term, twice, in reference to his war on terror. For European dismay at use of the term and its Catholic-Islamic historical roots, see Peter Ford, "Europe Cringes at Bush 'Crusade' against Terrorists," *Christian Science Monitor,* September 19, 2001; and James Carroll, "The Bush Crusade," *The Nation,* September 2, 2004.

46. Dan T. Carter, *From George Wallace to Newt Gingrich: Race in the Conservative Counterrevolution, 1963–1994* (Baton Rouge: Louisiana State University Press, 1996), 43 (first quotation). John Mitchell, U.S. attorney general in the Nixon administration and husband to Alabama native Martha Mitchell, understood Phillips's point well and agreed with it, but he put it in politer terms as the development of a "positive polarization" that would attract the vast majority of Wallace voters to the Republican Party. See Carter, *From George Wallace to Newt Gingrich,* 43–44; Dennis Crews, "Strange Bedfellows: Religion and Politics Are Becoming Too-Easy Partners in Today's—1984—America," *Yurica Report,* http://www.yuricareport.com, October 1984 (second quotation).

47. Kevin P. Phillips, *The Emerging Republican Majority* (New York: Anchor Books, 1970), 462–63 (quoted).

48. Harry Dent to Richard Nixon (memo), October 13, 1969, box 2, Harry Dent Files, Richard Nixon Presidential Materials, National Archives, College Park, Maryland. See also Carter, *From George Wallace to Newt Gingrich,* 28 and 44.

49. Joe McGinnis, *The Selling of the President, 1968* (New York: Trident Press, 1969), 125 (Phillips quoted).

50. John Brady, *Bad Boy: The Life and Politics of Lee Atwater* (Reading, Mass.: Addison-Wesley, 1997), 70 (Atwater quoted). On Atwater and Rove's relationship, see Robert Novak's syndicated column, *Birmingham News,* December 26, 2000, 15A. For Ailes's background and praise for his approach to "news," see Sean Hannity, *Let Freedom Ring: Winning the War of Liberty over Liberalism* (New York: Regan Books, 2002), 258.

51. Brady, *Bad Boy,* 96 (Atwater quoted) and 70 (quoted).

52. Ibid., 148 (quoted).

53. Carter, *From George Wallace to Newt Gingrich,* 118–19 (Gingrich et al., quoted).

54. Greenhaw, *Elephants in the Cotton Fields,* 97 (Wallace quoted). Wallace identified himself as a Republican before he died. His son, George Jr., serves as state treasurer in Alabama on the Republican ticket. See *Birmingham News,* November 6, 2002, 1P. Eugene "Bull" Connor's nephew, James T. "Jabo" Waggoner, is a Democrat-turned-Republican state legislator who openly admits that the number one conversion factor for old Southern Democrats to the modern Republican fold, at least in Alabama, has been race. Jabo Waggoner, oral interview conducted by Melody P. Izard, Birmingham, January 14, 2002, 1 (in possession of the author). Howard "Bo" Callaway, the Georgia political boss who left the Democratic Party to oversee the Republican Southern Strategy on the ground in the South during the Nixon years, agreed that

George Wallace's ideas about race and the federal government were the same ideas that attracted Southern whites to the modern Republican Party in droves. See Reg Murphy and Hal Gulliver, *The Southern Strategy* (New York: Charles Scribner's Sons, 1971), 1.

55. Notes from conversation with "JH," November 6, 2002, Birmingham. "Jared" on the *Paul Finebaum Show,* WERC 960 AM, November 7, 2002 (quoted), Birmingham.

56. Sheldon Hackney, *Populism to Progressivism in Alabama* (Princeton: Princeton University Press, 1969), 42 and 77.

57. On the evangelicalism of Baptists and Methodists constituting an official Southern religion, see Ownby, "Ethos Without Ethic," esp. 249. For fundamentalist views of Catholicism, see the work of Gershom Gorenberg. For example, Tim LaHaye—Reagan-Republican activist, founding member of the Moral Majority and the American Foundation for Traditional Values, and coauthor of the Left Behind series—described it as a "false religion." See Gershom Gorenberg, "Intolerance: The Bestseller: Book Review of the *Left Behind* Series," *American Prospect,* "One Year Later: America Alone," September 23, 2002 (quotation). Bob Jones III, president of Bob Jones University, termed Catholicism "a cult which calls itself Christian" and referred to the pope as "the Anti-Christ." Quotation in the *Associated Press,* April 8, 1994, September 11, 1987; the *Christian Century,* May 5, 1993; the *Atlanta Journal-Constitution,* June 30, 1991; the *Arizona Star,* March 7, 2000; and http://www.multiracial.com, August 31, 2000.

58. For an example of the relatively recent alliance between neoconservatives (including Jews) and fundamentalist Protestant groups enamored with Tim LaHaye and Jerry B. Jenkins's millennialist embrace of Jews and Israel as positive signs of the End Times, which include the forcible conversion of Jews to Christianity or the alternative of genocide, see the Norman Podhoretz interview conducted by Terri Gross, September 1, 2004, on National Public Radio's *Fresh Air* from Philadelphia, Pennsylvania.

59. For an example of the surreptitious endorsement of candidates and parties, see the morning announcements from the pulpit by the lector and "From the Pastor's Desk" by Rev. Martin M. Muller, Our Lady of Sorrows Catholic Church Sunday Bulletin, Homewood, Alabama, November 3, 2002. Of course, black churches do similar things on behalf of Democrats. Ironically, it has been conservatives, led by Alabama Republican Rick Sellers, who have filed lawsuits recently alleging violations of the tax code by black churches in the South. See Bill Walsh, "Republican Activist Cites Pulpit Speeches, " *New Orleans Times-Picayune,* December 13, 2002; and Melanie Hunter, "Activist Files IRS Complaint over Alleged Church Politiking," http://www.crosswalk.com, December 2002.

60. Landrieu narrowly won reelection over Republican Susie Terrell (a Lebanese American Catholic) because of a large black turnout, despite the fact that Louisiana Republicans engaged in a variety of strategies designed to suppress black voter turnout, including hiring blacks to stand in African American neighborhoods with placards smearing Landrieu and advising fellow blacks to vote against her. Terrell hedged her bets by stating that "As a practicing Catholic, I did not leave my faith, as did Mary Landrieu." Katharine Q. Seelye, "Senate Race Boils Over in Louisiana," *Birmingham Post-Herald,* December 6, 2002, B3 (all quotations). See also note 11 above.

61. See the pastor of Cross Creek Baptist Church, Pelham, Alabama, James L. Evans's objection to the direct nature of the voter guides as a violation of the tax code, in "Christian Coalition Breeches Trust," *Birmingham News/Birmingham Post-Herald,* December 7, 2002, D8 (first quotations); "The Riley Friends and Family Favorites Cookbook" (Birmingham: Bob Riley for Governor, 2002), back cover (second quotation) (in possession of the author). After moving to the pastorship of the First Baptist Church of Auburn, Alabama, Evans wrote that "Even though established as a nonprofit, nonpartisan voter education organization, everyone knows the [Christian] coalition is really a front for the Republican Party." See "Hypocrites Hide Goals in Cloak of Religion," *Birmingham News/Birmingham Post-Herald,* September 18, 2004, C10 (quoted in text).

62. See the Birmingham (Ala.) *One Voice,* August 25, 2000 (Curtiss quotation) and the plentiful, mostly positive, reaction to Curtiss's declaration, equating voting the Democratic ticket with sin and some going on to defend the Republican program on its issues, even economics, in subsequent issues of *One Voice,* September 8, 15, 22, and 29, and October 6, 2000; Seelye, "Senate Race Boils Over," B3 (Hannan quotation); "Bishop to Gov. Davis: Choose Abortion or Communion," http://www.NewsMax.com, January 23, 2003 (Weigand quotations); and "Bishop Says Pro-Abortion Politicians Should Not Receive Communion," *One Voice,* January 31, 2003, 5 (Weigand quotations repeated). In his usual fashion, far right Republican/Catholic theologian George Weigel dismissed any possible nuanced position on abortion as "morally incoherent" while sticking to his, ostensibly, consistent and coherent position of apologia for big business theology and prowar spirituality. See "The End of 'I'm Personally Opposed, But . . . ,'" *Catholic Difference,* syndicated column in the *One Voice,* February 14, 2003, 4 (quotations in note and also Weigand quotations repeated). Kirkpatrick, "Churches See an Election Role" (Ghio quotation), and Burke information. Marquette University political scientist and amateur Catholic theologian Christopher Wolfe virtually echoed Ghio's comments at a Birmingham religious conference held at the ultraconservative Briarwood Presbyterian Church, "Churches at the Crossroads in the Public Square." Wolfe told the assembled Protestants that he could not imagine how a serious Catholic could consider voting for John Kerry. See "Religion" section of the *Birmingham Post-Herald,* October 23, 2004.

Very few outlying voices of dissent have been heard. One is that of Fr. Andrew M. Greeley, the Chicago priest, sociologist, and best-selling novelist who dismissed as nonsense the idea that one is no longer Catholic for doctrinal differences with the pope such as those on abortion: "one stops being Catholic only when one formally renounces the Church or joins another Church." Greeley, "Why I'm Still a Catholic," http://www.agreeley.com, ca. 2004 (quoted). When the Rev. Richard J. Tillman, of St. Charles Borromeo Church in Missouri, spoke openly that Catholic issues of life also applied to the Iraq War, the Bush campaign disinvited him from delivering an invocation when Bush spoke in St. Charles, a St. Louis suburb. See Kirkpatrick, "Churches See an Election Role."

63. Ratzinger's remarks actually appeared at the bottom of a one-page confidential memo sent to Cardinal Theodore E. McCarrick of Washington, the chair of a committee of American bishops charged with exploring the role of Catholics in public life. The Italian press reported the remarks in June 2004, but they did not appear in the United States until the *Detroit Free Press* reported them on September 6. Out-

spoken St. Louis Archbishop Raymond L. Burke grudgingly admitted that "in theory" there might be such proportionate reasons but could not help but adding that in practice, "it is difficult to imagine" what they could be. Alan Cooperman, "Catholic Voters Given Leeway on Abortion Rights Issue," *Washington Post,* September 7, 2004 (Ratzinger and Burke quotations). Ultraconservative lay theologian George Weigel expressed doubt that proportionate reasons could even be found. See "Cardinal Ratzinger and the Conscience of Catholic Voters," Catholic Difference column in the *One Voice,* September 17, 2004, 4. Eleven days after Cardinal Ratzinger's confidential memo was made public, Atlanta archbishop John Donoghue instructed the faithful of his archdiocese that "You have an erroneous conscience if you think there is some case in which you can vote for a pro-abortion candidate. You're wrong as far as church teaching is concerned." It was permissible for Catholics to debate other issues and come to nuanced positions, "but there's no debate about abortion. It is intrinsically evil. It is way above other issues as far as evil is concerned." His comments relied partially on the views of a theologian with the highly conservative Catholic Eternal Word Television Network (EWTN), headquartered in Irondale, Alabama. Gayle White, "Let Abortion Guide Vote," *Atlanta Journal-Constitution,* September 17, 2004 (Donoghue quotations). A day later, after an uproar over the publication of Donoghue's comments in the *Georgia Bulletin,* the newspaper of the archdiocese, the archbishop backed down. Parsing his earlier statements, Donoghue said he did not mean to tell his flock how to vote but only "how to decide" how to vote. Although he insisted that abortion still outweighed every other single issue, Donoghue conceded that it did "not necessarily outweigh all other issues combined." Gayle White, "Catholic Voters Told to Carefully Sift Issues," *Atlanta Journal-Constitution,* September 18, 2004 (quoted). Burke, though, remained completely unrepentant. Timing his comments just two days before John Kerry and George W. Bush arrived in St. Louis for the second of their televised presidential debates, Burke spoke out as if Ratzinger's statement had never been made public, informing the half-million plus Catholics in his archdiocese that voting for a candidate who supported abortion rights, stem cell research, or same-sex marriage (which, by the way, Kerry does not) would constitute a "grave sin" and that abortion was clearly more important than other life issues such as war and the death penalty (commonly identified with George W. Bush). P. J. Huffstutter, "St. Louis Catholics Debate Political Directive," *Los Angeles Times,* October 7, 2004 (quotation).

64. Bumper stickers at Our Lady of Sorrows Catholic Church parking lot, Birmingham, September 21, 2004 (both quoted).

65. See *One Voice,* e.g., 27, 2002, 1 (anti–war in Iraq), November 15, 2002, 1 (environmental conservation) and 2 (race relations); November 22, 2002, 1 (anti–war in Iraq and poverty issues); November 8, 2002, 1 (charitable giving); August 9, 2002, 1 and 11 (abortion and pro–George W. Bush); November 1, 2002, 13 (abortion compared with the civil rights movement); December 20, 2002, 4 (abortion and the Democratic Party), December 27, 2002, 2 (abortion and homosexuality).

66. "It's Time to Elect Candidates Who Will Protect Life!," Priests for Life flyer, 2004 (quotations), in possession of the author.

67. Most Reverend David E. Foley, D.D., bishop of Birmingham in Alabama to Dear Family in Christ, *One Voice,* June 25, 2004, 1 (quoted). Foley maintained a deafening silence after the publication of Cardinal Ratzinger's confidential memo in September 2004, allowing archconservative lay theologian George Weigel to inter-

pret the memo and its implications for the diocese. See George Weigel, "Cardinal Ratzinger and the Conscience of Catholic Voters," 4.

68. Glenn Feldman, "'Voters Guide' Doesn't Give Official Catholic Position," *Birmingham Post-Herald,* October 28, 2004, A9; and Feldman, "Catholic Bishops Repudiating Church Teachings in Subservience to GOP," unpublished essay, ca. October 2004, in possession of the author.

69. George Weigel, "Parsing the Peace Movement," *One Voice,* May 9, 2003, 4. (quoted). On the raft of extreme right-wing supporters and individuals associated with the Ethics and Public Policy Center—such as Richard Mellon Scaife, Chuck Colson, Antonin Scalia, and Richard Perle—see http://www.eppc.org. Considerable Vatican opposition to America's plans to wage preemptive war against Iraq were made clear to the Bush administration and to the world. See the statement of Cardinal Pio Laghi, special envoy of John Paul II to President George Bush, March 5, 2003, declaration by the Holy See press office director Joaquin Navarro-Valls, March 18, 2003; declaration by the Secretariat of State on the Iraqi Conflict, April 10, 2003; address of John Paul II to the Bishops of Indonesia on Their Ad Limina Visit to Rome, March 29, 2003; address of Pope John Paul II to the Honorable George W. Bush, President of the United States of America, June 4, 2004; all documents available at http://www.vatican.va. See also "Saddam's Capture May Bring Peace, Doesn't Excuse War, Cardinal Says," ca. 2003, Catholic News Service, http://www.americancatholic.org. The article addressed the statements of Cardinal Renato R. Martino, head of the Pontifical Council for Justice and Peace, located in the Vatican.

A favorite sophistic tack of Weigel's has been to equate the pro-life movement (limited to abortion and not extending to war or capital punishment) with the civil rights movement, calling abortion "the great civil rights issue of our time" and spouting other slogans such as "A 'pro-choice Catholic' makes no more sense than a 'pro-segregation Catholic.'" See George Weigel, "Pro-Life Wins, Trouble for Catholic Democrats," syndicated column in *One Voice,* December 20, 2002, 4 (both quotations in note), "Roe v. Wade at 30," *One Voice,* January 17, 2003, 4 (first quotation in note repeated); and "Speaker [Father Richard John Neuhaus] Compares Pro-Life Struggle to 1960s Civil Rights Movement," *One Voice,* November 1, 2002, 13.

70. George Weigel, "No Just War Possible?," *One Voice,* April 4, 2003, 4 (quoted).

71. John S. Martignoni to Editor, *One Voice,* October 6, 2000, 5 (quoted).

72. ROF to author, 27, 2004 (quotation), forwarding message from Frankiebaby, e-mail in possession of the author.

73. Falwell commentary in http://www.WorldNetDaily (first quotation) and the *New York Times,* July 16, 2004 (second quotation), both on the *Sojourners* website, http://www.sojo.net, August 26, 2004. Falwell's comment about "thugs" came in relation to his determination to encourage evangelical pastors to involve themselves and their congregations in the 2004 presidential election without being "intimidate[d] . . . into silence" by threats of IRS penalties. Falwell's "Old-Time Gospel Hour" was fined by the IRS in the 1980s. Brian Faler, "Falwell on 'Thugs' and Taxes," *Washington Post,* 5, 2004 (third quotation).

74. Jerry Z. Muller, *The Mind and the Market: Capitalism in Modern European Thought* (New York: Alfred A. Knopf, 2002), 79 (quotations).

75. As an example of this, see Kenneth P. Lavelle, Birmingham, to Editor, *One Voice,* September 15, 2000, 4; Reed Billman, Huntsville, Alabama, to Editor, *One Voice,*

September 29, 2000, 5; John S. Martignoni, Pleasant Grove, Alabama, to Editor, *One Voice*, October 6, 2000, 5.

76. For examples of culture wars fought out in different places and times, see Darrin M. McMahon, *Enemies of the Enlightenment and the Making of Modernity* (New York: Oxford University Press, 2001); and for a recent individual example, see Sheldon Hackney, *The Politics of Presidential Appointment: A Memoir of the Culture War* (Montgomery, Ala.: NewSouth Books, 2002).

77. Gordon Ellis to Editor, *South: The News Magazine of Dixie,* February 1966, 4 (first quotation), Major Squirm's column, *South,* October 1966, 22 (second quotation); C. M. Cason Sr. to Editor, *South,* October 1965, 4 (third quotation); Fred Morrissey to Editor, *South,* December 1966, 4 (fourth quotation); and Rev. Fred Peters to Editor, *South,* May 1967, 4 (fourth quotation).

78. *Official Proceedings of the Constitutional Convention of the State of Alabama, May 21st, 1901 to Sept.3, 1901* (Wetumpka, Ala.: Wetumpka Printing Co., 1940), 3: 3079 (quoted).

79. Ibid., 3:2841 (quoted).

80. *Birmingham News,* September 13, 1951 (first quotation); Horace C. Wilkinson to Dr. Duke McCall, Southern Baptist Theological Seminary, ca. 1954 (second quotation); and Wilkinson, "One World in Christ," unpublished Sunday school lesson, July 19, 1953 (third quotation), both in the Papers of Horace W. Weissinger, in possession of the author.

81. Workplace safety is a definite consideration here. But work without civility, respect, or even dignity is an even more mundane possibility. See, for example, the Sunday homily of Father Michael J. Deering, ca. September 2002, Our Lady of Sorrows Catholic Church, Birmingham. Notes in possession of the author.

82. See notes 21–25 above.

83. Interview with Martha Hooper, 172 (first quotation) and interview with the Rev. Dr. Benny Hooper, 196 (second quotation); both interviews conducted in Brownsville, Tennessee, by Jan Voogt; Jan Voogt, "The War in Vietnam: The View from a Southern Community; Brownsville, Haywood County, Tennessee," unpublished manuscript in possession of the author; Mary Orndorff, "Commandments Monument to Go across Country," *Birmingham News,* July 16, 2004.

84. Cooperman, "Bush Tells Catholic Group"; and Cooperman, "Openly Religious, to a Point."

85. Natalie M. Davis, "Pine Tree Reveals Much about State," *Birmingham News,* November 26, 2000, C1. On this general topic, see also Nell Irvin Painter, *Southern History across the Color Line* (Chapel Hill: University of North Carolina Press, 2002); Glenda Elizabeth Gilmore, *Gender and Jim Crow: Women and the Politics of White Supremacy in North Carolina, 1896–1920* (Chapel Hill: University of North Carolina Press, 1996); Joel R. Williamson, *The Crucible of Race: Black/White Relations in the American South since Emancipation* (New York: Oxford University Press, 1984); and Jacquelyn Dowd Hall, *Revolt against Lynching: Jesse Daniel Ames and the Women's Campaign against Lynching* (New York: Columbia University Press, 1979),

86. On this subject, see Nancy MacLean, *Behind the Mask of Chivalry: The Making of the Second Ku Klux Klan* (New York: Oxford University Press, 1994); and Kathleen M. Blee, *Women of the Klan: Racism and Gender in the 1920s* (Berkeley: University of California Press, 1991).

87. Host Russ Fine soap comment about aerobic dance instructor and fitness

guru Richard Simmons on the *Russ and Dee Show,* WYDE, 101.1 FM, Birmingham, on December 19, 2002 (quoted). The Fines also had an "apoplectic" response to federal circuit court of appeals Judge Myron Thompson's order to Alabama supreme court Chief Justice Roy Moore, giving him thirty days to remove his granite monument, placed in the rotunda of the state judicial building in the middle of the night. Elaine Witt to author (e-mail), November 20, 2002 (quoted). The Fines also reacted negatively to Trent Lott's apologies and backing off of affirmative action: "It's [the issue] not important. . . . This weakens us [with regard to the looming war with Iraq]. . . . Lott is a four-letter word. . . . I just need to be angry right now." Dee Fine on December 17, 2002 (quoted). The Fines are conservative Southern Jews.

88. See note 83 above.

89. See note 5 above.

90. See note 22 above.

91. Of course, this was a clear Social Darwinist argument. See the classic study by Richard Hofstadter, *Social Darwinism in American Thought* (Boston: Beacon Press, 1955).

92. See text associated with note 86.

93. Along with Falwell, Tom Delay and Alabama supreme court Chief Justice Roy Moore (all of whom are Republicans) have articulated a view of "religion" that includes only Christianity. See Sarah Schulman, "Falwell Places Foot in Mouth," (Birmingham) *Kaleidoscope,* October 15, 2002, 4; Paul Krugman, "Gotta Have Faith," *New York Times,* December 17, 2002; and Witt, "Dispute Was Always about Judge Moore."

94. For example, see, among others, Ulrich Bonnell Phillips, "The Central Theme of Southern History," *American Historical Review* 34 (October 1928): 30–43; Kenneth M. Stampp, *The Peculiar Institution: Slavery in the Antebellum South* (New York: Alfred A. Knopf, 1956); George Brown Tindall, *The Ethnic Southerners* (Baton Rouge: Louisiana State University Press, 1976); Cash, *The Mind of the South;* C. Vann Woodward, *The Burden of Southern History* (Baton Rouge: Louisiana State University Press, 1960); Paul K. Conkin, "Hot, Humid, and Sad," *Journal of Southern History* 64 (February 1998): 3–22; and Charles Marsh, *God's Long Summer: Stories of Faith and Civil Rights* (Princeton: Princeton University Press, 1997); Sheldon Hackney, "The Ambivalent South," in *Warm Ashes: Issues in Southern History at the Dawn of the Twenty-first Century,* ed. Winfred B. Moore Jr., Kyle S. Sinisi, and David H. White Jr. (Columbia: University of South Carolina Press, 2003), 385–95.

95. Robert Reich, "Who Really Picks the Next President," August 26, 2004, and "The Real Battle in the Battle Ground," September 22, 2004, Public Radio's Marketplace Commentaries, http://www.robertreich.org; D. Stephen Voss, "Strength in the Center," http://www.digitas.harvard.edu, ca. 2004.

96. WMS to JMF et al., August 20, 2004 (first and second quotations) and WMS to EC, October 1, 2004 (third quotation), both in possession of the author.

97. Two books that very ably address this political topic are Dan T. Carter, *From George Wallace to Newt Gingrich;* and Wayne Greenhaw, *Elephants in the Cottonfields.* Author's conversations with ADH, Homewood, Alabama, October 1998 (quotation), and with RRR, Dawson Memorial Baptist Church picnic, Homewood, Alabama, April 3, 2004 (author's notes in possession of the author).

98. On the media aspect, see E. J. Dionne Jr., "The Rightward Press," *Washington Post,* December 6, 2002. The negative aspects of hate–talk radio character assassina-

tion are "easier for voters to understand" and provide a "good guy/bad guy" factor, according to Larry Powell, a communications studies professor. (Birmingham) *Kaleidoscope*, October 15, 2002, 1 (quoted). There are numerous examples of this type of tabloid politics. For example, see Hannity, *Let Freedom Ring*. Princeton economist Paul Krugman, in "Reading the Script," *New York Times*, August 3, 2004, commented that "FOX News is for all practical purposes a G.O.P. propaganda agency." On the repetitive nature of the right-wing propaganda on Fox News and AM radio, see Bob Herbert, "Admit We Have a Problem," *New York Times*, August 9, 2004. Arianna Huffington, a former Republican, lamented how the GOP "relentlessly hammer[s] home their lies, and the other side had to let them get away with it . . . pounded home, Rove-style, day after day, week after week, until it sinks in." As a result, she noted in September 2004, 42 percent of Americans "still think Saddam [Hussein] was 'directly involved in planning, financing or carrying out the terrorist attacks'" of 9/11. See Arianna Huffington, "Special Delivery: A Hogwarts Howler for the American Voter," http://www.ariannaonline.com, ca. September 15, 2004 (quoted).

99. Juan Gonzales in "Media *Is* the Issue," September 2, 2004 (quoted), http://www.freepress.net. For this type of underrreporting on the march to war in Iraq, see the interview with filmmaker Robert Greenwald about his documentaries *Outfoxed* and *Uncovered, Washington Post*, August 2, 2004; on the carnage in Iraq after the United States passed off sovereignty to an Iraqi government in June 2004, see Paul Krugman, "Taking on the Myth," *New York Times*, September 14, 2004. E. J. Dionne noted that "Limbaugh's new respectability is the surest sign that the conservative talk network is now bleeding into what passes for the mainstream media, just as the unapologetic conservatism of the Fox News Channel is now affecting programming on other cable networks. This shift to the right is occurring as cable becomes a steadily more important source of news." Dionne, "Rightward Press" (quoted in note). The *Columbia Journalism Review* concluded, after monitoring coverage of the 2004 Republican Convention, that CNN "has stooped to slavish imitation of Fox's most dubious ploys and policies." See Krugman, "Reading the Script" (quotation in note); Alessandra Stanley agreed that CNN had "not been much more helpful" even than Fox "in separating fact from fiction" in the media free-for-all after the dubious but damaging claims against John Kerry of the Swift Boat Veterans for Justice. See Stanley, "On Cable, a Fog of Words about Kerry's War Record," *New York Times*, August 24, 2004 (quoted in note).

100. C. Vann Woodward, *The Strange Career of Jim Crow* (1955; reprint, Baton Rouge: Louisiana State University Press, 1974), 166.

101. David R. Davies, ed., *The Press and Race: Mississippi Journalists Confront the Movement* (Jackson: University Press of Mississippi, 2001), 9 (Carter quoted).

102. Gunnar Myrdal, *An American Dilemma: The Negro Problem and American Democracy*, 2 vols. (New York: Harper and Brothers, 1944), 1:440 (quotation). Myrdal went on: "Part of the explanation is that Southern conservatism is 'reactionary' in the literal sense of the word. It has preserved an ideological allegiance not only to *the status quo*, but to *status quo ante*. The region is still carrying the heritage of slavery" (1:441).

103. Alexander P. Lamis, ed., *Southern Politics in the 1990s* (Baton Rouge: Louisiana State University Press, 1999), 21 (quoted).

104. John Dos Passos, *State of the Nation* (Boston: Houghton Mifflin, 1944), 82 (quotation). See also Tindall, *Emergence of the New South*, 709.

105. William Warren Rogers and Robert David Ward realized this tendency in Alabama history, particularly during its progressive era, that, "in retrospect it has been possible to affix the progressive label to all but the most cynical of reactionaries.... Historians have bestowed the sobriquet [too] liberally." William Warren Rogers, Robert David Ward, Leah Rawls Atkins, and Wayne Flynt, *Alabama: The History of a Deep South State* (Tuscaloosa: University of Alabama Press, 1994), 362 and 375 (quoted).

106. Bill Keller, "Reagan's Son: The Radical Presidency of George W. Bush," *New York Times Magazine*, January 26, 2003; and Garrison Keillor, "We're Not in Lake Wobegon Anymore," *In These Times,* August 26, 2004 (quotations). On Greenspan, see Edmund L. Andrews, "Warning Anew about Retiree Expectations," *New York Times,* August 28, 2004. Princeton economist Paul Krugman denounced Greenspan for "betray[ing] his principles" and lending "crucial aid and comfort to the most fiscally irresponsible administration in history. . . . He never said, 'Let's raise taxes and cut benefits for working families so that we can give big tax cuts to the rich!' But that's the end result of his advice." See "The Maestro Slips Out of Tune," *New York Times,* June 6, 2004 (quoted in note). See also John Eisenhower, "Another View: Why I Will Vote for John Kerry for President," (New Hampshire) *Union Leader,* September 28, 2004; and, by a former leading Republican strategist, Kevin Phillips, *American Dynasty: Aristocracy, Fortune, and the Politics of Deceit in the House of Bush* (New York: Viking Books, 2004).

107. Elaine Witt noted that Roy Moore's granite monument of the Ten Commandments was also pastiched with selected patriotic quotes in the *Birmingham Post-Herald,* November 19, 2002.

108. Populism sometimes, but rarely, bled into socialism. See Hackney, *Populism to Progressivism,* 115. But despite this reality, it was sometimes perceived as such. See Hugh C. Davis, "Hilary A. Herbert: Bourbon Apologist," *Alabama Review* 20 (July 1967): 222.

109. Unionist participant at the Politics and Labor Issues session at the North Carolina AFL-CIO Leadership School, at the University of North Carolina at Wilmington, July 21–23, 1999 (quoted). A white female member of the UAW in North Alabama explained that she voted Republican in the 2000 presidential election because of "Clinton's sexual escapades . . . moral issues." She voted Republican in the 2002 midterm elections because "I was scared" in a military/terrorism sense, and Democrats have never been known as "being safety-minded. . . . If Clinton had had another term, 9/11 would've been nothing compared to what would have happened." Paid Employment Leave class, United Auto Workers/Daimler-Chrysler Training Center, Huntsville, Alabama, December 3, 2002 (quoted).

110. Cash, *The Mind of the South.*

111. Caveat: because this theorem concerns human beings and their behavior as its subject matter, it is, unlike theorems in the hard sciences, subject to the whims, caprices, idiosyncrasies, predilections, and free will choices of human beings. That is, it is not foolproof—nor does it have to be. But it is an accurate indicator of how people behave in societies that is based on detailed historical observation.

112. Stan Bailey, "Damned to Hell," *Birmingham News,* July 14, 2004 (quotation). Of course, once contacted, Moore denied that he had made the comments, although they are, regrettably, in keeping with much of the sentiment of his other public remarks.

113. *Birmingham News,* September 10, 2003; Paul Krugman, "The Tax-Cut Con," *New York Times Magazine,* September 14, 2003 (quotation). For Riley's fiscally and social conservative career in Congress and the influence of University of Alabama tax law Professor Susan Pace Hamill's divinity school thesis on Riley, see Adam Cohen, "What Would Jesus Do? Sock It to Alabama's Corporate Landowners," *New York Times,* June 10, 2003.

114. Alabama's Democratic chair and the mostly Democratic Alabama Education Association endorsed the Riley initiative. See Dale Russakoff, "Alabama Tied in Knots by Tax Vote," *Washington Post,* August 17, 2003 (all quotations); and "Alabama Governor Ties $1.2B Tax Package Vote to Christian Duty," *Charleston Post and Courier,* July 30, 2003, http://www.charleston.net. See also *Birmingham News,* September 10, 2003; Krugman, "Tax-Cut Con." Marty Connors's excessive pride in Alabama's old Reconstruction-based defiance to federal authority would be perverse anywhere else for a Republican except, perhaps, in the Deep South. In denouncing the tax plan, Connors cheerfully boasted, apparently without a trace of irony, "In Alabama, it is part of our DNA to distrust government. We have a rich tradition of cynicism and defiance." Kyle Whitmire, "Reading, Riley, and Arithmetic: Governor's Tax Plan Faces Long Odds and Tough Opposition," *Birmingham Weekly,* July 17–24, 2003, 5 (quotation in note). For details of Malone's compensation, see Jerry Underwood, "SouthTrust Deal Hurts Rank-and-File," *Birmingham News,* July 18, 2004; and Ryan Mahoney, "Malone to Leave SouthTrust Board after Retirement," *Birmingham Business Journal,* April 21, 2004.

115. Russakoff, "Alabama Tied in Knots" (quotation).

116. Whitmire, "Reading, Riley and Arithmetic," 4 (quotation).

117. *Birmingham News,* September 10, 2003. "Governor Riley's State of the Union Address," February 1, 2005, http://www.governorpress.alabama.gov. For strong opposition to the Riley plan from among lower-middle-class and poor Alabamians, see Russakoff, "Alabama Tied in Knots" and "Alabama Governor Ties $1.2B Tax Package Vote to Christian Duty."

Selected Bibliography

Aamodt, Terrie Dopp. *Righteous Armies, Holy Cause: Apocalyptic Imagery and the Civil War.* Macon, Ga.: Mercer University Press, 2002.

Allen, Frederick Lewis. *Only Yesterday: An Informal History of the 1920s.* New York: Alfred A. Knopf, 1931.

Alvis, Joel L., Jr. *Religion and Race: Southern Presbyterians, 1946–1983.* Tuscaloosa: University of Alabama Press, 1994.

Ammerman, Nancy. *Baptist Battles: Social Conflict and Religious Conflict in the Southern Baptist Convention.* New Brunswick, N.J.: Rutgers University Press, 1990.

Applebome, Peter. *Dixie Rising: How the South Is Shaping American Values, Politics, and Culture.* New York: Times Books, 1996.

Atkins, Leah Rawls, William Warren Rogers, Robert David Ward, and Wayne Flynt. *Alabama: The History of a Deep South State.* Tuscaloosa: University of Alabama Press, 1994.

Ayers, Edward L. *The Promise of the New South: Life after Reconstruction.* New York: Oxford University Press, 1992.

Bailey, Fred Arthur. "'The Work among the Colored Brethren': Race, Religion, and Social Order in the New South, 1890–1920." *West Tennessee Historical Society Papers* 55 (2002): 55–71.

Bailey, Kenneth. *Southern White Protestantism in the Twentieth Century.* New York: Harper and Row, 1964.

Barkun, Michael. *Religion and the Racist Right.* Chapel Hill: University of North Carolina Press, 1994.

Bartley, Numan V. *The New South, 1945–1980.* Baton Rouge: Louisiana State University Press, 1995.

———. *The Rise of Massive Resistance: Race and Politics in the South during the 1950s.* Baton Rouge: Louisiana State University Press, 1969.

Bauman, Mark K., and Berkley Kalin, eds. *The Quiet Voices: Southern Rabbis and Black Civil Rights, 1880s to 1990s.* Tuscaloosa: University of Alabama Press, 1997.

Bauman, Mark K., and Arnold Shankman. "The Rabbi as Ethnic Broker: The Case of David Marx." *Journal of American Ethnic History* (Spring 1983): 71–95.

Black, Earl, and Merle Black. *Politics and Society in the South*. Cambridge: Harvard University Press, 1987.

Black, Gregory D. *The Catholic Crusade against the Movies, 1940–1975*. Cambridge: Cambridge University Press, 1997.

Blee, Kathleen M. *Women of the Klan: Racism and Gender in the 1920s*. Berkeley: University of California Press, 1991.

Bode, Frederick A. *Protestantism and the New South: North Carolina Baptists and Methodists in Political Crisis, 1894–1903*. Charlottesville: University Press of Virginia, 1975.

———. "Religion and Class Hegemony: A Populist Critique in North Carolina." *Journal of Southern History* 37 (August 1971): 417–38.

Boles, John B., and Evelyn Thomas Nolen, eds. *Interpreting Southern History: Historiographical Essays in Honor of Sanford W. Higginbotham*. Baton Rouge: Louisiana State University Press, 1987.

Boyer, Paul. *When Time Shall Be No More: Prophecy Belief in Modern American Culture*. Cambridge: Harvard University Press, 1992.

Branch, Taylor. *Parting the Waters: America in the King Years, 1954–1963*. New York: Touchstone, 1988.

Breslin, Jimmy. *The Church That Forgot Christ*. New York: Free Press, 2004.

Brownell, Blaine A., and David R. Goldfield. *The City in Southern History: The Growth of Urban Civilization in the South*. Port Washington, N.Y.: Kennikat Press, 1977.

Campbell, Ernest Q., and Thomas F. Pettigrew. *Christians in Racial Crisis: A Study of Little Rock's Ministry*. Washington, D.C.: Public Affairs Press, 1959.

Carpenter, Joel. *Revive Us Again: The Reawakening of American Fundamentalism*. New York: Oxford University Press, 1997.

Carter, Dan T. *From George Wallace to Newt Gingrich: Race in the Conservative Counterrevolution, 1963–1994*. Baton Rouge: Louisiana State University Press, 1996.

———. *The Politics of Rage: George Wallace, the Origins of the New Conservatism, and the Transformation of American Politics*. 2nd ed. Baton Rouge: Louisiana State University Press, 2000.

Cash, W. J. *The Mind of the South*. New York: Alfred A. Knopf, 1941.

Chappell, David L. *A Stone of Hope: Prophetic Religion and the Death of Jim Crow*. Chapel Hill: University of North Carolina Press, 2003.

Clark, Elmer T. *The Negro and His Religion*. Nashville: Cokesbury Press, 1924.

Clayton, Bruce. *The Savage Ideal: Intolerance and Intellectual Leadership in the South, 1890–1914*. Baltimore: Johns Hopkins University Press, 1972.

Collins, Donald. *When the Church Bell Rang Racist: The Methodist Church and the Civil Rights Movement in Alabama*. Macon, Ga.: Mercer University Press, 1998.

Cook, Elizabeth Adell, Ted G. Jelen, and Clyde Wilcox. "Issue Voting in Gubernatorial Elections: Abortion in Post-*Webster* Politics." *Journal of Politics* 56 (1994): 187–99.

Cook, Raymond A. *Fire from the Flint: The Amazing Career of Thomas Dixon.* Winston-Salem, N.C.: John F. Blair, 1968.

———. *Thomas Dixon.* New York: Twayne, 1974.

Crawford, Sue E. S., and Laura R. Olson, eds. *Christian Clergy in American Politics.* Baltimore: Johns Hopkins University Press, 2001.

Dailey, Jane. "Sex, Segregation, and the Sacred after *Brown.*" *Journal of American History* 91 (June 2004): 119–44.

Dailey, Jane, Glenda Elizabeth Gilmore, and Bryant Simon, eds. *Jumpin' Jim Crow: Southern Politics from Civil War to Civil Rights.* Princeton: Princeton University Press, 2000.

Dalhouse, Taylor. *An Island in the Lake of Fire: Bob Jones University, Fundamentalism, and the Separatist Movement.* Athens: University of Georgia Press, 1996.

Daniel, Pete. *Lost Revolutions: The South in the 1950s.* Chapel Hill: Smithsonian Institute and the University of North Carolina Press, 2000.

Deaton, Thomas M. "Atlanta during the Progressive Era." Ph.D. diss., University of Georgia, 1969.

Dent, Harry S. *The Prodigal South Returns to Power.* New York: Wiley, 1978.

Diamond, Sara. *Not by Politics Alone: The Enduring Influence of the Christian Right.* New York: Guilford, 1998.

Diefendorf, Barbara B. *Beneath the Cross: Catholics and Huguenots in Sixteenth-century Paris.* Oxford: Oxford University Press, 1991.

Dinnerstein, Leonard. *The Leo Frank Case.* New York: Columbia University Press, 1968.

Dittmer, John. *Black Georgia in the Progressive Era, 1913–1945.* Baton Rouge: Louisiana State University Press, 1977.

———. *Local People: The Struggle for Civil Rights in Mississippi.* Urbana: University of Illinois Press, 1994.

Doyle, Don H. *New Men, New Cities, New South: Atlanta, Nashville, Charleston, and Mobile, 1860–1910.* Chapel Hill: University of North Carolina Press, 1990.

Dunn, Charles W., ed. *Religion in American Politics.* Washington, D.C.: Congressional Quarterly Press, 1989.

Dunnavant, Anthony L. "David Lipscomb and the 'Preferential Option for the Poor' among Post-Bellum Churches of Christ." In *Poverty and Ecclesiology: Nineteenth-century Evangelicals in the Light of Liberation Theology,* edited by Anthony L. Dunnavant, 27–50. Collegeville, Minn.: Liturgical Press, 1992.

Eagles, Charles W. "The Closing of Mississippi: Will Campbell, the $64,000 Question, and Religious Emphasis Week at the University of Mississippi." *Journal of Southern History* 67 (May 2001): 331–72.

Egerton, John. *The Americanization of Dixie: The Southernization of America.* New York: Harper's Magazine Press, 1974.

———. *Speak Now against the Day: The Generation before the Civil Rights*

Movement in the South. Chapel Hill: University of North Carolina Press, 1994.

Eighmy, John Lee. *Churches in Cultural Captivity: A History of Social Attitudes of Southern Baptists.* Knoxville: University of Tennessee Press, 1972.

Elmer, Michael H., and Eugene M. Tobin. *The Age of Urban Reform.* Port Washington, N.Y.: Kennikat Press, 1977.

Feldman, Glenn. *From Demagogue to Dixiecrat: Horace Wilkinson and the Politics of Race.* Lanham, Md.: University Press of America, 1995.

———. *Politics, Society, and the Klan in Alabama, 1915–1949.* Tuscaloosa: University of Alabama Press, 1999.

———, ed. *Reading Southern History: Essays on Interpreters and Interpretations.* Tuscaloosa: University of Alabama Press, 2001.

———. "Soft Opposition: Elite Acquiescence and Klan-Sponsored Terrorism in Alabama, 1946–1950." *Historical Journal* 40, no. 3 (1997): 753–77.

Fink, Gary M. *The Fulton Bag and Cotton Mills Strike of 1914–1915: Espionage, Labor Conflict, and New South Industrial Relations.* Ithaca: Cornell University Press, 1993.

Flynt, Wayne. *Alabama Baptists: Southern Baptists in the Heart of Dixie.* Tuscaloosa: University of Alabama Press, 1998.

Frady, Marshall. *Billy Graham: Parable of American Righteousness.* Boston: Little, Brown, 1979.

Friedland, Michael. *Lift Up Your Voice Like a Trumpet: White Clergy and the Civil Rights and Antiwar Movements, 1954–1973.* Chapel Hill: University of North Carolina Press, 1998.

Gaston, Paul M. *The New South Creed: A Study in Southern Mythmaking.* New York: Alfred A. Knopf, 1970.

Gilmore, Glenda Elizabeth. *Gender and Jim Crow: Women and the Politics of White Supremacy in North Carolina, 1896–1920.* Chapel Hill: University of North Carolina Press, 1996.

Glass, William R. *Strangers in Zion: Fundamentalists in the South, 1900–1950.* Macon, Ga.: Mercer University Press, 2001.

Goldfield, David R. *Cotton Fields and Skyscrapers: Southern City and Region, 1607–1980.* Baton Rouge: Louisiana State University Press, 1982.

Graham, Hugh D., and Numan V. Bartley. *Southern Politics and the Second Reconstruction.* Baltimore: Johns Hopkins University Press, 1975.

Grantham, Dewey W. *Hoke Smith and the Politics of the New South.* Baton Rouge: Louisiana State University Press, 1958.

———. *Southern Progressivism: The Reconciliation of Progress and Tradition.* Knoxville: University of Tennessee Press, 1983.

Green, John C., James L. Guth, Cowin E. Smidt, and Lyman A. Kellstedt. *Religion and the Culture Wars.* Lanham, Md.: Rowman and Littlefield, 1996.

Greenberg, Mark I. "Creating Ethnic, Class and Southern Identity in the Nineteenth-century America: The Jews of Savannah, Georgia, 1830–1880." Ph.D. diss., University of Florida, 1997.

Greenhaw, Wayne. *Elephants in the Cottonfields: Ronald Reagan and the New Republican South.* New York: Macmillan, 1982.

Guth, James L., and John C. Green, eds. *The Bible and the Ballot Box.* San Francisco: Westview Press, 1991.

Guth, James L., John C. Green, Corwin E. Smidt, Lyman A. Kellstedt, and Margaret Poloma. *The Bully Pulpit: The Politics of Protestant Preachers.* Lawrence: University Press of Kansas, 1997.

Hackney, Sheldon. *The Politics of Presidential Appointment: A Memoir of the Culture War.* Montgomery: NewSouth Books, 2002.

Hall, Jacquelyn Dowd. *Revolt against Chivalry: Jesse Daniel Ames and the Women's Campaign against Lynching.* New York: Columbia University Press, 1979.

Hankins, Barry. *Uneasy in Babylon: Southern Baptist Conservatives and American Culture.* Tuscaloosa: University of Alabama Press, 2002.

Harper, Keith. *The Quality of Mercy: Southern Baptists and Social Christianity, 1890–1920.* Tuscaloosa: University of Alabama Press, 1996.

Harrell, David Edwin, ed. *Varieties of Southern Evangelicalism.* Macon, Ga.: Mercer University Press, 1981.

Harvey, Paul. *Redeeming the South: Religious Cultures and Racial Identities among Southern Baptists, 1865–1925.* Chapel Hill: University of North Carolina Press, 1997.

Heilbroner, Robert L. *The Worldly Philosophers: The Lives, Times, and Ideas of the Great Economic Thinkers.* 7th ed. New York: Simon and Schuster, 1999.

Hertzberg, Steven. "Southern Jews and Their Encounter with Blacks: Atlanta, 1850–1915." *Atlanta Historical Journal* (Fall 1970): 7–24.

———. *Strangers within the Gate City: Jews in Atlanta, 1845–1915.* Philadelphia: Jewish Publication Society of America, 1978.

Hill, Samuel S., Jr. *The South and the North in American Religion.* Athens: University of Georgia Press, 1980.

———. *Southern Churches in Crisis.* New York: Holt, Rinehart, and Winston, 1967.

———. *Southern Churches in Crisis Revisited.* Tuscaloosa: University of Alabama Press, 1999.

Hill, Samuel S., Jr., et al. *Religion and the Solid South.* Nashville: Abingdon Press, 1972.

Hunter, James Davison. *Before the Shooting Begins: Searching for Democracy in America's Culture War.* New York: Free Press, 1994.

———. *Culture Wars: The Struggle to Redefine America.* New York: Basic Books, 1991.

Kelley, Robin D. G. *Hammer and Hoe: Alabama Communists during the Great Depression.* Chapel Hill: University of North Carolina Press, 1990.

Kellstadt, Lyman A., et al. *Religion and the Culture Wars.* Lanham, Md.: Rowman and Littlefield, 1996.

Key, V. O., Jr. *Southern Politics in State and Nation.* New York: Alfred A. Knopf, 1949.

King, Keith Lynn. "Religious Dimensions of the Agrarian Protest in Texas, 1870–1908." Ph.D. diss., University of Illinois, 1985.

Kirby, Jack Temple. *Darkness at the Dawning: Race and Reform in the Progressive South.* Philadelphia: J. J. Lippincott, 1972.

Klaits, Joseph. *Servants of Satan: The Age of the Witch Hunts.* Bloomington: Indiana University Press, 1985.

Kostlevy, William C. "Benjamin Titus Roberts and the 'Preferential Option for the Poor' in the Early Free Methodist Church." In *Poverty and Ecclesiology: Nineteenth-century Evangelicals in the Light of Liberation Theology,* edited by Anthony L. Dunnavant, 51–67. Collegeville, Minn.: Liturgical Press, 1992.

Kousser, J. Morgan. *The Shaping of Southern Politics: Suffrage Restriction and the Establishment of the One-Party South, 1880–1910.* New Haven: Yale University Press, 1974.

Kuhn, Clifford M. *Contesting the New South Order: The 1914–1915 Strike at Atlanta's Fulton Mills.* Chapel Hill: University of North Carolina Press, 2001.

———. "'A Full History of the Strike as I Saw It': Atlanta's Fulton Bag and Cotton Mills Workers and Their Representatives through the 1914–1915 Strike." Ph.D. diss., University of North Carolina, 1993.

Larsen, Lawrence H. *Rise of the Urban South.* Lexington: University Press of Kentucky, 1985.

Lienesch, Michael. *Redeeming America: Piety and Politics in the New Christian Right.* Chapel Hill: University of North Carolina Press, 1993.

Link, Arthur S. *Wilson: The New Freedom.* Princeton: Princeton University Press, 1956.

———, ed. *The Papers of Woodrow Wilson.* 33 vols. Princeton: Princeton University Press, 1980 to date.

Lubell, Samuel. *Revolt of the Moderates.* New York: Harper and Brothers, 1956.

MacLean, Nancy. *Behind the Mask of Chivalry: The Making of the Second Ku Klux Klan.* Oxford: Oxford University Press, 1994.

———. "The Leo Frank Case Reconsidered: Gender and Sexual Politics in the Making of Reactionary Populism." *Journal of American History* 78 (December 1991): 917–48.

Malone, Bobbie. "Standing 'Unswayed in the Storm': Rabbi Max Heller, Reform and Zionism in the American South, 1860–1929." Ph.D. diss., Tulane University, 1994.

Manis, Andrew M. *A Fire You Can't Put Out: The Civil Rights Life of Birmingham's Reverend Fred Shuttlesworth.* Tuscaloosa: University of Alabama Press, 1999.

———. *Southern Civil Religions in Conflict: Black and White Baptists and Civil Rights, 1947–1957.* Athens: University of Georgia Press, 1987.

Marsden, George. *Fundamentalism and American Culture: The Shaping of Twentieth-century Evangelicalism, 1870–1925.* New York: Oxford University Press, 1980.

Marsh, Charles. *God's Long Summer: Stories of Faith and Civil Rights.* Princeton: Princeton University Press, 1997.

Martin, William. *With God on Our Side: The Rise of the Religious Right in America.* New York: Broadway, 1996.

McDowell, John Patrick. *The Social Gospel in the South: The Woman's Home Mission Movement in the Methodist Episcopal Church, Southern, 1889–1939.* Baton Rouge: Louisiana State University Press, 1982.

McMahon, Darrin M. *Enemies of the Enlightenment and the Making of Modernity.* New York: Oxford University Press, 2001.

Melnick, Jeffrey. *Black-Jewish Relations on Trial: Leo Frank and Jim Conley in the New South.* Jackson: University Press of Mississippi, 2000.

Morgan, David T. *The New Crusades, the New Holy Land: Conflict in the Southern Baptist Convention, 1969–1991.* Tuscaloosa: University of Alabama Press, 1996.

Muller, Jerry Z. *The Mind and the Market: Capitalism in Modern European Thought.* New York: Alfred A. Knopf, 2002.

Newman, Mark. *Getting Right with God: Southern Baptists and Desegregation, 1945–1995.* Tuscaloosa: University of Alabama Press, 2001.

Oney, Steve. *And the Dead Shall Rise: The Murder of Mary Phagan and the Lynching of Leo Frank.* New York: Pantheon, 2003.

Ownby, Ted. "'Ethos Without Ethic': Samuel S. Hill and the Search for Southern Religious History." In *Reading Southern History: Essays on Interpreters and Interpretations,* edited by Glenn Feldman, 247–59. Tuscaloosa: University of Alabama Press, 2001.

Palmer, Bruce M. *"Man over Money": The Southern Populist Critique of American Capitalism.* Chapel Hill: University of North Carolina Press, 1980.

Pegram, Thomas R. "Temperance Politcs and Regional Political Culture: The Anti-Saloon League in Maryland and the South, 1907–1915." *Journal of Southern History* 63 (February 1997): 57–90.

Perlstein, Rick. *Before the Storm: Barry Goldwater and the Unmaking of the American Consensus.* New York: Hill and Wang, 2001.

Phillips, Kevin P. *The Emerging Republican Majority.* New York: Anchor Books, 1970.

Plank, David N., and Rick Ginsberg. *Southern Cities, Southern Schools: Public Education in the Urban South.* Westport, Conn.: Greenwood Press, 1990.

Quinley, Harold E. *The Prophetic Clergy: Social Activism among Protestant Ministers.* New York: John Wiley, 1974.

Reed, John Shelton. *The Enduring South: Subcultural Persistence in Mass Society.* Lexington, Mass.: Lexington Books, 1972.

Roberts, Derrell C. *Joseph E. Brown and the Politics of Reconstruction.* Tuscaloosa: University of Alabama Press, 1973.

Rogin, Michael Paul. *Ronald Reagan, the Movie and Other Episodes in Political Demonology.* Berkeley: University of California Press, 1987.

Rozell, Mark J., and Clyde Wilcox, eds. *God at the Grassroots: The Christian Right in the 1994/5 Elections.* Lanham, Md.: Rowman and Littlefield, 1997.

Rozell, Mark J., and Clyde Wilcox. *Second Coming: The New Christian Right in Virginia Politics.* Baltimore: Johns Hopkins University Press, 1996.

Segers, Mary, ed. *Piety, Politics, and Pluralism: Religion in the Courts and the 2000 Election.* Lanham, Md.: Rowman and Littlefield, 2002.

Smith, Oran P. *The Rise of Baptist Republicanism.* New York: New York University Press, 1997.

Spain, Rufus. *At Ease in Zion: Social History of Southern Baptists.* Nashville: Vanderbilt University Press, 1967.

Sparks, Randy. *Religion in Mississippi.* Jackson: University Press of Mississippi, 2001.

Streiker, Lowell D., and Gerald S. Strober. *Religion and the New Majority: Billy Graham, Middle America, and the Politics of the '70s.* New York: Association Press, 1972.

Sullivan, Patricia. *Days of Hope: Race and Democracy in the New Deal Era.* Chapel Hill: University of North Carolina Press, 1996.

Thompson, James J., Jr. *Tried as by Fire: Southern Baptists and the Religious Controversies of the 1920s.* Macon, Ga.: Mercer University Press, 1982.

Thornton, J. Mills, III. "Alabama Politics, J. Thomas Heflin, and the Expulsion Movement of 1929." *Alabama Review* 21 (April 1968): 83–112.

Tindall, George Brown. *The Disruption of the Solid South.* New York: W. W. Norton, 1972.

———. *The Emergence of the New South, 1913–1945.* Baton Rouge: Louisiana State University Press, 1967.

Turley, Briane. *A Wheel within a Wheel: Southern Methodism and the Georgia Holiness Association.* Macon, Ga.: Mercer University Press, 1999.

Tyson, Timothy B. *Radio Free Dixie: Robert F. Williams and the Roots of Black Power.* Chapel Hill: University of North Carolina Press, 1999.

Walsh, Frank. *Sin and Censorship: The Catholic Church and the Motion Picture Industry.* New Haven: Yale University Press, 1996.

Watts, Eugene J. *The Social Bases of City Politics: Atlanta, 1865–1903.* Westport, Conn.: Greenwood Press, 1978.

Webb, Clive J. *Fight against Fear: Southern Jews and Black Civil Rights.* Athens: University of Georgia Press, 2001.

Wilcox, Clyde. *Onward Christian Soldiers? The Religious Right in American Politics.* Boulder, Colo.: Westview Press, 2000.

Williamson, Joel R. *The Crucible of Race: Black-White Relations in the American South since Emancipation.* New York: Oxford University Press, 1984.

Wilson, Charles Reagan. *Baptized in Blood: The Religion of the Lost Cause, 1865–1920.* Athens: University of Georgia Press, 1980.

Wolfe, Alan. *One Nation After All: What Middle-Class Americans Really Think about God, Country, Family, Racism, Welfare, Immigration, Homosexuality, Work, the Right, the Left, and Each Other.* New York: Viking, 1998.

Woodward, C. Vann. *American Counterpoint: Slavery and Racism in the Black-White Dialogue.* Boston: Little, Brown, 1971.

———. *Origins of the New South, 1877–1913.* Baton Rouge: Louisiana State University Press, 1951.

———. *Tom Watson: Agrarian Rebel.* New York: Macmillan, 1938.

Wuthnow, Robert. *Christianity in the Twenty-first Century: Reflections on the Challenges Ahead.* New York: Oxford University Press, 1993.

———. *The Restructuring of American Religion: Society and Faith since World War Two.* Princeton: Princeton University Press, 1998.

Contributors

FRED ARTHUR BAILEY is professor and chair of the Department of History at Abilene Christian University. He is the author of *William Edward Dodd: The South's Yeoman Scholar* (1997) and *Class and Tennessee's Confederate Generation* (1987).

MARK K. BAUMAN is professor of history at Atlanta Metropolitan College. He is the author of *Harry H. Epstein and the Rabbinate as Conduit for Change* (1994) and *Warren Akin Candler: Conservative Amidst Change* (1981).

CHARLES S. BULLOCK III is Richard B. Russell Professor of Political Science at the University of Georgia. He has written numerous books and articles, including *Elections to Open Seats in the U.S. House* (2000), *Runoff Elections in the United States* (1992), and *Public Policy and Politics in America* (1978).

NATALIE M. DAVIS is professor of political science at Birmingham-Southern College. She is the author of *National Defense: The Opinion-Policy Linkage* (1981) and was a candidate for the U.S. Senate in 1996.

GLENN FELDMAN is the author or editor of a number of books, including *Politics, Society, and the Klan in Alabama, 1915–1949* (1999), *Reading Southern History: Essays on Interpreters and Interpretations* (2001), and *The Disfranchisement Myth: Poor Whites and Suffrage Restriction in Alabama* (2004). He is associate professor at the Center for Labor Education and Research in the School of Business at the University of Alabama at Birmingham

JAMES L. GUTH is William Rand Kenan Jr. Professor of Political Science at Furman University. He is the coauthor of *The Bully Pulpit: The Politics of the Protestant Clergy* (1997) and the coeditor of *Religion and the Culture Wars: Dispatches from the Front* (1996) and also *The Bible and the Ballot Box: Religion in the 1988 Election* (1991).

PAUL HARVEY is associate professor of history at the University of Colorado at Colorado Springs. He is the author of *Redeeming the South: Religious Cultures and Racial Identities among Southern Baptists, 1865–1925* (1997) and *Freedom's Coming: Religious Culture and the Shaping of the South from the Civil War through the Civil Rights Era* (2005).

ANDREW M. MANIS is the author of *A Fire You Can't Put Out: The Civil Rights Life of Birmingham's Fred Shuttlesworth* (1999) and *Southern Civil Religions in Conflict: Black and White Baptists and Civil Rights* (1987). Manis is a lecturer in American history at Macon College.

STEVEN P. MILLER is a doctoral student on fellowship at Vanderbilt University studying under Don H. Doyle. His master's thesis was on "Billy Graham, Evangelicalism, and the Changing Postwar South."

TED OWNBY is professor of history and southern studies, and director of the Center for the Study of Southern Culture, at the University of Mississippi. He is the author or editor of a number of books, including *American Dreams in Mississippi: Consumers, Poverty, and Culture, 1830–1998* (1999) and *Subduing Satan: Religion, Recreation, and Manhood in the Rural South, 1865–1920* (1990).

MARK J. ROZELL is the author or coauthor of eight books, including *The Bush Presidency* (forthcoming), *Interest Groups in American Campaigns* (1999), *Second Coming* (1996), *In Contempt of Congress* (1996), and *The Press and the Bush Presidency* (1996). He is professor of politics at the Catholic University of America.

MARK C. SMITH is assistant professor of political science at Cedarville University. His dissertation was entitled "With Friends Like These . . . The Religious Right, the Republican Party, and the Politics of the American South." He received his doctorate in political science at the University of Georgia in 2001.

CLYDE WILCOX is professor of political science at Georgetown University. He is the author or coauthor of eight books, including *God's Warriors: The Christian Right in Twentieth-century America* (1992), *Between Two Absolutes: Public Opinion and the Politics of Abortion* (1992), *Second Coming: The New Christian Right in Virginia Politics* (1996), and *Onward Christian Soldiers: The Christian Right in American Politics* (1996).

Index